D1714717

HELENA OF BRITAIN
IN MEDIEVAL LEGEND

St Helena, mother of Constantine the Great and legendary finder of the True Cross, was appropriated in the middle ages as a British saint. The rise and persistence of this legend harnessed Helena's imperial and sacred status to portray her as a romance heroine, source of national pride, and a legitimising link to imperial Rome. This study is the first to examine the origins, development, political exploitation, and decline of this legend, whose momentum and adaptive power are traced from Anglo-Saxon England to the twentieth century. Using Latin, English and Welsh texts, as well as church dedications and visual arts, the author examines the positive effect of the British legend on the cult of St Helena and the reasons for its wide appeal and durability in both secular and religious contexts. Two previously unpublished *vitae* of St Helena are included in the volume: a Middle English verse *vita* from *The South English Legendary*, and a Latin prose *vita* by the early-thirteenth-century hagiographer Jocelin of Furness.

ANTONINA HARBUS is a Research Fellow in the Department of English, University of Sydney.

HELENA OF BRITAIN
IN MEDIEVAL LEGEND

Antonina Harbus

D. S. BREWER

First published 2002
D. S. Brewer, Cambridge

ISBN 0 85991 625 1

D. S. Brewer is an imprint of Boydell & Brewer Ltd
PO Box 9, Woodbridge, Suffolk IP12 3DF, UK
and of Boydell & Brewer Inc.
PO Box 41026, Rochester, NY 14604–4126, USA
website: www.boydell.co.uk

A catalogue record for this book is available
from the British Library

Library of Congress Cataloging-in-Publication Data
Harbus, A. (Antonina)
    Helena of Britain in medieval legend / Antonina Harbus.
        p. cm.
    Includes bibliographical references and index.
    ISBN 0–85991–625–1 (alk. paper)
    1. Helena, Saint, ca. 255–ca. 330.   2. Holy cross – Legends.   I. Title
    BR1720.H4 H37 2002
    270.1'092 – dc21   2002018577

This publication is printed on acid-free paper

Printed in Great Britain by
St Edmundsbury Press Ltd, Bury St Edmunds, Suffolk

Contents

Preface

I would like to acknowledge my thanks to the librarians of the British Library, London; the Bodleian Library, Oxford; and the Forschungs- und Landes-bibliothek, Gotha; and the Master and Fellows of Corpus Christi College, Cambridge, who made the relevant manuscripts available for consultation; provided copies of the the pages containing the texts edited in the appendices; and granted permission to publish those texts. I am grateful to the Rev. David Wiseman for granting permission to view and photograph the St Helena windows at the Parish Church of St Michael and All Angels, Ashton-under-Lyne, and to Karin Olsen and Jennifer Neville for accompanying me on a memorable journey there.

The consultation of manuscripts and other materials was made possible by the financial support of the Australian Research Council and the University of Sydney.

It is a pleasure to thank the many people who have discussed this project with me and offered valuable assistance: to Helen Fulton who generously made trans-lations from Welsh for me, and to my other colleagues at Sydney, Margaret Clunies Ross and Diane Speed, for their advice and assistance on various sections of this project. I gratefully acknowledge help and advice received from: Robert Bartlett, Helen Cooper, Jan Willem Drijvers, C.E.V. Nixon, George Rigg, Susan Rosser, John O. Ward, Jocelyn Wogan-Browne, Alex Woolf, and the anonymous reader for Boydell & Brewer. I am also happy to express my appreciation for the research assistance provided by Don Gillett in London and Carol Percy in Toronto, for proof-reading done by Craig Ronalds, and technical aid given by Beth Lewis in Sydney. Finally, I would like to express my thanks to Andrew Gillett for erudite advice on late Roman history and much other sound advice in the writing of this book. Any errors and infelicities remaining are my own responsibility.

Abbreviations

ASE	*Anglo-Saxon England*
ASPR	Anglo-Saxon Poetic Records, ed. G.P. Krapp and E.V.K. Dobbie (New York, 1931–53)
AASS	Acta sanctorum (Antwerp etc., 1643–1940; Paris, 1863–67)
BHL	*Bibliotheca hagiographica latina antiquae et mediae aetatis*, ed. Bollandists, Subsidia hagiographica 6 (Brussels, 1898–1901); *Novum supplementum*, ed. H. Fros, Subsidia hagiographica 70 (Brussels, 1986)
CSASE	Cambridge Studies in Anglo-Saxon England
CSEL	Corpus scriptorum ecclesiasticorum latinorum (Vienna, Leipzig, Prague, 1866–)
EETS	Early English Text Society (os = original series; ns = new series; ss = supplementary series)
GCS	Die griechischen christlichen Schriftsteller der ersten drei Jahrhunderte (Leipzig and Berlin, 1897–)
JEGP	*Journal of English and Germanic Philology*
MGH	Monumenta Germaniae historica (Hanover, Leipzig, Berlin, etc., 1826–)
NLA	*Nova legenda Anglie*
NM	*Neuphilologische Mitteilungen*
PL	Patrologiae cursus completus, Series latina, ed. J.-P. Migne, 221 vols. (Paris, 1841–64)
PLRE	*Prosopography of the Later Roman Empire*, vol. I, ed. A.H.M. Jones, J.R. Martindale, and J. Morris (Cambridge, 1971)
PMLA	*Publications of the Modern Language Association*
RE	*Realencyclopädie der classischen Altertumswissenschaft*, ed. A.F. von Pauly, G. Wissowa, et al., 2nd ed. (Stuttgart, 1893–1955)
SEL	*South English Legendary*
TYP	*Trioedd Ynys Prydein*
VC	*Vita Constantini*

Note: Where the cited edition contains a translation, that translation has been used; otherwise all translations are my own.

Introduction

St Helena's fame during the Middle Ages was assured both by the historical circumstance that she was the mother of Constantine the Great, and also by the legendary attribution to her of the finding of the Cross on which Jesus was crucified. Through accretion, her status was further elevated: she was considered to have actively participated in the conversion of Constantine to Christianity and thereby to have played a considerable part in the recognition of Christianity as the dominant religion of the Roman Empire. These excellent credentials for renown span both the secular and religious spheres and must have been very appealing to a wide range of communities wishing to associate themselves with Helena or to appropriate her more directly for their own rhetorical and political purposes. In the context of her multifaceted value as Roman empress and Christian saint, there arose in England from Anglo-Saxon times a further cause for Helena's celebrity: the audacious claim that she was a native of Britain, in some cases the daughter of King Cole of Colchester (the 'merry old soul' of the nursery rhyme). For at least one thousand years, this legend of a noble, British birth was invoked, modified, and elaborated by writers of histories, chronicles, poetry, saints' calendars, and hagiography, depicted by visual artists, and kept alive as a tradition, both in England and abroad.

Typically of both legend and hagiography, the story of Helena developed some outlandish manifestations: Helena as disguised princess, Jewish convert, or Welsh dawn goddess. The form of the legend changed as often as the vehicle for transmission, and varied according to genre, audience, and circumstances. Because the story was contingent upon the immediate factors of reception for its shape and contents, there is no single legend, but rather a large number of constructions of the idea of a British princess Helena which served a variety of uses. At some stages, the patriotic concept became subordinated to wider forces, such as the vigorous cycles of legends surrounding Constantine and Pope Silvester which were widely promulgated for ecclesiastical and political reasons. In other instances, Helena's life-story was given priority and was reconstructed by writers of the national literature of Francia and Wales as well as England. As the legend gathered momentum during the central Middle Ages, Helena came to be revered not only as a high-profile saint of the Christian church, but also, in a secular and political context, as the provider of an imperial link with Rome which outshone the legendary appeal even of King Arthur in British national consciousness.

Several scholars have discussed the origins and growth of the British legend, though only briefly or selectively, and almost exclusively as a minor part of the Constantine cycle of legends.[1] The legend is peripheral to two recent examinations of St Helena's alleged finding of the Cross, by Stephan Borgehammar and Jan Willem Drijvers,[2] and the studies by Susan Larkin and Hans Pohlsander make only preliminary investigations into Helena's British connections.[3] It is a fair indication of Helena's multivalent associations that all these examinations of her life and legends treat other aspects of her fame which have overshadowed the British legend. Relatively little attention has been paid to the persistent creations of a British Helena and the infiltration of the story into church and state records and histories as well as into more overtly creative texts and works of art.[4] One major reason for the reduced interest in her origins and in Helena herself is her usual roles as an auxiliary rather than the key figure in legendary narratives: she is an accessory rather than the centre of attention in the feast of the *Inventio crucis* (the finding of the Cross), as she is in legends treating Constantine's conversion in the cult of St Silvester. Certainly, her fame relies on her relationship with Constantine and his conversion to Christianity, topics which have received far more critical attention.[5]

---

1   Existing studies are quite brief or treat the British Helena legend only tangentially: W. J. Mulligan, 'The British Constantine: An English Historical Myth', *The Journal of Medieval and Renaissance Studies* 8 (1978), pp. 257–79; Geoffrey Ashe, *Mythology of the British Isles* (London, 1990), pp. 152–64; and Marie-Françoise Alamichel, 'La Légende de Sainte Hélène de Cynewulf à Evelyn Waugh', *Études Anglaises* 48 (1995), pp. 306–18. Mulligan's discussion includes a particularly valuable but necessarily selective treatment of the growth of the legend between the fifteenth and eighteenth centuries, though early sources are either omitted or treated scantily. Mulligan does not endeavour to uncover the origins of the myth and the contention that 'it is most likely that the legend developed innocently' through confusion and 'wishful thinking' (p. 258) is vague and unsupported. Ashe's claim that 'genuine misunderstanding may have played a part, since the legend adopted and confused other persons bearing the same names' (p. 156) may account to some extent for the rise of the legend, but does not factor in the political and rhetorical agendas of writers and users of the legend. Alamichel's article briefly recounts the Cross and British legends throughout the eighth to twentieth centuries, focusing on a comparison between the accounts of Cynewulf and Waugh.

2   Stephan Borgehammar, *How the Holy Cross was Found: From Event to Medieval Legend*, Bibliotheca theologiae practicae, Kyrkovetenskapliga studier 47 (Stockholm, 1991); Jan Willem Drijvers, *Helena Augusta: The Mother of Constantine the Great and the Legend of her Finding of the True Cross* (Leiden, 1992).

3   Susan Larkin, 'Transitions in the Medieval Legends of Saint Helena' (unpub. Ph.D. Diss., Indiana Univ., 1996). Larkin's concentration on the Anglo-Latin writers leads her to position the legend solely in the context of nationalism and romance. Hans A. Pohlsander, *Helena: Empress and Saint* (Chicago, 1995), examines cults and legends dealing with Helena, and their expression in art and literature, devoting only eleven pages to 'The Traditions of Britain', and accumulating rather than synthesising information or drawing conclusions from it. There are several other studies which examine a portion of the topic: F. Arnold Foster, *Studies in Church Dedications, or England's Patron Saints*, 2 vols (London, 1899), I.181–9; S. Baring-Gould and John Fisher, *The Lives of the British Saints*, 4 vols (London, 1911), III.255–60; and John J. Parry, 'Geoffrey of Monmouth and the Paternity of Arthur', *Speculum* 13 (1938), pp. 271–7.

4   The legend is often just briefly mentioned as a traditional tale: e.g. Mary-Catherine Bodden, ed. and trans., *The Old English Finding of the True Cross* (Cambridge, 1987), pp. 2, 54; and Michael Swanton, trans., *Anglo-Saxon Prose* (London, 1993), p. 114.

5   Amnon Linder, 'The Myth of Constantine the Great in the West: Sources and Hagiographic Commemoration', *Studi medievali*, 3rd ser. 16/1 (1975), pp. 43–95, at pp. 84–93; and John Matthews,

The British legend, however, developed a life of its own within the central Middle Ages and situated Helena in a position of importance in her own right in much the same way as the cult of Mary more spectacularly developed its own legitimacy, an analogy which was not lost on medieval writers about St Helena. The rise in her status as an individual saint is observable in the move from her role as an agent in the feast of the *Inventio* (3 May), to the later acquisition of her own *vitae* and feast day in the Western Church (18 August); in the Eastern Church, she shared and still shares Constantine's feast day, 21 May. The British legend played a demonstrable role in this shift of focus in the West. The sites of this legend are so numerous and diverse that the development of its rhetorical power deserves scrutiny, even if it cannot be completely disentangled from myths of Constantine and the legend of the *Inventio*. The creation of various Helenas is worth examining in detail not only because of her status as a saint and imperial progenitor, but also because of her wide appeal and flexible application to local, national, ecclesiastical, and political agendas.

The range of texts, artefacts, and cultures in which the British Helena legend is found suggests a level of importance and degree of transmission enjoyed by few saints, particularly because she is featured in historiographical as well as hagiographical traditions, in vernacular as well as Latinate discourse, in visual as well as textual representation, and in popular, oral contexts as well as learned, scribal ones. The many secular and religious witnesses to the legend show that it is both much older than is usually acknowledged and also was transmitted much farther afield than England. The full array of sources needs to be assembled and assessed in the light of all available evidence. The early written sources, particularly the Anglo-Saxon texts, have not yet been adequately explored, nor have their implications for vernacular literary culture been considered, probably because these allusions to Helena are brief and predate the major vehicle for the legend's dissemination, the *Historia regum Britannie* of Geoffrey of Monmouth (c. 1138). Cumulatively, the very early references to Constantine's British birth, and by implication Helena's British origins, are significant in that they indicate the growth of a new legend; sources include Aldhelm's *De virginitate* (c. 700), the Old English translation of Bede's *Historia ecclesiastica* (c. 890), and the tenth-century Welsh genealogies. The concept underpinning these manifestations, that there is rhetorical value in claiming a famous personage as a compatriot, becomes more widely appealing during this period of the growth of vernacular literature, including narrative hagiography. More intriguing still is the evidence that the legend was not confined to British sources and acquired the durability and wide dissemination of a traditional story. It motivated a conflict in the tenth century between York and Trier, and is alluded to in a thirteenth-century Latin redaction of a Byzantine obituary list (the *Necrologium*)

'Macsen, Maximus, and Constantine', *Welsh Historical Review* 11 (1983), pp. 431–48; repr. as text XII in John Matthews, *Political Life and Culture in Late Roman Society* (London, 1985).

originally compiled in the mid-tenth century.[6] These non-insular witnesses of the legend signal that the story survived, and perhaps even arose, outside British patriotic contexts. The concept was transferred between cultures, and association with Helena was sought intently enough to produce rivalry and to warrant official intervention. As the range of uses to which the legend was put grew, Helena's fame and therefore her rhetorical value also increased. The development of the legend, however, did not enjoy an unbroken upward trajectory, but rather was subject to the changing fortunes and the fluctuating degree of mutual tolerance between the forces with which it was inherently implicated: the perceived legitimacy of written sources, the cult of saints, the momentum of tradition, and the persuasiveness of nationalist rhetoric.

The British legend seems at times to have flourished independently of the myth that Helena found the Cross on which Jesus was crucified, although the two stories are often recounted together. The exclusive concentration on Helena's secular accomplishments is most prominent in the Anglo-Latin histories of the twelfth century, most notably Geoffrey of Monmouth's *Historia regum Britannie*, which develop the persona of a noble British princess. After Geoffrey, there are a great many redactions of the British legend, most of which are remarkable in that they share Geoffrey's secular focus on Helena's lineage rather than on her conversion, baptism, and finding of the Cross. This suppression of religious material arises from Geoffrey's vigorous and conscious nationalistic agenda, and affords Helena's supposed British origins even greater significance. It also allows Geoffrey to develop other aspects of the legendary persona which would be cited by later writers and eventually mesh with earlier portrayals: Helena's spotless character, noble birth, worldly accomplishments, and her location in Colchester.

Geoffrey's priorities, however, were not the only ones operating in the transmission of the British Helena legend during the Middle Ages. Alongside his version, there existed parallel biographies of Helena: the account based on Roman sources; a distinct hagiographic tradition of Helena; and her continued role in the feast of the *Inventio*. In the English religious context, the British legend helped Helena attain the credentials of sanctity; in turn, the legend was disseminated to an even wider range of contexts, including church dedications and visual art. Several extant saint's lives feature a British Helena. These, together with her (rather late) acceptance into saints' calendars and national legendaries and her representation in monuments, stained glass, and paintings reflect the developing, but fluctuating, interest in the subject.

The conventions of hagiography helped to shape the treatment of Helena's life and accomplishments in a broad range of medieval texts outside the strictly religious sphere. Indeed, the conceptual importance of the saint's birth and early experiences in the hagiographic tradition no doubt raised the issue of Helena's

---

6 This source merely says that Constantine was British, but implies that this nationality was acquired from his British mother, Helena.

origins to a position of significance in other biographical texts. Not only are her early circumstances and later achievements treated in the most favourable light in the hagiographic context and standard miracles claimed on her behalf, but a completely new biographical legitimacy is promoted. A royal pedigree is rebuilt from the ground up with little respect to historical veracity or logical likelihood. Such treatment is not unique, but in the case of Helena, her secular status and imperial position made this kind of fabrication particularly bold, even within the conventions of hagiography. The process was self-perpetuating: her British origins, once established, allowed her to be included in national legendaries and this led finally to her acceptance by the Church as a British saint. This dissemination of the legend in turn led to greater attention being paid to her by histories and a more general acceptance of the story as truth by both writers and congregations. For church-goers in particular, visual reminders of the saint's status and the local associations which these depictions implied would have reinforced the legend.

Because a large portion of the legend's vitality in the later Middle Ages depended upon ecclesiastical acceptance and commemoration in liturgy, authorised texts, and artistic representations, the Reformation had a detrimental impact upon further development. The confluence of historiographic, hagiographic and popular traditions, however, proved a durable combination, and the tale was kept alive in secular contexts. When it was questioned during the humanistic rigours of the eighteenth century, the legend did not succumb easily and prompted some fairly energetic argumentation before being discredited in historical accounts. Nevertheless, the legend continued to live on in less formal contexts, in popular imagination and visual representations in public places. Despite the general muting of the legend, the town of Colchester continued to regard Helena as its patron and erected a twelve-foot high bronze statue of her on the tower of the Town Hall in 1902.[7] Similarly, the sequence of 20 fifteenth-century panels of stained glass at St Michael's Church in Ashton-under-Lyne depicting Helena's British birth and later biography is a permanent visual reminder of the legend, though even this material manifestation of the story has been subject to modification as a result of fluctuating opinion.[8] Helena, for some of the British at least,

---

[7] In advertising material, Colchester promotes itself as 'Britain's oldest recorded town' (boasting an eleventh-century Norman castle) and still claims Helena as its patron saint. The other, smaller statues of the Town Hall similarly invoke prestigious historical connections: Queen Boadicea, King Edward the Elder, and Eudo Dapifer, Steward to William the Conqueror (on Eudo Dapifer, see below, p. 67).

[8] The windows can, and have been, changed to reflect changing public attitude. In 1872 they were dismantled from the east window of the church to make room for a memorial window and repositioned (out of order) in the windows of the south aisle. This cavalier treatment was subsequently counterbalanced by restoration work undertaken in 1913 (H. Reddish, 'The St Helen Window Ashton-under-Lyne: A Reconstruction', *Journal of Stained Glass* 18 [1986–87], pp. 150–61, at p. 151). Another indication of Helena's waning fortunes in this particular location is the likelihood that the church was rededicated from St Helena to a conventional choice, St Michael and All Angels, in the early fifteenth century; yet the stained glass was commissioned and produced in 1499, after the rededication (Alan F. Bacon, 'The History of the Windows', *The Saint Helen Windows in the Ancient*

had become a sort of national treasure not to be relinquished, thereby enabling the power of tradition to assume the force of historical validity.

Legends of a British St Helena evolved from her especially abundant and wide-ranging appeals as a literary and dedicatory figure: imperial connections, a significant contribution to the Christian Church, and a well-documented later life compared with obscure origins. The genesis of the legend, and more importantly its reception history and the circumstances of its ongoing momentum, deserve to be examined fully. The specific reconstructions of a local empress saint for diverse audiences and situations says much about the cultural milieux and encoded agendas of each of its manifestations. But more broadly, the legendary British St Helena functions as a repository of a wide range of unlikely but rhetorically useful secular and sacred attributes, as a protagonist in key narratives, and as a source of local importance and pride.

My examination of the development and deployment of the British Helena legend is chronological, though the material has been further divided according to geographic, generic, and thematic criteria. In Chapter I, I attempt to produce the most likely version of Helena's life based on the evidence of late Roman historical sources, moderated by modern interpretations. This chapter will also discuss myths of Constantine as they relate to Helena and the rise of the *Inventio crucis* legend, and the development of the cult of the Cross in Western Europe. Chapter II covers the manifestation of the legend in Anglo-Saxon England and in contemporary continental Europe, in an attempt to locate its written origins. The cult of the Cross seems to have overshadowed Helena's presence in Anglo-Saxon England, though she attracts reflected glory from this phenomenon. At the end of this period, Britain was competing with Trier as Helena's recognised place of origin, but both traditions worked together to bring Helena's birthplace to the West and to move her origins up the social scale. The chapter closes with an examination of this contest and its extraordinary outcome.

The Welsh also appropriated Helena, but the picture here is more complex because it incorporates the intermingling of imported Roman and British literary culture with native Welsh legend. In Chapter III, I try to gauge the Welsh contribution to the legend's heritage by disentangling the fusion of two identities in Welsh literature: the Welsh goddess Elen and the historical Helena transformed by the British legend. The place of King Cole and the rise of Colchester in the legend are also explored in this chapter, as well as the arrival of another borrowed Roman personage into the Welsh manifestations of the story, the imperial usurper Magnus Maximus. This chapter analyses the impact of the legend's Welsh reception and transformation on its subsequent career in England.

In Chapter IV, I discuss the popularisation of the British Helena legend in the

Parish Church of Saint Michael and All Angels Ashton-under-Lyne [Ashton-under-Lyne, 2000], pp. 7–8, at p. 7). On the windows, see below, pp. 94–5.

twelfth-century Anglo-Latin histories of Henry of Huntingdon, Geoffrey of Monmouth, and William of Malmsbury, and the life of the legend in later vernacular chronicles. These writers have been wrongly credited with the origins of the legend. Understanding their active embellishment of selective portions of the legend, rather than their creation of it, sheds new light both on their methodologies and agendas and also the status of the legend at this time. Helena has been reinvented in these texts as the daughter of 'Old' King Cole and is based in Colchester. From this time, a British Helena is firmly situated in the national consciousness and is now ripe for patriotic exploitation. The final sections of the chapter treat the fate of the legend in the Brut tradition and national chronicles of England. These vernacular texts are examined for their role in legitimating a British Helena as part of national history and their contribution to the rise of her star as a saint.

Chapter V explores the fate of the legend in religious literature, art, and culture. Helena's late entry into saints' calendars and legendaries was closely tied to the association of her legends with those of St Silvester, who is credited with curing Constantine from leprosy and converting both the emperor and Helena to Christianity. In this version of events, Helena is converted from Judaism; the cultural implications of this new legend are considered here. Two texts containing these episodes are examined in detail in the chapter, the prose Latin *Vita sancte Helene* by Jocelin of Furness, and the Middle English verse *St Elyn*. Both are previously unedited and unstudied. To facilitate discussion, I provide transcriptions of these two texts in my appendices. These texts are not only witnesses to the interconnectedness of Helena's fame with that of Constantine and Silvester, but are also examples of the medieval trend of taking Helena's British nationality for granted and using it for specific rhetorical reasons.

The legend's life beyond the Middle Ages in literature and popular culture is the subject of Chapter VI. The imperial connection to the British throne offered by a British Helena was exploited by the Tudors, and created a revival of interest in British history, at least amongst antiquarians. Later debate in which national pride was a key ingredient ensured the longevity of an otherwise unlikely story, which also enjoyed a subterranean existence in popular tradition. Even the subjection of the legend to humanist scrutiny in the seventeenth and eighteenth centuries did not immediately or permanently discredit it except in the most learned circles. The vigorous debate over the veracity of the British Helena story during the eighteenth century is explored, as well as the continuing vitality of the legend in popular imagination and, to a lesser extent, in literary culture. The mid-twentieth century witnessed a minor resurgence of interest in the legend, in the consciously theological productions of the well-known writers Evelyn Waugh (in his 1950 novel, *Helena*) and Dorothy L. Sayers (in her 1951 play, *The Emperor Constantine*). The chapter closes with a consideration of how several strands of the legend were manipulated by Waugh and Sayers to produce narratives for the twentieth century which proved too theological for modern tastes, but by no means too Anglocentric.

The rise and transmission of this legend rest on powerful but fluid forces: the cult of the saints, the development of national sentiment in Britain, the longevity of folk belief, the durability of visual commemorations, the interconnectedness of cycles of saints' legends, and the force of ecclesiastical and political agendas. It also relies on the appeal of a recognisable but not firmly detailed persona which lends itself to reconstruction and can be put to both secular and ecclesiastical uses. A British Helena was an attractive and lasting concept, able to be exploited even in the face of much counter-evidence. There are remnants of this tendency right into the late twentieth century.[9] As an idea, the legend has its own epic biography.

[9] Even if the British Helena/Constantine legend has been decisively debunked by now, the city of York is still celebrating its more legitimate connection with Constantine. Recently, a bronze statue commissioned by the York Civic Trust was unveiled outside York minster, near the site of Constantine's proclamation as emperor. The chairman of the Trust, John Shannon, explained why this had been done (inaccurately ignoring the local claims of Magnus Maximus and others), saying, 'Because York is the only English city in which a Roman emperor has been proclaimed, we felt that it was absolutely right to have this statue erected' (*The Times*, 25 July 1998, p. 6). Even though Constantine's presence in York is well supported by early historical sources, this civic gesture nevertheless expresses the desire to appropriate publically and visually a Christian Roman imperial figure by claiming a material connection with a local site. The same rationale lies behind many textual and artistic manifestations of the British Helena legend.

I

Helena in Late Antiquity and the Early Middle Ages

L EGENDARY ACCOUNTS of Helena's life and achievements arose during
Late Antiquity and the Middle Ages in the absence of reliable contemporary records. Despite her imperial status as Augusta, mother of the emperor
Constantine, most of the details of her biography are obscure. There are two
reasons for this: her humble origins, and Constantine's control over information
concerning the imperial family. Helena's early life is unrecorded because she
was simply socially unimportant until she made a liaison with a high-ranking
Roman soldier and official, Constantius 'Chlorus';[1] and her later life defines her
in terms of the achievements of her son, Constantine. Of course, this lack of information is not unusual. Some aspects of Constantine's own life, such as his
date of birth and baptism, are similarly unrecorded or contentious, not least
because of his policy of suppression of compromising information.[2] This
biographical vagueness left medieval writers free to construct the Helena of
their choice, modified by the early legends which arose within a century of her
death. The claims that Helena discovered the Holy Cross and facilitated the
spread of Christianity throughout the Roman empire were the most widely
disseminated of these stories (though they were certainly not the only ones, and
themselves were not consistently adopted). These legendary achievements
conferred the status of saint on Helena and initiated the creative processes of
hagiography, first within the cult of the *Inventio* and later in her own traditions.
Helena's status as a saint in her own right, however, was dependent upon the
development of other legendary achievements, which the hagiographic and also
the historiographic traditions were able to elucidate. With sacred biography
comes an interest in the origins and early experiences of the subject, which were
particularly elusive in Helena's case. Because the exact date and place of her

---

[1] 'Chlorus' was a nickname connoting 'green', first attested in the sixth century. It is not part of
Constantius's real name, but because it is traditionally treated as if it were, it is used here. Evelyn
Waugh, in his novel *Helena* (London, 1950) attempts to explain the origin of the appellation, as well
as the usual description of Helena as a *stabularia* ('stable-maid') in an imaginary scene. In this historical romance, Helena calls the hungover and queasy Constantius 'Green-faced', who in turn calls her
'Helen ostler' because he finds her in the stable. Waugh concludes whimsically: 'And so these two
names, "Chlorus" and "Stabularia", lightly blown, drifted away into the dawn and settled at last
among the pages of history' (p. 29). On Waugh's *Helena*, see below, pp. 134–8.

[2] See Bill Leadbetter, 'The Illegitimacy of Constantine and the Birth of the Tetrarchy', *Constantine:
History, Historiography and Legend*, ed. S.N.C. Lieu and D. Montserrat (London and New York,
1998), pp. 74–85.

birth were not known with certainty, even by contemporary writers, Helena was particularly vulnerable to being appropriated as a native of any land which desired imperial and sacred connections.

The Life of Helena According to Late Roman Sources

Even though Helena's activities during the imperial reign of her son Constantine are afforded some attention, authoritative details and reliable dates from Helena's biography were not transmitted by the ecclesiastical historians who provide the chief written witnesses to Constantine's reign. The contemporary Greek historian, Bishop Eusebius of Caesarea, is of very little help. He fails to mention Helena in his *Historia ecclesiastica*, the first institutional history of Christianity, initially composed before 300, but revised, after Constantine's rise to power, in 313 or later, and again in 325/6.[3] The closest Eusebius comes to mentioning Helena in his history is the comment that Constantine was 'the lawful son' of Constantius (VIII.13), a technical evasion of the dispute over whether or not Helena and Constantius were legally married which still occupies historians. In his *Vita Constantini*, however, a work eulogising Constantine as the ideal Christian emperor and completed just after the subject's death in May 337, he devotes quite a lot of space (III.42–7) to Helena's journey to the Holy Lands and her death.[4] Eusebius is vague about Helena's biography, though this tendency is characteristic of the conventional style of panegyric in which he composed the *Vita Constantini*,[5] where silence was preferable to unflattering details. Eusebius's presentation of Constantine in both the *Historia ecclesiastica* and *Vita Constantini* is dominated by the emperor's own propaganda. Constantine clearly suppressed details about his own and Helena's background, with the result that Eusebius omitted conventional biographical details where there was no information complimentary to the emperor. This contemporary vacuum created by Constantine's own agenda provided fertile ground for later legendary embroidery of Helena's life as well as his own.

---

3   Eusebius, *Historia ecclesiastica*, ed. E. Schwartz, *Die Kirchengeschichte*, 3 vols, GCS IX (Leipzig, 1903–09); Engl. trans.: H.J. Lawlor and J.E.L. Oulton (London, 1927–28).

4   *Vita Constantini*, ed. F. Winkelmann, *Über das Leben des Kaisers Konstantins, Eusebius' Werke*, I.1, GCS (Berlin, 1975); Engl. trans.: Averil Cameron and Stuart G. Hall, *Eusebius: Life of Constantine*, Clarendon Ancient History Series (Oxford, 1999). Eusebius also produced many other written works, including a chronicle, no longer extant, but partially preserved in Jerome's translation made in the late fourth century, and two panegyrics for Constantine. The latter are edited in *Laus Constantini*, ed. Ivar A. Heikel, *Eusebius' Werke*, I, GCS 7 (Leipzig, 1902), pp. 195–223; Engl. trans.: H.A. Drake, *In Praise of Constantine* (Berkeley, 1976), pp. 83–102. On Eusebius, see Robert M. Grant, *Eusebius as Church Historian* (Oxford, 1980); and T.D. Barnes, *Constantine and Eusebius* (Cambridge, Mass. and London, 1981).

5   Drake, *In Praise of Constantine*, describes Eusebius as 'infuriatingly indifferent to precise chronology (indeed to precision of any kind)' (p. 9).

Rufinus translated Eusebius's *Historia ecclesiastica* from Greek into Latin in about 403, compressing the original ten books into nine, and adding a further two of his own.[6] Rufinus's work, the major vehicle for the transmission of Eusebius's history to the medieval West, says little about Helena's origins, and defines her solely as Constantine's parent. The *Vita Constantini* itself was not available in Latin and was therefore virtually unknown in the West. The fifth-century Greek continuators of Eusebius's history – Socrates Scholasticus, Sozomen, and Theodoret – transmit some details from the *Vita Constantini*, as well as the legend of the finding of the Cross, of which Eusebius makes no mention.[7] At the request of Cassiodorus, these parallel accounts were compressed into a single narrative and translated into Latin in the mid-sixth century by Epiphanius Scholasticus, in a text known as the *Historia tripartita*.[8] By these means, substantial sections of the Greek Church historians came to be widely available in the medieval West. These authors, however, say nothing about Helena's early life, and omit many important details from her later biography, concentrating instead on the legend of the finding of the Cross, based on the details of her journey to Palestine recounted in Eusebius's *Vita Constantini*. Other sources also fail to mention Helena's early life.[9] Again, lack of definitive information, especially in the sources available to the Latin West, Rufinus's *Historia* and the *Historia tripartita*, facilitated attempts by later writers to appropriate Helena as a native of their own city or to fabricate details of her life (particularly once hagiographic considerations came into play).

---

6 Rufinus of Aquileia, *Historia ecclesiastica*, ed. E. Schwartz and T. Mommsen, *Eusebius' Werke*, II.2 (Leipzig, 1908), pp. 960–1040; Engl. trans. (partial): Philip R. Amidon, *The Church History of Rufinus of Aquileia: Books 10 and 11* (New York and Oxford, 1997). On Rufinus's translation of Eusebius's *History*, see Pierre Courcelle, *Late Latin Writers and their Greek Sources*, Engl. trans. Harry E. Wedeck (Cambridge, Mass., 1969), p. 143.

7 These three separate Greek continuations of Eusebius's history were all produced during the mid-fifth century. Sozomen and Theodoret reworked Socrates's material, but the three produced quite distinct versions. Socrates Scholasticus, *Historia ecclesiastica*, ed. R. Hussey, 3 vols (Oxford, 1853); Sozomen, *Historia ecclesiastica*, ed. J. Bidez, GCS 50 (Berlin, 1960); Theodoret, *Historia ecclesiastica*, ed. L. Parmentier, rev. F. Scheidweiler, GCS 44 (Berlin, 1954). An English translation of the histories of Socrates, Sozomen, and Theodoret is available in A Select Library of Nicene and Post-Nicene Fathers, 2nd ser., vol. II (A.C. Zenos, ed., *Socrates and Sozomon*) and vol. III (B. Jackson, ed., *Theodoret and Gennadius*), both repr. Grand Rapids, 1973. Details of the *Vita Constantini* are also preserved in the Arian ecclesiastical history of Philostorgius, a contemporary of Socrates and Sozomen. His work, though lost, is preserved in substantial fragments by the ninth-century summary of Photius: see Joseph Bidez, ed., *Kirchengeschichte*, 3rd ed., rev. F. Winkelmann, GCS (Berlin, 1981); Engl. trans.: E. Walford (London, 1855).

8 This text, also known as *Historia ecclesiastica tripartita*, is usually referred to as 'Cassiodorus–Epiphanius', even though Cassiodorus provided only the preface. Editions: J.-P. Migne, PL 69 (Paris, 1865), cols 879–1213; and W. Jacob and R. Hanslik, eds, CSEL 71 (Vienna, 1952).

9 See also the anonymous *Origo Constantini*, ed. I. König (Trier, 1987); Engl. trans. Jane Stevenson with introduction and notes by S.N.C. Lieu, *From Constantine to Julian: Pagan and Byzantine Views: A Source History*, ed. S.N.C. Lieu and Dominic Montserrat (London and New York, 1996), pp. 39–62. Other contemporary or near-contemporary sources on Constantine which omit reference to Helena are Lactantius, Eutropius, and Aurelius Victor. On these writers and their works, and for fuller details of editions and translations, see Lieu and Montserrat, *From Constantine to Julian*, and Barnes, *Constantine and Eusebius*.

Often, the desire to claim Helena was part of a larger campaign to situate Constantine's birth in a particular location. Modern scholarship has reflected this tendency by touching on Helena's nationality only within the study of legendary versions of the birth of Constantine.[10] Recent work by Borgehammar, Drijvers, and Pohlsander, however, has balanced the inquiry by focusing attention on the historical Helena, as well as on her legendary career.[11] These contributions, as well as valuable earlier work, enable a likely model of Helena's life to be configured from the existing documentary evidence coupled with scholarly inference.[12] Because these three studies, and others, have examined the primary sources in detail, only a brief review of the documented details of Helena's life is required here before turning to the construction of legendary Helenas.

Helena was probably born in Bithynia, within the province of Drepanum in Asia Minor, though the earliest authority for this information, the sixth-century historian, Procopius, is by no means contemporary and therefore needs to be treated with caution.[13] Earlier historians perhaps imply this place of origin when they mention that Constantine renamed Drepanum 'Helenopolis' in 328 after Helena's death, presumably, though not necessarily, because it was her birthplace.[14] He perhaps had other, political reasons for doing so, or sought merely to

---

10 Eduard Heydenreich, 'Constantin der Grosse in den Sagen des Mittelalters', *Deutsche Zeitschrift für Geschichtswissenschaft* 10 (1893), pp. 1–27, at pp. 3–10; Jean Pierre Callu, ' "Ortus Constantini": Aspects historiques de la légende', *Constantino il grande: Dall'antichità all'umanesimo*, Colloqio sul Cristianesimo nel mondo antico, ed. G. Bonamente and F. Fusco (Macerata, 1992), pp. 253–82, at pp. 258–62; and Amnon Linder, 'The Myth of Constantine the Great in the West: Sources and Hagiographic Commemoration', *Studi Medievali*, 3rd ser. 16/1 (1975), pp. 43–95.

11 Stephan Borgehammar, *How the Holy Cross was Found: From Event to Medieval Legend*, Bibliotheca theologiae practicae, Kyrkovetenskapliga studier 47 (Stockholm, 1991); Jan Willem Drijvers, *Helena Augusta: The Mother of Constantine the Great and the Legend of her Finding of the True Cross* (Leiden, 1992); and Hans A. Pohlsander, *Helena: Empress and Saint* (Chicago, 1995) concentrate on the *Inventio* legend rather then the British one. Similarly, the older and less critical study, Abbé R. Couzard, *Sainte Hélène d'apres l'histoire et la tradition* (Paris, 1911), makes only the briefest mention of the British legend (p. 7); and Jules Maurice, *Sainte Hélène: L'Art et les saints* (Paris, 1930), does not consider the legend at all.

12 For the known facts of Helena's life and the historical sources, see A.H.M. Jones et al., eds, *Prosopography of the Later Roman Empire*, 3 vols (Cambridge, 1971–92), I.410–11; O. Seeck, 'Helena 2', *RE*, vol. 7, cols 2820–3; and R. Klein, 'Helena II (Kaiserin)', *Reallexikon für Antike und Christentum*, ed. E. Dassman et al. (Stuttgart, 1987) vol. 14, cols 355–75, esp. 367–73. For evaluations of the sources, see Borgehammar, *How the Holy Cross was Found*, and Drijvers, *Helena Augusta*. The *Acta sanctorum* entry on Helena, under her feast day, 18 August ([Paris and Rome, 1867], Aug. III, pp. 548–651), though dated, is still extremely useful. It covers many of the pertinent issues and provides copies of several of the primary sources discussed here. It is to be used with caution, however, because some texts are conglomerates, created from a selection of sources by the Bollandists; other texts are divided and their parts relegated to different sections of the discussion.

13 Drijvers, *Helena Augusta*, p.11.

14 Eusebius, *Vita Constantini* (hereafter, *VC*), III.47; Socrates I.17; Sozomen II.2. See Barnes, *Constantine and Eusebius*, p. 221, on Constantine's refounding of the city. There was another Helenopolis in Palestine, though the exact location is unknown (E.D. Hunt, *Holy Land Pilgrimage in the Later Roman Empire: AD 312–460* [Oxford, 1982], p. 49). This city, as well as the province of Helenopontus, was probably named after Helena.

honour his mother rather than to identify the city as her place or origin, an action with imperial precedent.[15] Cyril Mango pithily sums up the status of Roman and modern knowledge on the place of Helena's birth and a likely reason for it: 'If we do not know where she came from, that is because she came from some pretty obscure place that no-one had heard of.'[16]

Working from Eusebius's comment that she was about 80 on her return from Palestine, a journey of about two years' duration commenced in 326, it appears likely that Helena was born between 248 and 250.[17] Her birth and early life are not recorded, probably suppressed by Constantine because she came from a family of low social standing. The fact that Helena sprang from humble origins and perhaps worked as a *stabularia* ('stable-maid' or 'inn-keeper') was widely acknowledged in the fourth-century sources.[18] Some writers attempted to make a virtue out of this fact; others ignore it or gloss over it, especially after Constantine had been proclaimed emperor.[19] We know that she was the partner of Constantius Chlorus (a Roman military commander and later emperor), though the exact nature of their relationship is in dispute. Helena's low social status and the terminology used in contemporary sources suggest that she was either the concubine or a 'common-law' wife of Constantius Chlorus, before he became caesar (293–305) and later emperor (305–6).[20] Helena bore a son, Constantine, to Constantius in 272 or 273 at Naissus in Dardania (modern Nish in Serbia).[21] Sources confirm that Constantius divorced or separated from her in 288 or 289 to marry Theodora, daughter of the emperor Maximian, for whom Constantius served as Praetorian Prefect in Gaul. Very likely, this marital change was a precondition of Constantius's subsequent elevation to caesar, as indicated

---

15 Cyril Mango, 'The Empress Helena, Helenopolis, Pylae', *Travaux et Mémoires* 12 (1994), pp. 143–58, argues that it is unlikely that Helena was born in Drepanum, and that Helenopolis was 'founded by Constantine with a view to improving the network of communications leading to a new capital' (p. 150), citing instances of imperial naming practices expressing maternal respect.

16 Mango, 'The Empress Helena', p. 150.

17 Eusebius, of course, might have exaggerated Helena's age for rhetorical reasons (Drijvers, *Helena Augusta*, p. 15).

18 This low social status was first alluded to by Eutropius in his *Breviarium* in the mid-fourth century (Constantine was born 'ex obscuriore matrimonio', 'from a rather ignoble marriage') and elaborated by Ambrose, the first to refer to Helena specifically as a *stabularia* (Drijvers, *Helena Augusta*, p. 15).

19 Ambrose refers to her as a 'good' stable-maid ('bona stabularia') (*De obitu Theodosii*, ed. O. Faller, *Sancti Ambrosii opera*, pars VII, CSEL 43 [Vienna, 1955]), § 42, p. 393); Engl. trans.: Mary Dolorosa Mannix, *Sancti Ambrosii oratio de obitu Theodosii: Text, Translation, Introduction and Commentary* (Washington, D.C., 1925). Linder, 'The Myth of Constantine', p. 84, describes a conscious programme of image reform: '[Constantine's] accession to the throne was followed . . . by an intensive state propaganda aimed at the creation of a new image of Helen.' See also Lieu and Montserrat, *From Constantine to Julian*, p. 49.

20 Drijvers, *Helena Augusta*, pp. 17–18; and Lieu and Montserrat, *From Constantine to Julian*, p. 49. For the view that Constantius and Helena were legally married, see T.D. Barnes, *The New Empire of Diocletian and Constantine* (Cambridge, Mass. and London, 1982), p. 36.

21 Barnes, *Constantine and Eusebius*, p. 3. See the brief but probably reliable account of the birth of Constantine in *Origo Constantini*, possibly composed c. 337 (Lieu and Montserrat, *From Constantine to Julian*, p. 40). The sources give the day and month of Constantine's birth, 27 February, but not the year.

by Jerome in his *Chronicon*.[22] Helena's humble origins would not necessarily have made her seem an unsuitable wife for Constantius once he had been made a member of Diocletian's tetrarchy in 289[23] (all of the Tetrarchs were of low birth, and Diocletian himself was known to be the son of peasants). She had to make way for Theodora, however, because all members of the Tetrarchy were tied to the others by marriage; as with Maximian and Constantius, emperors became fathers-in-law of present or intended caesars. When Diocletian and Maximian abdicated in 305, Constantius and his fellow caesar Galerius were promoted emperors of the West and East respectively.

Although sources do not comment on the period between her separation from Constantius and her reunion with Constantine after he had become emperor,[24] it is almost certain that Helena never set foot on British soil. She did, however, have a genuine, if indirect, connection with Britain: her former husband (or consort) Constantius Chlorus, then emperor, died in York, on 25 July 306. Constantius, along with his son Constantine, had been in York, then imperial capital of the province of Northern Britannia, campaigning successfully against the Picts. Immediately on the death of his father, Constantine was proclaimed Augustus in York by the troops.[25] The two events are well attested by historical sources and naturally are often mentioned together. Jerome's translation of Eusebius's chronicle, for example, places the two remarks side by side: 'Constantine died in Britain, in York, in the sixteenth year of his reign. After him, his son Constantius, born of his concubine Helena, seized rule.'[26] Similarly, Eutropius's *Breviarium*, an important digest of Roman history produced in the late fourth century, juxtaposes these two events, as do his many redactors.[27] It

---

22 Barnes, *Constantine and Eusebius*, p. 3; Lieu and Montserrat, *From Constantine to Julian*, p. 49; and Pohlsander, *Helena*, p. 17. In their attempts to claim Helena as a Briton, later English writers turned even this unpromising detail to their advantage. In the seventeenth century, the Stowe Manuscript of *Britannia sancta* (London, British Library, MS Stowe 949), based on the *Annales ecclesiastici* of the late-sixteenth-century writer Baronius, states that the reason behind Constantius's divorce of Helena was not her low social status but her nationality: that she was a British 'barbarian' ('The Life of St Helena Empress', *The Lives of Women Saints of Our Contrie of England*, ed. C. Horstmann [London, 1886], pp. 30–6, at p. 30). See below, p. 127.

23 This was the first ruling group of one Augustus and one Caesar in each of the Eastern and Western sections of the empire, to be distinguished from the second tetrarchy formed after Diocletian's retirement in 305.

24 See Drijvers, *Helena Augusta*, pp. 21–34.

25 The proclamation was later modified to Caesar by the emperor Galerius (Lieu and Montserrat, *From Constantine to Julian*, p. 52). Constantine's presence in York (Eboracum) was contentious, as he had been campaigning with the emperor Galerius in the East and suddenly requested leave to fight alongside his father, with whom he crossed the Channel to Britain. For a discussion of the official and probable versions of the story, see Barnes, *Constantine and Eusebius*, p. 27. Lieu interprets Constantine's behaviour as 'desertion by a serving officer' (*From Constantine to Julian*, p. 52).

26 'Constantinus XVI imperii anno diem obiit in Brittania Eboraci. Post quem filius eius Constantinus ex concubina Helena procreatus regnum inuadit' (ed. R. Helm, Hieronymus, *Chronicon*, in *Eusebius' Werke*, VII, GCS 47 [Berlin, 1956], p. 228, lines 20–1). Jerome was translating the *Canones chronici* of Eusebius, which is no longer extant.

27 Eutropius, *Breviarium ab urbe condita*, ed. F. Ruehl (Stuttgart, 1975); Engl. trans.: H.W. Bird, Translated Texts for Historians, vol. 14 (Liverpool, 1993). Book 10, Ch. 1, mentions that Constantine died

was the Constantine/York nub of this widely recounted pair of ideas which probably led some later English writers, motivated by patriotic zeal, to infer that there was some national connection between Helena and York.

There is another important collection of texts which came to play a key role in the development of the British Helena legend, particularly in early modern Britain. Several of the panegyrics originally declaimed before Constantine, and preserved in the late-fourth-century collection known as the *XII Panegyrici Latini*, include conventional praise of Britain as the place of Constantine's elevation. One anonymous panegyric of 310 says, 'O Britain, fortunate and happier now than all lands to have been the first to have seen Constantine Caesar!'[28] Another of these 'display pieces for grand occasions at court', written in 307, compares Constantius and Constantine: 'He (Constantius) liberated Britain from slavery; you (Constantine) ennobled it as well by emerging from there.'[29] Several early-modern scholars have assigned the beginning of the British Helena legend to a misreading of these panegyrics, where Constantine's emergence from Britain, it is assumed, was construed as his physical birth there.[30] Attractive though this theory is, it is untenable, since there is no evidence that the *Panegyrici Latini* circulated after their collection into one codex, probably by the panegyricist Pacatus sometime after 389; they were unavailable to medieval writers until their rediscovery in 1433 in a library in

in York. The *Breviarium* was a very widely disseminated survey of Roman history covering the period from the eighth century B.C. to 364 A.D. It was commissioned by Valens (364–78); translated almost immediately into Greek; and expanded by Paul the Deacon in the eighth century (L.D. Reynolds, 'Eutropius', *Texts and Transmission: A Survey of Latin Classics* [Oxford, 1983], pp. 159–62).

28 C.E.V. Nixon and Barbara Saylor Rodgers, eds, *In Praise of Later Roman Emperors: The Panegyrici Latini. Introduction, Translation, and Historical Commentary with the Latin Text of R.A.B. Mynors* (Berkeley, 1994): 'O fortunata et nunc omnibus beatior terris Britannia, quae Constantinum Caesarum prima uidisti' (VI.9.1, p. 576). This panegyric, presented in 310 after the treachery and death of Maximian, addresses the exploits of Constantius and Constantine, as well as the revolt of Maximian, and is difficult to interpret. It might be 'providing Constantine with a unique hereditary claim to rule' or merely be 'a fleeting by-product of an immediate political embarrassment' (Nixon and Rodgers, eds, pp. 215–16).

29 'Liberauit ille Britannia seruitute; tu etiam nobiles illic oriundo fecisti' VII.4.3 (Nixon and Rodgers, eds, p. 566; 'display pieces' definition, p. 26). Both panegyrics are anonymous, not by either Eumenius or Nazarius, as is often asserted. This earlier panegyric was delivered to mark Constantine's marriage to Maximian's daughter, Fausta, in 307, and his promotion to Augustus by Maximian at the same time (Nixon and Rodgers, eds, p. 179).

30 Francis A. Foster, *Studies in Church Dedications, or England's Patron Saints* (London, 1899), seems to make the mistake of thinking that the panegyrics were influential upon the development of the legend: 'Upon the slender basis of a phrase in two Latin authors, which speaks of Constantine as 'taking his rise from Britain,' a complete mythical history of S. Helena has been built up by Geoffrey of Monmouth and Henry of Huntingdon' (p. 185). Foster does not give the details of the Latin authors, saying only that they are 'quoted in Morant's "Essex"'. The eighteenth-century historian Phillip Morant mistakenly uses these texts as evidence that Constantine was a native of Britain (see below, p. 131). Certainly, *oriundo* is semantically ambiguous, but not in the context of the panegyrics. Edward Gibbon (*Decline and Fall of the Roman Empire*, 9 vols [London, 1776–88, repr. 1909], p. 428; see below, p. 133) notes both the appeal of these passages to English antiquarians and the probable reference to Constantine's proclamation as Caesar rather than to his birth.

Mainz.[31] The Helena legend was well developed by the time of this rediscovery, so no direct link with the *Panegyrici Latini* is likely, other than after this date. It is probable, however, that the resurgence of interest in the British Helena legend in the fifteenth century, due to contemporary political motivations in England and the rise of patriotic sentiment, was fuelled by the re-emergence of this group of texts, which was widely cited throughout the Early Modern period as evidence of Constantine's British birth.[32]

There are only sparse details of Helena's life between the time of her divorce or separation from Constantine Chlorus in 288 or 289 and her pilgrimage to Palestine in 327, or at least until Constantine's proclamation in 306. She perhaps spent most of her life at Drepanum,[33] though epigraphic evidence links her (at times tenuously) with Trier and Rome, both imperial residences of Constantine.[34] During this time, Constantine's activities are naturally the focus of contemporary sources. He exhibited a tolerance towards Christians, contrary to the edicts of the emperor Diocletian, a position which he continued to embrace during his own reign and to pursue more energetically after 312. The change of fortunes for Christians under the rule of Constantine from tolerance to official promotion was demonstrated most emphatically by the emperor's church-building programme and his arrangement of the first 'universal' church council, at Nicaea in 325.[35] Helena must have been in residence with Constantine during this time and been exposed to this pro-Christian environment, possibly undergoing conversion at the same time as her son, or perhaps both she (and previously Constantius) were already Christians.[36] Constantine's attitude towards his mother was clearly favourable, too, because he had Helena proclaimed Augusta (empress) in 324, as is evidenced by coinage issued in her honour.[37] Contemporary sources omit the four decades between Helena's liaison with Constantius Chlorus and her imperial elevation.[38] They record that Helena enjoyed the privileges of this elevated status, including access to the imperial

---

31 M. Winterbottom, '*Panegyrici Latini*', *Texts and Transmission*, ed. Reynolds, p. 289, confirms that the work was unavailable until 1433.

32 W.J. Mulligan, 'The British Constantine: An English Historical Myth', *Journal of Medieval and Renaissance Studies* 8 (1978), pp. 257–79, at pp. 273–4. See below, pp. 127–8.

33 Lieu and Montserrat, *From Constantine to Julian*, p. 143. Drijvers, *Helena Augusta*, p. 21, presents contradictory evidence.

34 Hunt, *Holy Land Pilgrimage*, p. 31. Later legends situating Helena's remains in Trier are discussed below, pp. 44–50.

35 On Constantine's conversion and its consequences, see Andrew Alföldi, *The Conversion of Constantine and Pagan Rome*, Engl. trans. Harold Mattingly (Oxford, 1948); A.H.M. Jones, *Constantine and the Conversion of Europe* (1948; repr. Toronto, 1982); and Barnes, *Constantine and Eusebius*, pp. 3–4, 43, and 48–53.

36 See Barnes, *Constantine and Eusebius*, pp. 4 and 49.

37 P.M. Bruun, *The Roman Imperial Coinage*, gen. eds, C.H.V. Sutherland and R.A.G. Carson, 10 vols, *Vol. VII: Constantine and Licinius, AD 313–337* (London, 1966), index of obverse legends (p. 727). Helena was elevated along with her son's wife, Fausta. Both had been proclaimed *nobilissimae feminae* in 318. Sozomen mentions the gold coins issued in Helena's honour (*Historia ecclesiastica*, II.2).

38 Jones, *Constantine and the Conversion*, p. 199, interprets this re-emergence of Helena only a short time prior to Fausta's death as suspicious.

treasury.[39] This position enabled her to act in the capacity of Constantine's representative on her journey to Palestine, most notably in establishing churches on sacred Christian sites.

The major episode in Helena's life, documented by contemporary and early sources, is her journey to the Holy Lands, in about 326, commencing when she was about 78 years old. There seem to have been political as well as personal motivations for this journey, both documented by early sources. Helena's great piety is celebrated by the ecclesiastical historians who stress her advanced age and great zeal for the undertaking. Those who attribute to her the finding of the Cross claim that she was encouraged by divine visions to visit Jerusalem,[40] but the contemporary historian Eusebius says rather that her journey was a pilgrimage motivated by a desire to demonstrate her gratitude to God and to experience the holy places first-hand:

> This lady, when she made it her business to pay what piety owed to the all-sovereign God, and considered that she ought to complete in prayers her thank-offerings for her son, so great an Emperor, and his sons, . . . came, though old, with the eagerness of youth to apply her outstanding intellect to enquiring about the wondrous land and to inspect with imperial concern the eastern provinces with their communities and peoples. (*VC*, III.42)

Eusebius recounts a brief summary of this tour of the eastern provinces, where Helena dedicated the churches which Constantine had ordered to be built, constructed other churches on the sites of important Christian events (over the cave of the nativity in Bethlehem and on the Mount of Olives), and bestowed largesse upon the poor and others (*VC*, III.42–5). Despite these claims and later hagiographical rhetoric based on them, the motivation for this journey might not have been primarily religious. E.D. Hunt outlines the domestic and imperial upheavals in Rome which might have precipitated Helena's journey, in particular her implication in the murder of Constantine's wife Fausta.[41] Hans Pohlsander likewise enunciates the prevailing critical view, that the journey itself was 'an act of expiation, either for her own sins or those of Constantine'.[42] Ostensibly, though, the journey was a public expression of thanks to God for the

---

39 See Paulinus, Bishop of Nola, Letter 31 (ed. W. Hartel, CSEL 29 [Vienna, 1894]; Engl. trans.: P.G. Walsh, *Letters of St. Paulinus of Nola*, 2 vols, Ancient Christian Writers [London, 1967]), (early fifth century) which recounts Helena's legendary finding of the True Cross, with the help of Constantine's funds. See Drijvers (*Helena Augusta*, pp. 113–15) for a discussion of this text.

40 Rufinus, 10.7; Socrates, I.17.

41 Hunt, *Holy Land Pilgrimage*, pp. 32–4. Constantine ordered his own (illegitimate) son Crispus to be put to death, for unrecorded reasons. Shortly afterwards, his wife Fausta was found suffocated in a steam bath. Barnes (*Constantine and Eusebius*, p. 221) argues that Fausta was implicated in the condemnation of Crispus, and when Helena revealed this to Constantine, she brought about Fausta's own downfall and suicide. Helena's journey to Palestine, undertaken immediately after these events, Barnes argues, was prompted by Constantine's 'political embarrassment' and desire to 'advertise the Christianity of the imperial court ostentatiously' (p. 221). Drijvers rejects, for lack of evidence, the suggestion that Helena's journey was 'an act of reparation' (*Helena Augusta*, p. 67), though the timing of the journey is certainly suspicious.

42 Pohlsander, *Helena*, p. 23.

good fortunes of her family and the means of overseeing Constantine's building works, especially the construction of churches at Bethlehem and the Mount of Olives. Constantine was particularly known for his building of churches, in Rome, Palestine, and Constantinople, but it was Helena's role as his representative in the construction of the three churches on sacred Christian sites in Palestine which sanctified her image and later made it appropriate that she in particular be credited with finding the Cross.[43] Eusebius does not mention Helena in relation to the excavation of the Holy Sepulchre and the building of a church at Golgotha. Only the later tradition of Rufinus and Socrates attributes to her these works, as well as the finding of the Cross.[44]

According to literary evidence, including Eusebius, Helena died at age 80 in Rome shortly after her return from Palestine. Again, the exact date and place are not known. The date of her death can be inferred from numismatic evidence as not later than 329 (after which coins bearing her image ceased to be produced),[45] and also prior to Constantine's renaming Drepanum 'Helenopolis' in 328, leaving 327 as the most likely date.[46] The place of Helena's burial is also in dispute. The earliest reference, by Eusebius, is ambiguous: he says her body was taken by 'a huge number guards to the imperial city and there placed in a royal tomb'.[47] Later writers, including Socrates in the fifth century, interpreted this to be Constantinople, and inferred that Helena had been buried in the mausoleum of the Holy Apostles. This version of events was repeated by medieval writers who used the widely circulated *Historia tripartita*, of which Socrates's history was a source. But Eusebius probably meant Rome, not Constantinople, the 'New Rome'. The sixth-century *Liber pontificalis* (the semi-official serial biographies of the bishops of Rome, compiled from earlier sources) mentions Constantine's mausoleum for his mother on the Via Labicana outside Rome, and this is now widely accepted as her place of burial.[48] The early confusion about the location of her resting place allowed medieval writers, influenced by hagiographical traditions which placed emphasis on the *locus* of a saint's tomb, the freedom to select a preferred site. Some medieval writers claim that she was buried at Rome and then transferred to Constantinople, but the fact that her feast day is joined with Constantine's in the East (21 May) indicates the absence of a local tradition

---

43 Jo Ann McNamara, '*Imitatio Helenae*: Sainthood as an Attribute of Queenship', *Saints: Studies in Hagiography*, ed. Sandro Sticca (Binghamton, 1996), pp. 51–80, takes this argument further, claiming that Helena became the 'original model for the saintly queen' (p. 52) and consequently, queenship during the Middle Ages 'became prominently associated with church building' (p. 62). On Helena as a model for queenly piety and pilgrimage, see also Drijvers, *Helena Augusta*, p. 182, and Drijvers, 'Helena Augusta: Exemplary Christian Empress', *Studia Patristica* 24 (1993), pp. 85–90. On Helena's role in the *Inventio*, see below, pp. 20–2.

44 Hunt, *Holy Land Pilgrimage*, p. 38.

45 Drijvers, *Helena Augusta*, p. 13.

46 Barnes, *New Empire*, p. 77.

47 *VC*, III.7.

48 M.J. Johnson, 'Where were Constantius I and Helena Buried?', *Latomus* 51 (1992), pp. 145–50, at p. 150; and Pohlsander, *Helena*, p. 149.

surrounding her burial, which would have afforded her a separate feast.[49] In accordance with her imperial status, Helena was honoured in statues, inscriptions, cameos, and coins produced during her lifetime and after her death (many of which also feature the Cross), though most of these are no longer extant and some of those which do still exist may represent other figures.[50] Most notably, Constantine erected a statue of his mother alongside one of himself in the forum at Constantinople, a pairing of images which was often repeated in contemporary and later art. It is likely that these visual representations of Helena's position as Augusta alongside Constantine in turn motivated the fabrication of the aristocratic origins perceived to be more appropriate to a woman of her rank during the Middle Ages and beyond.

The early historians spoke about Helena's achievements in a manner likely to encourage a close association with Constantine. Eusebius, in his widely emulated comparison of Constantine and Helena to Christ and Mary, calls her 'the God-beloved mother of the God-beloved emperor' (*VC*, III.43), who deserves to be remembered 'both for her own God-loving deeds and for those of the extraordinary and astonishing offspring which arose from her' (*VC*, III.47). In this remark, Helena acquires both glory by association with her famous and pious son, but also conventional, Marian maternal respect. Eusebius employs the conventional rhetoric of hagiography, 'wonderful woman' and 'thrice blessed', to describe Helena.[51] On the other hand, Linda L. Coon sees Helena's role in Eusebius's portrait of Constantine as a humanising one – 'Helena's philanthropy, humility, and ministry to the poor humanize Eusebius's supernatural portrayal of the divine Constantine'[52] – though in these respects, she is nevertheless extraordinary. Rufinus develops Eusebius's theme of a uniquely excellent character, describing Helena as 'a woman matchless in faith, devotion, and singular generosity, the sort of person whose son Constantine would be, and be considered to be'.[53] Helena, in part because of her association with Jerusalem, had become the ideal candidate for enriching the Christian empire with the discovery of the True Cross and the distribution of its relics, and became an exemplum for aristocratic female pilgrimage, humility, and charity.[54] This journey was to precipitate the construction of a major Christian celebration of her discovery, the feast of the *Inventio*.

---

[49] M.J. Johnson, 'Late Antique Imperial Mausolea', 3 vols (unpub. Ph.D. diss., Princeton Univ., 1986), I.265–7; and Pohlsander, *Helena*, p. 153.

[50] Drijvers, *Helena Augusta*, p. 189.

[51] Cameron and Hall, *Eusebius: Life of Constantine*, p. 295.

[52] Linda L. Coon, *Sacred Fictions: Holy Women and Hagiography in Late Antiquity* (Philadelphia, 1997), p. 97.

[53] *Historia ecclesiastica*, 10.7: 'Femina inconparabilis fide religione animi ac magnificentia singulari, cuius vere Constantinus et esset filius et crederetur' (Engl. trans.: Philip R. Amidon, *The Church History of Rufinus of Aquileia: Books 10 and 11* [New York and Oxford, 1997], p. 16).

[54] See Coon, *Sacred Fictions*, p. 99; and Leslie Brubaker, 'Memories of Helena: Patterns of Imperial Female Matronage in the Fourth and Fifth Centuries', *Women, Men and Eunuchs: Gender in Byzantium*, ed. Liz James (London and New York, 1997), pp. 52–75.

Inventio *Legends and the Cult of the Cross*

Helena came to be regarded as a saint of the Christian church on the basis of the legend that she found the Holy Cross, but this veneration did not commence during her lifetime, or even immediately after she had died. It was not until some 60 years after her death that the story first circulated of Helena's discovery during her pilgrimage to the Holy Lands of the Cross on which Jesus had been crucified. It is probable that the legend arose in Jerusalem, but was quickly transmitted throughout Christendom.[55] The earliest extant reference to this event is in Ambrose's *De obitu Theodosii*, a sermon delivered on 25 February 395 to mark the death of the emperor Theodosius, but this was not the first time the claim was made. Gelasius of Caesarea, author of a lost Greek ecclesiastical history, was probably the first to publish, around 390, the story of the Finding of the Cross, and although this source is no longer extant, at least some of it can be reconstructed from later recensions.[56] It is probable that the two books which Rufinus added to his translation of Eusebius's *Historia ecclesiastica* were derived from Gelasius's work,[57] affording the latter a prominent place in the Western transmission of legends concerning Constantine and Helena.

The only contemporary account of Helena's journey, Eusebius's *Vita Constantini*, makes no mention of the *Inventio*, and scholars have construed this omission as evidence of its falsehood. Borgehammar's argument that Eusebius had subtle reasons for avoiding the subject, but knew that Helena did find the Cross, are simply unconvincing.[58] If Helena had made this great discovery, it is improbable that Eusebius would have chosen to neglect it, given his desire to present Constantine as an individual afforded special favour by God, and his more general agenda of demonstrating the divine presence in miraculous events.[59] Despite the wide circulation and resilience of this legend, and its vigorous defence even today by Borgehammar and others,[60] in all probability

---

[55] Drijvers, *Helena Augusta*, p. 131.

[56] Drijvers, *Helena Augusta*, p. 97; and Borgehammar, *How the Holy Cross was Found*, pp. 7–56.

[57] Drijvers, *Helena Augusta*, p. 96.

[58] Borgehammar suggests that Eusebius might have felt some delicacy about mentioning a tangible symbol of Christianity within a theological discussion (*How the Holy Cross was Found*, pp. 115–20). Similarly unconvincing is the argument of H.A. Drake, *Constantine and the Bishops: The Politics of Intolerance* (Baltimore and London, 1999), that Eusebius knew about Helena's discovery of the Cross but made no mention of it in his *Vita Constantini* because 'his thinking, formed in an earlier age, did not give as much weight to the cross, much less to the cult of relics, as later ages were to do' (p. 275).

[59] Grant, *Eusebius*, p. 146.

[60] See P.W.L. Walker, *Holy City Holy Places? Christian Attitudes to Jerusalem and the Holy Land in the Fourth Century* (Oxford, 1990), p. 129. Drijvers modifies this view by claiming, unconvincingly, that Eusebius knew that the Cross had been discovered (though not by Helena), but omitted any reference to it because 'in Eusebius's opinion, reverence for a piece of wood would make Christianity dangerously primitive' (*Helena Augusta*, p. 88). It is far more likely that before Helena's name came to be associated with the discovery, the story was not widely circulated or believed and was therefore unavailable to Eusebius or dismissed by him as false.

Helena did not find the Holy Cross. The story is attractive, however, because it blends two proximate and credible events into a legendary narrative. The two parts of the story – the circulation of relics which were reputedly from the Cross, and Helena's journey to Jerusalem – are well attested by the contemporary sources. Constantine had indeed ordered excavations of sacred sites in Palestine, and Helena did in fact go there to supervise building works on his behalf, so it was not placing a great strain on credulity to credit her with unearthing the Cross during these activities. It is possible, indeed likely, that wooden fragments, which were reputedly part of the Cross, were found during the excavations by Constantine's builders around Golgotha long before Helena visited the region, as reported by Cyril of Jerusalem in the 340s. Cyril claimed that there were pieces of the Cross, discovered during the reign of Constantine, scattered throughout the world.[61]

Alleged fragments of the Cross might have been found, but it is unlikely that Helena had anything to do with their discovery. With progress of time, however, the attractiveness of linking Helena with the *Inventio*, and thereby crediting the first Christian emperor, Constantine, with the possession of this most powerful symbol, became irresistible. When Ambrose specifically names Helena as the finder of the Cross in 395, this sort of rhetorical agenda can be construed. Ambrose transforms the Christian symbol into an imperial one when he recounts that Helena sent the nails from the Cross back to Constantine, who incorporated them into his bridle and diadem. Ambrose's version of events, 'the Christian empire inaugurated by Constantine and sealed by Helena's alleged discovery', was widely transmitted.[62] The legend quickly replaced the historical version of events: by the end of the fourth century, the *Inventio* was accepted as fact. Ecclesiastical outcomes included the proliferation of Cross relics throughout the empire and the inclusion of the *Inventio crucis* in the liturgy. Liturgical celebrations, documented in the West from the early eighth century, probably originated in northern Italy from around the fifth century.[63] Helena's role as agent of the *Inventio* constituted her only liturgical acknowledgment at this stage.

The *Inventio* legend proved extremely durable and was transmitted very widely in several versions. The two main offshoots are both Syrian in origin and both developed during the early fifth century: the Protonike and the Judas Cyriacus versions of the story.[64] In the former, the imaginary queen Protonike (allegedly married to the emperor Claudius) finds the Cross. This version, in which Helena plays no part, is primarily confined to Eastern sources, but the other legend, in which Helena is directed to find the Cross by the Jew Judas

61 Drijvers, *Helena Augusta*, p. 81.
62 Hunt, *Holy Land Pilgrimage*, p. 41. Ambrose recounts the events as a fulfilment of Zechariah's prophecy: 'By finding the Cross and the nails, Helena rescued the emperors' (Drijvers, *Helena Augusta*, p. 112).
63 Borgehammar, *How the Holy Cross was Found*, p. 188.
64 Drijvers, *Helena Augusta*, p. 147.

Cyriacus, spread to the West and became the most popular version of the *Inventio* in the Christian Middle Ages and was transmitted in several vernacular languages.[65] The ecclesiastical historian Sozomen refers to this legend, though he denies its accuracy, when he relates that Helena was lead to the Cross by divine signs, not by a Jew.[66] The Cyriacus version, however, became the orthodox account of the *Inventio* and is recounted in influential early medieval sources, including the *Liber pontificalis* and Gregory of Tours in the sixth century.[67] Over 200 manuscript accounts of this form of the legend are extant from the sixth century onwards, as well as its frequent treatment in sermon literature, particularly in Anglo-Saxon England.[68] Possibly this popularity derived from the blatantly anti-Jewish character of the story in which the Jew, Judas, leads Helena to the Cross and is subsequently baptised and renamed Cyriacus.[69] The Cross becomes in this miraculous tale the means of establishing Christianity over Judaism, and the accounts of Helena's pilgrimage to the Holy Lands and legendary finding of the Cross served to shift the focus of the newly Christian Roman Empire towards Jerusalem, which had become the new major site of Christian pilgrimage.[70]

As the one who brought about this revelation of the most important Christian symbol, Helena was destined for sainthood. That transformation, however, was to take some considerable time, especially because her spiritual status at the time of her journey was dubious. Despite the legendary embellishment of her activities in Palestine, though, it is probable that the historical Helena made her journey as a Christian, and that it was a form of pilgrimage, even if there were other motivations as well. It remains unclear, however, at what stage she embraced Christianity. Eusebius claims that she had been converted to Christianity by Constantine prior to this journey, but does not provide a date.[71] Later writers were to offer different circumstances for her conversion, and the motivation for her own and Constantine's baptism.

---

[65] Drijvers, *Helena Augusta*, p. 165. The versions are linked to one another: in some versions, the discovery of the Cross under the direction of Judas Cyriacus is subsequent to the initial finding of the Cross by Protonike. For a full treatment of the two versions, see Drijvers, *Helena Augusta*, pp. 147–80. The *Actus Cyriaci* is available in AASS, May I (Antwerp, 1680), pp. 445–8; Engl. trans. M.J.B. Allen and D.G. Calder, *Sources and Analogues of Old English Poetry: The Major Latin Texts in Translation* (Cambridge, 1976), pp. 60–8.

[66] Drijvers, *Helena Augusta*, p. 174, citing Sozomen, *Historia ecclesiastica*, II.1.4. This use of the legend in Sozomen's history (written c. 440) dates the origin of the legend to at least the early fifth century.

[67] Drijvers, *Helena Augusta*, p. 175, cites *Liber pontificalis*, I.167, and Gregory of Tours, *Libri historiarum*, X.I.36a.

[68] Borgehammar, *How the Holy Cross was Found*, pp. 202 and 191. The Cyriacus legend is also the basis of the Old English poem *Elene*, by Cynewulf, discussed below on pp. 36–7.

[69] Drijvers, *Helena Augusta*, p. 165.

[70] Coon, *Sacred Fictions*, p. 99.

[71] *VC*, III.47.

Legends of Constantine and Pope Silvester

One group of legends claims that Helena had been converted to Judaism prior to her Christian conversion by her son Constantine and Pope Silvester and, in this context, the reliance of her fame on that of her son is most evident. Constantine, even more so than his mother, was the subject of a vigorous cycle of legends throughout Late Antiquity and the Middle Ages, particularly in the Eastern Church.[72] Alexander Kazhdan has discussed the development of individual elements of these legends in Byzantine chronicles and hagiography from the fourth to the ninth century.[73] He concludes from the textual accounts that 'the peak of interest in the Constantine-story occurs approximately in the ninth century when most of them [the Byzantine texts] were compiled', including the version of Constantine's life given in the *Chronographia* of Theophanes.[74] Although Kazhdan treats Eastern sources, the same is true for the West, as indicated by the church dedications and literary evidence of Anglo-Saxon England, discussed in the following chapter.

In the most famous manifestation of the legendary Constantine, the emperor is cured from leprosy and baptised by Pope Silvester (Bishop of Rome 314–35). Garth Fowden has examined in detail the origins and development of this legend surrounding Constantine's baptism, the actual date and circumstances of which are unknown.[75] As with many other details of Constantine's and Helena's lives, a lack of agreement between recorded details gave rise to incompatible versions of events modified by legendary additions. Eusebius of Caesarea (*VC*, IV.61–2) and the ecclesiastical historians recount that Constantine was baptised in 337 at Nicomedia on his deathbed as was then the custom, though by the Arian bishop Eusebius of Nicomedia, not by Silvester (the bishop is unnamed in some accounts). Historians from the fifth century, unable to accept Constantine's delay in seeking baptism and his baptism at the hands of an Arian, report different details.[76] John Malalas, writing in Constantinople in the sixth century,

---

[72] See Samuel Lieu, 'From History to Legend and Legend to History: The Medieval and Byzantine Transformation of Constantine's *Vita*', *Constantine: History, Historiography and Legend*, ed. Lieu and Montserrat, pp. 136–76.

[73] ' "Constantine Imaginaire": Byzantine Legends of the Ninth Century about Constantine the Great', *Byzantion* 57 (1987), pp. 196–250. On the cycle of Silvester legends, see W. Pohlkamp, 'Tradition und Topographie: Papst Sylvester I (314–35) und der Drache vom Forum Romanum', *Römische Quartalschrift für die christliche Altertumskunde und für Kirchengeschichte* 78 (1983), pp. 1–100; and W. Pohlkamp, 'Textfassungen, literarische Formen und geschichtliche Funktionen der römischen Silvester-Akten', *Francia* 19 (1992), pp. 115–96.

[74] Kazhdan, 'Constantine Imaginaire', p. 211. For a specific examination of the role of the Constantine legend in the sixth-century chronicle of Malalas and the ninth-century chronicle of Theophanes, see: Roger Scott, 'The Image of Constantine in Malalas and Theophanes', *New Constantines: The Rhythm of Imperial Renewal in Byzantium, 4th–13th Centuries*, ed. Paul Magdalino (Aldershot, 1994), pp. 57–71.

[75] Garth Fowden, 'The Last Days of Constantine: Oppositional Versions and their Influence', *Journal of Roman Studies* 84 (1994), pp. 146–70, at pp. 153–8.

[76] See E.J. Yarnold, 'The Baptism of Constantine', *Studia Patristica* 26 (1993), pp. 95–101.

transmitted the earliest extant version of the more popular form of the story, which has Constantine baptised by Silvester in Rome according to orthodox rites.[77]

The legendary version of the Silvester baptism was first articulated in the Latin *Actus beati Silvestri* of unknown date, possibly as early as 450, which is extant in over 350 Latin manuscripts, 90 Greek, as well as Syriac and Armenian versions.[78] It most probably had its origins in the West and was imported into Eastern traditions.[79] At any rate, it was extremely widely transmitted, and, according to Fowden's evaluation, 'provided, until the Renaissance, the sole widely-known account of the first Christian emperor', for whom 'posterity emphasized God's direct intervention in his reign'.[80] The *Actus beati Silvestri* is of particular importance as it provided the legendary basis for the famous eighth-century forgery, the Donation of Constantine, which allegedly documents how the emperor repays Silvester for this miracle by granting considerable secular powers and privileges to the Papacy in Italy.[81] This purportedly legal document of Constantine's renunciation of power in the Western Empire was widely disseminated within medieval canon law and generally believed to be genuine, despite intermittent dissenting voices, until it was convincingly challenged on philological grounds by Lorenzo Valla in 1440.[82]

According to the Silvester legend, Constantine, suffering from leprosy, refuses at the last minute to undergo the treatment recommended by his physicians: bathing in the blood of infants. For his pity and magnanimity towards the children and their distressed mothers, the same evening he is instructed in a vision by St Peter and St Paul to seek out St Silvester, who has fled to the hills during the time of Diocletian's persecution. Constantine does so, and is not only cured, converted, and baptised, but arranges for Helena's conversion too; he later undertakes an energetic programme of conversion to Christianity and establishes the basilica of St Peter in Rome.[83] As Fowden notes, the mythical leprosy provided a neat symbol of the moral corruption of Constantine's paganism and a vehicle for God's intervention; the use of this symbol thereby constitutes a 'serious attempt to create symbolic events around which to articulate . . . a Christian view of history'.[84] An influential early channel of transmis-

---

[77] Scott, 'The Image of Constantine', p. 59.

[78] Ed. Boninus Mombritius, *Sanctuarium sive vitae sanctorum*, 2nd ed. (Paris, 1910). See Fowden, 'The Last Days', pp. 154–5; and Drijvers, *Helena Augusta*, p. 37.

[79] Linder, 'The Myth of Constantine', p. 55.

[80] Fowden, 'The Last Days', pp. 154 and 170.

[81] On the significance of this document, which was originally considered authentic, but proved to be a forgery in the fifteenth century, see W. Levison, 'Konstantinische Schenkung und Silvester-Legende', *Miscellanea Francesco Ehrle*, 2, Studi e testi 38 (Rome, 1924), pp. 159–247. More recent is Lieu, 'From History to Legend', esp. pp. 136–49. On the Donation of Constantine, see L. Duschesne, ed., *Le liber pontificalis*, 3 vols, 2nd ed. (Paris, 1957), I.cvii–cxx.

[82] *De falso credita et ementita Constantini donatione declamatio*, ed. and Engl. trans. Christopher B. Coleman (1922; repr. Toronto, 1993).

[83] Cf. the Middle English verse *St Elyn*, discussed below, pp. 111–18 and transcribed in Appendix 2.

[84] Fowden, 'The Last Days', p. 170.

sion, the sixth-century *Liber pontificalis*, articulates the kernel of the legend in its papal biography of Silvester: '(Silvester) baptized the emperor Constantine, whom the Lord cured from leprosy <by baptism>, and from whose persecution he is known to have fled in exile.'[85] This story was widely repeated throughout the Middle Ages in saint's lives of Silvester, including those in hagiographic collections such as the *Legenda aurea* and *The South English Legendary*. Of the historical person Silvester, relatively little is recorded, and during the development of the legend, historical details, particularly the dates of his pontificate, were treated flexibly.[86]

The *Actus beati Silvestri* was responsible for disseminating the apocryphal story that Helena was Jewish prior to her conversion by Silvester. The origin of this legend is unknown, but is perhaps based on Helena's association with Jerusalem, the ancient Jewish capital, locating the site of the Cross, and also in her act of pilgrimage, which might be construed (in the mind of a Christian writer) as reparation for her former Judaism. Because her family origins are unknown, we cannot be certain that she was not Jewish, but the absence of any hint of this in the earlier sources makes it unlikely.[87] As a later accretion, however, this narrative item was both widespread and durable. Later manifestations of the British Helena legend occasionally presented her as susceptible to Jewish influences (i.e. conversion, preference for Jerusalem as a residence, ability to negotiate with/influence Jewish groups), without trying to reconcile this with her alleged British origins, a sign of the degree to which the Jewish factor had become ingrained and unquestioned. In the Silvester legend, which is the basis of the two texts transcribed in the Appendices below, Helena has become a convert to Judaism and initially attempts to convert Constantine to this religion, whereas Silvester urges the case for Christianity. To decide the matter, Constantine organises a public debate between twelve Jewish rabbis and Pope Silvester, adjudicated by two pagans. The rabbis kill a bull by whispering 'Jehovah' into its ear; Silvester resuscitates it with the words 'Jesus Christ'. In some versions a dragon is involved, and in the Middle English *St Elyn*, Silvester exposes the demonic possession of an animated brass bull.[88] In all versions, Silvester's greater miracle converts both Helena and Constantine to Christianity. It is easy to see how this legend became a vehicle for anti-Jewish polemic during the

---

[85] 'Baptizavit Constantinum Augustum, quem curavit Dominus a lepra, cuius persecutionem primo exilio fuisse cognoscitur' (Duschesne, ed., p. 170; Engl. trans.: Raymond Davis, *The Book of the Pontiffs*, Translated Texts for Historians, Latin Series, 5 [Liverpool, 1989], p. 14).

[86] See Fowden, 'The Last Days', p. 154.

[87] See AASS, Aug. III, pp. 558–61. Modern arguments that Helena might in fact have been Jewish are unconvincing. Drijvers, *Helena Augusta*, p. 36, and Pohlsander, *How the Holy Cross was Found*, p. 6, reject these claims, enunciated in J. Vogt, 'Helena Augusta, das Kreuz und die Juden', *Saeculum: Jahrbuch für Universalgeschichte* 27 (1976), pp. 211–22.

[88] See Appendix 2 below, lines 205–22.

Middle Ages.[89] The miraculous details, which are accretions of the Silvester cycle of legends, appealed to graphic as well as literary artists.[90]

The nature of Constantine's conversion in this narrative is different from that in the 'Vision of Constantine' recounted by Lactantius and Eusebius in which Constantine is converted by a vision of the Cross or the Chi Rho symbol (a monogram constructed from overlapping the Greek symbols for the first two letters of the word 'Christ'). The earlier version by the Christian rhetorician Lactantius, in his account of the imperial persecution of Christianity up to 313, *De mortibus persecutorum*, reports that Constantine had a vision of the Chi Rho the night before the decisive battle against his rival Maxentius at the Milvian bridge.[91] Eusebius, on the other hand, claims that the Cross appeared to the whole army in broad daylight, bearing the inscription 'in this sign, you will conquer' and was interpreted by a nocturnal vision.[92] Combinations and permutations of these two accounts, which exclude the participation of Helena in the conversion and reduce that of Silvester to the officiator at the baptism, were widely disseminated throughout the Middle Ages, for example in Cynewulf's *Elene*. A strong causal connection developed between the *Visio* legend and the *Inventio*, in which Constantine is first introduced to the symbolic value of the Cross and Helena is encouraged to find the physical object, both by divine inspiration.[93] From the early fourth century, the *Visio* was attached as an introduction to written accounts of the *Inventio*, the legend of Helena's discovery of the True Cross with the help of Judas Cyriacus, and is also found appended to manuscripts of the *Actus beati Silvestri*.[94] Both legends were widely believed, and undoubtedly drew credibility from one another.

The *Visio* legend might even have some basis in fact, at least to the extent that Constantine dramatically adopted the Christian symbol. Andrew Alföldi argues that there must have been some authenticity in the account of Constantine's *Visio* because numismatic evidence indicates that Constantine bore the Chi Rho on his own helmet at the Milvian Bridge and afterwards used the symbol on his imperial banner.[95] Of course, other less divine circumstances might have occasioned the adoption of this sign, though none is suggested in the early sources. Most compellingly, Constantine's propaganda lay behind his published association with the Cross. This symbol, rather than the Chi Rho, became widely promulgated as the official image of the empire in Constantine's promotion of

---

89 See Drijvers, *Helena Augusta*, p. 187.

90 The scene is recounted in many later sources, including the mid-ninth-century *Chronicle* of George the Monk (Lieu and Montserrat, *From Constantine to Julian*, p. 28); and the *Legenda aurea* (on which, see below, pp. 108–9). The same scene is depicted in the eleventh-century frescoes in the Chapel of Saint Sylvester in the Church of the Quattro Coronati in Rome (reproduced in Drake, *Constantine and the Bishops*, p. 394).

91 Ed. and Engl. trans. J.L. Creed (Oxford, 1984), § 44.5, pp. 62–3.

92 *VC*, I.28–9.

93 Linder, 'The Myth of Constantine', p. 66.

94 Borgehammar, *How the Holy Cross was Found*, p. 302.

95 Alföldi, *The Conversion of Constantine*, p. 17.

Christianity as a state religion, thereby lending credence to the accounts of Eusebius and Lactantius.

These groups of legends co-existed and developed separately as Helena's fame grew, especially in the West. In the East, Constantine had been canonised and was the more important member of the pair, whereas in the West, Helena, not Constantine, was recognised as a saint.[96] In most manifestations, though, Helena is associated with Constantine's conversion and is thereby instrumental in the legitimation of Christianity as an official and privileged religion of the Roman Empire. The changing roles of Constantine and Helena in various versions of these legendary strands indicate the shifting historical circumstances and rhetorical agendas of the producers of the texts and visual commemorations of their lives. Because most of the details of Helena's biography were unrecorded, and specifically because the place of her birth was implied rather than stated in the early sources, her early life was invented according to the immediate requirements of individual writers and artists, guided by hagiographic conventions and the legendary accounts of Constantine and Silvester transmitted in a wide range of media. A variety of legendary Helenas of varying prominence were constructed and developed throughout the Middle Ages, in which selected portions of historical and legendary accounts were rearranged and supplemented by the creative powers and interpretive processes of individual visual and literary artists, themselves influenced by (and in turn no doubt affecting) the more amorphous vacillations of tradition. In the chapters which follow, one particular strand in this complex of stories, the British legend, is isolated for investigation, though not without recognising the organic nature and interdependence of several vigorous traditions surrounding Helena.

---

[96] Linder, 'The Myth of Constantine', p. 61.

II

The Legend in Anglo-Saxon England and Francia

FINDING A BEGINNING to the British Helena legend is impossible, as it most probably grew in oral rather than in scribal circumstances. There is no doubt, however, that the legend was already widely known, if not wholly believed, well before the Anglo-Norman writers Henry of Huntingdon and Geoffrey of Monmouth popularised the story in the early twelfth century. There is certainly sufficient evidence to show that Henry and Geoffrey were developing rather than creating mythological narratives of a British Helena. Earlier references to Helena suggest that her legendary origins as a British princess (as well as other legendary and historical versions of her biography) had been in circulation both in England and abroad since at least the eighth century.

The British legend, which was by no means the dominant narrative, seems to have grown out of tales or perhaps a misunderstanding that Constantine was born in Britain. The advantages of claiming a connection with the first Christian emperor and the Roman Empire itself were sufficiently attractive to encourage writers and others to extrapolate elements of Helena's biography to fit with the model of a British Constantine. This claimed connection with Roman Britain, which would not have been necessarily desirable to early Anglo-Saxon writers, eventually achieved the force of tradition and credibility as the historical details receded to the more remote past.

The Cross and Helena in the North

Constantine was closely linked with York in the minds of the English from Anglo-Saxon times because his proclamation as caesar there was widely known.[1] His involvement with the discovery of the True Cross was also accepted, at least in learned circles. This well-documented association between the first Christian emperor and York might have influenced the manner in which the cult of the Cross was deployed in Anglo-Saxon England after its importation from the Continent along with other manifestations of Christian worship with

---

[1] Constantine celebrated the day of his proclamation in York, 25 July, as his imperial anniversary (C.E.V. Nixon and B.S. Rodgers, *In Praise of Later Roman Emperors: The Panegyrici Latini* [Berkeley and Los Angeles, 1994], p. 183). British historians from Gildas onwards record his activities in York.

Augustine in 597.[2] The York connection perhaps accounts for the apparent regional interest in this cult in Northumbria from the seventh century. This phenomenon is strikingly suggested by the evidence of huge stone preaching crosses, of which more than 1500 are still extant, most of them in the north, dating from the ninth century.[3] Considering the early political and intellectual dominance of the kingdom of Northumbria and the spread of Christianity in this region,[4] the location of these crosses in the north is an unsurprising artistic expression, though the sustained local interest in this artform is notable: stone crosses continued to be the favoured sculptural form in the North throughout the pre-Conquest period.[5]

Within the wider context of Anglo-Saxon veneration of this symbol, the early and enthusiastic Northumbrian interest in the cult of the Cross suggested by the sheer number of these crosses shows the remarkable power of the symbol in this region. This interest is evidenced in other sources also. Bede recounts in his *Historia ecclesiastica* (III.2) that King Oswald of Northumbria imitated Constantine's vision of the Cross before battle in 633, by erecting a wooden cross which later was credited with miraculous powers.[6] This dramatic participation in the cult of the Cross predates other recorded Anglo-Saxon devotions to this Christian symbol, which are concentrated between the eighth and the tenth centuries. The major sources are the two extant poetic celebrations mentioned below, *The Dream of the Rood* and *Elene*, the former of which perhaps originated in Northumbria.[7] Numismatic evidence supports the impression that the Cross was a popular iconographic symbol in the north, though not exclusively in this region. Early coins originating in Northumbria frequently include a representation of the Cross, as do many other Anglo-Saxon coins and their Merovingian, Byzantine and late-Roman antecedents and models.[8]

---

2   The ongoing interdisciplinary project 'The Cross in Anglo-Saxon England' co-ordinated by K. Jolly, C.E. Karkov, and S.L. Keefer, will make a timely contribution to the study of the vernacular deployment and veneration of this important symbol.

3   Rosemary Cramp, *Corpus of Anglo-Saxon Stone Sculpture*, vol. 1: *County Durham and Northumberland* (Oxford, 1984), esp. p. 20; and Barbara C. Raw, *Anglo-Saxon Crucifixion Iconography and the Art of the Monastic Revival*, CSASE 1 (Cambridge, 1990), pp. 40–1. The total figure cited does not include those crosses made of wood which have not survived. See *The Dream of the Rood*, ed. M. Swanton (rev. ed., Exeter, 1987), pp. 42–52. The most famous of these crosses is the Ruthwell Cross, which contains, inscribed in runes, an analogue to part of the text of the Old English poem *The Dream of the Rood*, discussed below. See Brendan Cassidy, ed., *The Ruthwell Cross* (Princeton, 1992).

4   See, e.g., F.M. Stenton, *Anglo-Saxon England*, 3rd ed. (Oxford, 1971), pp. 74–95, and most recently J. Fairless, *Northumbria's Golden Age: The Kingdom of Northumbria, AD 547–735* (York, 1995).

5   Richard Gameson, *The Role of Art in the Late Anglo-Saxon Church* (Oxford, 1995), p. 240. See also R. Bailey, *Viking Age Sculpture* (London, 1980), pp. 143–75.

6   Noted also by Swanton, ed. (*The Dream of the Rood*), p. 45.

7   Sandra McEntire, 'The Devotional Context of the Cross before AD 1000', *Sources of Anglo-Saxon Culture*, ed. Paul Szarmach, Studies in Medieval Culture 20 (Kalamazoo, 1986), pp. 345–56, at p. 351; and Swanton, ed., p. 39. Cynewulf, the author of *Elene*, is generally considered to have been a Mercian, though this is on the basis of the dialectal features of the poem; nothing is known of him.

8   Philip Grierson and Mark Blackburn, *Medieval European Coinage, with a Catalogue of the Coins in the Fitzwilliam Museum, Cambridge*, 13 vols, vol. I, *The Early Middle Ages (Fifth to Tenth Centuries)*

The Cross figured prominently in the Anglo-Saxon imagination as a specific image of divine splendour. Michael Swanton interprets the evidence of Oswald's regnal ritual, as well as the imagery in the Old English poem *The Dream of the Rood*, to infer that 'it was this Constantinian vision of the Ravennate cosmic symbol aligned with sun, moon, and stars, which seems to have arrested the Anglo-Saxon mind', to which the image of the Cross soaked in blood was the original insular contribution to Cross iconography, articulated in this poem.[9] With its focus on the symbolic power of the physical object, *The Dream of the Rood* represents an insular interest in the cult of the Cross rather than in the Crucifixion as expressed in both literary and pictorial arts.[10] The crucifix is widely used only from the tenth century.[11] This absolute and synecdochical quality of the Cross, without the image of the crucified Christ, suggests adoption of the symbolic value of the sign into the vernacular religious literary tradition.

This interest in the Cross is supported by liturgical evidence: the feast days of the *Inventio*, *Exaltatio*, and *Adoratio Crucis* (3 May, 14 September, and Good Friday, respectively) were observed by the Church in Anglo-Saxon England.[12] The *Inventio* feast was observed from the early eighth century. The evidence of church calendars suggests the inclusion of the feast of the *Inventio* might have been observed earlier than that of the *Exaltatio*. The feast of the *Inventio*, but not the *Exaltatio*, appears in Willibrord's early-eighth-century *Calendar*, though its inclusion under the date observed in the Eastern Church, 7 May, suggests to the work's modern editor 'the existence in England of a peculiar combination of Eastern and Western usage'.[13] On the other hand, Bede does not mention the

---

(Cambridge, 1986; repr. 1991), pp. 119–20, 158, 161, 170, and plate 31. What were once considered to be early Nothumbrian coins bearing the name 'Ecgfrith' (670–85) depicting a Cross surrounded by light and the word 'lux' (cited by Swanton, ed., p. 45) are now generally considered, on the basis of style and metrology, to be modern forgeries (e.g. C.S.S. Lyon, 'A Reappraisal of the Sceatta and Styca Coinage of Northumbria', *British Numismatic Journal* 28 [1956], pp. 227–42, at p. 229; and more recently and dismissively, James Booth, 'Sceattas in Northumbria', *Sceattas in England and on the Continent: The Seventh Oxford Symposium on Coinage and Monetary History*, ed. David Hill and D.M. Metcalf [Oxford, 1984], pp. 71–111, at p. 71). Helena herself does not make an appearance on a coin until the thirteenth century, and then it is on a Thessalonican one with Constantine (Philip Grierson, *Byzantine Coins* [London, 1982], p. 242, and plate 79, nos 1264, 1266).

9   Swanton, ed., p. 45.

10 Barbara C. Raw, '*The Dream of the Rood* and its Connections with Early Christian Art', *Medium Ævum* 39 (1970), pp. 239–56, at p. 249.

11 Raw, *Anglo-Saxon Crucifixion Iconography*, p. 12 and passim. For artistic representations of the Crucifixion from pre-Viking Northumbria, see Elizabeth Coatsworth, 'The Robed Christ in Pre-Conquest Sculptures of the Crucifixion', *ASE* 29 (2000), pp. 153–76, at pp. 158–63.

12 The actual dates of adoption are difficult to identify, given the nature of the extant evidence. Susan Rosser at the University of Manchester is currently preparing a much-needed monograph on the legends of the Cross in Anglo-Saxon England. I am grateful to Dr Rosser for discussing her forthcoming work with me.

13 H.A. Wilson, ed., *The Calendar of St. Willibrord From MS. Paris Lat. 10837: A Facsimile with Transcription, Introduction, and Notes*, Henry Bradshaw Society 55 (1918; repr. Woodbridge, 1998), p. 29. The manuscript and scribal additions date from the mid-eighth century at the latest (Wilson, p. xi).

Inventio in his *Martyrology*, though he does mention the *Exaltatio*.[14] He does, however, transmit the legend in his *Historica ecclesiastica* (V.16) and at greater length in his homily, 'De inventione sanctae crucis'.[15] Both feasts appear in all 19 of the pre-Conquest calendars edited by Francis Wormald, dating from the ninth to the eleventh centuries.[16] The more elaborate mid-ninth-century calendar known as the Old English *Martyrology* also includes the *Inventio* under 3 May, but Helena is not mentioned, nor is she honoured under her feast day, 18 August, and the *Exaltatio* is likewise absent.[17] The inclusion of the feast of the *Inventio* in these sources demonstrates that the Cross was celebrated liturgically in Anglo-Saxon England.[18] This feast had been part of the Western liturgy and celebrated in Italy from the fifth century and in Gaul from the eighth century.[19] The earliest insular reference to the *Inventio* occurs in the Lindisfarne Gospels, dated at c. 700, in a list of feasts at which gospel readings are to be used; this may reflect local observation of this feast.[20] Later pre-Conquest calendars show that the *Inventio* became more widely an established component of Anglo-Saxon liturgical observance. Towards the end of the Anglo-Saxon period, veneration for the Cross was also expressed in the form of prayers addressed to it.[21]

As in many other regions of the Christian world, physical relics of the Cross were highly prized in Anglo-Saxon England. Alcuin, after he moved from York to Tours, apparently requested a relic in 796,[22] and William of Malmesbury reports in his *Gesta regum Anglorum* (c. 1126) that the Frankish king Hugh made a gift of a Cross-nail to King Æthelstan in Malmesbury in 926 as part of

---

[14] Frederick M. Biggs, 'Inventio Sanctae Crucis', *Sources of Anglo-Saxon Literary Culture: A Trial Version*, ed. F.M. Biggs, T.D. Hill, and P.E. Szarmach (Binghamton, 1990), pp. 12–13.
[15] PL 94, cols 494–5.
[16] Francis Wormald, ed., *English Kalendars Before A.D. 1100*, Henry Bradshaw Society 72 (1934; repr. Woodbridge, 1988).
[17] Günter Kotzer, ed., *Das altenglische Martyrologium*, 2 vols (Munich, 1981). The passive construction of the 3 May entry, 'seo rod wæs gemeted', 'the Cross was discovered' (II.78, lines 15, 16), puts the emphasis on the act not the identity of the person involved.
[18] Thus, McEntire, 'Devotional Context'; contra Raw, '*The Dream of the Rood* and its Connections', p. 251. Compare the contemporary *Martyrologium* by the Continental monk Hrabanus Maurus, who is known to have studied with the Anglo-Saxon Alcuin at Tours: under 3 May, he includes the *Inventio*, with two references to Helena and one to Constantine within the space of a few lines, and a brief entry on the Exaltation under 14 September (ed. John McCulloh, Corpus christianorum, Continuatio mediaevalis 44 [Turnhout, 1979]).
[19] Stephan Borgehammar, *How the Holy Cross was Found: From Event to Medieval Legend* (Stockholm, 1991), p. 188.
[20] Leaf 23, printed in *The Holy Gospels in Anglo-Saxon, Northumbrian and Old Mercian Versions, Synoptically Arranged*, ed. W.W. Skeat (Cambridge, 1871–87), p. 23: 'Inventio crucis domini nostri iesu christi'. Borgehammar, *How the Holy Cross was Found*, p. 188, cites this text as proof that lectionaries are the earliest documentary evidence of the celebration of the *Inventio*. Of course, the existence of this reference in this list might be the result of copying from a Continental exemplar rather than a reflection of local usage. The Lindisfarne Gospels are based on a seventh-century or older Neapolitan original. See also *Dictionnaire d'archéologie chrétienne et de liturgie*, vol. 12.1 (Paris, 1935), s.v. Naples, cols 756–60.
[21] Raw, '*The Dream of the Rood* and its Connections', pp. 250–1.
[22] Swanton, ed., p. 48.

his suit for the king's sister.[23] The *Anglo-Saxon Chronicle* states under the entry for 885: 'The good pope Marinus . . . sent [Alfred, king of Wessex] great gifts and a fragment of the Cross on which Christ suffered.'[24] This story was elaborated in the tenth-century *Chronicle* of Æthelweard and manuscript marginalia of *The Anglo-Saxon Chronicle*.[25] This Cross relic is possibly preserved in the late-tenth-century Brussels Cross.[26] Æthelwold, Bishop of Abingdon, near Oxford (c. 955–63), gave prominence to the cult of the Cross, especially the *Crux nigra*, an iron cross believed to contain a nail from the True Cross and exhumed near the site traditionally ascribed to a nunnery dedicated to St Helena.[27] This object of veneration also served as a reliquary. Similarly, a later, more northern cross in the Church of St Helena at Kelloe in County Durham doubles as a medium for the depiction of scenes from the *Inventio*. The illustrative panels, believed to have been carved in the twelfth century,[28] do not make any reference to the British Helena legend; the location of this votive cross within a church dedicated to her suggests a strong association with this saint and explicit recognition in the region of her role in the *Inventio*.

Meditation on the Cross was also facilitated by written texts, many of which were produced within the monasteries of Northumbria. At the end of the seventh century, King Aldfrith ordered copies of a text describing cross relics, Arculf's *De locis sanctis* (translated and adapted by Adamnan, Abbot of Iona 679–704), to be circulated.[29] This text was abridged by Bede, which probably promoted an even wider transmission.[30] In the late eighth century, Alcuin (735–804), educated at the cathedral school of York, composed hymns and an acrostic poem venerating the Cross, imitating the style of Venantius Fortunatus.[31]

---

23 *Gesta regum Anglorum*, ed. and Engl. trans. R.A.B. Mynors, completed by R.M. Thomson and M. Winterbottom, 2 vols (Oxford, 1998–99), II.135.2, pp. 218–19. See also David Rollason, *Saints and Relics in Anglo-Saxon England* (Oxford, 1989), p. 161: 'Its possession by an English king who liked to model himself on Charlemagne must have been an important asset to that king's prestige.'

24 'Se goda papa Marinus . . . sende him micla gifa & þære rode dæl þe Crist on þrowode' (*The Anglo-Saxon Chronicle: A Collaborative Edition*, ed. David Dumville and Simon Keynes, vol. 3, *Ms A*, ed. Janet M. Bately [Cambridge, 1986], pp. 52–3).

25 Swanton, ed., p. 48.

26 Bruce Dickens and Alan S.C. Ross, eds, *The Dream of the Rood*, 4th ed. (London, 1954), p. 15.

27 *Chronicon Monasterii de Abingdon*, ed. J. Stevenson, Rolls Series, 2 vols (London, 1858), I.7–8; II.269–70, cited by Alan Thacker, 'Æthelwold and Abingdon', *Bishop Æthelwold: His Career and Influence*, ed. Barbara Yorke (Woodbridge and Wolfeboro, N.H. 1988), pp. 43–64, at p. 59. See also M.A. Meyer, 'Patronage of the West Saxon Royal Nunneries in Late Anglo-Saxon England', *Revue Bénédictine* 91 (1981), pp. 332–58, at p. 345; and F.M. Stenton, *The Early History of the Abbey of Abingdon* (Stamford, repr. 1989), p. 3.

28 James T. Lang, 'The St. Helena Cross, Church Kelloe, Co. Durham', *Archaeologia Aeliana*, 5th ser., 5 (1977), pp. 105–19.

29 Swanton, ed., p. 45. Adamnan's text is edited in P. Geyer, CSEL 39 (Vienna, 1898), pp. 219–97.

30 Bede quotes from his own abridgement in his *Historia ecclesiastica gentis Anglorum*, ed. and Engl. trans. Bertram Colgrave and R.A.B. Mynors (Oxford, 1969), V.17.

31 Acrostic poem: 'Versus de sancta cruce ad Carolum', *Poetae latini aevi Carolini*, ed. E. Dümmler, MGH (Berlin, 1881, repr. 1964), p. 225. Alcuin's poem is mentioned also in Swanton, ed., p. 49. See also D. Schaller and E. Könsgen, *Initia carminum Latinorum saeculo undecimo antiquiorum:*

As an extension of this Anglo-Saxon cult of the Cross in the north of England, and on the basis of the association between Constantine and York, this region also became particularly receptive to the veneration of Helena. Church dedications to her, rather than to the Cross, are disproportionately numerous in the north. Frances Arnold Foster has calculated that approximately half of the extant (and mainly very early) dedications to Helena are in Yorkshire and Lincolnshire. He concludes from this evidence that Helena herself was revered in the north of England whereas the Cross was venerated in the south; clearly this dichotomy is not entirely valid as the Cross was also intensely venerated in the north.[32] Although Foster's work has been shown to be somewhat unreliable because it does not distinguish medieval evidence from later interpolations,[33] it is nevertheless still of value in identifying areas of interest in particular saints. There appears to have been a certain degree of continuity of dedication or association between Roman and Anglo-Saxon places of worship and pre- and post-Conquest churches. In particular, Steven Bassett has demonstrated that 'several churches of Anglo-Saxon origin which carried a dedication to Helena had a direct physical relationship with a former Roman structure'.[34] It is tempting to infer from the evidence of church dedications that the British Helena legend has its origins in the north of England from the early Anglo- Saxon period.

In the eighth century, feasts for Helena appear in Continental liturgies. Her prior role in liturgical celebrations had been confined to that of an agent in the feast of the *Inventio*.[35] It was in the eighth and ninth centuries too that claims for a western origin for Helena, either in Britain or Trier in Gaul, were first disseminated. These two phenomena are likely interrelated. After these tales of Continental or British birth became widely circulated, Helena's position as a venerable figure in her own right developed.

Helena's name is found in petitions or litanies to saints, which were becoming popular within the devotions of the Western Church, especially in Anglo-Saxon England from the eighth century.[36] During the later Anglo-Saxon period, Helena's status as a saint seems to have become more firmly established. She is mentioned in several Latin litanies of saints, in mostly eleventh-century manuscripts (though the litanies may originate earlier), with a variety of prove-

---

Bibliographisches Repertorium für die lateinische Dichtung der Antike und des früheren Mittelalters (Göttingen, 1977), p. 137, no. 1.

32 Frances Arnold Foster, *Studies in Church Dedications, or England's Patron Saints*, 3 vols (London, 1899), I.188–9.

33 Nicholas Orme, *English Church Dedications, with a Survey of Cornwall and Devon* (Exeter, 1996), p. 56.

34 Steven Bassett, 'Churches in Worcester before and after the Conversion of the Anglo-Saxons', *The Antiquaries Journal* 69 (1989), pp. 225–56, at p. 246, with details at n. 128, p. 255.

35 Amnon Linder, 'The Myth of Constantine the Great in the West: Sources of Hagiographic Commemoration', *Studi Medievali*, 3rd ser. 16/1 (1975), pp. 43–95, at p. 86.

36 Michael Lapidge, ed., *Anglo-Saxon Litanies of the Saints*, Henry Bradshaw Society 106 (London, 1991), p. 25.

nances: Worcester, Winchester, Exeter, Brittany, and Bury St Edmunds.[37] Although local views on her sanctity are suggested by this evidence, the belief that she was British is not apparent. In only one of the litanies is her name alongside those of native Anglo-Saxon saints,[38] and none originates in the north of England.

Helena's growing popularity and recognition as a saint is also suggested by the evidence of Church calendars, particularly by their annotations and additions. Her name appears on three eleventh-century pre-Conquest calendars: London, British Library, MS Cotton Nero A.II, fol. 6b, under 19 August (though her Western feast day was 18 August), perhaps included by a later hand; under her correct feast day in Oxford, Bodleian Library, MS Douce 296, fol. 4v; and also as an addition to 18 August in London, British Library, MS Cotton Vitellius A.XVIII, fol. 6b (11thC).[39] She is occasionally included in slightly later calendars: London, British Museum, MS Cotton Cleopatra B.IX, fol. 58; Cambridge, University Library, MS Kk.I.22, fol. 5; and London, Lambeth Palace, MS 873.[40]

Helena in Old English Literature

The British Helena legend does not feature in the earliest extant Anglo-Saxon literary texts, Old English poetry; it is, however, alluded to in the later prose tradition. It is reasonable to assume that the legend arose during the Anglo-Saxon period, and was not an idea circulating earlier which was absorbed into Anglo-Saxon literary culture. In view of the importance of the cults of both Helena and the Cross, any pre-existing suggestion that Helena was British by birth would likely be attested in Old English sources. The vigorous traditions surrounding Helena and the Cross in England, and to a lesser extent the historical interest in Constantine, however, provided a fertile context for the later growth of the British legend. Apart from the Latin treatments of the *Inventio* by Bede and Alcuin, the Cross in particular was the subject of considerable interest to writers of the vernacular, both in prose and in poetry.

In the extant Old English prose corpus, there are two homiletic celebrations of the *Inventio*: the anonymous *Finding of the True Cross* and Ælfric's *The Finding of the Holy Cross*.[41] Neither refers to the British Helena tradition,

---

[37] Anglo-Saxon litanies: VI.132 (12thC); VIII.ii.75 (11thC); XXIII.307 (11thC); XXXIII.98 (11thC); XLIV.267 (10/11thC); and XLV.98 (11thC) (Lapidge, ed.). Some provenances are uncertain or unknown.

[38] Anglo-Saxon Litany XLV.98 (Lapidge, ed.). Her name is conspicuously absent from XLIII (late 10thC), where many Anglo-Saxon saints are mentioned.

[39] Wormald, *English Kalendars before A.D. 1100*, pp. 37, 107, and 261.

[40] Francis Wormald, ed., *English Benedictine Kalendars after A.D. 1100*, vol. 1: Abbotsbury-Durham (London, 1939).

[41] Edited, respectively, by Mary-Catherine Bodden, ed. and Engl. trans., *The Old English Finding of the True Cross* (Cambridge, 1987); and Malcolm Godden, ed., *Ælfric's Catholic Homilies, The Second*

though there is some evidence within these texts that she was a figure of interest. The homily by Ælfric, abbot of Eynsham (c. 996–1010), attributes the desire to find the Cross to Helena rather than to Constantine. In his *The Finding of the Holy Cross*, Ælfric follows the *Historia tripartita* in recounting that Helena was prompted to this journey by a divine vision (lines 39–42), but he follows Rufinus's account of the Vision of Constantine:

> His mother was Christian. She was called Helena. . . . Then she went to Jerusalem, with great faith, intending to find the Cross on which Christ suffered. She came to the place which God indicated to her in a divine vision.[42]

The other homily, the anonymous *The Finding of the True Cross*, states that Helena did not make the pilgrimage on her own initiative, aided by divine inspiration, but was sent by Constantine in order to establish churches upon the holy sites.[43] A recent editor of this second homily, Mary-Catherine Bodden, suggests there was 'a native homiletic tradition for the narrative [of the Finding of the Cross] which stretches from Cynewulf to Ælfric'.[44] These two homilies show the co-existence in Anglo-Saxon England of two parallel versions of the *Inventio* legend, which differ somewhat in the motivation of Helena's trip to the Holy Lands, but clearly indicate her involvement in the discovery.

There are many other references to the Cross in Old English prose literature, but few to Helena. In another sermon by Ælfric celebrating the return of the Cross to Jerusalem, called in modern editions *The Exaltation of the Holy Cross* (as a sequel to *The Finding of the Holy Cross*), Helena is mentioned by name but Constantine is not. He is called 'her dear son',[45] suggesting that his relationship to Helena was so well known as not to require mention by name, or perhaps that she, rather than Constantine, was the focus of the sermon. Constantine's daughter, Constantia (or Constantina) is also the subject of Old English homily on St Agnes: Constantine suffers leprosy, which is cured by St Agnes by means of a dream (there is an obvious parallel with Constantine's disease and cure in the Silvester legend).[46] In this version, Constantine's daughter, not his mother, brings about his conversion and requests that her father establish a church to honour St Agnes.

In the relatively smaller number of poetic texts from Anglo-Saxon England (comparable in size to the complete works of Chaucer), the Cross is the thematic

---

Series, EETS, ss 5 (London, 1979), pp. 174–76. The former, in translation, is also in Michael Swanton, *Anglo-Saxon Prose* (London, 1993), pp. 114–21.

[42] Godden, ed., p. 175: 'His modor wæs cristen. Elena gehaten . . . þa ferde heo to hierusalem. mid fullum geleafan. wolde ða rode findan. ðe crist on ðrowode. Heo becom to þære stowe swa hire geswutelode god. þurh heofonlicere gebicnunge' (lines 38–42).

[43] Bodden, ed., pp. 68–71.

[44] Bodden, ed., pp. 54–5. Bodden suggests that this continuity might in part spring from the belief that Helena was British, but does not investigate this matter further. The idea is unsustainable, because there is no reference within the homilies to Helena's supposed British origins.

[45] 'Hire leofan sunu' (*Ælfric's Lives of the Saints*, ed. and Engl. trans. Walter W. Skeat, 4 vols, EETS, os 76, 82, 94, 114 [London, 1881–1900; repr. in 2 vols, 1966], II.144–58 [p. 144, line 13]).

[46] Skeat, ed., I.170–87; pp. 184–86, lines 261–95.

focus of two poems, *The Dream of the Rood* and *Elene*. In the former, an alternatingly bejewelled and blood-soaked cross recounts its own experience of the Crucifixion to a dreamer.[47] This poem does not mention the legendary finder of the Cross, Helena, though the discovery itself is alluded to briefly (lines 75–7). The date of composition and the identity of the author are unknown, though the manuscript in which the poem is contained is dated palaeographically to the late tenth century.[48] Swanton argues on linguistic grounds for an earlier, specifically northern, exemplar for *The Dream of the Rood*, a direct product of 'the flowering of the cross cult in Northumbria'.[49] The innovative viewpoint of the Crucifixion taken in this poem, where the Cross itself is an animated entity enunciating its empathetic participation in Christ's suffering to a dreamer–narrator, is a meditation on the object's symbolic power unmatched in literary treatments of the subject.[50] In this text, there is a far greater interest in the Cross as Christian symbol than in the provenance of the physical object.

The story of the *Inventio* is recounted in greater detail in the long poem called in modern editions *Elene*.[51] This ninth-century poetic account omits any reference to Constantine's or Helena's origins.[52] This poem was written by Cynewulf, who signs his name in runes at the conclusion of this and three other verse texts. He was probably 'a west Mercian poet writing in the first half of the ninth century', though nothing is known about him for certain.[53] But even though the poem recounts Constantine's vision of the Cross and Helena's discovery of it, the nationality of the two protagonists is not of interest. *Elene* is heavily based on the widely popular *Acta Cyriaci*: the narrative follows the discovery of the Cross by Helena with the assistance of Judas Cyriacus. It also recounts at length Lactantius's version of Constantine's vision, subsequent conversion, and baptism by Silvester (lines 69–192).[54] In *Elene* as in the source text,

---

47 Recent editions include those by Swanton (rev. 1987) and Dickins and Ross (4th ed. 1954).

48 Swanton, ed., *The Dream of the Rood*, p. 1. As mentioned above, part of the text is inscribed in runes on the faces of a monumental stone cross in Ruthwell, though the chronological relationship between the two texts is still disputed. The runes were probably added after the cross had been built in the mid-eighth century (Douglas MacLean, 'The Date of the Ruthwell Cross', in Cassidy, ed., *The Ruthwell Cross*, pp. 49–70).

49 Swanton, ed., p. 39. Cf. Raw, '*The Dream of the Rood* and its Connections', where a later date (early tenth century) is suggested, less convincingly, on the grounds that it would then be contemporary with other written devotions to the Cross (p. 251).

50 There is an enormous secondary literature on the poem (for which see Swanton's edition and the annual listings in *Anglo-Saxon England* and *Old English Newsletter*). For a discussion of the literary role of the dream framework in a poetic meditation on the Cross, see A. Harbus, 'Dream and Symbol in *The Dream of the Rood*', *Nottingham Medieval Studies* 40 (1996), pp. 1–15.

51 It is unnamed in the single extant manuscript witness, but editions, from the nineteenth century on refer to the poem by this name (see P.O.E. Gradon, *Cynewulf's Elene* [London, 1958], pp. 7–9).

52 Jane Chance, *Woman as Hero in Old English Literature* (Syracuse, 1986), mistakes the British Helena legend for fact and argues from this misconception that Cynewulf 'anglicises' her confrontation with the Jews as well as Constantine's conversion (pp. 38–9).

53 Gradon, ed., p. 23.

54 There is other evidence that the legend of St Silvester was known in Anglo-Saxon England. The late-eleventh-century codex of a possibly earlier collection of saints' lives known as the Cotton-Corpus Legendary (London, British Library, MS Cotton Nero E.I, pt ii, fols 168r–180r)

finding the Cross is the prearranged object of the journey, and Helena acts merely under Constantine's order to travel to Jerusalem and search out the Cross (line 214). In this, *Elene* agrees with the homily *The Finding of the True Cross*. The *Inventio* (occupying 84 percent of the poem, according to one calculation[55]), rather than Helena, is the main subject of the poem. This momentous event in Christian history is at the forefront of the narrative, and shapes the presentation of both Helena and Constantine. In a detailed and convincing consideration of Cynewulf's alterations to his source text, Gordon Whatley argues that Constantine is presented as a typological 'New Israel' involved in 'a profoundly significant and portentous moment in the history of his own culture'.[56] That culture is the imperial Christian Church, not Anglo-Saxon England. Cynewulf's presentation of Helena in his poem includes alterations to his source relating to the development of an appropriate saintly persona rather than to any issues of national identification. Karin Olsen has shown that Cynewulf's Helena is moulded into a less temporally powerful, less emotional figure than her counterpart in the Latin analogues.[57]

The British Helena legend, then, is not invoked within these extant Old English poetic and homiletic texts, although Helena herself and the Cross are topics of considerable interest and liturgical veneration. There is evidence in other texts, however, of the belief that Constantine at least was born in Britain.

Aldhelm, Histories, and Chronicles

The earliest recorded reference to a local connection with Helena is in Aldhelm's prose version of *De Virginitate*, a collection of saints' lives produced at the end of the seventh or the beginning of the eighth century. Aldhelm (d. 709) was Abbot of Malmesbury and later Bishop of Sherborne. In his prose text, he situates Constantine's birth in Britain and specifically mentions the name and status of his mother. In his 'Vita Constantinae', a section of his *De virginitate*

---

includes the legend as the *Gesta S. Siluestri*, which 'has been extensively altered and added to in a hand of the second quarter of the twelfth century, probably that of John of Worcester' (Peter Jackson and Michael Lapidge, 'The Contents of the Cotton-Corpus Legendary', *Holy Men and Holy Women: Old English Prose Saints' Lives and their Contexts*, ed. Paul E. Szarmach [Albany, N.Y., 1996], pp. 131–46, at pp. 143–4). More generally, Silvester rather than this particular legend about him is commemorated on his feast day, 31 December, in the extant Anglo-Saxon calendars, including Willibrord's, the Old English *Martyrology*, and all nineteen pre-Conquest calendars edited by Wormald (*English Kalendars before 1100*), though Silvester's name has been added in a later hand in one, London, British Library, MS Arundel 155, fol. 7b.

55 Marie-Françoise Alamichel, 'La Légende de Sainte Hélène de Cynewulf à Evelyn Waugh', *Études Anglaises* 48 (1995), pp. 308–18, at p. 313.

56 Gordon Whatley, 'The Figure of Constantine the Great in Cynewulf's "Elene"', *Traditio* 37 (1981), pp. 161–202, at p. 202.

57 Karin Olsen, 'Cynewulf's Elene: From Empress to Saint', *Germanic Texts and Latin Models: Medieval Reconstructions*, Germania Latina IV, ed. K. Olsen, A. Harbus, and T. Hofstra (Louvain, 2001), pp. 141–56.

regarding Constantina, the daughter of Constantine, Aldhelm remarks, 'Constantine, son of Constantius [was] born in Britain from the concubine Helena.'[58] Perhaps Aldhelm was implying that Helena was British, or was construed by others to be suggesting this. Aldhelm also subsequently produced a poetic version of the *De virginitate*, which does not repeat the statement ('Vita Constantinae', lines 2051–120), though the two works appear to have been based on the same untraced source and transmit other more orthodox traditions.[59] It is interesting that Aldhelm cites the tradition that Helena was a concubine rather than the wife of Constantius Chlorus, in accordance with the version of Jerome, Cassiodorus– Epiphanius, and others.[60] There is no attempt to elaborate the story, enhance Helena's social status, or justify the remarks, which are presented as undisputed fact.

The statement that Constantine was born in Britain might be Aldhelm's own misreading of his unidentified source. Jean Pierre Callu suggests that Aldhelm's idea might stem from 'une mauvaise interprétation' of the Latin panegyric on Constantine,[61] but since these texts went out of circulation and were not attested after the fourth century, this source of inspiration for Aldhelm is impossible.[62] Callu also suggests that the development of the legend might owe something to the similarity of the words 'Bithinia' and 'Britannia', but this cannot be entertained seriously. The degree of learning and the awareness of world geography demonstrated by Anglo-Saxon scholars like Aldhelm, Bede, and Ælfric would have disallowed an error of this sort, especially because the early sources reduce the opportunity for ambiguity by using the terms 'Drepanum' and 'Helenopolis' in addition to 'Bithinia'.

The source, if any, of Aldhelm's comment that Constantine was British remains unclear. He might have had access to a lost or obscure text. Aldhelm's excellent education and extensive knowledge of Latin texts, and possibly Greek also,[63] admits a range of possibilities. In particular, Aldhelm is known to have collected materials on Silvester's baptism of Constantine and used the *Actus beati Silvestri* for his *De virginitate*.[64] He might have become aware of the British legend during his studies at the school of Theodore and Hadrian in

---

58 'Constantinus, Constantii filius in Britannia ex pellice Helena genitus' (*Aldhelmi Opera*, ed. R. Ehwald, MGH, Auctores Antiquissimi, XV [Berlin, 1919], p. 302, lines 20–1).

59 Michael Lapidge and Michael Herren, Engl., trans., *Aldhelm: The Prose Works* (Cambridge, 1979), p. 178.

60 See above, p. 13.

61 Jean Pierre Callu, ' "Ortus Constantini": Aspects historiques de la légende', *Constantino il grande: Dall'antichità all'umanesimo*, Colloquio sul cristianesimo nel mondo antico, ed. G. Bonamente and F. Fusco (Macerata, 1990), pp. 253–82, at p. 259.

62 See above, p. 15.

63 Lapidge and Herren, eds, *Aldhelm*, p. 8.

64 Samuel Lieu, 'From History to Legend and Legend to History: The Medieval and Byzantine Transformation of Constantine's *Vita*', *Constantine: History, Historiography and Legend*, ed. S.N.C. Lieu and Dominic Montserrat (London and New York, 1998), pp. 136–76, at p. 136.

Canterbury, where a separate Byzantine legend relating to St Helena was in existence.[65] Legends relating to Constantine were particularly numerous in Byzantine texts, which themselves provided the main source of myths relating to Constantine in the medieval West.[66] Remarkably, Constantine's British origin is claimed in one of these Eastern sources. This myth is preserved in a Latin redaction of a now lost tenth-century (or earlier) Greek text, a list of the dates of death or deposition of the emperors from Constantine, the *Necrologium imperatorem*. The casual reference to Constantine's British birth suggests acceptance of this view at least as far back as the original time of compilation, and probably much further: 'Constantine, son of Constantius, was born of the concubine Helena in Britain.'[67] The wording is very similar to that used by Aldhelm, suggesting a possible common source. Even so, the evidence of the *Necrologium* that the legend was believed outside Britain indicates the great fluidity and wide transmission of myths relating to Constantine in the early Middle Ages, and increases the likelihood that Aldhelm or one of his sources had some access to an earlier version of the story, from which this detail has been acquired.[68]

Whatever his source or reason for the remark that Constantine was born in Britain, it appears to have been overlooked or rejected by Aldhelm's literary descendants, of whom there were many. Aldhelm's work was widely disseminated during the Middle Ages, becoming a 'curriculum text', though it did not significantly affect the liturgy.[69] His *De virginitate* was certainly known to Bede, who makes no reference to Constantine's claimed British birth in his extremely influential *Historia ecclesiastica*. Given his very clear consciousness of the distinction of Roman and post-Roman Britain from Anglo-Saxon England, Bede

---

65 The 'Theodore Glosses' contain a reference to Helena (Gn-EX-EvIa 36): 'Twelve baskets and six water-pots which contained 150 bushels; as some people aver, they were brought by the dowager empress Helena to Constantinople' (Bernard Bischoff and Michael Lapidge, eds, *Biblical Commentaries from the Canterbury School of Theodore and Hadrian*, CSASE 10 [Cambridge, 1994], p. 395). In their commentary, Bischoff and Lapidge adduce from this gloss that 'Theodore spent some time in Constantinople' (p. 550), where he might have become aware of many other legends relating to Constantine and Helena.

66 Linder, 'The Myth of Constantine', p. 49. See also S.N.C. Lieu and Dominic Montserrat, eds, *From Constantine to Julian: Pagan and Byzantine Views. A Source History* (London and New York, 1996), pp. 24–5; A. Kazhdan, ' "Constantin Imaginaire": Byzantine Legends of the Ninth Century about Constantine the Great', *Byzantion* 57 (1987), pp. 196–250; and Roger Scott, 'The Image of Constantine in Malalas and Theophanes', *New Constantines: The Rhythm of Imperial Renewal in Byzantium, 4th–13th Centuries*, ed. Paul Magdalino (Aldershot, 1994), pp. 55–71.

67 'Constantinus, Constancii filius, ex concubina Helena in Britannia natus' (*Necrologium imperatorem et catalogus eorum sepulchrorum*, ed. R. Cessi, *Origo civitatem Italie seu venetiarum: Chronicon Altinate et chronicon Gradense* Fonti per la storia d'Italia, Istituto storico italiano [Rome, 1933], p. 104). Transmission details and summary of the contents of this text are in Philip Grierson, 'The Tombs and Obits of the Byzantine Emperors (337–1042)', *Dumbarton Oaks Papers* 16 (1962), pp. 3–60.

68 The cult of Constantine itself, however, is recognised as being primarily Roman rather than Eastern (Linder, 'The Myth of Constantine', p. 75). This fact does not disallow a different origin for the remark about Constantine's birthplace.

69 Michael Lapidge and James J. Rosier, Engl. trans., *Aldhelm: The Poetic Works* (Cambridge, 1985), p. 101.

would have had little interest in appropriating Constantine or Helena.[70] Using late Roman historical sources such as Orosius and Eutropius, Bede simply mentions the widely recorded details that Britain was the place in which both Constantius died and Constantine was created emperor:

> Constantius . . . died in Britain. He left a son, Constantine, who was made emperor of Gaul, being the child of his concubine Helena. Eutropius writes that Constantine was created emperor in Britain and succeeded to his father's kingdom.[71]

Like the earlier ecclesiastical historians, Bede pays little attention to Constantine's or Helena's origins; Procopius, the first writer to mention her birth in Drepanum, was unavailable in Anglo-Saxon England. In fact, Bede is not particularly interested in Constantine at all. As Jane Stevenson has argued, Bede accepts the relative local insignificance of Constantine compared with Magnus Maximus (a late-fourth-century Roman general who usurped imperial power in Britain in 383 and ruled most of the West until his defeat by Theodosius I in 388). In this he follows the sixth-century *De excidio Britannie* of Gildas.[72] Bede recounts the same details in his influential chronicle the *Chronica maiora*, adding details supported by earlier historians that Helena was buried in Rome and that Constantine renamed Drepanum 'Helenopolis' after her.[73] This text, along with the *Historia ecclesiastica*, promulgated the historically accurate version of the Constantinian biography throughout Anglo-Saxon England.

The Old English translation of Bede's *Historia*, made in the late ninth or early tenth century, departs from the source text and claims that Constantine was born in Britain. This translation, once considered the work of King Alfred or his collaborators in his educational programme, is now considered by most readers to have been made independently of Alfred.[74] It is generally characterised as a careful and consistent adaptation rather than a translation, with an even more

---

[70] On Bede's wide knowledge and rhetorical agenda, see (among many studies) James Campbell, 'Bede I' and 'Bede II', in his *Essays in Anglo-Saxon History* (London and Ronceverte, 1986), pp. 1–27 and 29–48; and more recently, the articles in *Beda Venerabilis: Historian, Monk and Northumbrian*, ed. L.A.J.R. Houwen and A.A. MacDonald (Groningen, 1996). For the argument that the *Historia ecclesiastica* reflects Bede's own concern with Northumbrian ecclesiastical politics, see Walter Goffart, *The Narrators of Barbarian History (D.D. 550–800): Jordanes, Gregory of Tours, Bede and Paul the Deacon* (Princeton, 1988), pp. 235–328.

[71] Colgrave and Mynors, ed. and Engl. trans.: 'Constantius . . . in Britannia morte obiit. Hic Constantinum filium ex concubina Helena creatum imperatorem Galliarum reliquit. Scribit autem Eutropius quod Constantinus in Brittania creatus imperator patri in regnum successerit' (I.8). Constantine was in fact proclaimed by the troops in Britain and accepted the title caesar, only later becoming emperor.

[72] Jane Stevenson, 'Constantine, St Aldhelm and the Loathly Lady', *Constantine: History, Historiography and Legend*, ed. Lieu and Montserrat, pp. 189–206, at p. 190.

[73] Ed. T. Mommsen, MGH Auctores Antiquissimi, XIII (Berlin, 1898), pp. 295–6; Engl. trans.: Faith Wallis, *Bede: On the Reckoning of Time* (Liverpool, 1999), pp. 157–237, at p. 213.

[74] Dorothy Whitelock, 'The Old English Bede', *Publications of the British Academy*, 48 (1962), pp. 52–90, at p. 74; and more recently, see Janet M. Bately, 'Old English Before the Reign of Alfred', *ASE* 17 (1988), pp. 93–108, at pp. 123–5. Cf. the alternative view asserted by Sherman M. Kuhn, 'The Authorship of the Old English Bede Revisited', *NM* 73 (1972), pp. 172–80.

pronounced English perspective than the original.[75] This new agenda is demonstrated most frequently by the omission of material which does not pertain to the English,[76] but with reference to Constantine, it is manifest in the alteration of the source text. The translator specifically says that Constantine was British, and sources this piece of information, erroneously, to Eutropius: 'Eutropius writes that Constantine was born in Britain and succeeded to the kingdom after his father.'[77] The translator has evidently misconstrued the Latin 'creatus (imperator)', 'raised as (emperor)' to mean 'born', as the Old English term *acenned* exists in the extant corpus only with the latter connotation.[78] If there remains any doubt that this is the connotation, the immediately preceding sentence uses the same word to express the idea that Constantine was born to Constantius and his wife Helena (though he actually calls both men 'Constantinus', a common mistake, understandable given the similarity of the two names).[79] This change might be deliberate like the change from 'concubine' in the Latin Bede to the more acceptable 'wife' in the Old English version.[80]

The purposefulness of the change is indicated by the syntactic rearrangement of the Old English translation. In the Old English version of Bede's *Historia ecclesiastica*, the sense of *imperator* has been moved to the head of the clause to form part of the subject 'Constantinus se casere'. This syntactic recasting, quite characteristic of this translator's method, indicates a complete reworking of the Latin. The previous sentence offers the comparison of the translator's rather free rendering of the expression 'creatum imperatorem Galliarum', 'to him who had been made emperor of the Gauls' as 'þam godan casere' (1.8) 'to the good emperor'. This example indicates that whatever other nuances of Latin might have escaped this translator, the meaning of *imperator* is clear, though it is difficult to be sure whether the rendering of the Latin details of Constantine's elevation is the result of poor translation skills or a misunderstanding of the Latin

75 Whitelock, 'The Old English Bede', pp. 66 and 74.
76 Whitelock, 'The Old English Bede', p. 66, and Stanley B. Greenfield and Daniel G. Calder, *A New Critical History of Old English Literature* (New York, 1986), p. 58.
77 'Writeð Eutropius þæt Constantinus se casere wære on Breotone acenned, & æfter his fæder to rice feng' (*The Old English Version of Bede's Ecclesiastical History of the English People*, ed. and Engl. trans. Thomas Miller, 4 vols [Oxford, 1890, repr. Millwood, N.Y., 1978], I.VIII, 42.17).
78 *The Dictionary of Old English*, A. diP. Healey, et al., Fascicule A (Toronto, 1994), s.v. *acennan*: A.1 'to bear or bring forth, give birth (to)'. All recorded connotations of the term (many of which are in the past-participle form, like this example) relate to this primary meaning of physical birth, or to figurative connotations such as spiritual rebirth through baptism, birth into eternal life through martyrdom, or to the capacity of inanimate things 'to produce, generate', or of the Christian Church, 'to come into being'. The Old English Bede frequently glosses *natus* with *acenned*. The gloss pair *acenned* and *creatus* is unique to this text.
79 'Constantinus . . . ferde he forð on Breotone; & Constantinus his sunu þam godan casere, se wæs of Elena þam wife acenned' (1.42).
80 Although *wif* can and often does denote 'woman' rather than 'wife', it generally denotes 'wife' in possessive constructions like this one (J. Bosworth and T.N. Toller, *An Anglo-Saxon Dictionary* [Oxford, 1898], s.v. *wif*, III).

prejudiced by local tradition.[81] The error of rendering *creatus* 'created' with *acenned* 'born' is repeated in the list of chapter headings which prefaces some manuscripts of the Old English *Historia ecclesiastica* and may or may not have been the work of the original translator.[82] In a reference to a later Constantine (III), who, like Constantine I, was elevated along with Gratian by the army in Britain (in 407), the heading says, 'Gratianus ond Constantius wæron on Breotene acende' (6.25) 'Gratian and Constantius were born in Britain', rendering 'Gratianus et Constantinus in Brittania tyranni creati', 'Gratian and Constantine were set up as dictators in Britain' (Colgrave and Mynors, ed. and trans, p. 8). The application of the British reference to the wrong Constantine as well as Gratian II here strongly suggests linguistic confusion over the connotation of *creatus*.[83]

The person responsible for the Old English Bede, in rendering *creatus* as *acenned* on these occasions, was probably unconsciously creating the legendary location of Constantine's birth in Britain through inaccurate translation choices. This accidental or incidental appropriation also occurs in relation to another Roman figure, Magnus Maximus.[84] Unfortunately, the relevant section has been omittted from the Old English Bede, though it is referred to in the list of chapter headings prior to Book 1, where the same translation choice is made: 'Maximus se casere wæs on Breotene acenned' (6.21) 'Maximus the caesar was born in Britain', for '. . . imperator creatus', 'created emperor' (Colgrave and Mynors, ed. and trans., pp. 8–9). Since it is evident throughout the Old English Bede that the translator was consistent in his renderings, this may be no more than evidence of his regular but erroneous translation choice for *creatus*, though this sort of error is uncharacteristic of this translator. Perhaps his willingness to leap to conclusions regarding both Constantine and Magnus Maximus may acknowledge the existence of rumours that they were born in Britain, or in turn might have helped feed the idea among later writers that these Roman leaders had been born in Britain.

The writers of both the *Anglo-Saxon Chronicle* (first copied and disseminated soon after 890 and continued in distinct local versions until the late eleventh century)[85] and Æthelweard's late-tenth-century *Chronicle* both use Bede's

---

81 J.W. Pearce, 'Did King Alfred Translate the *Historia Ecclesiastica*?', *PMLA* 8 (1883), pp. vi–viii, calls the mistranslation 'the error of a beginner, a blunderer' (p. viii).

82 See Dorothy Whitelock, 'The List of Chapter-Headings in the Old English Bede', *Old English Studies in Honour of John C. Pope*, ed. Robert B. Burlin and Edward B. Irving, Jr (Toronto, 1974), pp. 263–84, at p. 277.

83 Gratian is not mentioned in the Old English translation which omits the relevant portion of Bede's chapter: 'Apud Brittanias Gratianus municeps tyrannus creatur et occiditur', 'Gratian, a citizen, was set up here in Britain as dictator and killed' (Colgrave and Mynors, ed. and Engl. trans., I.11). Up to I.23, several incidents which have been left out of the vernacular translation appear in the list of chapter headings (Whitelock, 'The List of Chapter Headings', p. 277).

84 On the legendary British Magnus Maximus, see below, pp. 55–61.

85 *The Anglo-Saxon Chronicle, A Revised Edition*, ed. D. Whitelock, D.C. Douglas and S.I. Tucker (London, 1961), p. xxi. There are extant seven distinct manuscripts and two fragments of the *Chronicle*, with entries reflecting regional tastes, interests, and chronicling methods.

Historia ecclesiastica as a source, and extant versions might have been influenced by the Old English translation, though no reliance one way or the other has been demonstrated.[86] The entries for 380/81 in all manuscripts of both the *Anglo-Saxon Chronicle* and Æthelweard's Latin *Chronicle* state that Magnus Maximus was 'born in Britain', 'on Breten londe geboren'[87] and 'natus in Britannia erat'.[88] Bede has 'imperator creatus' (1.9). In both cases, the wording unambiguously refers to physical birth. Bede's *creatus* has been misconstrued by the Old English translator as 'created/born', either accidentally or purposefully. Since this change occurs in the work of more than one translator, it is more likely the result of translation error, perhaps influenced by the Old English Bede, than a conscious alteration of the source text. The imperfect grasp of Latin by writers of Old English adaptations might very well supply the key to the origin of the British Helena legend. This sort of mistranslation was also the source of the later (perhaps wilful) misuse of the fourth-century Latin panegyrics in the fifteenth century as evidence of Constantine's British birth. Contrary to later interpretations, the origins of the legend appear to be more closely linked with mistranslations of Eutropius's *Breviarium* (which was available, indeed widely disseminated, throughout the Middle Ages) than to a misconstrual of the *Panegyrici Latini* (which were not).

Other Anglo-Saxon accounts of Constantine did not make the same mistake. The ninth-century Old English translation of Orosius's *Historia adversus paganos* merely says that Constantius bequeathed Britain to Constantine, son of his concubine Helena: 'Constantius . . . gave his realm to his son Constantine, whom he had by his concubine, Helena', [89] and later that 'he was killed there'.[90] The same is true for the earliest Welsh source. The text of the *Historia Brittonum*, produced in Wales around the beginning of the ninth century, says, like Bede's *Historia ecclesiastica*, that 'Constantius . . . died in Britain'.[91] In Anglo-Saxon England, then, there was a fairly low-level adoption of Constantine through the accidental misconstrual of his status in Britain. This error implying British birth might have helped, by extension, to project the idea of British heritage onto Helena herself. The notion that Constantine was born in

---

86 Whitelock, 'The Old English Bede', pp. 72–4.

87 See also *The Anglo-Saxon Chronicle*, Whitelock, Douglas and Tucker, eds, p. 9. C. Plummer, ed., *Two of the Anglo-Saxon Chronicles Parallel*, 2 vols (Oxford, 1892–99), where the same point is made (II.9).

88 *The Chronicle of Æthelweard*, ed. A. Campbell (London, 1962), p. 5. On Æthelweard, see pp. xii–xiv.

89 'Constantius . . . gesealde his suna þæt rice Constantinuse, þone he hæfde be Elenan his ciefese' (Janet Bately, ed., *The Old English Orosius*, EETS, ss 6 [London, 1980], p. 148, lines 7–9 [VI.30]).

90 'He þær ofslagen wearð' (p. 148, line 20). The original Latin text of Orosius's *Historia adversus paganos*, Bede's main source for this section, has a slightly different emphasis, setting down only the two historically verified facts: 'Constantius . . . in Britannia mortem obiit. qui Constantinum filium ex concubina Helena creatum imperatorem Galliarum reliquit' (ed. Caroli Zangemeister [Leipzig, 1889] VII.25.19–22) 'Constantius died in Britain. Constantine, his son born of the concubine Helena, was made emperor of Gaul.'

91 'Constantius . . . obiit in Britannia' (John Morris, ed. and Engl. trans., *Nennius: British History and Welsh Annals*, History From the Sources [London, Chichester, and Totowa, 1980], § 25).

Britain was promulgated as a minor variation of the historically accurate version that Constantius died and Constantine was proclaimed caesar in Britain. The wide dissemination of these facts would later interact with the hopeful belief that Helena was British. If there was an earlier oral history of the British Helena legend, it is not recoverable from extant sources.

Helena in Trier and Hautvillers

Oral traditions lay behind the earliest hagiographic celebrations of Helena's achievements, as was typical with medieval saints' lives.[92] When Helena became the subject of *vitae* in her own right, rather than as an agent in the *Inventio* (as in the Old English *Elene*), the documentation of oral traditions brought renewed legitimacy and renown to her legends. Hagiographic discourse was deployed as a tool for appropriating Helena as a local saint and, therefore, the shape of the subject's biography was manipulated to suit the particular rhetorical needs involved. As Helena's life was modelled according to the conventions of this highly stylised genre, new emphasis came to be laid on her origins and place of burial: the locations with which a physical connection with her could be established. Because the cult of saints, and especially the cult of relics, placed great significance on the physical remains of the saint as the object of devotional pilgrimage and the site of successful miracles, the place of burial was crucial. Almost as important were the place of birth and local associations of the saint. Saints were traditionally appropriated through claims of proximity, but his or her general provenance participated in this process as well. Part of this local attribution involved the inclusion of the saint into the liturgy and local saints' calendars and the production of local saints' *vitae*.[93]

There is considerable evidence that the early English claims on Helena were part of a larger and mainly undocumented competition for claiming her as a patron, which extended to the furthest corners of both the Eastern and the Western halves of the globe.[94] Acquiring St Helena for local ecclesiastic purposes had been attempted by Continental writers wishing to claim that she was a native of Trier, one of Constantine's early imperial residences, because

---

[92] See Evelyn Birge Vita, 'From the Oral to the Written in Medieval and Renaissance Saints' Lives', *Images of Sainthood in Medieval Europe*, ed. R. Blumenfeld-Kosinski and T. Szell (Ithaca and London, 1991), pp. 97–114.

[93] There is an enormous literature on this subject: see, e.g., André Vauchez, *Sainthood in the Later Middle Ages*, Engl. trans. Jean Birrell (Cambridge, 1997); Stephen Wilson, 'Introduction', in *Saints and their Cults: Studies in Religious Sociology, Folklore and History* (Cambridge, 1983), pp. 1–53; Blumenfeld-Kosinski and Szell, *Images of Sainthood*; Alison Goddard Elliott, *Roads to Paradise: Reading the Lives of the Early Saints* (Hanover and London, 1987); and Barbara Abou-El-Haj, *The Medieval Cult of Saints: Formations and Transformations* (Cambridge, 1994).

[94] See Hans Pohlsander, *Helena: Empress and Saint* (Chicago, 1995), p. 11, on the claims of Edessa in modern Turkey.

Helena is believed to have resided there.[95] Although traditionally the cathedral in Trier was considered to be a gift from Helena to that city,[96] there is no firm evidence of her association with Trier despite reputed visual depictions of her there.[97] The Benedictine monastery of Hautvillers near Reims in West Francia made a more concerted effort to appropriate Helena, though not by arguing that it was her birthplace. This monastery claimed to have her relics, and legitimated this possession by situating her birth in the relatively nearby city of Trier. This story was supported by the tradition that part of her relics were reputedly stolen from her original burial place in Rome by the monk Theogisus and taken to Hautvillers in the diocese of Rheims in 840.[98] This translation is usually accepted as genuine, by both medieval and modern writers,[99] and the date, 7 February, is widely recorded and celebrated.[100] The translation of Helena's remains was part of a wider phenomenon of relic theft in post-Carolingian Europe, which reached its peak in the ninth century.[101] Claims to the physical possession of the saint's relics indicate the fervour behind the local saintly association and the demand for relics. As Barbara Abou-El-Haj plausibly suggests, the theft also provided a dramatic quality to the possession of relics and further enhanced the value of a saint to an ecclesiastical establishment.[102]

Hautvillers had its own competitors for Helena's relics, especially as that institution was known to possess only part of her body. The idea that she had been buried in Constantinople persisted, growing out of the vague references in the fourth-century sources to her entombment. This uncertainty about her resting place gave rise to many claims on her relics. In a late account, after the Frankish conquest of Constantinople in 1204, Helena's relics were allegedly translated from Constantinople to Venice.[103] Well before the thirteenth century,

---

[95] See the Bollandists' discussion in AASS, Aug. III, pp. 550–2.

[96] Jan Willem Drijvers, *Helena Augusta: The Mother of Constantine the Great and the Legend of her Finding of the True Cross* (Leiden, 1992), p. 22. See Altmann's *Vita*, AASS, Aug. III, p. 583B.

[97] The ceiling fresco excavated beneath the cathedral in Trier is often claimed as proof that Helena lived there, but there is no convincing evidence to suggest that Helena is depicted in this fresco or was connected with the cathedral (*pace* Drijvers, *Helena Augusta*, p. 26).

[98] Recounted in the late-eleventh-century *Chronica Sigeberti*, under the year 849: 'Sancta Helena imperatrix . . . ad Franciam a Theogiso monacho transfertur, et in diocesi Remensi magna Francorum veneratione excolitur [in Altuillari]' (ed. L.C. Bethmann, PL 160 [Paris, 1880], cols 57–240, at col. 162; and MGH Scriptores VI [Hanover, 1884], pp. 300–74, at p. 339). Altmann, however, says it occurred in 840 (AASS, Aug. III, p. 601F); see Pohlsander, *Helena*, p. 158.

[99] The translation of Helena's relics, which may or may not have occurred, is treated as factual in J.B. (l'Abbé) Manceaux, *Histoire de l'abbaye et du village de Hautvillers*, 1 (Epernay, 1880), p. 202; Abbé R. Couzard, *Sainte Hélène: D'après l'Histoire et la Tradition* (Paris, 1911), p. 219; Linder, 'The Myth of Constantine', p. 87; and Drijvers, *Helena Augusta*, p. 75. Pohlsander more convincingly suggests that 'Theogisus perpetrated a hoax' (*Helena*, p. 158).

[100] AASS, Aug. III, p. 600E.

[101] See Patrick J. Geary, *Furta sacra: Thefts of Relics in the Central Middle Ages* (Princeton, 1978; rev. ed. 1990).

[102] Abou-El-Haj, *Medieval Cult of Saints*, p. 10.

[103] Cited in Andrea Dandulus, *Chronicon Venetum* 10.4.20 (Johnson, 'Where were Constantius I and Helena Buried?', *Latomus* 51 [1992], pp. 145–50, at p. 147). Bertrandon de la Broquière, who recorded his 1433 visit to Venice in his *Travels*, tells the story he had heard there that after the fourth

there arose so many accounts of the placement of her remains in diverse places that it became widely believed that her relics had been separated into portions which were held in different locations,[104] and her tomb at Hautvillers continued to be disturbed, presumably to enable the further distribution of pieces of her skeleton.[105] In this gruesome fashion, tradition in Rome claimed that those relics not held at Hautvillers, including her head, were moved to the Church of St Maria Ara Coeli in Rome in 1140.[106] Because there existed a good deal of scepticism about the authenticity of the relics in Hautvillers, Trier, Venice, and Rome, there arose a pressing need for written corroboration of relic possession (and thereby saintly patronage), particularly because Helena came to be confused with other saints of the same name.[107]

The task of establishing the authenticity of Hautvillers's claim to Helena's relics was undertaken by the monk Altmann (c. 830–89) when he wrote his *vita* of Helena, modified from details provided by the Cassiodorus–Epiphanius, to which he appended an account of the translation of her relics (reportedly to have occurred in 840) and the later miracles asociated with them.[108] As Altmann announces in his prefatory epistle (p. 581), this work had been commissioned by the illustrious and powerful Hincmar, Archbishop of Reims (845–82) in 868. It must have constituted part of Hincmar's agenda for raising the status of the see of Reims to one of ecclesiastical and political pre-eminence, which he achieved very successfully.[109] More specifically, the intention of Altmann's *vita* must have been to increase the prestige of the monastery of Hautvillers.[110] In a typical hagiographical manipulation of information, Altmann achieves these goals in an extravagant fashion. His account of Helena's life not only claims that the relics in Hautvillers were hers, but extrapolates that Helena had been a native and patron of Trier, originating from an aristocratic family. Altmann appears to be keen to press the local connection, as his opening line emphatically establishes Helena's credentials and the city's debt to her generous public donations of property:

---

crusade (1204), the body of Helena was stolen from the imperial mausoleum built in Constantinople by Constantine and taken to Venice (*Voyage d'Outremer*, ed. G.R. Kline [New York, 1988], p. 5).

104 Johnson, 'Where were Constantius I and Helena Buried?', p. 149.

105 AASS, Aug. III, p. 604.

106 Drijvers, *Helena Augusta*, p. 75.

107 Giles Constable, 'Troyes, Constantinople, and the Relics of St Helen in the Thirteenth Century', *Mélanges Rene Crozet* (Poitiers, 1966), pp. 1035–42; repr. in Constable, *Religious Life and Thought (11th–12th Centuries)* (London, 1979), item XIV; see esp. p. 1039.

108 *Historia translationis ad cenobium Altivillarense*, AASS, Aug. III, pp. 580–99 (*Vita*), BHL 3772; pp. 601–3 (*Translatio*), BHL 3773; and pp. 612–17 (*Miracula*), BHL 3774–5. On Altmann, see *Lexikon des Mittelalters* (Munich and Zurich, 1980), I.445–6; and *Dictionnaire de biographie Française* (Paris, 1936), II.263–5.

109 Rosamond McKitterick, 'The Carolingian Kings and the See of Rheims, 882–987', *Ideal and Reality in Frankish and Anglo-Saxon Society*, ed. Patrick Wormald and Donald Bullough (Oxford, 1983), pp. 228–49, at p. 228. On Hincmar, see also Janet L. Nelson, 'Kingship, Law and Liturgy in the Political Thought of Hincmar of Rheims', *English Historical Review* 92 (1977), pp. 241–79.

110 Franca Ela Consolino, 'L'Invenzione di una biografia: Almanno di Hautvillers e la vita di sant' Elena', *Hagiographica* 1 (1994), pp. 81–100, at p. 83.

The blessed Helena, originating from Trier, was of such nobility, according to the rank and dignity of this present life, that almost the whole city of this great magnitude could be reckoned within the bounds of her estate.[111]

This, the first Latin *vita* of Helena, is also the earliest extant text explicitly to situate her birth in the West and elevate her origins to aristocratic levels,[112] two new aspects of her biography which were developed enthusiastically by later English writers and seemed to fit with the known details of her imperial status. Altmann's *Vita Helenae* resulted in the creation of a special service to honour the saint within the church of Reims and must have increased the status of the monastery as the site of devotional pilgrimage. This attention to Helena suggests that the acquisition of her relics was energetically promoted at Hautvillers and was typically a political as well as a spiritual issue. Later liturgical and literary tradition surrounding Hautvillers draws upon this revival of interest in Helena and the numerous later miracles attributed to her.[113] The claims of Hautvillers to possession of Helena's relics were further reinforced by the tenth-century account of Flodoard, the abbot of Reims, in his *Historia Remensis ecclesiae*,[114] which provided an account of the translation based on Altmann's text.

Altmann's *vita* appears to have effectively stimulated a cult of Helena in Hautvillers, which must have further enhanced an already wealthy and powerful see.[115] The success of Altmann's biography lay in establishing a strong connection between Helena and Hautvillers, through the selective and creative amalgamation of details derived from the historical sources and the diverse and well-established legends of Silvester and Constantine.[116] Moreover, he deploys his rhetorical tools effectively when he recounts that there was some doubt as to the authenticity of the relics, but that proof was provided by emissaries to Rome.[117] In asserting the authenticity of the relics held at Hautvillers, Altmann was effectively undermining the credibility of Trier's claims to Helena's remains, thereby fuelling the already intense rivalry between these two dioceses.[118] In a more positive and widely influential light, Altmann's *Vita Helenae* also brought about her acceptance as a saint in her own right rather than as an agent in the feast of the *Inventio*. Her feast day, 18 August, is first recorded

---

111 'Beata igitur Helena, oriunda Trevirensis, tantæ fuit nobilitatis secundum honestatem et dignitatem præsentis vitæ, ut pene tota ingentis magnitudinis civitas computaretur in agrum sui prædii' (AASS, Aug. III, p. 583B).

112 Linder, 'The Myth of Constantine', p. 87.

113 AASS, Aug. III, pp. 612 ff.

114 Martina Stratmann, ed., *Flodoard von Reims: Die Geschichte der reimser Kirche* (Hanover, 1998), MGH, Scriptores XXXVI, II.8 (pp. 150–3).

115 Couzard, *Sainte Hélène*, pp. 219–31.

116 Consolino, 'L'Invenzione', p. 89.

117 AASS, Aug. III, p. 602C. This key piece of information is repeated by Flodoard in his much briefer account of the translation (Stratmann, ed., p. 152), and also appears briefly in the version by Jocelin of Furness (see Appendix 1 below, lines 1044–5).

118 Pohlsander, *Helena*, p. 202.

in the *Martyrology* of Usard, dated to around 875, very soon after the publication of Altmann's work in 868.[119] Manuscript evidence suggests that Altmann's *vita* continued to be influential in Gaul, at least until the twelfth century,[120] and her cult remained strong in Hautvillers during that time.[121] Altmann's claim that Helena was born in Trier was reiterated in the twelfth-century *Gesta Trevorum*, a local chronicle.[122] By this time, Helena had become a more popular figure in European religious art, most notably in Reims, where she is depicted with the Cross in a relief in the cathedral.[123] Given the local claims of Hautvillers and Trier, this representation of her role in the *Inventio* might be interpreted as a further attempt at local appropriation rather than a more general celebration of her accomplishment, though the latter motivation is widely evident in the High Middle Ages. Iconographically, she came to be associated almost exclusively with the Cross and often with Constantine as well, these unique attributes making her a particularly identifiable saint.[124]

Altmann transmits other legendary material while creating new elements for the legendary biography of Helena. He presents the story of Constantine's conversion according to the *Actus beati Silvestri* and Constantine's vision according to Rufinus. For Helena's finding of the Cross, on which he focuses a great deal of attention, Altmann follows the version of Cassiodorus–Epiphanius. Most of his text, however, is devoted to conventional hagiographic praise of Helena's virtues and accomplishments. Altmann provides an account of the place of Helena's death which only partially explains away Constantine's renaming of Drepanum 'Helenopolis'. He says, somewhat confusedly, that she returned to Rome after her pilgrimage to Palestine and was buried in the 'Via Lavicane, between two laurels, in the district of Drepanum, which the emperor Constantine dedicated Helenopolis in his mother's name'.[125]

Altmann's hagiographic treatment brought about some major and durable changes to Helena's biography. He observes conventional practices when he presents an aristocratic subject on whose ethnic origins he concentrates. Like many writers of hagiography, Altmann enhances the formative circumstances and natural attributes of his subject, drawing a connection between worldly and

---

119 Pohlsander, *Helena*, p. 189.
120 See BHL, p. 563; and Novum Supplementum, p. 413. Manuscript details in Bollandists, *Catalogus codicum hagiographicorum latinorum antiquorum saeculo XVI . . . Bibliothèque Nationale*, 3 vols (Brussels, 1889), II.591; III.97, 113, 129, 348, and 393.
121 See AASS, Aug. III, pp. 603–47, for texts detailing the miracles attributed to Helena which continued to be recorded; and, more recently, P.-A. Sigal, 'Les Miracles de sainte Hélène à l'abbaye d'Hautvillers au Moyen Age et à l'époque moderne', *Assistance et assistés jusqu'à 1610: Actes du 97ᵉ Congrès national des sociétés savantes* (Paris, 1979), pp. 499–513.
122 Pohlsander, *Helena*, p. 7.
123 See Hans Reinhardt, *La Cáthedrale de Reims* (Paris, 1963), p. 168; and Peter Kurmann, *La Façade de la cathedrale de Reims*, 2 vols (Paris, 1987), I.198–200 and II, plates 401–4.
124 See Louis Réau, *Iconographie de l'art Chrétien* (Paris, 1958), III.635–6, s.v. Hélène; and *Bibliotheca Sanctorum*, IV.992–5, s.v. Elena.
125 'In Via Lavicane inter duas lauros, in vico Drepani, quem vicum princeps Constantinus cognomine matris dedicavit civitatem Helenopolim' (p. 598A).

spiritual nobility.[126] Later English writers particularly retained this new element of an aristocratic Helena, the wife of Constantius, even if they rejected many other aspects of her story. In this new manifestation, Helena had become extremely desirable as a local patron. She represented the ideal of virtuous, aristocratic sainthood: finder of the Cross, mother of the ideal Christian emperor, and paragon of noble virtue. In these respects, her new character resembles those of a romance heroine, a phenomenon which later secular historians were to exploit, while frequently ignoring the major motif of romance in her biography, her quest for the Cross.

Altmann's attempt to claim Helena as a native of Trier was instrumental in invigorating the cult of Helena in Western Europe and establishing her sovereign status as a saint rather than as an auxiliary in the feast of the *Inventio*. Altmann's *vita*, however, also had political ramifications when it brought about an energetic counter-claim by clerics at York, manifest in their increased liturgical interest in Helena and in Cross relics from the eleventh century.[127] The vigorous claims of York eventually overcame the rival claims of Trier, with the official acceptance by the sees of Reims and Trier of Helena's British origins. Both specifically refer to Helena as daughter of the British King Cole. Showing the influence of later embellishments to the biography, the Reims breviary states, 'Helena, native of Britain, was the daughter of one Cole, king of the island.'[128] The same idea appears in the liturgical offices of Hautvillers and Reims: 'Helena, daughter of Cole, king of the English'.[129] Although both of these texts are from editions published in the early seventeenth century, they can be traced back to manuscripts produced in the twelfth century;[130] the precise date of their inclusion into the offices is unknown. At some stage, however, the British Helena legend was accepted by York's rivals, Hautvillers and Reims. Perhaps as an expression of only incomplete acquiescence, Trier boasts a tomb-stone from the eleventh century claiming inhumation of Constantius in

---

126 Many medieval saints were either royal or aristocratic: see Vauchez, *Sainthood*, p. 158; Elliott, *Roads to Paradise*, p. 78; and Wilson, *Saints and their Cults*, p. 37. Early English saints were more likely to have been rulers than not: see Susan Ridyard, *The Royal Saints of Anglo-Saxon England: A Study of West-Saxon and East Anglian Cults* (Cambridge, 1988).

127 There are no contemporary English documents for this exchange, which must be inferred from the Continental reactions. The English position is also evident in the sudden appearance of church dedications to St Helena dating from the eleventh century, especially in Yorkshire and Lincolnshire (Linder, 'The Myth of Constantine', p. 92). Her popularity in this respect appears to have escalated in the following centuries. In church dedications from the thirteenth century, Helena is the most frequently named of the saints whose *vitae* are later recounted in the collection called the *Nova legenda Anglie* (Manfred Görlach, ed., *The Kalendre of the Newe Legende of England* (Heideberg, 1994), p. 39, using data from Foster, *Studies*, II.365–6); see below, p. 106.

128 'Helena, patria Britannia, filia fuit unius ex insulæ regulis nomine Coël' (AASS, Aug. III, p. 651A).

129 'Helena, Coëlis a Anglorum regis filia' (AASS, Aug. III, p. 648C).

130 MSS listed in Bollandists, *Catalogus*, II.598; and in U. Chevalier, *Sacramentaire et martyrologe calendrier, ordinaire et prosaire de la Metropole de Reims (VIIIe–XIIIe siècles)* (London, 1910). In the Martyrology entry for 7 February, Helena is described as British (p. 30). See further Ch. IV below, pp. 64–5, on the twelfth-century development of the legend featuring Cole.

that city,[131] and a dual saint's life of Helena and Agricius, Bishop of Trier, was produced at the same time for presumably the same purpose.[132] This dialogue between Trier and York, fuelled by the conflicting claims of local interests, and later the capitulation by the religious establishment in Trier, shows that serious consideration of Helena as a Briton was not confined to northern England and had acquired a wide-ranging traditional force.[133] The liveliness of this legend, though, did not altogether hinder the transmission of other stories in Western Europe featuring Helena as a native of Trier.[134]

The claims of Hautvillers to the possession of Helena's relics did not diminish the growth of the British Helena legend in England. On the contrary, the transferral of the focus of her cult to the West, the promotion of her memory in Francia, and the elevation of her social status all enhanced her reputation in England and increased the desirability of appropriating her locally. As the hagiographical tradition gained momentum, her place of birth became an important element in Helena's value as a saintly patron, of equal importance with the final resting place of her relics. In this way, Helena was appropriated at both ends of her long life in the energetic competition to acquire her as a local patron by establishing her physical association with a particular place, just as, according to legend, she sought a connection with the physical Cross. Even within the context of the cult of the saints developing throughout Christendom, this appropriation of Helena was particularly vigorous and manifest in a wide range of genres.

The fluctuating dynamics of claiming Helena as a local patron must have been closely associated with her growing reputation as a venerable figure. As an idea, St Helena gained prominence the more she was connected with local traditions and institutions, which in turn wove her story into the legendary history of the vicinity. Her own reputation continued to rely heavily upon the cult of the Cross; the continued rival claims for her relics, as well as the proliferation of Cross relics, assisted in the promotion of her cult throughout Western Christendom. England, however, did not participate in the competition for her remains, even though Cross relics were much valued there. Helena's less tangible legendary British nationality was far more useful to the particular agendas of English writers, especially the secular historians who would not have been interested in relics and saintly miracles but were more concerned with

---

131 Linder, 'The Myth of Constantine', p. 93.

132 Paris, Bibliothèque Nationale, Cod. 9740, item 10 (fols 91r–106v), BHL 3776.

133 A later manifestation of the currency of the British legend in Trier is the thirteenth-century text on King Cole, called *De gestis patris Helene*, which is placed alongside other saints' *vitae* including one for Katherine and an office for Helena (listed in Van Acker, K.G., 'Ein weiterer Kodex aus dem Bistum Trier [Universitätsbibliothek Gent, Ms. 245]', *Scriptorum* 28 [1974], p. 74, fols 79v–80r), BHL 3790d.

134 The fourteenth-century *vita* of Constantine, *Incerti auctoris de Constantino Magno eiusque matre Helena libellus*, ed. E. Heydenreich (Leipzig, 1879), describes how Helena, a Christian pilgrim from Trier to Rome, is raped by Constantius and then offered a costly ornament and ring as recompense (p. 3), BHL 3780. On the gift motif, see also note 20 to Appendix 1 below.

dynastic traditions. Nevertheless, her growing international reputation as a saint enhanced her profile in general, particularly the aristocratic status and local activities asserted by Altmann. A cult had grown up around Helena which was to be developed quite separately from hagiographic and *Inventio* traditions. Later Anglo-Norman and English writers concentrated on developing the idea of a royal, virtuous, and specifically secular Helena, but before they reconfigured the legend, it had undergone further curious transformation and elaboration within the Welsh tradition.

III

Magnus Maximus and the Welsh Helena

THE WELSH TRADITION adopted and transmitted the British Helena legend with substantial local modifications, incorporating a new set of associations. The Welsh version of this tale depicts a woman called Elen as the progenitor of the race, leader of hosts, builder of roads, and wife of another Welsh appropriation from Roman history, Magnus Maximus. Because all the extant manifestations of this legend are relatively late (i.e. tenth century or later) and belong to literary fiction or the rhetoric of nationalism, the Welsh contributions to the development of the narrative are distinctively and extravagantly creative. Tony Curtis provides a convincing context for this particular appropriation of a figure who combines British, Roman, and Christian elements. He describes the importance of legends to the creation of that 'elaborate structure of ideas', Welsh national identity:

> The retreating, ever more constricted, Welsh people were sustained by telling themselves that they were the primary people of the British Isles, . . . that the origin of their government and ruling families was Roman and Imperial . . . and that they had been Christians for centuries, perhaps since the visit of Joseph of Arimathea to Britain, and that they were utterly different from the pagan Anglo-Saxons with their recent veneer of Christianity.[1]

The Welsh Elen legend, particularly her role as glorious ancestor of one powerful dynasty, plays a significant role in this construction of the nation.

Elen in the Welsh Genealogies

The earliest Welsh source for the British Helena legend deploys her name in an extremely unlikely yet rhetorically powerful way within a semi-fictitious genealogical list. St Helena is presented here as the noble British ancestor of a Welsh leader, as well as the finder of the Cross. This reference to Helena is contained in a late-eleventh-century manuscript of the *Historia Brittonum* (London, British Library, MS Harley 3859), within some appended Welsh genealogies,

---

1 Tony Curtis, *Wales: The Imagined Nation: Studies in Cultural and National Identity* (Bridgend, 1986), pp. 40 and 22.

compiled shortly after 954.[2] This particular manuscript of the early-ninth-century text is important as it is the only complete extant copy of that version of the *Historia Brittonum* which is usually ascribed to Nennius.[3] The second genealogy appended to this manuscript is for Owain in the Dyfed dynasty, and traces his line back to St Helena, finder of the True Cross:

> Ovein, ... from Arthur, ... from Maxim Guletic, ... from Constantine the Great, from Constantius and Helen Luitdauc, who travelled from Britain as far as Jerusalem seeking the cross of Christ and carried it with her from there as far as Constantinople where it is today.[4]

This is the earliest extant attestation of the British Helena legend. Helena's British origins are implied both by the existence of this remark in the context of a Welsh genealogical list, and the reference to Britain as the origin of her pilgrimage to Jerusalem. Her finding of the Cross is the focus of the reference to Helena, placing the dynasty firmly within a Christian context.

The genealogies work on several other rhetorical levels as well. As David Dumville says, these lists do not constitute a 'historical record', but rather 'express a legal or political claim', in this case by Owain of Deheubarth (950–88) to a large portion of Wales.[5] With Helena as an ancestor, the dynasty of Owain claims for itself both imperial and Christian legitimacy, analogous to the long Byzantine tradition of establishing political credibility through claimed descent from Constantine.[6] This position is strengthened by the factual portion of the genealogies. The identities on this list are verifiable at least back to the sixth century.[7] Beyond that point, historical fact is treated more flexibly, and possibly the genealogies were read with this in mind. As Miller has argued, 'it is almost a rule of interpretation of pedigrees to look for the eponym lowest in date' and to regard the Roman names added above as part of a 'eulogy exploiting

2 Kathleen Hughes, 'The Welsh Latin Chronicles: *Annales Cambriae* and Related Texts', *Proceedings of the British Academy* 59 (1973), pp. 233–58, at p. 234.
3 H.M. Chadwick, 'Vortigern', *Studies in Early British History*, ed. H.M. Chadwick et al. (Cambridge, 1954), pp. 21–46, at p. 24. The text is usually referred to as Nennius's own, but David Dumville, ' "Nennius" and the *Historia Brittonum*', *Studia Celtica* 10/11 (1975/76), pp. 78–95, has demonstrated that this attribution is mistaken. He argues elsewhere that 'the primary version ... was written in Wales by a multilingual cleric in the year 829/30' (Dumville, ed., *Historia Brittonum*, vol. 3: The 'Vatican' Recension [Cambridge, 1985], p. 3).
4 'Ouein ... map Arthur ... map Maxim Guletic (MS *Gulecic*) ... map Constanini Magni map Constantii et Helen Luitdauc, que de Brittannia exiuit ad crucem Christi querendam usque ad Jerusalem et inde attulit secum usque ad Constantinopolin et est ibi usque in hodiernum diem' (P.C. Bartrum, *Early Welsh Genealogical Tracts* [Cardiff, 1966], p. 10). See also Edmond Faral, *La Légende Arthurienne: Études et documents*, 3 vols. [Paris, 1929], III.50–7; this genealogy [no. II] p. 51).
5 David Dumville, 'Sub-Roman Britain, History and Legend', *History* 62 (1977), pp. 177–92, at p. 178.
6 Amnon Linder, 'The Myth of Constantine the Great in the West: Sources and Hagiographic Commemoration', *Studi Medievali*, 3rd ser. 16/1 (1975), pp. 43–95, at p. 60.
7 Peter Hunter Blair, 'The Origins of Northumbria', *Archaeologia Aeliana*, 4th ser. 25 (1947), pp. 1–51; repr as text III, *Anglo-Saxon Northumbria*, ed. M. Lapidge and P. Hunter Blair (London, 1984), p. 24, citing H.M. and N.K. Chadwick, *The Growth of Literature* (Cambridge, 1936), pp. 151–2.

and elaborately decorating pedigree technique'.[8] Because many Britons had Roman names, it was easy enough to slip a few illustrious and temporally remote Romans into genealogies. The other examples in this collection show that this was often done.[9] Arthur is also included in this particular list as a descendant of Helena, one legendary ancestor acquiring imperial legitimacy and importance from the other. Since another important figure, Maxim (or Macsen) Guletic (i.e. Magnus Maximus; see below), is also included on this list, it seems that the compiler was loading this genealogy with all the legendary heavyweights available. Helena's name, though, is in the significant last position: it is to her glorious name, not to Constantine's, that Owain's lineage is traced and her entry is the lengthiest.[10] Although Helena's parentage is not mentioned, her legendary father, 'Old King Cole', is not far away. In several other genealogies in this group, none of which mentions Helena, the family line is traced back to Cole Hen, a figure with whom Helena comes to be associated in the twelfth-century histories.[11]

The genealogies consort well with the rhetorical agenda of the text to which they have been appended, the *Historia Brittonum*,[12] which also contains information on Magnus Maximus. As Antonia Gransden argues, this text sought to show that 'the Britons had a long and famous history, comparable to the history of the biblical people and of the Greeks and Romans'.[13] It focuses on the important British military contribution to the Roman empire, most notably in the lengthy section on the Roman emperors who ruled from Britain, listing seven of them, in Chapters 19 to 30. Among these emperors are Constantine (Ch. 25) and Maxim(ian)us, or Magnus Maximus (twice: Chs 26 and 27), who is afforded the longest summary and is referred to again in Ch. 29.

In the genealogy, Helena is provided with her usual Welsh epithet, 'Luitdauc' (or 'Luyydog'), connoting 'with a host'.[14] The combination of this appellation with an explicit reference to the finding of the Cross and maternity of Constantine is the earliest and most explicit proof that the Helena of the Welsh

8 M. Miller, 'Date Guessing and Dyfed', *Studia Celtica* 12/13 (1977/78), pp. 33–61, at p. 37.
9 See Rachel Bromwich, 'The Character of the Early Welsh Tradition', *Studies in Early British History*, ed. H.M. Chadwick et al. (Cambridge, 1954), pp. 83–136, for the argument that 'a favourite device is the introduction of characters famous in mythology and floating saga tradition, whose indefinite remoteness in time constituted their recommendation to be designated as the founders of dynasties' (p. 93).
10 The previous genealogy in this group (Gen. 1), for Ouen, likewise concludes with a longer entry, suggesting that this progenitor is the important one. This genealogy outlandishly claims a cousin of the Virgin Mary as the key ancestor, and other examples in the group list Roman or Biblical figures in the final position.
11 Gen. 9, 11, 12, and 19; he is also on the list in Gen. 10 (Bartrum, ed.). On Cole and the genealogies, see further below, p. 65.
12 John Morris, ed. and Engl. trans., *Nennius: British History and the Welsh Annals* (London, Chichester, and Totowa, 1980).
13 Antonia Gransden, *Historical Writing in England, c. 550–c. 1307* (Ithaca, 1974), p. 10.
14 Rachel Bromwich, ed. and Engl. trans., *Trioedd Ynys Prydein: The Welsh Triads*, 2nd ed. (Cardiff, 1978) (hereafter, *TYP*), p. 452.

tradition was modelled on St Helena. Before this issue is explored more fully, we need to examine Helena's relationship to Maxim Guletic in Welsh literature.

Magnus Maximus and The Mabinogion

The same tenth-century Welsh genealogy mentions Maxim Guletic as a descendant of Helena. This relationship is a variation on the usual model: the two are frequently portrayed as husband and wife in Welsh literature, most notably and at greatest length in a tale from the most famous collection of early Welsh stories, *The Mabinogion*. Maxim Guletic (or 'Wledig', connoting 'a leader of a local, or native, militia'[15]), is a Welsh legendary figure based loosely on the usurping emperor, Magnus Maximus (emperor 383–88) who was held in high esteem in Welsh tradition. His name is on the genealogical list for the same reason that Helena's appears there. Maxim Guletic provides not only a convenient analogy with St Helena as a Welsh appropriation of a Roman personage, but also offers further evidence of the construction of a national heritage out of conflated legendary and historical material.

The historical Magnus Maximus was a native of Spain, though, like Constantine, he did have some legitimate connection with Britain. He campaigned there against the Picts and Scots, probably from 369, and probably became commander of the British troops, *dux Britanniarum*.[16] Like Constantine in 306, Magnus Maximus was proclaimed augustus by the troops in Britain in 383, usurping the imperial title from the ruling Western augustus, Gratian.[17] Also like Constantine, Maximus ruled Gaul, Britain, and Spain after the murder of Gratian, taking as his main residence the city of Trier,[18] a place with which Helena came to be associated. These similarities alone might have assisted the mythical union of Maximus and Helena in the Welsh tradition. Magnus Maximus invaded Italy in 387, but was defeated and put to death by the Eastern emperor Theodosius I the following year.

The activities of Magnus Maximus in Britain and on the Continent are documented by Orosius, the ecclesiastical historians, and other early sources.[19] For the Welsh tradition, however, the sixth-century invective text, *De excidio*

---

15 Bromwich, ed., *TYP*, p. 434.
16 A.H.M. Jones et al., *Prosopography of the Later Roman Empire*, vol. I (Cambridge, 1971) (hereafter, *PLRE*), p. 588 (citing Zosimus IV.25 and Latin Panegyric XII as two key sources). See also W. Ensslin, 'Maximus (Usurpator)', *RE*, vol. 14, cols 2546–55. Michael G. Jarrett, 'Magnus Maximus and the End of Roman Britain', *Transactions of the Honourable Society of Cymmrodorion* (1983), pp. 22–35, notes that Maximus's exact position prior to 369 is unclear (p. 29).
17 See John Matthews, 'Macsen, Maximus, and Constantine', *The Welsh Historical Review* 11 (1983), pp. 431–48; repr as Text XII, Matthews, *Political Life and Culture in Late Roman Society* (London, 1985).
18 Matthews, 'Macsen, Maximus, and Constantine', p. 435.
19 See Jones, *PLRE*, I, s.v. Magnus Maximus 39.

Britannie, by the British cleric Gildas (d. c. 570), was more influential. According to Gildas, Maximus was a tyrant with no right to bear the imperial title, who led an army permanently from Britain to the Continent:

> At length the tyrant thickets increased and were all but bursting into a savage forest. The island was still Roman in name, but not by law and custom. Rather, it cast forth a sprig of its own bitter planting and sent Maximus to Gaul with a great retinue of hangers-on and even the imperial insignia, which he was never fit to bear: he had no legal claim to the title, but was raised to it like a tyrant with a rebellious soldiery. Applying cunning rather than virtue, Maximus turned the neighbouring lands and provinces against Rome, and attached them to his kingdom of wickedness with the nets of his perjury and lying . . . After that Britain was despoiled of her whole army, her military resources, her governors, . . . and her sturdy youth, who had followed in the tyrant's footsteps, never to return home.[20]

In a way characteristic of his polemical agenda, Gildas harshly criticises Maximus for denuding Britain of its troops in this manner, though his suggestion that Maximus took and kept away the entire army is probably an exaggeration.[21] Strikingly, Gildas refers to Maximus as 'a sprig of its [i.e. Britain's] own bitter planting'. There was no ambiguity about this in Gildas's mind that Maximus merely staged a rebellion and was proclaimed emperor in Britain rather than being a native of that place. Later readers of his text, however, of which there have been many, might have misconstrued this comment to mean that Magnus Maximus was born in Britain, as some did with reference to Constantine's proclamation as caesar there. Like Constantine, Maximus was 'created' emperor in Britain, and therefore, according to Gildas, was an imperial product of that nation. Gildas's wording certainly provides later readers with the opportunity of fashioning Maximus as a British-born Roman emperor.

Magnus Maximus's activities are described in the later but extremely influential *Historia Brittonum*, produced by an unknown Welsh author around 830.[22] This is the text to which the Welsh genealogies, discussed above, were appended in the tenth century. The *Historia Brittonum* situates Maximus within its prominent list of Roman emperors who ruled in Britain:

---

[20] Michael Winterbottom, ed. and Engl. trans., *Gildas: The Ruin of Britain and Other Works* (London, 1978), Chs 13–14 (pp. 20–1); Latin text is at p. 93:

> Itemque tandem tyrannorum virgultis crescentibus et in immanem silvam iam iamque erumpentibus insula, nomen Romanum nec tamen morem legemque tenens, quin potius abiciens germen suae plantationis amarissimae, ad Gallias magna comitante satellitum caterva, insuper etiam imperatoris insignibus, quae nec decenter usquam gessit, non legitime, sed ritu tyrannico et tumultuante initiatum milite, Maximum mittit. Qui callida primum arte potius quam virtute finitimos quosque pagos vel pronvincias contra Romanum statum per retia periurii mendaciique sui facinoroso regno adnectens, . . . Exin Britannia omni armato milite, militaribus copiis, rectoribus . . ., ingenti iuventute spoliata, quae comitata vestigiis supra dicti tyranni domum nusquam ultra rediit.

[21] Jarrett, 'Magnus Maximus and the End of Roman Britain', p. 30. See also Bromwich, ed., *TYP*, p. 317; and Matthews, 'Macsen, Maximus, and Constantine', p. 443.

[22] One recension is ascribed to 'Nennius' from the eleventh century (Dumville, ' "Nennius" and the *Historia Brittonum*', p. 94).

The seventh emperor to rule in Britain was Maxim(ian)us. He went forth from Britain with all the troops of the British and killed Gratian, the king of the Romans, and held the empire of all Europe. He refused to send the soldiers who had gone forth with him back to Britain, . . . but gave them many districts from the lake on the top of Mount Jove to the city called Quentovic, as far as the Western mass, that is the Western Ridge. For the Armorican British, who are overseas, went forth there with the tyrant Maximus on his campaign . . . They are the Armorican British, and they never came back, even to the present day. That is why Britain has been occupied by foreigners, and the citizens driven out, until God shall give them help [*he was the last emperor to rule the British in Britain*].[23]

Maximus is credited here with having established Breton colonies on the Continent with the troops he led from Britain and later as 'the founding figure of independent post-Roman Britain'.[24] He was important enough for the *Historia Brittonum* to recount further his proclamation in Britain, his murder of Gratian, and his own execution by Theodosius (Ch. 28). The writer confuses the matter by splitting the character of Magnus Maximus into two emperors. The author refers in Ch. 26 to 'Maximus', the sixth emperor to rule Rome from Britain, described as a contemporary of St Martin of Tours (d. 397), and to 'Maxim(ian)us', the seventh emperor, in Chs 27 and 29.

Because the *Historia Brittonum* was so widely circulated, and it specifically identified Maximus as the last Roman emperor ruling in Britain, the Welsh tradition 'came to associate the transition from Roman to native rule with the death of Magnus Maximus'.[25] For the Welsh, Maximus was remembered as 'the founding figure of independent post-Roman Britain'.[26] Considering this status, it is hardly surprising that the name of Magnus Maximus finds its way onto a politically motivated genealogical list.[27] Because he was credited politically with founding the Welsh nation, it is only natural that his name is exploited in the Welsh genealogical lists on several occasions. Developing this idea, David Dumville goes so far as to claim that 'Maximus is arguably the literary source of

---

23 Morris, ed., Ch. 27 (pp. 24–5). The final sentence is misplaced after the next paragraph in Morris's translation (his italics):
> Septimus imperator regnavit in Britannia Maximianus. Ipse perrexit cum omnibus militibus Brittonnum a Brittannia, et occidit Gratianum, regem Romanorum, et imperium tenuit totius Europae, et noluit dimittere milites, qui perrexerunt cum eo, ad Brittanniam, . . . sed dedit illis multas regiones a stagno quod est super verticem Montis Jovis usque ad civitatem quae vocatur Cant Guic, et usque ad cumulum occidentalem, id est Cruc Ochidient. Britones namque Armorici, qui ultra mare sunt, cum Maximo tyranno hinc in expeditionem exiuntes . . . Hi sunt Brittones Armorici, et nunquam reversi sunt hucusque in hodiernum diem. Propter hoc Brittannia occupata est ab extraneis gentibus et cives expulsi sunt, usque dum Deus auxilium dederit illis. [*Britonibus in Brittania imperator ultimus praefuit*]. (p. 65)

24 Dumville, 'Sub-Roman Britain', p. 180.

25 David N. Dumville, 'Kingship, Genealogies and Regnal Lists', in *Early Medieval Kingship*, ed. P.H. Sawyer and I.N. Wood (Leeds, 1977), pp. 72–104, at p. 81.

26 Dumville, 'Sub-Roman Britain', p. 180.

27 His name is in the significant final position on another of the Harley genealogies (Gen. 4), which traces the descent of Iudgual (according to Bromwich, an 'identified northern genealogy' ['Character of Early Welsh Tradition', p. 94]). Bromwich also notes that the name Maxim Guletic has replaced Ceredig Gwledig as the founder of the Strathclyde dynasty (p. 94).

inspiration for Geoffrey of Monmouth's Arthur, who does such great – but ultimately unsuccessful – deeds as a British emperor on the Continent.'[28] The
appearance of Arthur's name on this genealogical list certainly lends support to
the idea that Magnus Maximus was in the same rhetorical league as Arthur.

The presence of Maximus's name in the same list as Helena's contributes to
the impression that she is being claimed as a Briton, and also demonstrates a
variant construction of their legendary relationship. According to the later and
more widespread Welsh legend, the usurper Magnus Maximus married a Welsh
princess called Elen, the daughter of the leader Eudaf. Here, the legendary
history of the British Helena becomes more complicated as the Welsh offshoot
develops a life of its own. This woman, known in Welsh legend as 'Elen of the
Hosts' (Elen Luitdauc or Luyddog), was remembered as a builder of roads and
mother of five children, including a boy called Constantine (though this was a
popular name in Britain from the fourth to the sixth centuries, even becoming
'one of the main pan-Celtic saints' and the name of a Cornish king).[29]

The story of the union of Magnus Maximus and Elen, daughter of Eudaf, is
recounted in 'The Dream of Macsen Wledig' in the collection of texts
commonly known as *The Mabinogion*.[30] This late-twelfth-century literary
version of events was produced in Gwynedd.[31] It conveniently unites two
legendary Welsh progenitors in one marriage.[32] In this account, Elen, as the
daughter of the British chieftain Eudaf, and wife of the Roman military
commander Magnus Maximus, is linked with two founders of Brittany.[33] This
version of events elevates Maximus's status by portraying him as emperor
before he reaches and conquers Britain, rather than presenting him as a usurper
who seized power once there. It also concentrates thematically on the union of
Maximus and Elen. The story is told as a romance: Maximus falls in love with
Elen in a dream and pursues her thereafter. As Loth says, this Maximus is 'un
personage imaginaire',[34] whom Matthews interprets as 'an expression of the
surviving memory of the Roman empire, put to political use by the Celtic dynasties'.[35] Unlike the Gildas account of a deceitful Maximus, here the hero is
presented as a legitimate emperor of Rome, embodying the popular belief in his

---

28 Dumville, 'Sub-Roman Britain', p. 181.
29 Linder, 'The Myth of Constantine', p. 79. See also P.C. Bartrum, *A Welsh Classical Dictionary*
(Aberystwyth, 1993), s.v. Custennin; and B.L. Olsen and O.J. Padel, 'A Tenth-Century List of Cornish
Parochial Saints', *Cambridge Medieval Celtic Studies* 12 (1986), pp. 33–71, at p. 57, on the confusion
surrounding the name 'Elenn' in Wales, Brittany, and Cornwall.
30 Ifor Williams, ed. *Breuddwyd Maxen*, 3rd ed. (Bangor, 1928); Engl. trans.: Gwyn Jones and Thomas
Jones, *The Mabinogion*, 2nd ed. (London, 1974). See also J. Gwenogvryn Evans, *The White Book
Mabinogion* (Pwllheli, 1907), cols 178–91; and *The Red Book of Hergest*, vol. 1 (Oxford, 1887), pp.
82–92.
31 Andrew Breeze, *Medieval Welsh Literature* (Dublin, 1997), p. 82.
32 Bromwich, 'Character of Early Welsh Tradition', p. 108.
33 George F. Brewer and Bedwyr Lewis Jones, 'Popular Tale Motifs and Historical Tradition in
Breudwyt Maxen', *Medium Ævum* 44 (1975), pp. 23–30, at p. 28.
34 J. Loth, ed., *Les Mabinogion*, 2 vols (Paris, 1913), I.211.
35 Matthews, 'Macsen, Maximus, and Constantine', p. 447.

British nationality.[36] As in Geoffrey of Monmouth's *Historia regum Britannie* and later derivative versions of this account, Elen is styled as a typical romance heroine.[37]

The *Mabinogion* version completely alters the historically established series of events, conflating the historical figure of Maximus with that of Maxentius, defeated by Constantine at the Battle of the Milvian Bridge, and further confusing the portrait by ascribing some of Constantine's and Constantius's attributes to Maximus.[38] The reason for the confusion with Constantine may stem from the reference in the Harley manuscript of the *Historia Brittonum* that 'Constantinus' is buried near Cair Segeint (or Segontium, now Caernarfon), a place with which the real Maximus probably had a connection, though it was not the place in which he died: 'Constantine was the son of Constantine the Great, and he died here and his tomb is to be seen by the city called Caer Seint, as the letters on its stonework show.'[39] This entry exemplifies the ease with which Roman names with similar stems could become confused with one another, though just a little later in the text the name *Constantius* is used correctly.[40] Further on, in the list of cities of Britain in the *Historia Brittonum*, this same Cair Segeint (Segontium) is listed as a separate place from both Cair Colun (Colchester) and Cair Custoeint (Constantine's Fortress), both of which will later become involved in the legend of the British Helena.[41] Such a tomb might have once existed, if later corroboration is to be believed. In the thirteenth century, the discovery of a tomb at Caernarfon, reportedly containing the body of Constantius, was documented, along with the translation of the remains to a local church.[42] Because both Constantine and Magnus Maximus were associated with Caernarfon in medieval tradition, the two naturally became intermingled, especially with respect to their relationship with Helena, and consequently

[36] See Gwyn Thomas, 'O Maximus I Maxen', *Transactions of the Honourable Society of Cymmrodorion* (1983), pp. 7–21.

[37] St Mary of Egypt is similarly transformed in medieval accounts. See Simon Lavery, 'The Story of Mary the Egyptian in Medieval England', *The Legend of Mary of Egypt in Medieval English Hagiography*, ed. Erich Poppe and Bianca Ross (Dublin, 1996), pp. 113–48, and the other articles in that volume.

[38] C.E. Stevens, 'Magnus Maximus in British History', *Études Celtiques* 3 (1938), pp. 86–94, at pp. 87–8.

[39] 'Constantinus, Constantini magni filius fuit, et ibi moritur, et sepulchrum illius monstratur juxta urbem quae vocatur Cair Segeint ut litterae, quae sunt in lapide tumuli, ostendunt' (Morris, ed., Ch. 25). Other manuscripts have 'Constantius, son of Constantine . . .' or 'Constantine, father of Constantine the Great' (John J. Parry, 'Geoffrey of Monmouth and the Paternity of Arthur', *Speculum* 13 [1938], pp. 271–7, at p. 274). The historical Maximus was executed in northern Italy; there was no tradition of his being buried in England.

[40] 'Constantius . . . obiit in Britannia', 'Constantius . . . died in Britain'. See Matthews, 'Macsen, Maximus, and Constantine', p. 439; and Linder, 'The Myth of Constantine', p. 79.

[41] Nos. 19, 6, and 8 respectively (Morris, *Nennius*, § 80).

[42] *Flores historiarum*, of c. 1283, ed. Henry Ward, Rerum Britannicarum medii aevi scriptores 95 (London, 1890), p. 59 (cited in M.J. Johnson, 'Late Imperial Mausolea', 3 vols [unpub. Ph.D. diss., Princeton Univ., 1986], I:263). See also Williams, ed., *Breuddwyd Maxen*, pp. xviii–xix.

Maximus acquired legendary attributes from narratives dealing with Constantine.[43]

That Magnus Maximus was British by birth was apparently also believed in Anglo-Saxon England.[44] In all the extant manuscripts of the *Anglo-Saxon Chronicle*, the listing for 380/81 reads: 'He was born in Britain.'[45] The same statement is contained in the Latin *Chronicle* of Æthelweard, produced between 978 and 988, and based on the *Anglo-Saxon Chronicle* and Bede's *Historia*: 'He was born in Britain'.[46] Æthelweard is perpetuating an error that is made in the contemporary Old English translation of Bede's *Historia ecclesiastica,* where the expression 'creatus imperator' relating to Constantine, not Maximus, is similarly construed as 'born'.[47] Possibly, both mistranslations are based on the belief that Roman commanders of British troops had to be British. Like the origin of the British Helena legend, the source of the British Maximus legend is obscure, though it is likely that simple mistranslation or misconstrual of Gildas's 'sprig of its own bitter planting' is again at the base of the story. Maximus also provides a parallel appropriation of a late imperial Roman figure for Britain, and the elaboration of that individual's *vita* in Welsh legendary history.

The relative dates of the Harley genealogy (tenth century) and 'The Dream of Macsen Wledig' (twelfth century) indicate that, in the development of the Welsh Elen legend, the native Elen acquired the attributes of St Helena at some stage before Maximus and Helena were paired.[48] This means that by the time Elen came to be remembered as the wife of Maximus, she already possessed the attributes of St Helena. Although the 'Dream of Maxim Wledig' is later than Geoffrey of Monmouth's *Historia regum Britannie*, there appears to have been no borrowing from it, and the task of reconciling the two versions fell to the redaction of the Welsh Brut, known as the *Brut Dingestow*, which has two distinct characters, Coel's daughter, Elen, and Maxim's wife, Helena.[49] The

---

43 Matthews, 'Macsen, Maximus, and Constantine', p. 447, and Stevens, 'Magnus Maximus in British History', p. 88.

44 This legend was not believed by Bede, who omits any reference to Maximus's origins (*Ecclesiastical History*, 1.9). His source is Orosius's *Historia adversus paganos*, VII.35.

45 'He wæs in Bryten lande geboren' (Oxford, Bodleian Library, MS Laud Misc 108, ed. Charles Plummer, *Two of the Saxon Chronicles Parallel*, 2 vols [Oxford 1892], 1.11). The same sense is conveyed in all manuscripts (Plummer 2.9, and Dorothy Whitelock et al., ed. and Engl. trans., *The Anglo-Saxon Chronicle* [London, 1961], p. 9). Cf. details on p. 43 above.

46 'Natus in Brittannia erat' (A. Campbell, ed. and Engl. trans., *The Chronicle of Æthelweard* [London, 1962], p. 5). Campbell argues that Æthelweard uses a version of the A manuscript of the *Anglo-Saxon Chronicle* as his source, from which he 'deviates little' in general, though in the entry for 381, 'the conquests of Maximus are grandiloquently extended' (p. xxi).

47 Plummer notes that 'creatus imperator' is mistranslated in the *Anglo-Saxon Chronicle* and the Old English version of Bede's *Historia ecclesiastica* (2.9). The Old English translation of Bede's *Historia* does not, unfortunately, treat events concerning Maximus at all, so there is no occasion for this error to be repeated in this text.

48 Bromwich, 'Character of Early Welsh Tradition', p. 108.

49 Bromwich, 'Character of Early Welsh Tradition', pp. 126–7; *Brut Dingestow*, ed. Henry Lewis (Cardiff, 1942).

'Dream of Maxim Wledig', though, might have been the product of the general interest in the 'pseudo-history of Britain' generated by Geoffrey's *Historia*.[50]

The connection between Magnus Maximus and a British princess is entirely fabricated in the Welsh tradition, although, like the British Constantine story, it is based on the known military leadership of the Roman emperor in Britain. We know that Magnus Maximus was married, but the ancient sources, including Gildas, Bede, and the *Historia Brittonum*, make no reference to the name or origins of Maximus's wife.[51] In the only near-contemporary reference to her, she, like St Helena in some legendary incarnations, is associated with Trier rather than Britain. In the *Dialogues* on the life of St Martin of Tours, produced in the early fifth century, Sulpicius Severus does mention Maximus's wife, in the context of the kindness of the Empress towards St Martin in Trier.[52] But there is absolutely no evidence that this woman was from Britain or was called Helena or Elen.[53]

Helena and Elen

The precise relationship between the Welsh Elen and the legendary Helena is convoluted. Perhaps there was a pre-existing Welsh figure, historical or legendary, who was conflated with her more famous namesake, or perhaps the Welsh Elen was contrived in the context of St Helena's fame. Rachel Bromwich argues that the Welsh Elen was 'in origin a character of early Welsh mythology', one who acquired her status from confusion with St Helena and was 'renowned as an ancestral deity'.[54] Bromwich accepts the unsubstantiated claims by Rhys that Elen was a 'dawn goddess' with a 'mythical host',[55] agreeing with Ifor Williams's similar remark that she was probably a 'goddess of war',[56] based on her name element, 'Luyddog' connoting 'of hosts'. Williams argues that there must have been a pre-existing Welsh Elen, because St Helena was not known as a leader of hosts or as a builder of roads.[57] But the historical Helena, who undertook a pilgrimage to the Holy Lands, certainly acted as Constantine's representative in his church-building programme and controlled his treasury during her journey, so therefore she might have been seen in this light (and is portrayed as such in the Old English poem, *Elene*). Bromwich similarly suggests that Elen might have acquired her reputation (and epithet) for road-building from

---

50 Williams, ed., p. xxi.
51 The woman is appropriately called 'Anonyma 4' in *PLRE*, I.1038.
52 *Dialogi*, II.7 (PL 20 [Paris, 1845], col. 206; Engl. trans.: F.R. Hoare, *The Western Fathers* [London, 1954], pp. 68–144).
53 See *PLRE*, I.588.
54 Bromwich, ed., *TYP*, p. 341.
55 Bromwich, 'Character of Early Welsh Tradition', p. 161, citing John Rhys, *Lectures on the Growth of Religion as Illustrated by Celtic Heathendom* (London, 1888), p. 167.
56 Williams, ed., p. xvi.
57 Williams, ed., p. xiv.

Constantine's road-building in Britain.[58] Rhys vaguely attributes this characteristic to her reputation as 'this vagrant goddess of dawn and dusk' and as the
source of the place names 'Sarn Helen' or 'Helen's Road'.[59] A far more likely
source of the attribution lies in the existence of the Welsh word 'elin' connoting
'elbow/angle' and used to describe angular sections of road.[60] As Brewer and
Jones argue, there is absolutely no evidence to support the claim that Elen was
believed to have been a Welsh dawn goddess.[61]

John Matthews's argument that the historical Helena was appropriated by
Welsh legendary tradition and later transmuted into the character of Elen of
Hosts deserves more serious consideration.[62] The late date of the Harley genealogies and the even later *Mabinogion* reference to the Welsh Elen provide ample
opportunity for the appropriation of St Helena, and the subsequent back-forma-
tion of a local version of the character. The added detail of Elen's son being
called Constantine suggests that the story was fabricated in order to provide an
impressive genealogy for Owain which includes Arthur. Welsh poets, like other
peoples, were inclined to adopt national stories from Roman history, modified
for a local audience.[63] In this general context of foreign borrowing, Helena must
have been acquired as a mythological component in the mixture of history and
legend from which Welsh vernacular literature was created, along the lines
described above by Curtis.

All the evidence suggests that the legendary Welsh Elen was created from
stories treating St Helena at some time prior to or during the tenth century (i.e.
the date of the genealogies), and was thereafter deployed rhetorically for
specific local political reasons. The compilation of the genealogies themselves,
in all their fictional glory, probably provided sufficient impetus to crystallise the
figure of a Welsh Helena. It is unlikely that there was a pre-existing goddess of
the same name who was conflated with the saint. No such explanation is
required, because St Helena herself, with her new placement in the West and
aristocratic origins supplied by Altmann of Gaul, was an attractive figure,
capable of flexible regional interpretation. The free use made of the figure of
Magnus Maximus provides a close analogy to the way in which Helena was
appropriated and moulded according to immediate literary and rhetorical needs.

The Welsh manifestation of St Helena had important ramifications for later
versions of the story. Most importantly, the genealogies link her name with
Arthur and feature Cole prominently. These connections in particular were

---

58 Bromwich, ed., *TYP*, p. 341.
59 Rhys, *Lectures on the Growth of Religion*, p. 167.
60 Meic Stephens, *The Oxford Companion to the Literature of Wales* (Oxford, 1986), s.v. Elen Luyddog.
   See *Geiriadur Prifysgol Cymru: A Dictionary of the Welsh Language*, ed. R.J. Thomas (Caerdydd,
   1960), s.v. elin, 'elbow; forearm; also transf. angle, bend' with listings from the ninth century.
61 Brewer and Jones, 'Popular Tale Motifs', p. 27.
62 Matthews, 'Macsen, Maximus, and Constantine', p. 439.
63 John Morris, *The Age of Arthur: A History of the British Isles from 350 to 650* (London, 1973), p. 416.

exploited elaborately by Henry of Huntingdon and Geoffrey of Monmouth in their imaginative and durable portrayal of princess Helena of Colchester, daughter of King Cole. Ultimately, too, Constantine's legendary British heritage through his mother acquired propagandistic value to the (originally Welsh) Tudors who wished to claim imperial status for the British monarchy.

IV

Popularisation in the Anglo-Latin Histories and the English Brut Tradition

DURING THE MIDDLE AGES, new legendary Helenas had been constructed in Francia and Wales with two biographical elements in common: her alleged royal origins and local birth. Her actual status as Augusta in later life and the documented or alleged associations between members of her family and these regions must have made narrative developments like these credible. Within this context of legendary accretion, she was successfully appropriated by both Altmann and the Welsh genealogists and refashioned to reflect local tastes and individual rhetorical needs within both the hagiographical and historiographical traditions. This fluid regional association continued to characterise the depiction of Helena throughout the early Middle Ages, though one decisive connection was to be wrought which firmly situated her in Britain: her supposed kinship with the legendary King Cole of Colchester.

Helena at Colchester

At about the same time that the tenth-century Welsh genealogies were claiming Helena as an ancestor of one of the nation's royal lines, another initially unrelated change occurred which was to have a lasting effect on the British Helena legend: the town of Cair Colun (or Colne-cester, named after the River Colne, perhaps from the Roman term *colonia*)[1] in Essex came to be known as Colchester.[2] Although the change probably exemplifies the common linguistic development of the simplification of consonant clusters (*-lnch-* to *-lch-*) in the middle of a word,[3] by the early twelfth century a new folk etymology had been

---

[1] Charles Kightly, *Folk Heroes of Britain* (London, 1982), pp. 81 and 98.

[2] Amnon Linder, 'The Myth of Constantine the Great in the West: Sources and Hagiographic Commemoration', *Studi Medievali*, 3rd ser. 16/1 (1975), pp. 43–95, at p. 92, citing P.H. Reaney, *Place Names of Essex* (Cambridge, 1969), p. 368.

[3] On simplification, see Fernand Mossé, *A Handbook of Middle English*, Engl. trans. James A. Walker (Baltimore, 1952), § 49.4; and A. Campbell, *An Old English Grammar* (Oxford, 1959), § 476. On post-Conquest developments in OE names with the element *-ceaster*, see Cecily Clark, 'Towards a Reassessment of "Anglo-Norman Influence on English Place-Names"', repr. in *Words, Names and History: Selected Writings of Cecily Clark*, ed. Peter Jackson (Cambridge, 1995), pp. 144–55, at pp. 151–2.

constructed around this name, based on the belief that it denoted 'fortress of Cole'. This interpretation conveniently finds a new local base for Coel Hen,[4] the legendary fifth-century Pennine ruler from whom several Welsh genealogies are traced.[5] This Coel, who is probably 'an eponymous invention',[6] achieved his own lasting fame in British folk history, and was honoured in the eighteenth-century nursery rhyme commencing 'Old King Cole was a merry old soul.'[7] Colchester was a plausible choice of residence for this leader, not only because of the similarity of the names, but also because it had been the site of an important Roman town, Cair Colun (also known earlier as Camulodunum).[8] Of course, if Cole had existed, he would not have had any contact with this town, as the Welsh genealogies which mention him place him in the North, coincidentally in the region of York, the sole legitimate Constantinian location in Britain.[9]

It is likely that prior to the twelfth century the town of Colchester became the new site of the developing local, oral legends concerning Helena, which were later adopted and elaborated by the Anglo-Norman historians Henry of Huntingdon and Geoffrey of Monmouth. By construing the name *Colchester* as the town of the legendary leader Cole, these writers provide an 'etymological explanation' for the new name,[10] which was probably already the basis of local legends. With a new location, and a firm connection with a legendary Welsh

---

4   On Coel Hen, see Rachel Bromwich, 'The Character of Early Welsh Tradition', *Studies in Early British History*, ed. H.M. Chadwick et al. (Cambridge 1954), pp. 83–136, at pp. 93–4; and John Morris, *The Age of Arthur: A History of the British Isles from 350 to 650* (London, 1973), p. 213, where it is claimed that Coel Hen was possibly the 'last regularly appointed *dux*'. This view is not substantiated by evidence more reliable than the tenth-century Welsh genealogical tables. Peter Hunter Blair, 'The Origins of Northumbria', *Archaeologia Aeliana*, 4th ser. 25 (1947), pp. 1–51, repr. as text III in *Anglo-Saxon Northumbria*, ed. Michael Lapidge and Pauline Hunter Blair (London, 1984), pp. 45–8, argues that Coel Hen was 'responsible for bringing the Saxons to the North'; was a possible rival of Vortigern for this honour; and was born c. 380, though these details are all educated conjecture. So also H.M. Chadwick, *Early Scotland: The Picts, the Scots, and the Welsh in Southern Scotland* (Cambridge, 1949), p. 143: 'Of Cole himself we have no record', but 'there seems to be no reason for doubting the historical character of the genealogy'. In a lengthy treatment of Cole, Kightly argues (on the basis of poetic references, believed to be from the sixth and seventh centuries) that he was a genuine leader from the early fifth century, defending the British against the Picts and Scots (*Folk Heroes of Britain*, pp. 90–1).

5   These genealogies include those in MS Harley 3859 (8, 9, 10 [seventh from last name]), 11, 12, and 19 [spelt Gyl Hen], edited in P.C. Bartrum, *Early Welsh Genealogical Tracts* (Cardiff, 1966). Other genealogies tracing the family line back to Coel Hen occur in the thirteenth-century codex containing a much earlier text known as *The Descent of the Men of the North* (ed. and Engl. trans. W.F. Skene, *The Four Ancient Books of Wales*, 2 vols [Edinburgh, 1868], II.454–65; discussion I.165–70).

6   W. Gurney Benham, 'Legends of Coel and Helena', *Journal of the British Archaeological Association* 25 (1919), pp. 229–44, at p. 239.

7   First published by William King in his *Useful Transactions in Philosophy*, in 1709. See 'Cole' in Iona and Peter Opie, eds, *The Oxford Dictionary of Nursery Rhymes* (Oxford, 1951), pp. 134–5. Kightly, *Folk Heroes of Britain*, p. 83, challenges the idea that the nursery rhyme relates to the legendary King Cole of Colchester, claiming that it is about a Scottish king. See also Geoffrey Ashe, *Mythology of the British Isles* (London, 1990), pp. 152–4.

8   On Cair Colun, see Kightly, *Folk Heroes of Britain*, p. 81.

9   Hunter Blair, 'The Origins of Northumbria', p. 47; and Bromwich, 'Character of Early Welsh Tradition', pp. 94–5.

10   Linder, 'The Myth of Constantine the Great', p. 92.

leader, governed by parochial interests, the Helena legend was now ready for more energetic dissemination and rhetorical exploitation in the secular, historical sphere. Henry of Huntingdon and Geoffrey of Monmouth deploy the legendary figures of Cole and Helena as part of their new national histories of England, providing an ideal home for the legendary princess by linking her with a famous Welsh progenitor, based in Colchester. This version of the story, which was in competition with the version recounted by both late Roman historians as transmitted by Bede and others and also that of the Welsh 'Dream of Macsen Wledig' (Elen, daughter of Eudaf of Cair Segeint), became the dominant narrative in the British Helena tradition, from the time it was popularised in the twelfth century to its invocation by Evelyn Waugh and Dorothy L. Sayers in the mid-twentieth century. It was precisely on account of the new imaginative basis promulgated by the British histories in the twelfth century that this version became more widely circulated. Helena had become a figure alive in literary fiction and also a political tool.

With the move from York to Colchester during the early twelfth century, the Helena legend loses the only tenuous link it had with historical veracity during Anglo-Saxon times: Constantine's proclamation in York. The change also brings with it a complete refashioning of Helena's circumstances. As she is represented in Altmann's ninth-century *vita*, and no doubt directly resulting from the liturgical and literary adoption of this rhetorical portrait, Helena is now aristocratic, well educated, and virtuous (unlike the early historical portraits of a stable-maid or concubine). In the tradition of the romance heroine, she has become the talented daughter of King Cole of Colchester, heir to his throne, political pawn of Constantius, and by her marriage to him, the direct link between Britain and imperial Rome. These departures from previous traditions greatly enhanced the attractiveness and usefulness of the Helena story in post-Conquest England, the time of the fullest and most secular expression of the legend. The latent suggestions of the legend in Anglo-Saxon England, which were probably the result of mistranslation sourced in oral traditions, grow into more conscious and specifically scribal myth-making in the twelfth century.

This was a time in which a general interest in the past, and more specifically in British history, was a new focus for insular writers who wished to produce these 'serious entertainments', in Nancy Partner's well-known phrase.[11] Arising out of the traditions of Bede and the *Anglo-Saxon Chronicle*, historical writing took a sudden leap forward in the twelfth century. The new taste for long, comprehensive accounts of the history of Britain, with a secular focus, valued tales such as those about Helena and King Cole because they glorified Britain's past. More precisely, these stories demonstrated that Britain played a vital role in the business of the Roman Empire. Susan Larkin has considered the social and

---

[11] Nancy F. Partner, *Serious Entertainments: The Writing of History in Twelfth-Century England* (Chicago and London, 1977), p. 5. See also Robert W. Hanning, *The Vision of History in Early Britain: From Gildas to Geoffrey of Monmouth* (New York and London, 1966), p. 127.

political forces which helped to shape the new image of Helena promulgated during the twelfth century. She cites three main elements acting upon the development of the legend: 'the growth of nationalism', 'the rise of romance style', and, less convincingly, the ramifications of 'papal politics' (specifically the Investiture Controversy).[12] There is certainly evidence that these factors are motivations for the shape the Helena narrative took during the Middle Ages, but there is a variety of more individual and literary forces at work in addition to these general movements as well as the pervasive influence of local traditions.

The three main Anglo-Latin texts[13] dealing with Helena are contemporary with each other, and each underwent a series of revisions, so that a distinct chain of reliance is difficult to ascertain, but it is generally acknowledged that William of Malmesbury's *Gesta regum* (1125, rev. to 1135)[14] was published just prior to Henry of Huntingdon's *Historia Anglorum* (1131, rev. to 1154),[15] which in turn appeared shortly before Geoffrey of Monmouth's *Historia regum Britannie* (1136–38).[16] We know that Geoffrey used Henry's text as a source for his own history, and that Henry revised his work several times to 1154, during which time he had read Geoffrey (but not apparently William of Malmesbury).[17]

Just prior to these histories, though, the Abbey of St John was built in Colchester (c. 1120) and within the history of its foundation by the king's steward, Eudo Dapifer, is a reference to the Princess Helena of Colchester story, which may or may not be contemporary. The document, part of *The Chronicle of Colchester or Oath Book*, says that princess Helena was born in Colchester and that Constantius won Britain not by force but by a marriage alliance with her:

> Colchester is situated in the eastern part of Britain. The city is close to the harbour, pleasantly located, irrigated throughout with spring-waters, with a most wholesome atmosphere, constructed with the strongest fortifications. The city would be numbered among the most eminent, had not old age, fires, floods, even invasions of pirates, and the various ravages of events destroyed all memorials of the city. Indeed it is related that Helena, later mother of the empire, was born and brought up in this city. It was of

12 Susan Grace Larkin, 'Transitions in Medieval Legends of St Helena' (unpub. Ph.D. diss., Indiana Univ., 1995), pp. 94–5.
13 Another near-contemporary writer, Orderic Vitalis (1075–c. 1142), recounts the Constantine/Helena narrative, though his version is of little interest as he mostly transmits the genuine historical version of events in his *Historia ecclesiastica* (ed. and Engl. trans. M. Chibnall, Oxford Medieval Texts, 6 vols [Oxford, 1968–80], I.23). Orderic Vitalis does, however, situate Helena's birth in Gaul: Constantius is said to have taken a concubine named Helena, mother of Constantine, from a city he founded in northern Gaul (Neustria), and named after himself as 'Coutances' (V.9). Chibnall regards the source of this idea to be a lost legendary text, the *Gesta Romanorum* (p. 48). This version shares some similarities with earlier legends basing Helena in Trier (such as the ninth-century *vita* by Altmann, discussed on pp. 46–9 above). Orderic Vitalis also recounts at length Constantine's baptism by Pope Silvester (II.18), an element of the legendary history of Constantine which was widely transmitted during the Middle Ages.
14 Antonia Gransden, *Historical Writing in England c. 550–c. 1307* (Ithaca, 1974), p. 168.
15 Diana E. Greenway, ed. and Engl. trans., *Henry, Archdeacon of Huntingdon, Historia Anglorum* (Oxford, 1996), pp. lxvii–lxix.
16 Gransden, *Historical Writing in England*, p. 210.
17 A.G. Rigg, *A History of Anglo-Latin Literature, 1066–1422* (Cambridge, 1992), p. 36.

great merit, as can be seen from the fact that Constantius, father of Constantine the Great, is said to have besieged this city for three years, but was unable to win it except finally by marrying Helena. Indeed, this is conjectured from those things which people digging have excavated from the earth: iron, precious stones, and minted coins, and buildings found beneath the earth.[18]

Helena is presented here as an attractive part of Colchester's history, a reason for the town's earlier eminence, along with the archaeological evidence adduced as proof of the town's historical status. As such, this section fits into the larger narrative well enough, though as a diversion from the main area of interest. But because it is a thematically discrete unit in the text, this legendary material might be a later interpolation. The general description of the town of Colchester is itself a digression from the main topic of the text, the history of the founding of the Abbey of St John and the biography of its founder. If the Helena material was not part of the original text, it is impossible to say just when it is likely to have been included. It might contain a floating oral tale which was also the basis of the longer treatments given the legend by Henry of Huntingdon and Geoffrey of Monmouth, or it might have borrowed the details from one of those histories prior to its inclusion here. The author claims that the entire document is drawn from Book 3 of the *Chronicle* of Marianus Scotus (1028–82), but the material is not from that source, nor from the text which is often cited as 'Marianus', John of Worcester's adaptation of the *Chronicle*, so the dating remains uncertain.[19]

The manuscript evidence is of little help in this regard. The sole manuscript witness of the document, London, British Library, MS Cotton Nero D. VIII, is a compilation of three separate booklets bound together, the first from the twelfth or thirteenth century, the second from the fourteenth or fifteenth century, and the Colchester document from the seventeenth century, written in Humanist Caroline minuscule.[20] It is probable that the codex was compiled in Colchester during the seventeenth century, as this account of St John occupies the final gathering, which constitutes a separate booklet, and is accompanied by an engraving of the monastery and an elaborate list of the abbots within circles in

---

18   Est igitur Colcestria civitas in orientali parte Brittaniæ posita; civitas vicina portui, situ ameno, fontibus undique scaturentibus irrigua; aere saluberrimo, mœnibus firmissimis constructa; civitas inter eminentissimas numeranda, si non vetustas, conflagrationes, eluviones, denique piratarum immisiones, variæque casuum afflictationes omnia civitatis memoralia delivissent. Traditur tamen Helenam, quondam imperii matrem, ex hac civitate natam et educatam; quæ quanti fuerit, vel eo con[j]icitur, quod Constantius Constantini magni genitor, triennio dicitur, hanc obsedisse; nec optinuisse, nisi tandem per Helenæ nuptias. Con[j]icitur etiam ex his, quæ de terra fossores eruerunt; tam ferrum, quam lapides, quam æra signata, quam ædificia sub terra inventa.
     (From London, British Library, MS Cotton Nero D. VIII, fol. 345b, ed. William Dugdale, *Monasticon Anglicanum: A New Edition*, ed. John Caley, H. Ellis, and B. Bandinel, 8 vols (London, 1846), IV.607 (my translation). The text is also edited and translated in H.J.D. Astley, 'Mediaeval Colchester – Town Castle and Abbey – From MSS in the British Museum', *Transactions of the Essex Archaeological Society*, s. 8 (1903), pp. 117–38 (text at pp. 122–35).

19   Astley, 'Mediaeval Colchester', p. 120.

20   Julia C. Crick, *The Historia regum Britannie of Geoffrey of Monmouth, III: A Summary Catalogue of the Manuscripts* (Cambridge, 1989), pp. 149–52.

the margin (fols 345r–347r). This manuscript arrangement implies that by the time this version was penned, the monastery document was important, but it is not immediately obvious why it has been bound with the other two booklets. Many, though not all, of the other texts in both sections are related specifically to British history and legend: Geoffrey of Monmouth, *Historia regum Britannie*; the *Historia Brittonum*; a list of Bede's works; and two brief texts on 'the origins of giants in Albion' and 'the longitude and latitude of Anglia'.[21] The reference to a British Helena might account for this otherwise curious manuscript context for the account of a monastery. If this legend was rhetorically important to a codex compiled in Colchester, the reference to Helena might well have been inserted after Henry of Huntingdon and Geoffrey of Monmouth had popularised the story that she hailed from Colchester. Conversely, the historians might have had access to the same oral tales which informed this manuscript account, should it be early.[22]

Turning to the details of the Helena interpolation into the Colchester document, we can see that this brief account shares many similarities with that in Geoffrey of Monmouth's *Historia* (discussed below). Helena's 'merits' are greatly elaborated by Geoffrey who develops a more prominent political role for her, though even in the Colchester document she is presented as a powerful force and the direct link between Britain and Rome (even being referred to as 'mother of the empire').[23] Unlike Geoffrey's *Historia*, there is no mention of Cole in this document, but Helena's royal status is implied by her role in the marriage alliance which brings Britain into the hands of Constantius. This assumption of knowledge about Cole on the part of the document-writer might indicate that he was referring to a well-known narrative of a British princess, Helena, daughter of Cole. More significant omissions, especially in a document which recounts the history of the foundation of a monastery, are Helena's sanctity and her legendary finding of the True Cross. This accords with the treatment in Geoffrey's *Historia*, where she is presented merely as a political figure by which Colchester gains a firm connection with the Roman Empire. These similarities between the Colchester document and the *Historia regum Britannie* might suggest a direct link between the two, but it is unclear in which direction the reliance runs.

If the Colchester document was composed around the year 1120 (and the

---

21 Crick, *A Summary Catalogue*, p. 150. Geoffrey's *Historia* is the first text, and is accompanied by a note on Geoffrey in an early-modern hand. The other items include Dudo of Saint-Quentin, *Historia Normannorum* (including portions of later redactions), the *Iuli Valeri Alexandri Polemi res gestae;* the *Epistola Alexandri;* Geoffrey of Monmouth, *Prophecies of Merlin;* Gerald of Wales, *Descriptio Kambrie;* Higden, *Polychronicon;* and an account of a land dispute.

22 Edmond Faral, *La Légende Arthurienne: Études et documents*, 3 vols (Paris, 1929), III.188.

23 She is 'imperii matrem', 'mother of the empire', not 'imperatoris matrem', 'mother of the emperor' as she is referred to on most other occasions. Although *imperium* can be used in a transferred sense meaning 'emperor', it denotes 'empire' in an overwhelming majority of cases, of which there are many in classical and medieval Latin (see C.T. Lewis and C. Short, *A Latin Dictionary* [Oxford, 1879]) and J.F. Niermeyer, *Mediae Latinitatis lexicon minus* [Leiden, 1976], s.v. *imperium*).

detailed account of the circumstances of the monastery's foundation suggest that it was),[24] the reference to Helena might have been original, and predate the *Historia* which was written c. 1136. Kightly, Pohlsander, and Larkin all assume that the Helena section dates from c. 1120, without defending the date.[25] But if the document were intended for local use, why are the situation of Colchester and its natural beauties mentioned, unless as a trope of *laus civitatis*, in which a city or town is praised as a matter of rhetorical convention? If this is the reason for the inclusion of these details, and if the legend was part of the original text, it would be the earliest documented account of the legend, but this is highly dubious. The section on Helena, which is a very brief interpolation of no direct relevance to the narrative of the arrangement for the foundation of a monastery and the fate of Eudo Dapifer and his wife, might have been inserted at any time during the history of the text and was very probably later.[26] Within a tangential paragraph on Colchester, the digression on Helena looks even more like a barely relevant interpolation, interrupting the list of the material evidence of the town's former pre-eminence. It is highly likely, then, that it is not original, and was perhaps inserted during the fourteenth century when Colchester seems to have made a bid to appropriate Helena as a local patron, suggested by another written account of her alleged association with the abbey in *The Chronicle of Colchester or Oath Book*. This early-fourteenth-century document contains the claim that Helena was born and died in the town of Coel, Duke of the Britons.[27]

Although this is a likely time for its composition, the dating of the Colchester document must remain inconclusive. But even though there is no proof of the existence of early written versions of the story, it remains probable that the British Helena legend was first in circulation, at least in the capacity of folktale or traditional belief in that town, by the early eleventh century, and that the Anglo-Norman historians developed a pre-existing story of local significance. The legend appears to have been widely or at least officially credible, as Helena's image featured in the corporate seals of the town from the twelfth century,[28] suggesting some form of local appropriation. On these grounds, Kightly regards the Colchester document as the result of local traditions which finally found their way into printed history,[29] an idea which is borne out by the existence of a chapel dedicated to Helena dating from late Anglo-Saxon times,

---

[24] See Dugdale, *Monasticon Anglicanum*, pp. 601–6.

[25] Kightly, *Folk Heroes of Britain*, p. 60; Hans A. Pohlsander, *Helena: Empress and Saint* (Chicago, 1995), p. 65; Larkin, 'Transitions in Medieval Legends of St Helena', p. 108.

[26] Faral, *La Légende Arthurienne*, II.187, n. 2, also considers that the Helena reference is a later addition. This later date becomes even more probable in view of the fictitious reference to Helena's personal involvement with the abbey made in the fourteenth-century *Chronicle of Colchester*. This text is edited in W. Gurney Benham, ed. *The Oath Book or Red Parchment Book of Colchester* (Colchester, 1907) (fol. 20r), p. 27. See also Pohlsander, *Helena*, p. 10.

[27] Ed., J.H. Round, *St Helen's Chapel, Colchester* (London, 1886), p. 21. Round, p. 2, dates the charter to the early fourteenth century. Noted also by Pohlsander, *Helena*, p. 10, and Kightly, *Folk Heroes of Britain*, p. 63.

[28] Gurney Benham, 'Legends of Coel and Helena', p. 230.

[29] Kightly, *Folk Heroes of Britain*, p. 61.

and at one stage connected with St John's Abbey.[30] Colchester's claim to Helena appears to have been an attempt to situate her birth in a particular place, within the context of the more general legend that she was British, in circulation from Anglo-Saxon times (Aldhelm seems to have been aware of the legend, as does the Anglo-Saxon translator of Bede's *Historia ecclesiastica*).[31] Colchester appears to have jumped at this civic opportunity, provided by the fortuitous confluence of legend, luck, and onomastic circumstance. Clearly there was a more specific local benefit available in claiming Helena for Colchester, a boon which is still exploited today.[32] She was claimed as the patron saint of the town throughout the Middle Ages, and is mentioned as such on a charter granted by Henry V in 1413.[33] By this time, the legend of Helena's British birth had been widely disseminated by three Anglo-Latin histories and had found a place also in the vernacular chronicles of Britain.

William of Malmesbury and the British Constantine

William, monk and librarian of Malmesbury abbey (c. 1090–1142), first completed his *Gesta regum* in 1125, and later revised it twice. William was an 'omnivorous' reader.[34] His 'sober secular history, based on earlier sources or site visits'[35] and heavily influenced by Bede's *Historia ecclesiastica*, tells the conventional account of Constantius's death and Constantine's proclamation in York, as provided by Eutropius and Jerome:[36]

> Constantius, who was reputed a most cultivated prince, left as his heir a young man of great promise, Constantine, his son by Helena, a stable-girl. Constantine, having been acclaimed emperor by the army, planned an expedition against the Continent, and took a large body of British troops away with him.[37]

---

[30] Janet Cooper, ed., *A History of the County of Essex*, vol. ix, *The Borough of Colchester* (Oxford, 1994), p. 20.

[31] See pp. 37–42 above.

[32] The present-day coat of arms of the town features the Medieval design of the Cross and nails; Helena herself figures on the early-twentieth-century town hall (see Cooper, *Borough of Colchester*, p. 277).

[33] The charter, of 7 July 1413, features a historiated initial containing a portrait of Helena styled as a medieval princess, with her connection to Colchester stated explicitly in a scroll text within that initial: 'Sancta Elena nata fuit in Colcestria. Mater Constantini fuit et sanctam crucem inuenit Elena', 'Saint Helena was born in Colchester. Helena was the mother of Constantine and found the Holy Cross.' A large Cross extends beyond the borders of the initial, with a smaller figure of Constantine holding on to the right-hand arm. The charter is on display at the Castle Museum, Colchester. See Gurney Benham, 'Legends of Coel and Helena', pp. 230–1.

[34] Rodney Thomson, *William of Malmesbury* (Woodbridge, 1987), p. 12. See his Appendix I, 'Handlist of works known to William at first hand'.

[35] Rigg, *A History of Anglo-Latin Literature*, p. 34.

[36] On William and his historical method, see Thomson, *William of Malmesbury*, pp. 1–97; and Gransden, *Historical Writing in England*, pp. 166–85.

[37] 'Constantius, ut aiunt, uir magnae ciuilitatis Constantinum ex Helena stabularia susceptum, egregiae spei iuuenem, reliquit herdem; qui ab exercitu imperato consalutatus, expeditione in superiores terras indicta, magnam manum Britannorum militum abduxit' (*William of Malmesbury, Gesta regum*

Like many of his sources, William's account praises Constantine, presenting him as the ideal Christian emperor, though omitting any reference to his place of birth. He epitomises Constantine's fame in Britain and echoes Orosius's comment by mentioning the rise of a 'second Constantine', who was 'chosen emperor there for the promise of his name'.[38] As an example of his use of genuine sources, William mentions Helena's low social status: a *stabularia* (stable-maid or inn-keeper), the term most used in the earliest documents to describe Helena's occupation.[39] His sometime adherence to verifiable historical remarks is attributable to William's familiarity with the sources such as Rufinus and Cassiodorus–Epiphanius, and to the fact that he had produced, with his collaborators, a version of Eutropius's *Breviarium* in 1125.[40]

Despite this knowledge of the sources, the appeal of a British Constantine seems to have been irresistible for William, who sets the legendary material alongside more factual information in an offhand manner. When he returns to the subject of Constantine in Book IV, he explicitly says that the emperor was a native of Britain. He remarks, somewhat incongruously, that 'the emperor's heart was especially content to be founding a city at Heaven's bidding in a place where fertile soil and temperate climate conspired to make men healthy, for being born in Britain, he hated excessive heat',[41] thereby finding the allegedly 'moderate climate' of Constantinople ideal for his needs. This casual reference to the emperor's British birth is not repeated elsewhere or elaborated upon here, and its presence is curious. Indeed the allusion to the emperor's delicate sensibilities is somewhat at odds with the vigorous military leader depicted in William's history and his sources, and may be a somewhat strained way of introducing Constantine's legendary Britishness in a casual manner.[42] William does not claim that Helena was British, only that Constantine was born in Britain: she might have borne him there while visiting, or it might have been her native country. On the subject of Constantine's British birth, William seems to be referring to a well-known tradition which needs no elaboration or explanation, just like the reference to her discovery of the True Cross. He dates Macarius's time as patriarch of Jerusalem by adding parenthetically that 'in his time the

---

Anglorum: A History of the English Kings, ed. and Engl. trans. R.A.B. Mynors, completed by R.M. Thomson and M. Winterbottom, 2 vols [Oxford, 1998–99], I.1, pp. 16–18).

[38] 'Spe nominis imperato allectus' (Mynors, ed., I.2, pp. 18–19).

[39] See above, p. 13.

[40] L.D. Reynolds, *Texts and Transmission: A Survey of Latin Classics* (Oxford, 1983), p. 160. See also Thomson, *William of Malmesbury*, p. 67.

[41] 'Gratumque admodum fuisse ferunt imperiali animo ut illic urbem diuino iussi fundaret ubi et soli ubertas et caeli temperies mortalium saluti conueniret; quia enim in Britannia natus fuerat, ardores solis exosus erat' (Mynors, ed., IV.355, pp. 624–5).

[42] On the other hand, William might be imitating classical and later biographies, especially of emperors, which offset the robustness of their characters with some sort of delicacy as a standard trope. Suetonius, in his *De uita caesarum*, was particularly noted for including details of physical weakness (see Andrew Wallace-Hadrill, *Suetonius: The Scholar and his Caesars* [London, 1983], pp. 67–8); the trope was also used by Einhard. Even if William is observing this practice, the British detail is odd.

Holy Cross was discovered by Helena'.[43] Both legends – of the *Inventio* and Constantine's British origins – are tangentially important to William's agenda of presenting British history in its Roman, Christian context. William exalts Constantine in an understated effort to feature Britain's role prominently in the history of Rome, a cause which his contemporary historians undertake with more vigour.

Henry of Huntingdon and Old King Cole of Colchester

Henry of Huntingdon (c. 1088–1164)[44] was archdeacon in the diocese of Lincoln, and was writing at almost exactly the same time as William of Malmesbury. His *Historia Anglorum*, a long chronological account of the history of the British from Roman times up to his own day, was commissioned by Bishop Alexander of Lincoln shortly after 1123. The first version, down to the year 1129, was finished in 1131, and Henry continued revising and supplementing his text through at least five further versions until 1154.[45] Henry compiled his history from existing sources, particularly Bede's *Historia ecclesiastica* and the *Anglo-Saxon Chronicle*. Diana Greenway characterises his method of composition as that of a 'weaver compiler' because he depends on the work of other writers for about 75 percent of his text.[46] Henry's aim to write for a wide audience was evidently realised, as there are more than thirty copies of the complete manuscript extant and his work was frequently adapted by medieval writers.[47]

Henry interprets the successive invasions of Britain as deserved punishments by God, presenting history as an incentive for his readers to reform their lives.[48] Within this schema, Henry portrays the creation of order via his central theme of kingdom (*regnum*) in his elaborate 'story of the unification of the English monarchy'.[49] It is extremely significant that he situates the origins of this process during the reign of Constantine. Henry recounts the story of Constantine, son of the British princess Helena, in order to base the future

---

43 'Huius temporibus inuenta est sancta crux ab Helena' (Mynors, ed., IV.368, pp. 644–5).

44 The dates are uncertain. For details of Henry's life, see Greenway, ed., 'Introduction', pp. xxiii–lvii.

45 Greenway, ed., 'Introduction', pp. lxvi–lxxvii.

46 25% Bede, 40% *Anglo-Saxon Chronicle*, and 10% other writers (p. lxxv). In his Prologue, Henry says: 'I have followed the venerable Bede's *Ecclesiastical History* where I could, selecting material also from other authors and borrowing from chronicles preserved in ancient libraries' ('Bede uenerabilis ecclesiasticam qua potui secutus historiam, nonnulla etiam ex aliis excerpens auctoribus, inde cronica in antiquis reseruata librariis compilans') (Greenway, ed., pp. 6–7). See also Diana E. Greenway, 'Henry of Huntingdon and Bede', *L'Historiographie médiévale en Europe*, ed. J.-P. Genet (Paris, 1991), pp. 43–50.

47 Greenway, ed., 'Introduction', p. lxi.

48 Greenway, ed., 'Introduction', p. lix.

49 Greenway, ed., 'Introduction', p. lx. Partner, *Serious Entertainments*, pp. 11–48, explores the thematic concentration of Henry's *History* which she regards as one of *contemptus mundi*, 'contempt of the world'.

destiny of Britain firmly on home soil. Henry is the first writer actively and transparently to exploit the British Helena story, deploying it within the rhetoric of nationhood when he provides Constantine with a British pedigree. In Henry's version of events Britain, not Drepanum, produced the first Christian emperor, who set out from his native soil to conquer the empire, constructed churches in the Holy Lands, founded Constantinople, and is remembered as the ideal, inimitable leader whose like has not been seen in Britain since. Henry transmits the standard accounts of Constantine's vision and baptism by Pope Sylvester, but introduces a new element into the narrative, that Helena is the daughter of King Cole of Colchester:

> Constantius . . . received in marriage the daughter of Cole, the British king of Colchester, that is Helena whom we call 'Saint', and by her he fathered Constantine the Great. Constantius . . . died in Britain in York . . . Constantine, the flower of Britain, reigned for thirty years and ten months. Of British stock and origin, whose equal Britain has not produced before or since, he led an army from Britain and Gaul into Italy.[50]

Henry could not have read the fourth-century Latin panegyrics, yet because he employs the rhetoric of this genre, his remarks on Constantine mirror their tone and sentiments. Such effusive praise and the emphatic claim to British origins (mentioned three times in the extract and alluded to twice more) suggests an apologetic and nationalistic agenda. It is as if Henry is appealing to and promoting a well-known but perhaps not fully accepted story, adding legitimacy and coherence to floating folk belief.

Despite this rhetoric, Henry seems to invoke the British Helena legend cautiously: he is more sure that his readers will know of Helena's sanctity than her British origins. Revering and employing Bede's *History* to the extent which he does, he must have been aware of Bede's silence on her origins and the legendary nature of the King Cole connection. Henry, however, suppresses the detail that Helena had been born in Drepanum, from Bede's *Chronica maiora* (and ultimately, from Jerome's *Chronicon*), but does include the authentic detail that Constantine renamed Drepanum in Bithinia after his mother: 'Constantine, . . . in restoring the city of Drepana in Bithinia in honour of the martyr Lucian who was buried there, gave it the name of Helenopolis after his mother.'[51] There was a legendary connection between Helena and her favourite martyr, Lucian,

---

[50] 'Constantius . . . accepitque filiam regis Brittannici de Colcestre, cui nomen erat Coel, scilicet Helenam, quam sanctam dicimus, et genuit ex ea Constantinum magnum. Obiit autem Constantius . . . in Britannia Eboraci . . . Constantinus flos Brittannie regnauit triginta annis et decem mensibus. Hic igitur Brittanicus genere et patria, ante quem nec post similis egressus est de Brittannia, duxit exercitum a Britannia et Gallia in Italiam' (Greenway, ed., 1.37–8, pp. 58–9). The last sentence has no parallel in Geoffrey's *Historia Regum Britannie*, unlike the others (Greenway, ed., p. 60, suggests the idea might have an analogue in Paul the Deacon's version of Eutropius's *Historia Romana*, X.2–4).

[51] 'Constantinus . . . Depranum ciuitatem Bithinie in honorem martyris Luciani ibi conditi instaurans, ex uocabulo matris sue Helenopolim uocauit' (Greenway, ed., 1.38, p. 62). Henry incorporates Bede's text exactly (ed. T. Mommsen, MGH, Auctores antiquissimi, XIII [Berlin, 1898], p. 296; Engl. trans.: Faith Wallis, *Bede: On the Reckoning of Time* [Liverpool, 1999], pp. 157–237, at p. 213).

though this tradition is not explicitly invoked by Henry. He does not explain the connection between Helena and Drepanum or tackle the incongruity of his remark, 'gave it the name of Helenopolis after his mother', with his claims of her British birth, but rather copies Bede's text. In the next sentence but one, however, he interpolates some remarks about Helena which further connect her with Britain rather than Drepanum:

> Now Helena, the high-born daughter of Britain, is said to have encircled London with a wall, which is still there, and to have furnished Colchester with town walls. Among her many deeds she also restored Jerusalem and cleansed it from idols, and embellished it with many basilicas.[52]

The source of these details has not yet been identified.[53] Perhaps Henry is conflating the Welsh 'Elen of Hosts' legend (which includes road-building) with those about St Helena, relying on earlier, and perhaps orally transmitted, legendary material.[54] There is no reason to suppose that Henry did not have access to the Welsh genealogies (and legends), as his contemporary Geoffrey of Monmouth certainly did.[55] Henry's insistence on Helena's 'high birth' is in stark contrast to Bede's reference to her as a *stabularia* 'stable-maid' or 'inn-keeper', and, like the comments on Constantine, has an apologetic ring to it. Helena is more useful rhetorically as a 'high-born daughter of Britain' than as a 'stable-maid' from Drepanum, so Henry interpolates high social status into the details provided by Bede.

While revising his text, Henry came across two further sources relevant to Helena: Paul the Deacon's *Historia Romana* (a supplemented continuation of Eutropius's *Breviarium*), and Geoffrey of Monmouth's *Historia regum Britannie* (discovered by him during his visit to Bec in 1139).[56] Henry did not alter his account of Constantine and Helena in the light of these new sources. He ignored the legitimate references to Constantine's origins in the former text (though he does incorporate the formal statements of praise, *laudes*, of Constantine and others) and found a version already very similar to his own in the latter document. Henry recounts the story of his astonishing discovery of Geoffrey's text through Robert of Torigni in Bec, and provides in his *Epistola ad Warinum*[57] an

---

52 'Helena uero Britannie nobilis alumpna, Lundoniam muro quod adhuc superest cinxisse fertur, et Colcestriam menibus adornasse. Sed et inter alia multa Ierosolim instaurauit, mundatamque idolis, basilicis pluribus adornauit' (Greenway, ed., 1.38, pp. 62–3).

53 Greenway, ed., p. 62, n. 195, suggests that, given Henry's method of composition based heavily on other sources, there might be a lost 'Life of St Helena' upon which he has based this section. Cf. the remark made by Jocelin of Furness on his source (Appendix 1 below, lines 35–7).

54 See above, p. 58.

55 J.S.P. Tatlock, *The Legendary History of Britain* (Berkeley and Los Angeles, 1950), p. 236; and Michael J. Curley, *Geoffrey of Monmouth* (New York, 1994), p. 12.

56 Greenway, ed., 'Introduction', pp. lxxxix and ci.

57 Ed. and Engl. trans. in Greenway ed., pp. 558–83. See also Neil Wright, 'The Place of Henry of Huntingdon's *Epistola ad Warinum* in the Text-History of Geoffrey of Monmouth's *Historia regum Britannie*: A Preliminary Investigation', *France and the British Isles in the Middle Ages and Renaissance: Essays by Members of Girton College, Cambridge, in Memory of Ruth Morgan*, ed. G. Jondorf and D.N. Dumville (Woodbridge, 1991), pp. 71–113.

edited summary of the narrative matter covering the period between the legendary Brutus and Caesar missing from his own *Historia*. Geoffrey's account of Constantius's subjection of Duke Cole and marriage to Helena in Colchester is contained in a very abbreviated fashion in his *Epistola ad Warinum*, along with an account of King Arthur.[58] Henry, however, omits several episodes from Geoffrey's text, many of which contain a supernatural element, including Arthur's vengeance for the death of a different Helena on the giant of Tumba Helene (though these items might not have been included in his exemplar).[59] Neil Wright has concluded from this and other evidence that Henry deliberately rejected the more spurious elements of Geoffrey's *Historia*, and that his own *Epistola ad Warinum* was the earliest demonstration of the dubious response of some medieval historians to Geoffrey's veracity.[60] Clearly, Henry did not regard the British Helena material in the same light.

Geoffrey's text did not seem to exert an influence over Henry's own account of the brief Constantine/Helena section of his *Historia*. Even though Henry revised his *History* many times, so much so that Diana Greenway calls it 'a steadily growing and changing text',[61] he does not seem to have altered this part throughout the revision process. In fact, considering the similarity of the wording of the two accounts, and their respective dates of composition, it is likely that Geoffrey of Monmouth used Henry as a source of the British Helena legend rather than vice versa.[62] It was left to later writers to combine all the narrative elements offered by the two writers into a coherent account.

If Henry did not derive the Helena legend from Geoffrey of Monmouth, his source is uncertain. Diana Greenway's proposal that, given Henry's heavy reliance upon other sources, he perhaps used a *Life of St Helena*, now lost,[63] is a possibility, but there is no evidence for it. There is the chance that a version of the Colchester account of the founding of St John's Abbey of c. 1120 which contained the reference to Helena was already in circulation before Henry came to write his *Historia*. Even if it were original, however, it is unlikely that Henry had ever seen this document, though he might have heard the oral tales which were behind it. The reference in *The Colchester Chronicle* to Constantius's siege of the town, wholly missing from Henry's account, and a general lack of similarity in the wording makes it unlikely that Henry was drawing on such a document. His version, however, does agree with the substance of the account, in

58 Greenway, ed., pp. 574–5 (c. 8); and 578–81 (c. 9).
59 Wright, 'The Place of Henry of Huntingdon's *Epistola ad Warinum*', p. 77.
60 Wright, 'The Place of Henry of Huntingdon's *Epistola ad Warinum*', p. 91.
61 Diana Greenway, 'Henry of Huntingdon and the Manuscripts of his *Historia Anglorum*', *Anglo-Norman Studies, IX: Proceedings of the Battle Conference*, ed. R. Allen Brown (Woodbridge and Wolfeboro, N.H., 1987), pp. 103–27, at p. 111.
62 Greenway, ed., p. 60, citing Tatlock, *The Legendary History of Britain*, p. 34. Henry does make one significant change, writing 'Maximus' for Geoffrey's 'Maximianus' (son of Ioelinus), to correspond with 'Magnus Maximus' (Greenway, ed., p. 575, n. 121; and Wright, 'The Place of Henry of Huntingdon's *Epistola ad Warinum*', p. 83).
63 Greenway, ed., 'Introduction', p. civ, and ed., pp. 60 and 62.

presenting a princess Helena based in Colchester. The legend might be entirely the product of his own imagination and patriotic sentiments, or more plausibly he might have developed his own version of the legend from oral traditions about the saint.

There is a tantalising connection between Henry and Robert de Torigni (d. 1186), abbot of Mont Saint Michel and historian. It was Robert who had made Henry aware of Geoffrey's *Historia regum Britannie* for the first time in Bec in 1139, and Robert copied into his own chronicle Henry's edited summary of the novel parts of this text, his *Epistola ad Warinum*.[64] We know also that Robert had a manuscript of Henry's *Historia* at Mont Saint Michel from c. 1154,[65] but a closer connection with the Helena legend has been attributed to him. Sabine Baring-Gould claims that the earliest written reference to the legend that Helena was daughter of Old King Cole is found in the *Chronicle* of Mont Saint Michel of 1056.[66] Robert of Torigni is known to have updated this chronicle, from 1135 to 1173, as well as to have produced many other chronicles and histories, including a revision of the *Gesta Normannorum ducum* of William of Jumièges.[67] There is, however, no reference to the British Helena legend in any of his extant works. The only plausible association is the inclusion of a portion of Robert's redaction of the *Gesta Normannorum ducum* in the same manuscript in which the Colchester document appears.[68] Although these two fragments date from different periods (twelfth or thirteenth century and seventeenth century respectively) and are separated by nearly two hundred folios in the manuscript (London, British Library, MS Cotton Nero D.VIII, fols 147r–159v and fols 345r–347v), Baring-Gould has apparently interpreted them as contemporary witnesses to the British Helena legend, though the absence of any documentation in his work leaves this as supposition.

There was, however, apparently an assumed connection between Helena and Mont Saint Michel in popular tradition by the 1130s. Geoffrey of Monmouth, in his *Historia regum Britannie*, recounts a story of another Helen, daughter of Duke Hoel of Brittany, whose death Arthur avenges on the giant of Mont Saint Michel.[69] Although Geoffrey has probably invented the entire episode as an

---

64 Patricia Stirnemann, 'Two Twelfth-Century Bibliophiles and Henry of Huntingdon's *Historia Anglorum*', *Viator* 24 (1993), pp. 121–42, at p. 141.

65 Paris, Biblothèque Nationale, MS Latin 6042 (Greenway, ed., 'Introduction', pp. cxxii–cxxiii).

66 S. Baring-Gould, *Lives of the Saints*, 16 vols (Edinburgh, 1914), IX.164, designates the Mont Saint Michel *Chronicle* (dated to 1056) as the origin of the British Helena story. This view is reiterated by J. Giesen, 'Die Helena de Britannia: Des Meisters von St. Severin', *Jahrbuch des kölnischen Geschichtsvereins* 25 (1950), pp. 142–52, at p. 148, though no source details or quotations are provided by either scholar.

67 *Annalibus Montis S. Michaelis*, ed. Léopold Delisle, *Chronique de Robert de Torigni*, 2 vols (Rouen, 1872–73), II.207–36. On Robert and his work, see Gransden, *Historical Writing in England*, pp. 261–63; and E.M.C. Van Houts, ed., *The Gesta Normannorum ducum (of William of Jumièges, Orderic Vitalis, and Robert of Torigni)*, 2 vols (Oxford, 1992), 'Introduction', esp. pp. lxxvii–lxxix.

68 See Van Houts, ed., p. xcvi.

69 Neil Wright, ed., *The Historia regum Britannie of Geoffrey of Monmouth: I: Bern Burgerbibliothek, MS 568* (Cambridge, 1984), § 165 [X.3], pp. 117–18.

etymological explanation for Tumba Helene, he might have used oral tales as the basis of his invention.[70] In Geoffrey's *Historia*, this Helena is distinct from her namesake the mother of Constantine, though the similarity of the names *Cole* and *Hoel* suggests contact and the possible blending of the two legends at some point.

If Henry had heard the tales which inspired the production of the Colchester document, he certainly refashions them to suit his own wider and more national-istic agenda. He is also very selective about what information on Helena to include. Somewhat surprisingly, there is no mention of Helena's main cause of fame in the Middle Ages, her discovery and veneration of the True Cross, though this incident is also missing from the Colchester document. Both texts are more concerned with establishing Constantine's British nationality via Helena's British origins than with any hagiographic agenda. The rich opportuni-ties provided by conflating both legendary strands seem not to have been real-ised, though Henry does not altogether neglect to mention her saintly status, referring to her as 'Helena, whom we call Holy'.[71] This neglect of the *Inventio* legend is further evidence of the separate growth of the British Helena legend from the transmission both of other thriving mythical tales and of the historical version of events. It also demonstrates how far removed the rhetoric of sainthood is from Henry's main theme, the development of British monarchy. The sacred theme is divorced from the nationalistic agenda at work here. In his argument for an early development of national consciousness during the Middle Ages, John Gillingham has remarked that 'in the works of Henry of Huntingdon, as in those of William of Malmesbury, we can trace a developing sense of Englishness'.[72] Certainly, the praise of Constantine and the claim that he was born of an English mother are deployed to this end, and are extremely powerful rhetorical tools in Henry's hands. It is Geoffrey of Monmouth, though, who exploits the national-istic potential of the Helena legend more fully.

Geoffrey of Monmouth and the Arthurian Connection

Geoffrey of Monmouth (c. 1090–1155), was Bishop of St Asaphs in North Wales. He produced, around 1136–38, his *Historia regum Britannie*, a legendary history of the British from pre-history to the late seventh century.[73] This work was highly popular and influential, and is extant in over two hundred

---

[70] Geoffrey's version is in turn the source of the *Roman du Mont S. Michel* (c. 1154–86), lines 458–64. See Tatlock, *The Legendary History of Britain*, p. 87.

[71] 'Helenam, quam sanctam dicimus' (1.37).

[72] 'Henry of Huntingdon and the English Nation', *Concepts of National Identity in the Middle Ages*, ed. S. Forde, L. Johnson, and A.V. Murray, Leeds Texts and Studies, ns 14 (Leeds, 1995), pp. 75–101, at p. 88.

[73] His other two extant works are *Prophetiae Merlini* and *Vita Merlini*. For biography, see Curley, *Geoffrey of Monmouth*.

manuscripts.[74] Siân Echard calls it 'arguably the most influential product of British Latin writing in the twelfth century'.[75] Geoffrey claims to be translating an ancient Breton book (from Brittany), but scholars no longer accept this statement as truth.[76] Although Geoffrey admits to using William of Malmesbury's and Henry of Huntingdon's histories, and other sources can be traced, he undoubtedly made more use of his imaginative powers than of any literary source, and moreover cites writers inappropriately in order to lend authority (if not genuine information) to his history.[77] Geoffrey's highly fictional account of Britain's history is now widely regarded as a work of literature rather than history, and also as a cultural mirror of his own day.[78] Geoffrey is best known for his elaborate and very influential treatment of the legend of King Arthur within his elaborate glorification of Britain's past. In this creative approach to the writing of history he is unlike his predecessors, who strove to construct a legitimate history out of earlier sources with a lesser degree of imaginative input, though of course their presentation of material was not necessarily impartial or close to verifiable facts. Geoffrey is also different in that he chose not to write a Christian history, preferring instead to provide for the growing demand among his contemporaries for 'romance history', in order to entertain rather than edify.[79]

Geoffrey's portrait of Helena consorts well with this agenda. She is presented not as an insignificant *stabularia* or humble finder of the Cross, but as a romance heroine.[80] Like Henry, Geoffrey omits any reference to the *Inventio* legend. He is more interested in Helena's role as the ideal progenitor of English kings. This woman is not only exceptionally talented, beautiful, and wise in this version, but has been groomed for monarchy:

> Constantius . . . married the daughter of Coel, who was called Helena. Her beauty surpassed that of the other local girls, and there could not be found anywhere another considered more learned in musical instruments or in the liberal arts. Her father had no other child to take the throne, so he had striven to instruct her so that she would be able to rule the country without any difficulty after his death.[81]

74 Crick, *A Summary Catalogue*, pp. xv–xxii, lists 217 MSS.

75 Siân Echard, *Arthurian Narrative in the Latin Tradition* (Cambridge, 1998), p. 31.

76 It is possible, though less likely, that the wording connotes a Welsh book: 'Quemdam Britannici sermonis librum uetustissimum' (Wright, ed., § 2, p. xvii). On the probable fictionality of the source, see Rigg, *A History of Anglo-Latin Literature*, p. 41; and Christopher N.L. Brooke, 'Geoffrey of Monmouth as a Historian', *The Church and the Welsh Border in the Central Middle Ages*, Studies in Celtic History 8, ed. D.N. Dumville and C.N.L. Brooke (Woodbridge and Wolfeboro, N.H., 1986), pp. 95–106, at p. 97.

77 Brooke, 'Geoffrey of Monmouth as a Historian', p. 96.

78 See Gransden, *Historical Writing in England*, p. 206; and Wright, ed., p. xviii: 'Geoffrey's achievement . . . was primarily as a creative artist.'

79 Gransden, *Historical Writing in England*, p. 201.

80 See also Larkin, 'Transitions in the Medieval Legends of Saint Helena', p. 114.

81 'Constantius . . . duxitque filiam Coel cui nomen erat Helena. Pulchritudo eius prouinciales puellas superabat nec uspiam repperiebatur altera que in musicis instrumentis siue in liberalibus artibus doctior illa censeretur. Caruerat pater alia sobole que solio regni potiretur; unde eam ita docere

Geoffrey concentrates on Helena's accomplishments as those we would recognise of a typical heroine of medieval romance, though an unusually powerful one. She is one of four queens (with Cordelia, Gwendolen, and Marcia) in the *Historia* 'who govern Britain and are famed for their wisdom, righteousness and fidelity'.[82] This new portrait of Helena springs from the secular focus which characterises Geoffrey's narrative. Within this scheme, Geoffrey portrays an important role for Britain in Rome's history.[83] He manipulates and creates his narrative with this overriding agenda, which he executes extremely successfully. By presenting his imaginative biography of Britain as genuine history, Geoffrey has constructed British history as a legitimate subject of literature, what has been called 'the Matter of Britain'.[84] Specifically, he promoted the figure of King Arthur into the limelight as not only a genuine historical figure, but the greatest leader in British history. Constantine and Helena provide the British origins of this story.

Arthur, as he is reported as saying himself in this text, is a descendant of both Constantine and of Magnus Maximus of the Welsh tradition. When he argues that Rome ought to pay him tribute, Arthur, King of the Britons, says, 'Indeed, Constantine, son of Helena, and Maximianus, both closely related to me, wearing the crown of Britain one after the other, each sat on the throne of the Roman Empire.'[85] Arthur is establishing his right to Roman imperial status on the basis of his ancestors' British origins and alleged Roman positions. Geoffrey is conflating two traditions relating to Helena in this reference: the actual Roman Augusta (though it was an honourary position only) and the Welsh Elen Luyydog, daughter of Eudaf and wife of Magnus Maximus (i.e. Macsen Guletic). Geoffrey confuses the connection even further by presenting Maximianus as the cousin of a second Constantine (V.9), and also recounting the story of another Helena, niece of King Hoel of Brittany, whose murder by the giant of Mont Saint Michel Arthur himself avenges (X.3).[86] To make matters worse, Geoffrey introduces a third Constantine, King of Brittany and

---

laborauerat ut regimen patrie post obitum suum facilius tractare quiuisset' (Wright, ed., § 79 [V.6], pp. 50–1).

82 Curley, *Geoffrey of Monmouth*, p. 23.

83 Geoffrey further exaggerates Britain's role in Rome's history by making Britain the place to which the Roman nobles flee from the dictatorship of Maxentius: 'Incumbente igitur seuicia ipsius diffugiebant exterminati as Constantinum in Britaniam et ab ipso honorifice excipiebantur' (Wright, ed., § 79 [V.7], p. 51). 'Therefore, those exiles escaping his (Maxentius's) severity fled to Constantine in Britain and were received honourably by him.' See Curley, *Geoffrey of Monmouth*, p. 32, who similarly construes this addition as Geoffrey being 'always alert for opportunities to supply evidence of Britain's glorious role as a cradle of civilization'.

84 Brooke, 'Geoffrey of Monmouth as a Historian', p. 106.

85 'Constantinus etiam Helene filius necnon Maximianus, uterque michi cognatione propinquus, alter post alterum diademate Britannie insignitus, thronum Romani imperii adeptus est' (Wright, ed., § 159 [IX.16], p. 114).

86 Geoffrey has probably invented this episode to account for the name of the peak, once Tumbellana, construed by him as 'Tumba Helena' (Helen's Tomb), and his account proved attractive and became traditional (Curley, *Geoffrey of Monmouth*, p. 92).

grandfather of Arthur (VI.5). Geoffrey has created many links between the kings of Britain and Roman imperial leaders in his 'invention of a pedigree for Arthur',[87] as well as in his reiteration of those evocative names, Constantine and Helena.

Modern critics have been quick to call Geoffrey a liar,[88] because he was passing off fiction as fact, but this presupposes a great deal about medieval textual practice in general and Geoffrey's intentions in particular. Many critics have challenged or modified this interpretation.[89] Valerie Flint has suggested Geoffrey's conscious parody of the genre of history.[90] Siân Echard has refined this argument, proposing a methodology entailing 'a thoroughgoing subversion of conventions of historiography with serious implications'.[91] But it is not necessary to assume a parodic or satirical agenda, and is very difficult to prove it. Geoffrey's *Historia* might be construed instead as a patriotic romance, modelled on the shape of a history, and citing other authorities in order to add legitimacy to its own ideas, which are based on the premiss that tradition is history. If so it might be concluded that Geoffrey has actually deployed historical and legendary material extremely effectively. He grounds his literary creations firmly within known stories, as his presentation of the Constantine/Cole/Helena legends within his Arthurian narrative demonstrates. These legends provide the genealogical basis for Arthur's claim to Roman status, as well as his British origins. The existence of earlier versions of these tales, some of them in the Welsh tradition, made Geoffrey's version sound reliable, even though it was not. Because there are sufficient earlier references to the legend to demonstrate its livelihood in popular imagination and occasional admission to written accounts, Geoffrey's narrative of Constantine and Helena might be viewed as an elaborate culmination and expansion of earlier traditions, as well as a starting point for wider dissemination.

Geoffrey's plausible narrative was very entertaining and widely read. The degree of its success and influence can be gauged from the manuscript evidence: the *Historia* is extant in 217 manuscripts, which are grouped according to several variant versions.[92] As a secular history, it is unconcerned with the *Inventio* legend, though a Breton poem produced as a metrical paraphrase of Geoffrey's text in the mid-thirteenth century, called *Gesta regum*

---

87 John J. Parry, 'Geoffrey of Monmouth and the Paternity of Arthur', *Speculum* 13 (1938), pp. 271–7, at p. 277.

88 E.g. Gurney Benham, 'Legends of Coel and Helena', p. 235; and Brooke, 'Geoffrey of Monmouth as a Historian', p. 95: 'There has scarcely, if ever, been a historian more mendacious.'

89 See Rigg, *History of Anglo-Latin Literature*, p. 43; and Gransden, *Historical Writing in England*, esp. pp. 201–2.

90 Valerie Flint, 'The *Historia regum Britannie* of Geoffrey of Monmouth: Parody and its Purpose. A Suggestion', *Speculum* 54 (1979), pp. 447–68; and Echard, *Arthurian Narrative*, esp. pp. 35–7.

91 Echard, *Arthurian Narrative*, p. 36.

92 Julia C. Crick, *The Historia regum Britannie of Geoffrey of Monmouth: IV, Dissemination and Reception in the Later Middle Ages* (Cambridge, 1991), p. 215. For full details of the manuscripts, see Crick, *A Summary Catalogue*.

Britannie, remedies the omission: she is 'stamped with the sign of Christ', [93] and more cautiously, 'she is the one who was said once to have found the Cross of Christ'.[94] This is an unusual example of the prolific offspring of Geoffrey's influential text, most of which share his secular interests and omit these details.[95]

Helena in the Brut Tradition

Geoffrey of Monmouth's *History* was extremely popular, widely disseminated, and almost universally treated as genuine history, though its reliability was challenged by a few writers who compared his version of events with that presented by Bede's *Historia ecclesiastica*, especially in Bede's home territory of Northumbria, including Ailred and William of Newburgh.[96] On the whole, however, his version of events, including the King Cole legend, was accepted. The narrative was transmitted in Norman French, English, and Welsh translations, and adapted in part by many later writers, particularly chroniclers.[97] Geoffrey made Helena's desirable British pedigree, along with many other ideas, available for exploitation to a wide range of writers. These literary descendants included John of Salisbury, who in the Prologue of his *Policraticus*, produced in 1159, specifically states that Constantine was of British stock.[98] But the legend was not all-pervasive. A near-contemporary English historian, Ralph of Diceto, in his *Abbreviationes chronicorum* of about 1188, presents the story according to Jerome's *Chronicon*: 'On the death of Constantius, Constantine, the son of his ignoble marriage, is created emperor in Britain.'[99] Ralph shows that the legendary version did not completely efface the more historically accurate version of events, which was, however, disseminated as a minority view.[100]

---

[93] 'Signata caractere Christi' (Neil Wright, ed. and Engl. trans. *The Historia regum Britannie of Geoffrey of Monmouth: V, Gestum regum Britannie* [Cambridge, 1991], line 309).

[94] 'Hec est que dicitur olim/ Inuenisse crucem Domini' (lines 311–12).

[95] See Crick, *Dissemination*, passim.

[96] Antonia Gransden, 'Bede's Reputation as an Historian in Medieval England', *Journal of Ecclesiastical History* 32 (1981), pp. 397–425; repr. in *Legends Traditions and History in Medieval England* (London and Rio Grande, 1992), pp. 1–29, at pp. 19–23.

[97] See Laura Keeler, *Geoffrey of Monmouth and the Latin Chroniclers, 1300–1500* (Berkeley, 1946).

[98] C.J. Nederman, ed. and Engl. trans., *Policraticus* (Oxford, 1990), I.13, p. 3.

[99] 'Constantio mortuo Constantinus ex obscuriore matrimonio ejus filius, in Britannia est creatus imperator', ed., W. Stubbs, 2 vols (London, 1876), 1.73, entry for the year 308.

[100] W.J. Mulligan, 'The British Constantine: An English Historical Myth', *The Journal of Medieval and Renaissance Studies* 8 (1978), pp. 257–79, maintains that Ralph of Diceto was the sole exponent of the genuine version in the twelfth century, but this is unlikely in view of the wide dissemination of the genuine sources, especially Eutropius's *Breviarium*, and its redactions and continuations, including that made by William of Malmesbury and his collaborators in c. 1125 (London, British Library, MS Harley 2729 and Oxford, Lincoln College, MS Latin 100: see H.W. Bird, Engl. trans., *Eutropius, Breviarium ab urbe condita*, Translated Texts for Historians 14 (Liverpool, 1993), 'Introduction', pp. lv–lvii; and Reynolds, *Texts and Transmission*, pp. 159–62).

Geoffrey's version became very appealing and useful to those producing historical texts or chronicles both in Latin and in the vernacular.[101] The latter group is the more interesting: those writing British histories in the vernacular and thereby contributing to the Brut tradition, so-called from Geoffrey of Monmouth's false etymology of the word 'Britain' from its legendary founder, 'Brutus'.[102] When an English redaction of his *Historia* was made around the beginning of the thirteenth century, it absorbed and elaborated the British Helena legend. This text, Laȝamon's *Brut*, is important as it contains the earliest existing vernacular account of the British Helena legend. The *Brut*, a variety of national chronicle in verse, is extant in two manuscripts dating from the middle of the thirteenth century, so must have been produced prior to 1250, though probably after the death of Henry II in 1189.[103] Little is known about the author other than what he tells us in the opening lines, that he was a priest at Ernley, near Worcester. His text is based on Wace's Anglo-Norman *Roman de Brut* (of 1155),[104] which itself derives from Geoffrey's *History*, though Laȝamon has by no means made a close translation of Wace's text.[105] This extended alliterative account of British history (more than 16,000 long lines) differs from Geoffrey's and Wace's narratives in its focus on the English people rather than on Britain's relations with Rome, in 'an attempt to create a new foundation myth'.[106]

Laȝamon mentions Constantine's British mother on two occasions: once when the history of Britain is being recounted; and again when Arthur is enumerating the past glories of Britain.[107] In the earlier section, Laȝamon transmits Geoffrey's account, via Wace, of Helena, daughter of King Cole,[108] though with some changes:

---

101 Latin chronicles continued to be prolific during the Middle English period, and most frequently based their narratives on Geoffrey's version of events. The *Eulogium*, for example, produced in 1367 by a monk at Malmesbury, though it relies heavily on the local history, William of Malmesbury's *De gesta*, transmits Geoffrey's narrative of Helena and Cole (ed. F.S. Haydon, 2 vols [London, 1858], Ch. 32). See Gransden, *Historical Writing in England*, pp. 212 ff.

102 On the Brut texts, see E.D. Kennedy, *Chronicles and Other Historical Writings: A Manual of the Writings in Middle English 1050–1500*, vol. VIII, gen. ed., Albert E. Hartung (New Haven, 1939), pp. 2611–27.

103 Dating is still being disputed, but see Françoise H.M. Le Saux, *Laȝamon's Brut: The Poem and its Sources* (Cambridge, 1989), pp. 1–10.

104 Ed. and Engl. trans., Judith Weiss (Exeter, 1999).

105 Le Saux, *Laȝamon's Brut*, p. 42.

106 Le Saux, *Laȝamon's Brut*, p. 230. She adds: 'The poet's loyalties are not expressed in ethnic terms, but proceed from a sense of institutional continuity and the acceptance of cultural admixtures' (p. 227).

107 G.L. Brook and R.F. Leslie, *Laȝamon: Brut*, EETS, os 250, 277, 2 vols (London, 1963, 1978), London, British Library, MS Cotton Caligula A.IX, lines 5503 and 12,509. The following citations are to this edition of the Caligula version, generally considered to be the better text. See also the new edition of the Caligula text only, with translation: W.R.J. Barron and S.C. Weinberg, ed. and Engl. trans., *Laȝamon: Brut* (Harlow, 1995).

108 Laȝamon follows the version of the story extant in the majority of Wace manuscripts, situating Coel in Gloucester from the line of Gloi, whence its name (line 5418). Cf Wace, line 5594 and note, Weiss, ed., p. 141.

This king had a daughter, who was very dear to him, and he bequeathed all this land into the maiden's keeping. . . . That maiden was called Helena. She was afterwards queen in the land of Jerusalem, to the great bliss of its people. This maiden was well-educated, and she was well versed in book-learning and dwelt in this land with her powerful father.[109]

Although the stress on Helena's education and wisdom are derived from Wace (lines 5605–14), Laȝamon has added the detail that Helena later ruled as queen in Jerusalem. This expatriot status is curious, especially as it is mentioned prior to the enumeration of Helena's now traditional romance attributes and accomplishments, though evidently it is not coincidental.

Later Laȝamon expands Wace's brief account of Helena's arrival at Jerusalem and discovery of the Cross by the Jewish community (lines 5565–73), expanding the four lines in Wace,[110] and also elaborating on this earlier reference of a contented Helena in residence there:

And the lady Helena, the holy queen, went to Jerusalem with a magnificent troop, and spoke with the courageous Jewish elders, and she promised them a great many things if they should advise her on how to find the cross on which Christ our lord redeemed the earth. The Jews sought it and bestowed it on the queen. Then she was happier than she had ever been in her life and she remained there for many years.[111]

At this point in the *Brut*, Helena is said to be overjoyed at seeing and being given the Cross, but rather than take it back to Constantine as she does in many other renditions of the legend, here, she stays with it in Jerusalem for many years. Although in the early historians, Helena's journey to and from the Holy Lands takes a few years, Laȝamon's wording suggests a longer residence. This portrait of Helena remaining in Jerusalem with the Cross is extremely unusual and perhaps suggests the absorption of another legendary tale. Laȝamon might have been influenced by medieval legends of Helena as a Jewish proselyte, only later converted to Christianity by Pope Sylvester.[112] This version of events makes explicit Helena's affinity with the Jewish people and possibly hints at the

---

[109] Þes king hæfuede enne dohter   þe wes him swiðe deore.
       & he al þis kinelond   bitahte þan maidene an hond . . .
       Þat mæide hehte Elene   seoððen heo wes quene
       i þan londe of Ierusalem   leoden to blissen.
       Þis maiden wes wel itæhte,   on bocken heo cuðe godne cræft
       & wunede in þisse londe   mid hire fader stronge. (lines 5443–8)

[110] Wace lines 5721–4. Le Saux, *Laȝamon's Brut*, p. 171, claims that this is the only such elaboration of the accounts of British saints in the *Brut*.

[111]   & þa læuedi Ælene   þa halie quene.
       to Ierusalem wende   mid richere genge.
       & spæc wi[ð] þan elde   of þan Iudean þe weoren balde.
       & heo heom bihehte   swiðe muche æhte.
       þat heo hire sceoldon ræden   to vinden þa Rode.
       þe Crist ure Lauerd   alisden on þes middelærd.
       þeo Iudeus heo sohten   & þere quene heo itæhten.
       þa was heo swa bliðe   swa heo nes neuere ær on liue
       & heo vele ȝere   þurh þan wune<de> þere.   (lines 5565–73)

[112] See Ch. I above, p. 25.

The Anglo-Latin Histories and the Brut Tradition

integration of the cult of Helena with that of Silvester, or perhaps represents an unacknowledged remnant of the legend that Helena was Jewish. On the other hand, the reference to Helena's role as queen of Jerusalem might be a contemporary reflection of the new status of the city as a Latin kingdom, captured during the First Crusade of 1099, lost and won again by the Christians in the late twelfth and early thirteenth centuries.[113]

In Laȝamon's *Brut*, the *Inventio* is a non-event compared with Helena's settlement in Jerusalem: the Jews seek out the Cross and present it to Helena and her journey is a rich display of wealth and power rather than an act of pilgrimage. There is, however, some reference to the *Inventio* in this text, demonstrating that Laȝamon does not confine himself to secular interests as Geoffrey does. Laȝamon at least acknowledges Helena's sanctity, calling her 'the holy queen' (line 5565),[114] and gives more space to the *Inventio* episode than Wace did. But, as Le Saux remarks, 'religion in the *Brut* is a practical matter',[115] and in the Cross episode, Helena's majesty of the situation, rather than the symbolic significance of the Cross or its value as a relic, is the thematic focus.

In Laȝamon's narrative, the circumstances of Helena's marriage to Constantius (Custance) are similar to those in the earlier histories, with the exception that Laȝamon has created a new scene where Coel offers his daughter and the realm to Constantius at the advice of his counsellors, rather than Constantius's seizing both on Coel's death (lines 5495–503).[116] Regarding Constantine, 'son of the wisest woman who had ever lives in Britain' (line 5504), we are told that 'God Himself had chosen him' (line 5506), and his birth brings joys to all of Britain (line 5507), where he was born. He is beloved by all the British people, specifically because 'his mother Helena was queen of this land' (line 5513). Laȝamon elaborates this idea by explaining that it is only natural for Constantine, son of a British woman, to be loved by her kinsmen: 'The Britons were compliant to him and he loved them very much; they were his mother's kinsmen, (as) she was a native of Britain.'[117]

In the later reference to Helena in Laȝamon's *Brut*, the author's nationalistic bent is even more overt in his insistence on Constantine's pure-bred Britishness. Arthur says 'He was Helena's son, fully British',[118] putting aside Constantine's

---

113 The recapture of the city by Saladin in 1187 and Christian possession from 1229–39 and 1243–44 would have been recent history for Laȝamon, who was known to have reflected contemporary history in his presentation of the past (on which, see Leslie Johnson, 'Reading the Past in Laȝamon's *Brut*', *The Text and Tradition of Laȝamon's Brut*, ed. Françoise Le Saux [Cambridge, 1994], pp. 141–60).

114 Cf. Wace, 'sa bone mere', 'the good mother' (Weiss, ed., line 5720).

115 Le Saux, *Laȝamon's Brut*, p. 178.

116 Rosamond Allen, Engl. trans., *Lawman: Brut* (London, 1992), p. 430.

117 'Bruttes him weoren liðe & he hon luuede swiðe;/ heo weoren his moder cunnes men, icomen heo wes of Brutten' (lines 5515–16). Cf. Wace: 'He loved the Britons because of his mother' (Weiss, ed., line 5687).

118 'He was Helena sune, al of Brutten icome' (line 12,509). Cf. Wace: 'Constantine, who came from Britain and was Helena's son' (Weiss ed., lines 10,866–7).

85

Roman father in this rhetorical gesture, and exaggerating the stress on Britain of his source. This comment serves not only to position the national focus of the text, but also to justify the inclusion of the earler material on Constantine and Helena.

In expanding the importance of Constantine's British origins, and possibly by analogy with the British Helena legend, Laȝamon adds the detail that Constantine's wife, as well as his mother, was a Briton of high birth and great virtue: 'They later gave him a wife who was very well-bred, born of the noblest and the best of Britons.'[119] Laȝamon's alterations to his source have been shown to have stemmed from conscious invention rather than error or recourse to other material.[120] In this context, Laȝamon might be seen to be exploiting the British Helena legend in the creation of a new national history. This text became the centre of Brut history and myth, the primary manifestation of the absorption of British history into English history, and thereby a major vehicle in the dissemination of the British Helena legend, especially in the Brut chronicles.[121] Because it transmits the legend in the vernacular, Laȝamon's *Brut* opens up the readership of the story beyond the learned elite possessing Latin literacy. Although the Helena component is not particularly prominent in the text as a whole, its existence here as well as in other literature must have cemented the tale as fact in the minds of many readers or hearers and also assured its position in later works.

Later Vernacular Chronicles

Chronicle writing flourished during the later Middle Ages in England, particularly in the vernacular, as translations from Latin and French were made to satisfy the growing demand for readable histories during the fourteenth and fifteenth centuries.[122] This phenomenon provided a ready vehicle for the wide dissemination of legendary stories from Brut history such as Arthurian narratives, and to a lesser extent the British Helena legend, as genuine elements of the nation's past. Because most of these chronicles made use of Geoffrey of Monmouth's *Historia regum Britannie* as a chief source of information, they transmit the version he popularised of Helena as the daughter of King Cole of Colchester, and they frequently borrow Geoffrey's presentation of an accomplished, beautiful romance heroine. The writers of these texts, however, had access to a wide range of other written sources (as well as, undoubtedly, oral

---

119 'Seoððen heo him ȝefuen wif, wunder ane hende/ iboren of þan hæsten of Bruttene þan alre bezsten' (lines 6433–4).
120 Derek Brewer, 'The Archaic and the Modern in Laȝamon's *Brut*', *From Anglo-Saxon to Early Modern English: Studies Presented to E.G. Stanley*, ed. M. Godden et al. (Oxford, 1994), pp. 188–205, at p. 192.
121 Diane Speed, 'The Construction of the Nation in Medieval Romance', *Readings in Medieval English Romance*, ed. Carol M. Meale (Cambridge, 1994), pp. 135–57, at p. 141.
122 Kennedy, *Chronicles and Other Historical Writings*, p. 2597.

traditions) which they use in addition to Geoffrey. Frequently, the result in the case of sections of the texts dealing with Helena is a less secular portrayal of her life than Geoffrey provides, as the *Inventio* legend, omitted by him, was often incorporated into these chronicles, and the appellation 'saint' was typically applied to Helena. The frequent portrayal of Helena in religious art, usually with the Cross though also with Constantine or holding a book, must also have kept her holy status and significant accomplishments constantly in the minds of worshippers and thereby supported the transmission of her sacred reputation and narratives concerning her.[123]

This ecclesiastical acknowledgment of her status, if not her nationality, and the flourishing of hagiography at the same time (especially relating to St Silvester) must have positioned Helena firmly within sacred as well as historiographic traditions and the two probably worked in concert in the promotion of her identity. Even the relatively early metrical chronicles produced in England during the later Middle Ages present a confluence of religious and secular traditions relating to Helena as an integral part of the nation's past. In the early fourteenth century, Robert of Gloucester's *Metrical Chronicle* (c. 1300), recounts the story of Helena, daughter of Cole, mother of Constantine (later converted to Christianity and baptised by St Silvester).[124] The daughter of Cole is referred to as 'Seynt Helene' who 'fond þe swete holy rode'.[125] Her dual reasons for fame in Britain continued to be disseminated, as Robert's *Chronicle* was much revised and became the source of several prose paraphrases during the fifteenth century.[126] Similarly, Robert Mannyng of Brunne's poetic chronicle *The Story of England* (c. 1338), recounts both the *Inventio* and British Helena legends,[127] and the story found its way into more imaginative texts, such as the Middle English prose fictitious travel digest *Mandeville's Travels*.[128] This popular text was originally written in French in the mid-fourteenth century, and was translated into many languages, including English. The British Helena legend (as well as the legend that Helena translated the body of St Ann from Jerusalem to Constantinople) is mentioned several times within the section dealing with the Holy Land:

---

123 See below, pp. 92–5. The *Inventio* legend is mentioned briefly (and crudely) in Chaucer's *Canterbury Tales*. At the end of *The Pardoner's Tale*, the Host refuses the offer of a pardon, swearing that he would prefer to emasculate the offensive Pardoner: 'By the croys which that seint Eleyne fond/ I wolde I hadde thy coillons in myn hond' (VI.951–2) (*The Riverside Chaucer*, gen. ed. Larry Benson, 3rd ed. [Boston, 1987], p. 202).

124 Ed. T. Hearne, 2 vols (Oxford, 1724), I.82–7.

125 Hearne, ed., p. 84.

126 See Kennedy, *Chronicles and Other Historical Writings*, pp. 2621–2.

127 Ed. T. Hearne, *Peter Langtoft's Chronicle as Illust. and Improv'd by Robert of Brunne (AD 689–1307)*, 2 vols (Oxford, 1725); see Kennedy, *Chronicles and Other Historical Writings*, pp. 2625–8.

128 The c. 1400 version in London, British Library, MS Cotton Titus C.XVI is edited by M.C. Seymour (Oxford, 1967).

> This holy cros . . . lay there cc. yeer and more into the tyme of Seynt Elyne, that was moder to Constantyn the emperour of Rome. And sche was doughter of kyng Cool born in Colchester, that was kyng of Engelond that was clept thanne Brytayne the More, the whiche the emperour Constance wedded to his wif for her bewtee and gat vpon hire Constantyn, that was after emperour of Rome and kyng of Englond.[129]

Helena's dual prominence – as founder of the True Cross and mother of a Roman emperor – is succinctly captured in these remarks, which manipulate the combination of several legendary strands to promote the primacy of England in the sequence of events.

A roughly contemporary example of the manner in which Geoffrey of Monmouth's legend was integrated into vernacular Brut texts along with the *Inventio* legend is the lengthy poetic history of Britain combining traditional, legendary, and historical information, known as *Castleford's Chronicle* (c. 1327). Like most of the chronicles produced in England during the fourteenth century, this one follows in Geoffrey's historiographical footsteps, specifically in the presentation of Britain in its relations with Rome.[130] The author of this chronicle elaborates Geoffrey's portrait of a romance heroine: Helena, daughter of King Cole, is the fairest maiden in Britain and the most accomplished musically, who has been trained to be queen.[131] Like some other English chronicles, this one contains the Christian element which Geoffrey and some other Brut chronicles lack. We are told 'she understood the belief of Christ',[132] and her Finding of the True Cross, at Constantine's instruction, is related in some detail (lines 10,732–89). She is called 'Saint Helene' within this section.[133] The many sacred and secular references to the *Inventio* are referred to in the final lines which proclaim the primarily textual basis of saints' cults:

> So in the legends of the saints is it seen
> And is read among the deeds of the emperors
> And one may read it in stories of the church.[134]

Similarly, John Trevisa's English translation of Ranulph Higden's *Polychronicon* (of c. 1327–60), produced at the end of the fourteenth century (c. 1387), remedies the religious omissions of Geoffrey's text. Trevisa's translation of this world history was widely circulated and an influential source for a

---

129 Seymour, ed., p. 9, lines 3–8.
130 Caroline D. Eckhardt, 'The Presence of Rome in the Middle English Chronicles of the Fourteenth Century', *JEGP* 90 (1991), pp. 187–207, at p. 194. Eckhardt calls this the 'anxious evidence of the strength of Rome as a subject' (p. 207).
131 Caroline D. Eckhardt, ed., *Castleford's Chronicle or The Boke of Brut*, 2 vols (3rd volume forthcoming), EETS, os 305, 306 (Oxford, 1996), III. xxviii, lines 10,431–60.
132 'Þe troght of Criste scho vnderstode' (line 10,458).
133 Lines 10,689, 10,732, 10,742, 10,786. The first of these, in a section title, reflects the spelling of her name in the earlier Middle English poem, *St Elyn*, treated in Ch. V below and transcribed at Appendix 2.
134 So in legent of saintes es sene,
And redde amanges emperours dedes,
And in kirkes stories men redes. (lines 10,787–9)

wide range of writers, though it was not copied as prolifically as was its Latin source.[135] Both contain a reference to the British Helena legend, sourced to Geoffrey of Monmouth's *Historia regum Britannie*. The English translation of this section is typically faithful to the Latin:

> About þat tyme þe Romanys sente oon Constancius for to make Coelus kyng of Britayne sogette, and forto fonge tribut þat was i-werned. But Coelus was dede after þe monþe of his comynge, and Constancius hadde te kyngdom, and wedded þis Coelus his douȝter Helene, and gat on hire þe grete Constantyn.[136]

Helena's ecclesiastical building programme in Jerusalem and the *Inventio* are briefly mentioned in other parts of the text, as well as her burial in Rome.[137] Somewhat unusually, both the Latin and English versions contain an account of Constantine's later career as emperor in Europe, whereas most other chronicles recount only that part of Constantine's life relating to Britain.[138] This focus on his glorious career emphasises Constantine's importance outside Britain and lends international significance to this claimed local product.

By far the most popular English chronicle, and indeed the most influential secular text of Middle Ages, was the anonymous Middle English Prose *Brut* (c. 1400). First translated from the Anglo-Norman prose *Brut*[139] around the end of the fourteenth or the beginning of the fifteenth century, with original additions, this chronicle recounts the history of Britain from its legendary founding down to 1333.[140] It demonstrates the established place of the Helena legend in the Brut tradition, recounting the princess's marriage to Constantius and Constantine's rule in Britain and later Rome: 'The Kyng Coel ȝaf his douȝter Elyne to Constance' and 'Constantyne, his sone of seynt Elyne, þat founde þat

---

135 Fourteen manuscripts and four fragments are extant; cf. 118 manuscripts and nine fragments of Higden's text: see Kennedy, *Chronicles and Other Historical Writings*, pp. 2656–57. One Latin chronicle produced in Wales in the fifteenth century, by Adam Usk, is of particular interest, as it reports that contemporary Greeks recognise their descent from a British Constantine. See C. Given-Wilson, ed. and Engl. trans., *The Chronicle of Adam Usk, 1377–1421* (Oxford, 1997), p. 198 (entry for the year 1405): 'Some of these Greeks also told me that the entire nobility of Greece is descended from the aforesaid Constantine, his three uncles, . . . and the other thirty thousand Britons whom he took with him when he went there from Briton.'
136 *Polychronicon Ranulphi Higden monachi cestrensis, Together with English Translations of John Trevisa and of an Unknown Writer of the Fifteenth Century*, ed. Churchill Babington and J.R. Lumby, 9 vols, Rolls Series 41 (London, 1865), V.97. The Latin is very similar: 'Circa hoc dies Constantius quidam missus a Romanis ad subigendum regum Britonum Coelum, et ad recipiendum tributum denegatum; sed mortuo post mensem adventus sui Coelo, Constantius regno politus, copulavit sibi Helenam filiam Coeli prædicti, de qua Constantinum magnum procreavit' (V.96).
137 Babington and Lumby, ed., I.181 and IV.375.
138 Mulligan, 'The British Constantine', p. 265.
139 A compilation of French versions of Geoffrey's *Historia*, including the chronicles of Wace and Pierre Langtoft; 47 manuscripts of this text are extant (Kennedy, *Chronicles and Other Historical Writings*, p. 2630).
140 Ed. F.W.D. Brie, 2 vols, EETS, os 131, 136 (London, 1906–08). The Prose *Brut* was far more widely disseminated than other Brut texts: more than 172 manuscripts survive, many of which contain continuations beyond 1333, and Caxton's publication of printed versions of this text in 1480 and 1482 enhanced its circulation (Kennedy, *Chronicles and Other Historical Writings*, pp. 2629–30).

croice in þe holy londe ... bicome Emperoure of Rome.'[141] This version reflects its relatively late date of composition at a time when Helena's position as a saint was becoming more firmly recognised. In this text, Helena is a Christian from the outset, is revered for her role in the *Inventio*, and is taken by her son from Britain to Rome on account of her great wisdom. Fifteenth-century prose and metrical chronicles such as John Capgrave's *Abbreuiacion of Chronicles* (c. 1462)[142] place less emphasis on Helena's sanctity, but acknowledge it as well as her Colchestrian origins.[143] Similarly, John Hardyng's *Chronicle* (1457, rev. 1464) transmits the narrative, but with greater contextual significance, by positioning it amongst other legendary material which was generally of less interest to chronicles, such as accounts of Joseph of Arimathea and of Galahad's quest for the Grail.[144]

The chronicle tradition provided ongoing validity for the story that Helena was a princess of Colchester, a heritage which was to be exploited by later writers as part of the rhetoric of hagiographic and patriotic discourse. Throughout this time, the British legend was not receiving any particular emphasis in these texts, but was nevertheless being kept alive in popular culture while interest in St Helena was maintained in Christian iconographic representations with the chief symbol of that religion, the Cross, as well as in more formal vehicles for dissemination. During the three centuries between the date of Geoffrey's *Historia* (c. 1138) and these chronicles, the *Inventio* legend in particular was being celebrated by ecclesiastical writers and more generally within Christian culture, liturgically and in visual representations. As the following chapter will argue, Helena's growing fame allowed her an increased legitimacy within the ecclesiastical establishment which in turn was beginning to accept the British legend. But it was not until well into the fifteenth century that the legend of her British origins received official recognition within the Church, and her status as an English saint thereby became established.

---

[141] Brie, ed., Chs 45–6, I.39–40.
[142] Ed. P.J. Lucas, EETS, os 285 (Oxford, 1983), p. 61; on p. 85 is a reference to the relics of 'Seynt Heleyn' being translated from Rome to France. Capgrave refutes the story of late-Roman historians that Constantine was baptised on his deathbed, stressing that Silvester baptised him.
[143] On the genre at this time, see C.L. Kingsford, *English Historical Literature in the Fifteenth Century* (New York, 1913; repr. 1972) and Antonia Gransden, *Historical Writing in England II: c. 1307 to the Early Sixteenth Century* (Ithaca and New York, 1982).
[144] Ed. H. Ellis (London, 1812: repr. New York, 1974), p. 97. See Kennedy, *Chronicles and Other Historical Writings*, pp. 2644–7.

V

Late Medieval Saints' Legendaries

DESPITE THE INTEREST in Helena in the Brut tradition, she was never a popular subject of religious literature in England, yet her role in the *Inventio* legend continued to be recounted widely textually and iconographically. Helena is not often found in English saints' calendars before the fifteenth century,[1] and features in only one genuine *vita*, by Jocelin of Furness (see below), in England prior to the sixteenth century.[2] The Middle English verse *St Elyn*, discussed below, can hardly count as a *vita*, since, despite its manuscript title, it deals with the cure and conversion of Constantine by St Silvester rather than with Helena's life.

Even though her cult was evidently not one of the most vibrant during the early Middle Ages and the Church did not promote the alleged British connection, Helena's presence was maintained in a secondary capacity. She was a reasonably popular dedicatory saint in post-Conquest England, the subject of about 135 church dedications dating from the eleventh century onwards, most of which are in the north of England.[3] At least one of these, St Helen's Worcester, appears to have been a British church and a parochially powerful establishment which was probably dedicated to Helena before the earliest extant record of this name in the eleventh century.[4] It is likely too that St Helena was chosen as the dedicatee of other Anglo-Saxon churches as part of a programme of establishing some continuity with the Roman Church in Britain, including the deliberate

---

[1] For exceptions, see the eleventh-century calendars mentioned above, p. 34.

[2] S. Baring-Gould and J. Fisher, *The Lives of the British Saints*, 4 vols (London, 1911), III.260. Helena does, however, feature as the addressee in a rare extant prayer: a six-line prayer to her and the Cross in a manuscript held at York Minster (MS XVI.K.6, fol. 98v). This text is listed in Carleton Brown and R.H. Robbins,*The Index of Middle English Verse* (New York, 1943), as no. 2893 and is edited in Frank A.P. Patterson, *Middle English Penitential Lyrics* (New York, 1911), p. 72.

[3] Francis Bond, *Dedications and Patron Saints of English Churches: Ecclesiastical Symbolism, Saints and their Emblems* (London, 1914), p. 72; and Frances Arnold Foster, *Studies in Church Dedications, or England's Patron Saints* (London, 1899), p. 188. Although this figure might be slightly inflated with post-medieval evidence not distinguished by Bond and Foster and unrecorded rededications, it still represents a fair degree of interest in the saint. The situation is further complicated by the loss of dedications to St Helena through later rededications, as exemplified by the former St Helen's, Ashton-under-Lyne which became known as St Michael and All Angels (a standard dedication) in the fourteenth century (see above, p. 5, n.8).

[4] Steven Bassett, 'Church and Diocese in the West Midlands: The Transition From British to Anglo-Saxon Control', *Pastoral Care before the Parish*, ed. John Blair and Richard Sharpe (Leicester, 1992), pp. 13–40, at p. 22.

situation of churches on the sites of former Roman buildings.[5] The dates of later dedications and rededications to her are difficult to track, though sometimes material traces remain which are of assistance. The originally Anglo-Saxon Church of St Helen, Darley Dale, Derbyshire, appears to have once owned the service book Cambridge, Corpus Christi College, MS 422, Part II (dateable to c. 1061 and containing masses and other offices). Prayers for a mass for Helena, lections for the Feast of the *Inventio*, and antiphons for Helena in her role as *Inventrix* were added to the manuscript in the twelfth century, evidence of its having been 'refurbished for continued, and changing, use', specifically for use by a community dedicated to Helena.[6] These manuscript additions suggest that this particular church was known as St Helen's by the early twelfth century, by which time provision was being made for the formal veneration of this saint, specifically in her capacity of Finder of the True Cross.

Helena's role in the *Inventio*, as well as the importance of her relics, is implied by the additions to another manuscript, Oxford, Bodleian, MS Bodley Tanner 169*. Thirteenth-century additions to this twelfth-century Psalter from Chester include Latin metrical hymns honouring the Cross ('In exaltatione sancte Crucis'), and St Oswald, and a separate addition, 'Translacio sancte Elene', a fragmentary English alliterative poem on Helena's posthumous miracles, with musical annotation.[7] In the same mode, this manuscript also contains a painted miniature of the Crucifixion.[8]

These reminders of Helena's identity and elements of her cult must have been supported by visual depictions in stained glass and on painted rood screens and murals, of which there are many extant, particularly from the fifteenth century.[9] St Helena is represented in extant painted glass, mainly of the fifteenth century, in at least 12 locations.[10] These frequently feature Helena in her typical icono-

---

5   Steven Bassett, 'Churches in Worcester before and after the Conversion of the Anglo-Saxons', *The Antiquaries Journal* 69 (1989), pp. 225–56, at p. 246.

6   Mildred Budny, *Insular, Anglo-Saxon, and Early Anglo-Norman Manuscript Art at Corpus Christi College, Cambridge: An Illustrated Catalogue*, Medieval Institute Publications, 2 vols (Kalamazoo, 1997), I.648.

7   The text is fragmentary and the manuscript damaged, but traditional healing miracles are mentioned, similar to those recounted by Jocelin of Furness (see Appendix 1 below, lines 996–1043). The title, 'Translacio sancte Elene', has been added by a later hand. The manuscript contents are listed in Falconer Madan, *A Summary Catalogue of Western Manuscripts in the Bodleian Library at Oxford*, vol. III (Oxford, 1895), p. 86; the kalendar is edited in Francis Wormald, ed., *English Benedictine Kalendars After A.D. 1100*, vol. 1: Abbotsbury–Durham (London, 1939), pp. 100–11. The inclusion of a prayer to St Oswald in this collection recalls Bede's account of this king and martyr's ritualistic veneration of the Cross (*Historia ecclesiastica*, III.2, and see p. 29, above).

8   On the style of this painting, see L.M. Ayres, 'A Tanner Manuscript in the Bodleian Library and some Notes on English Painting of the Late Twelfth Century', *Journal of the Warburg and Courtauld Institutes* 32 (1969), pp. 41–55.

9   On mural paintings, see Frank Kendon, *Mural Paintings in English Churches during the Middle Ages: An Introductory Essay on the Folk Influence in Religious Art* (London, 1923), who cites lists of the frequency with which saints are depicted on murals, according to the calculations of C.E. Keyser's *List of Buildings Having Mural Decorations* (London, 1883). Helena is in 15th place on the list, with 23 identified instances (cf. St Christopher in first place with 186 and St George in second with 72).

10   Morley, Derbyshire ('modern' Holy Cross window); Exeter Cathedral (H. with Cross); Bristol, St

---

graphic environment with the Cross or Constantine, or both, crowned and nimbed (indicating both royal and holy status).[11] Helena was often depicted with either Constantine or with both him and St Silvester. One early example of this conventional representation is in the Stone Cross in the Parish Church of Kelloe, in Durham (c. 1200), which depicts the *Inventio*, and contains a separate panel showing Helena (holding a small cross) and Constantine together, as in Byzantine miniatures, possibly capturing the moment at which the emperor asks his mother to find the Cross.[12]

Unlike Roman portrayals of her, which depict Helena in aristocratic clothing and with no distinguishing features other than perhaps a characteristic hair-style,[13] in the Middle Ages, she has one of the clearest sets of iconographic symbols available. Helena is unmistakable, particularly in those representations which feature a large Cross or a depiction of her presenting the Cross nails to Constantine.[14] Her devotion to scripture is frequently encoded in images in which she is shown holding a book.[15] Associations or local claims are expressed in the placement of her name among those of other saints also found in inscrip-

---

Mary's, Redcliffe, Gloucestershire (H. with Cross); Fromond's Chantry, Hampshire (H.); St Weonard's, Herefordshire (H.); St Michael and All Angels, Ashton-under-Lyne, Lancashire (several panels depicting H.'s life: see below, pp. 94–5); Wiggenhall, St Mary Magdalene (H. with Cross); Oxford, All Souls College (H. with Cross); Ludlow, Shropshire (H. with Cross); Langport, Somerset (H. crowned, with Cross); Mells, Somerset (H. with Cross and book); York Minster (14thC: H. with stars) (details collected from listings in Philip Nelson, *Ancient Painted Glass in England, 1170–1500* [London, 1913], passim).

11 See for example, the fifteenth-century stained glass in Minster Lovell, St Kenelm and Hardwick St Mary (Peter A. Newton, *The County of Oxford: A Catalogue of Medieval Stained Glass* [London, 1979], pp. 105 and 150). On Helena's iconography throughout medieval and early-modern Europe, see F. Werner, 'Helena Kaiserin', in *Lexikon der christlichen Ikonographie* (Rome, 1974), vol. 6, cols 483–90, Elene Croce, 'Elena', in *Bibliotheca sanctorum* (Rome, 1961–68), vol. 4, cols 988–95; and Louis Réau, *Iconographie de L'Art chrétien* (Paris, 1958), IV.635–6, s.v. Hélène.

12 Barbara Baert, '*In hoc vinces*: Iconography of the Stone Cross in the Parish Church of Kelloe (Durham, ca 1200)', *Archaeological and Historical Aspects of West-European Societies*, ed. Marc Lodewijckz, Acta archaeologica lovaniensia monographie 8 (Louvain, 1996), pp. 341–62; and James T. Lang, 'The St Helena Cross, Church Kelloe, Co. Durham', *Archaeologia Aeliana*, 5th ser. 5 (1977), pp. 105–19.

13 Jan Willem Drijvers, *Helena Augusta: The Mother of Constantine the Great and the Legend of her Finding of the True Cross* (Leiden, 1992), p. 190.

14 For example, the late-fifteenth-century depiction of the *Inventio* and *Exaltatio* in the stained glass of the Collegiate Church of the Holy Trinity, Tattershall, in Lincolnshire (on which see Penny Hebgin-Barnes, *The Medieval Stained Glass of Lincolnshire* [Oxford, 1996], p. 306, and plate 3d, p. 319) features Helena presenting the nails and part of the Cross to Constantine; and R.C. Marks, *The Stained Glass of the Collegiate Church of the Holy Trinity, Tattershall (Lincs.)*, Outstanding Theses from the Courtauld Institute of Art (New York, 1984), pp. 208–15. Although the windows are no longer all extant, Marks has calculated that they constituted 'the largest known cycle devoted to this subject in English medieval art' (p. 213). The *Inventio* and *Exaltatio* are also the subjects of the contemporary series of windows from the cloister of Dale Abbey at Morley, Derbyshire (Marks, p. 213), and a slightly earlier depiction of the *Inventio* (fourteenth-century) is at St Mary's Abbey, York (Marks, p. 214).

15 E.g. in the east windows of Exeter Cathedral. This iconography has also been used in the nineteenth-century restoration of the window featuring Helena in St Albans Cathedral (see Francis W. Skeat, *Stained Glass Windows of St Albans Cathedral* [Chesham and Luton, 1977], p. 76).

tions and represented on painted glass in words and pictures.[16] As Richard Marks has argued, these visual reminders of a saint's identity, along with their inscriptions, could be symbolically and rhetorically powerful in their localised communitites: 'Even if stained glass did not rank high in terms of affective piety, it should not be assumed that windows had a negligible effect on their audiences.'[17] Some labels and inscriptions, he says, are exhortative; others 'proclaimed the rights (sometimes exclusive) of individuals and groups, such as fraternities, to particular areas in churches', or by donor inscriptions ensured that churches became 'theatres of memory'.[18] Because those who financed the painting of glass or other materials most often chose the subject matter, and probably also selected the type of representations and iconography, the form of the finished product encodes considerable information about the preferences of the local donors as well as the oral traditions and written sources available to them in their construction of saintly patronage.[19] Subjects might be chosen as a result of some family association with a particular saint, other local affiliations, or the presence of a relic of the saint (as was the case with the image of Helena in the Tattershall window, the site of an alleged Cross relic).[20]

These visual contexts promote the cult of Helena, position her as empress and saint, and also participate in promoting the cult of the Cross but, with one exception, do not communicate the British legend. The exception is a series of late-fifteenth-century stained glass windows at Ashton-under-Lyne in Greater Manchester, in the parish church of St Michael's, which, by means of donor inscriptions, also dedicates the sequence to the Ashton family.[21] Although some of the panels have been lost or damaged, and they were releaded in the nineteenth century before being replaced out of order, the original sequence, complete with inscriptions, has been reconstructed with the help of details in a sixteenth-century manuscript description.[22] Here, Helena's life-story is depicted in 20 panels of painted glass, which helpfully include written information, including the claim that she was born in Colchester, daughter of King Cole, and other details from the legend promulgated by Geoffrey of Monmouth.[23] The first

---

16 For example, her name is included on a fragmentary list of inscriptions dated to the early fifteenth century in the Crypt, St Gabriel's Chapel, at Christ Church Cathedral, Canterbury (see Madeline Harrison Caviness, *The Windows of Christ Church Cathedral, Canterbury* [London, 1981], p. 298).
17 Richard Marks, *The Medieval Stained Glass of Northamptonshire* (London, 1998), p. lvi.
18 Marks, *The Medieval Stained Glass*, p. xlix.
19 Richard Marks, *Stained Glass in England during the Middle Ages* (London, 1993), p. 61.
20 Marks, *Stained Glass in England*, p. 64.
21 See Philip Nelson, 'The Fifteenth-Century Glass in the Church of St. Michael, Ashton-under-Lyne', *The Archaeological Journal* 70 (1913), pp 1–10.
22 See Nelson, 'The Fifteenth-Century Glass'; and H. Reddish, 'The St Helen Window Ashton-under-Lyne: A Reconstruction', *Journal of Stained Glass* 18/2 (1986–87), pp. 150–61; and the colour booklet available from the church, *The St Helen Windows in Ashton-under-Lyne Parish Church* (Ashton-under-Lyne, 2000), which includes colour plates, transcriptions and translations of the text, and introductory material.
23 Nelson suggests that the source is the *Nova legenda Anglie*, but since the Helena legend was not added until at least after 1499 (See C. Horstmann, ed., *Nova legenda Anglie* [Oxford, 1901], p. vxii),

panel is inscribed: 'Hic nascitur elene. Coyle regis filia', 'here Helena is born, daughter of King Cole'. The second and third depict her education in the liberal arts and music and her care of prisoners, the fourth her betrothal to the emperor Constantius, the fifth her marriage, the sixth the birth of Constantine. The later panels depict Constantine's battle against Maxentius, his baptism, the Council of Nicaea, Helena's visit to Jerusalem, her interrogation of Judas, then the *Inventio* (four panels), the founding of the Church at Jerusalem, Silvester's resuscitation of the bull (two panels), and a final panel shows Helena at prayer.

The selection of scenes from her legendary *vita* builds a portrait of an orthodox romance heroine, whose legitimacy rests on her associations with Constantine and Silvester and on her prime accomplishment of finding the Cross. The stress in the sequence on her pious upbringing and traditional marriage to Constantius is in keeping both with hagiographic conventions and with narrative mythmaking. These visual reminders of Helena's respectability and orthodoxy might also have contradicted any rival stories of low origins and concubinage. The co-existence of the Latin inscriptions with the images proclaims the legendary attributes of Helena in this context, in which the British element and noble birth are key features. Although the national connection might have been suggested more subtly in the occasional portrayal of Helena among other recognisably English saints,[24] this phenomenon no doubt reinforced prevailing views of the saints' origins rather than actively promoted them.

Notwithstanding this one set of relatively late stained glass widows, the primary vehicle for the dissemination of the British legend was the written text, especially in the form of histories and chronicles. With the production of these texts, supported by the fact that her royal and saintly image rather than her specifically British legendary connection was kept before the church-going populace visually, Helena became a more familar figure during the later Middle Ages, and for the ecclesiastical establishment, eventually familiarity and sheer repetition of the legend produced legitimacy. Although we have no record of this change of heart, we do possess evidence that the legend had been absorbed by hagiographers. Helena's British origins are celebrated incidentally in two previously unpublished texts: the Latin *vita* written by Jocelin of Furness in Cumbria in the early thirteenth century; and later in the Middle English verse *St Elyn* (extant in manuscripts from the late-fourteenth century) which was a marginal component of the very influential national collections of Saints' legends, the *South English Legendary*. This unspectacular entrance into the ecclesiastical establishment suggests that Helena's status as a national saint continued to be questioned by the religious communities of England, and therefore her feast day

and the glass and inscriptions probably date from 1480, according to Nelson ('The Fifteenth-Century Glass', p. 2), another source must be found. One need look no further than the later redactions of Geoffrey's *Historia*.

24 See, for example, the Great East Window at Exeter Cathedral, which features, as well as Helena, the English saints St Edward the Confessor, St Edmund, and St Sidwell (C. Brooks and D. Evans, *The Great East Window of Exeter Cathedral* [Exeter, 1988], p. 70).

of 18 August came to be incorporated into church calendars and national legendaries only gradually. Her name is missing from many of the calendars (which often leave 18 August blank) prior to the fifteenth century.

Before this level of legitimacy was reached, however, Helena's image had to undergo major changes. Her worldly accomplishments and social standing were less important in this context than her conversion and spiritual integrity while searching for the True Cross. In order to construct a new Helena for a religious audience, her legends underwent a change of focus during the Middle Ages from Helena's secular to her religious accomplishments. The most significant change made in this redevelopment of the legendary Helena was in her relationship to Pope Silvester, who according to one legend, baptised both Constantine and Helena. Silvester's role in the spiritual life of Constantine, Helena, and therefore the Empire as a whole, became more pronounced. The development of the Helena legend thereby became more closely involved with the vigorous cycle of legends surrounding St Silvester. From the very early Middle Ages, Silvester had been the subject of an extremely prolific collection of legends based on the original *Actus beati Silvestri*.[25] The thematic reorientation produced by Helena's connection with Silvester must have played a role in her gradual acceptance by the English religious establishment and thereby facilitated her way into official church calendars. But this association, and the hagiographical momentum which it occasioned, came at a heavy price to Helena's own reputation: she had become a secondary character to Silvester's own hagiographical existence, as well as to Constantine's, as her early *vitae* demonstrate. This subordination, as well as her now heavily religious associations, inhibited the growth of the legend beyond the fifteenth century, though the alleged connection established between Rome and Britain proved useful enough for occasional revisitation. These later formal invocations of the legend as well as its retention in traditional tales allowed survival in a more muted manner beyond its hagiographic exploitation.

The Vita sancte Helene *of Jocelin of Furness*

The ealiest *vita* of Helena by Altmann in the ninth century was incorporated into the double *vita* of Sts Helena and Agricius produced in Trier in the eleventh century (c. 1050–72),[26] and continued to be copied and adapted on the Continent, particularly in the twelfth century.[27] In England, however, Helena was ignored by hagiographers until Jocelin of Furness, a Cistercian monk based in

---

[25] See above, p. 24.

[26] Hans Pohlsander, *Helena: Empress and Saint* (Chicago, 1995), p. 203.

[27] For a list of the versions and the manuscripts in which they are found, see Bollandists, *Bibliotheca hagiographica latina antiquae et mediae aetatis*, 2 vols (Brussels, 1898–1901), I.563–5, and H. Fros, ed., *Novum supplementum* (Brussels, 1986), p. 413 (*BHL*).

Cumbria, wrote an extant prose *vita* in Latin during the period c. 1198–1207.[28] Little is known about Jocelin of Furness, and less still about his *Vita sancte Helene*, which has previously been unedited, and is often ignored by scholars of the Helena traditions.[29] A transcription of this text, which includes an account of the *translatio* of Helena's remains, loosely derived from Altmann's version, is available in Appendix 1 below. Jocelin is mentioned as the author within his text, which is extant in full in two manuscripts (Cambridge, Corpus Christi College, MS 252, fols 166v–183v [MS C]; and Gotha, Forschungs- und Landesbibliothek, MS Memb. I 81, fols 203r–213v [MS Go]) and in an abbreviated form in a third into which other material has been interpolated (Oxford, Bodleian Library, MS Bodley 240 (SC 2469), pp. 801–8 [MS B]). The text is attributed to Jocelin in the rubrics of both the Gotha and Bodley manuscripts.[30]

The manuscript contexts of these three witnesses to Jocelin's text are valuable sources of information. All are compilations of religious material produced during the fourteenth century. The Cambridge manuscript (C) is a miscellaneous collection of religious documents, including the *Stimulis amoris, Planctus . . . de passione Christi*, a copy and discussion of the *Rule of St Benedict* made by Brother John de Reynham, monk of Norwich, at the beginning of the fourteenth century.[31] Jocelyn's *vita* of Helena is the last item in the codex and is in some respects thematically anomalous in a collection of otherwise expository works. The Gotha manuscript (Go), on the other hand, is devoted almost exclusively to hagiography. It was produced in England (exact location unknown) at the beginning of the fourteenth century and contains 64 *vitae* of British saints, including three by another Jocelin, of Canterbury, and several by John of Tynemouth.[32] The large Oxford codex (B) of 899 pages, datable to 1377 from Bury St Edmunds, contains the earliest extant manuscript of John of Tynemouth's chronicle of the world, the *Historia aurea* (in abbreviated form, filling the first 582 pages), various miscellanies, poetry, and ecclesiastical documents, as well as many saint's lives.[33] The organisation of this manuscript is somewhat haphazard, at least towards the end, where the account of Helena's *translatio* is separated from the *vita* by several unrelated homiletic fragments.[34] The inclu-

---

28 George McFadden, 'The *Life of Waldef* and its Author, Jocelin of Furness', *Innes Review* 6 (1955), pp. 5–13, at p. 10.
29 Even scholars who treat legends of St Helena in detail, such as Pohlsander, Larkin, Drijvers, Linder, and Borgehammar, do not mention Jocelin's text.
30 Gotha, fol. 203v: 'Incipit prologus Iocelini monachi de Fornesio in vite sancte Helene Regine'; and Bodley, fol. 801: 'Excerpta de prologo Jocelini monachi Fornensio in vita sancte Helene'.
31 M.R. James, *A Descriptive Catalogue of the Manuscripts in the Library of Corpus Christi College Cambridge*, 2 vols (Cambridge, 1912), II.3.
32 Contents listed in detail in P. Grosjean, 'De codice hagiographico Gothano', *Analecta Bollandiana* 58 (1940), pp. 90–103.
33 MS contents listed in Horstmann, ed., *Nova legenda Anglie*, I.lviii–lxv. Horstmann argues that this manuscript is 'a depository of documents of that abbey (of Bury St Edmunds) and not the work of one individual' (p. lviii).
34 Other such fragments occur earlier in the manuscript, at fols 793–8, and complete sermons and similar documents constitute a considerable portion of the codex.

sion of Jocelin's *vita* of Helena within these three collections of texts was probably simply a result of its generic status as hagiography, though other factors might also have had some influence. The most suggestive context is the Go manuscript where the presence of the text might be attributed either to the similarity of Jocelin's name to that of Jocelin, or Goscelin, of Canterbury, the celebrated writer of three other saints' lives in the codex, or to the concentration specifically on English saints in the collection.[35] At the very least, the three compilers of these manuscripts seem to have construed Jocelin's text as worthy of inclusion with orthodox religious texts, particularly other saints' lives.

Jocelin is known as the author of three other hagiographical texts: *Vita sancti Kentigerni episcopi* (datable to c. 1175–99);[36] *Vita sancti Waldevi abbatis* (c. 1207);[37] and most notably, *Vita sancti Patricii episcopi* (c. 1180–1201).[38] The subjects of these three hagiographies are all male religious leaders, unlike Queen Helena, the subject of his fourth text.[39] The dedications of these works explain Jocelin's selection of topics, as well as providing our only information on the man himself. Jocelin is of uncertain origin, perhaps an Englishman, though he might have been a Norman, Irishman, or a Scot.[40] It is even possible,

---

[35] M.L. Colker, 'A Gotha Codex Dealing with the Saints of Barking Abbey', *Studia Monastica* 10 (1968), pp. 321–4. On Goscelin, see Richard Sharpe, *A Handlist of the Latin Writers of Great Britain and Ireland before 1540* (Turnhout, 1997), s.v., pp. 151–4.

[36] Ed. A.P. Forbes, *Lives of S. Ninian and S. Kentigern* (Edinburgh, 1874), pp. 159–242. For full details of editions and commentary on Jocelin's work, see Michael Lapidge and Richard Sharpe, *A Bibliography of Celtic-Latin Literature, 400–1200* (Dublin, 1985), pp. 283–4; and Istituto Storico Italiano (A. Potthast), *Repertorium fontium historiae medii aevi* (Rome, 1990), s.v. Iocelinus Furnesiensis (though the *Vita sanctae Helene* is omitted from this entry).

[37] Edited in AASS, Aug. I, pp. 248–76; and, with translation and notes, in George McFadden, 'An Edition and Translation of the Life of Waldef, Abbot of Melrose, by Jocelin of Furness' (unpub. Ph.D. diss., Columbia, 1952). On the date, and on the text itself, see Derek Baker, 'Legend and Reality: The Case of Waldef of Melrose', *Church, Society, and Politics: Papers Read at the Thirteenth Summer Meeting and the Fourteenth Winter Meeting of the Ecclesiastical History Society*, ed. Derek Baker (Oxford, 1975), pp. 59–82. See also J.P. Bulloch, 'Saint Waltheof', *Records of the Scottish Church History Society* 11 (1952), pp. 105–32; and McFadden, 'The *Life of Waldef*'.

[38] Ed. J. Colgan, *Trias thaumaturga vitae, Acta sanctorum Hiberniae*, II (Louvain, 1647), pp. 64–116. Ludwig Bieler has written extensively on Jocelin of Furness, especially his *Vita sancti Patricii*. His many contributions to this subject and others have been collected in two Variorum reprint editions, edited by Richard Sharpe: *Studies on the Life and Legend of St Patrick* (London, 1986); and *Ireland and the Culture of Early Medieval Europe* (London, 1987). For ease of reference, in the discussion below only Bieler's title and the text number in the Sharpe volumes will be given. Bieler calls Jocelin's *Vita sancti Patricii* 'by far the fullest and most elaborate life of St Patrick, but also the least trustworthy' ('*Trias Thaumaturga, 1647*', in Sharpe, ed., 1987, text XVI, pp. 41–9, at p. 44). Robert Bartlett mentions that this was the first text to claim that Patrick banished snakes from Ireland (*New Dictionary of National Biography* [forthcoming], s.v. Jocelin of Furness; I am grateful to the author for an advance copy of this entry).

[39] According to the early-seventeenth-century chronicler John Stowe, Jocelin of Furness was also the author of a work which he calls *The Book of Brittish Bishoppes*, though this text is no longer extant (*Survey of London* [1603], ed. C.L. Kingsford, 2 vols [London, 1908], I.194 and II.125).

[40] Mc Fadden, 'The *Life of Waldef*', p. 10. A.G. Rigg, *A History of Anglo-Latin Literature, 1066–1422* (Cambridge, 1992), lists Jocelyn under Northern England/ Lancashire (p. 98); and Lapidge and Sharpe, *Bibliography*, lists him under Scotland (p. 283). In his later work, Richard Sharpe resists suggesting a national affiliation (*A Handlist*, p. 198). Bieler calls him 'an English Cistercian' ('Did

given the range and location of his associations, that he was Manx, especially in view of the administrative arrangements between Furness abbey and the Isle of Man.[41] This possibility is even more likely given the fact that Jocelin's *vita* of St Patrick is the only version to feature the saint's visit to Man.[42] In the preface to his *Vita Waldevi*, he refers to himself as 'Monk of Furness', and the author is called 'Jocelin of Furness' in the titles of two manuscripts of his *vita* of Helena, indicating that he belongs to the Cictercian (originally Savignac) monastery founded in 1127,[43] situated on the south-western tip of the Cumbrian coastline, in northern England; and in *Vita Kentigerni*, he mentions that he is a priest.[44] The latter work is dedicated to Jocelin's namesake, Jocelin, abbot of Melrose and later bishop of Glasgow (1175–99), and recounts the life of 'the founding father of the diocese'.[45] Through this connection, Jocelin came to be associated with Melrose, in Scotland.[46] Similarly, his later account of Waldef, abbot of Melrose, links him with that place. Jocelin is connected with Ireland too, because he travelled to Down with John de Courcy in 1180.[47] Here, he wrote his *Vita sancti Patricii*, dedicated to John de Courcy, who, along with the bishop of Down and the archbishop of Armagh, had apparently commissioned the work (c. 1180–1201).[48] Jocelin then wrote his *Vita sancte Helene*, though whether this was while he was in Down, or after his return to Furness, is uncertain.[49] His last extant work was the *Vita Waldevi* (c. 1207–14), and since he styles himself 'of Furness', presumably he returned from Ireland prior to the composition of this work.

Unlike Jocelin's other hagiographies, the *Vita sancte Helene* is dedicated to a group of religious people rather than to an individual, though their location is unknown. Jocelin merely says:

> And however much a devotion conceived deservedly for the holy woman incited me personally to this task, nevertheless, I am urged on by the entreaties of venerable and religious persons who have subjugated themselves obediently to Christ under the yoke of the rule under the name of St Helena.[50]

Jocelin of Furness Know the Writings of St. Patrick at First Hand?', in Sharpe, ed., 1986, text XV, pp. 161–7, at p. 162) and 'an Anglo-Norman, . . . the last great figure in the literary tradition of Celtic hagiography' ('The Celtic Hagiographer', in Sharpe, ed., 1987, text X, pp. 243–65, at p. 261).

[41] I am grateful to Alex Woolf for this idea and for an advance copy of his article. The monks of Furness abbey were granted the right to appoint the bishop of Sodor on Man (Alex Woolf, 'The Diocese of Sodor', *A New History of the Isle of Man*, vol. 3: *The Medieval Period, 1000–1406*, ed. Seán Duffy (Liverpool, forthcoming). See also R. Andrew McDonald, *The Kingdom of the Isles: Scotland's Western Seaboard, c. 1100–c. 1336* (East Linton, 1998), p. 207.

[42] Woolf, 'The Diocese of Sodor'.

[43] Woolf, 'The Diocese of Sodor'.

[44] McFadden, 'The *Life of Waldef*', p. 9.

[45] Bartlett, 'Jocelin of Furness', *New Dictionary of National Biography*.

[46] Baker, 'Legend and Reality', p. 59.

[47] Bieler, 'Celtic Hagiographer', p. 261.

[48] Bartlett, 'Jocelin of Furness', *New Dictionary of National Biography*.

[49] Bieler, 'Celtic Hagiographer', p. 261.

[50] Lines 41–4. A full transcription of the Latin text is at Appendix 1 below.

Robert Bartlett has suggested, quite reasonably, that this might refer specifically to the nuns at St Helen's Bishopsgate (London), as the time at which that institution flourished coincides with the time at which Jocelin was writing, although he was known to be based in the North of England.[51] Another possible reference is to the community of canons at Darley, Derbyshire (est. 1137), or the priory at Burstall, Yorkshire (first recorded reference 1218).[52] Of course, with many other religious institutions dedicated to Helena in Yorkshire and elsewhere, there are several other possibilities.[53] Jocelin's situation in the north of England is itself suggestive, as this region was one of the key regions in the growth of the cult of Helena, and might have accounted for his choice of subject matter.[54] Because his other three hagiographical texts recount the lives of specifically local saints, it is likely that Jocelin's *Vita sancte Helene* was produced as another parochial commemorative text. If this were the case, there is a degree of incongruity in the appropriation of Helena as a British princess situated in Colchester far away in the south. Perhaps here is a relic of the older tradition that she was from York, a legend produced in the north of England, where interest in Helena, rather than a more exclusive concern with the Cross, flourished throughout the early Middle Ages.[55]

Jocelin has been described as a 'professional hagiographer' who adheres to the rigid conventions of the genre.[56] His *vita* of Helena follows the structural schema of his other hagiographies: the provision of full biographical information, including the places of birth, death, and burial, followed by later miracles attributed to the saint. He was probably an established writer within the northern Cistercian communities by the time his *vita* of Helena was produced.[57] His style is elegant though often outlandish, characterised by a fondness for 'rare and novel words'.[58] He writes carefully and rhetorically, often with the aim of 'explicit moralisation'.[59] His *vita* of St Helena follows this stylistic pattern, characterised by the rhetorical embellishments,[60] including alliteration (e.g. lines 79, 241–2, 253, 587, 596, 879, 923–4, and 937), parallel constructions (e.g. lines 177–8, 226–7, and 920–3), parataxis (e.g. lines 517–18, 726–9, and 792–7), and elaborate descriptions (e.g. lines 13–21 and 346–54), as well as

---

[51] Private correspondence, 1997.

[52] Listed in Alison Binns, *Dedications of Monastic Houses in England and Wales 1066–1216* (Woodbridge, 1989), pp. 131 and 95.

[53] Francis Bond calculates the total number of dedications to Helena to be 135, and in Yorkshire Helena's name is 'sixth in order of popularity' (*Dedications and Patron Saints*, p. 75).

[54] See above, p. 33.

[55] Foster, *Studies in Church Dedications*, p. 188.

[56] McFadden, 'The *Life of Waldef*', p. 13. Cf. David McRoberts, 'The Death of St Kentigern of Glasgow', *Innes Review* 24 (1973), pp. 43–50: 'a well known littérateur' (p. 44).

[57] Baker, 'Legend and Reality', p. 59.

[58] McFadden, 'The *Life of Waldef*', pp. 5 and 12. Bieler concurs: 'elaborate and mannered style' ('Celtic Hagiographer', p. 261); as does McRoberts: 'very much concerned with literary style' ('The Death of St Kentigern', p. 44).

[59] Bieler, 'Jocelin von Furness als Hagiograph', in Sharpe, ed., 1986, Text XVI, pp. 410–15, at p. 414.

[60] Bartlett, 'Jocelin of Furness', *New Dictionary of National Biography*.

biblical references (e.g. lines 70, 342, 397, 556, and 763). The following lines exemplify Jocelin's vigorous prose style which favours paratactic syntax and description, particularly of visual splendour or beauty, coupled with a sense of awe at Helena's superlative achievements:

> Congregans igitur beata Helena undique latomos et artifices ac lignarios ecclesias multas et magnas construxit in quibus decoris eximii et operis preciosi templum domini et alterum in Golgotha et aliud circa sepulcrum domini mirandi operis edificauit. (lines 726–9)

> Therefore, gathering together from all parts stone-cutters and sculptors and carpenters, the blessed Helena constucted many and great churches, in which she built a temple of the Lord of extraordinary beauty and splendid workmanship and another in Golgotha and another near the sepulchre of the Lord with workmanship to be marvelled at.

Jocelin claims that his text is based on a range of sources, including histories and chronicles, and an English translation of a Brittonic (i.e. Welsh) text. If they ever existed, both the English and the Welsh texts are now presumably lost.[61] He says, 'Indeed, in a certain little book, composed in English, her life is recounted in sequence, whose author claims to have translated it from the Brittonic language' (lines 35–7). This comment is probably a screen for Jocelin's own imaginative input into the story, especially since he seems to resort to spurious sources in his other works.[62] On the other hand, such a text might have existed. Jocelin claims to have used another vernacular source for his *Vita sancti Kentigerni*.[63] The unsourced additional text provided after line 502 in MS B (provided in a note to the edition, below) further suggests that a text uniting the British legend with Byzantine narrative material and the motif of Constantius's post-coital gift to Helena was used in the compilation of this manuscript version. The story of Constantine's birth is summarised here in a brief paragraph, concluding with the word *etcetera*. This material does not occur in either of the other two manuscripts containing Jocelin's *Vita sancte Helene*, so was perhaps of limited circulation and not part of the original text. The placement of this extract and another treating Constantine's vision and baptism in MS B in lieu of the rest of the text found in MSS C and Go suggests a distinct agenda in the composition of the B version of the legend.

If Jocelin was drawing upon a genuine vernacular source for his *Vita sancte Helene*, perhaps this text also lies behind the version of events recounted by Geoffrey of Monmouth, and was the same lost text which Diana Greenway suggested lay behind Henry of Huntingdon's account.[64] Even if this were not the

---

61 R.M. Wilson, 'Some Lost Saints' Lives in Old and Middle English', *Modern Language Review* 36 (1941), pp. 161–72, at p. 163.

62 Bieler, 'Did Jocelin', p. 164. Cf. Bulloch, 'Saint Waltheof', p. 131, where Jocelin is presented as a careful and unimaginative transcriber of his sources who uncritically accepts even the wildest stories. See also K.H. Jackson, 'The Sources for the *Life of St Kentigern*', *Studies in the Early British Church*, ed. N.K. Chadwick et al. (Cambridge, 1958), pp. 273–357, on Jocelin's method and historical sources.

63 McFadden, 'The *Life of Waldef*', p. 10.

64 See above, p. 76.

case, Jocelin was writing a few generations after these writers, so might have been influenced himself by their histories. He has also had access to Altmann's *vita* or a text based on it, as he briefly recounts the translation of her relics from Rome to Hautvillers and a few of the later miracles there (lines 932–1056), though with no evident stylistic or close narrative dependence on the source text. Jocelin refers to Aldhem's *De virginitate* by name (line 442) when discussing the construction of Constantinople, and has used the ecclesiatical historians (lines 443 and 745). Whatever his source, Jocelin follows the details of Geoffrey's narrative of Helena, daughter of King Cole, and finder of the True Cross, though there are sufficient significant departures from the popular Anglo-Latin history to suggest either the existence of a separate, possibly orally transmitted source, or a major imaginative input on the part of Jocelin himself.

It is no surprise that this hagiographical treatment of Helena's life features the two key legitimating elements of ecclesiastical representations: her baptism by St Silvester, and her legendary finding of the True Cross. But Jocelin supplies or adapts some new elements in the legend, most of which contribute to an extremely favourable portrait of Helena. This text is worth examining more closely, not only because it is the earliest extant *vita* of Helena which bases her in Colchester, but also because it demonstrates one of the ways in which the legend was constructed and exploited during the Middle Ages: within the conventions of hagiography.

Jocelin stresses very early in the piece that Helena is of royal birth, the daughter of Cole of Colchester (lines 28, 48–57), and is very well educated academically, morally, and in the liberal arts (lines 57–65). Jocelin adds elements from late-Roman historical sources to this portrait, which he later uses to fashion a new plot element: Helena is particularly sympathetic to the poor (lines 65–9). She is also a catechumen (line 79), again a religious inclination to be later elaborated on (and at variance with some versions which feature a native Jewish Helena, though in this text she later incongruously converts to Judaism before returning to Christianity: see lines 280–7). Jocelin also attributes unbeliev-able power to Helena's looks: her beauty is so great, he says, that it is frequently the cause of conversion to the Christian faith: 'The beauty of our Helen caused the occasion of the promotion of the Christian faith, the exaltation of the church of God, the end of idolatry, the depression of the Jewish sect, and the elimina-tion of many heresies' (lines 93–5; see also lines 87–9, where the value of her beauty is compared favourably with the destructive force of that of her namesake Helen of Troy). This breathtaking claim is at any rate novel, and it has the virtue of addressing most of the negative legends surround St Helena in a single stroke. This portrayal owes a good deal to Geoffrey of Monmouth's romance heroine, typically beautiful and accomplished, though it turns around the conventional power of beauty to operate on the moral and spiritual planes. Here, in an explicit act of appropriation, Jocelin calles her 'Helene de Britannia' (line 89).

Jocelin follows Geoffrey of Monmouth in the circumstances leading to Constantius's presence in Britain, but adds another twist to the story in his account of the marriage of Helena and Constantius. After Coel's death, when the Roman Constantius succeeds to the throne, Helena, wishing to preserve her chastity, pretends to be a stable girl, ministering to the poor (lines 115–21). This ingenious explanation for her role as *stabularia* in the early sources has the added advantage of demonstrating Helena's virtues: her charity to the poor and her desire to remain chaste. Jocelin even echoes Ambrose (who is referred to by name in line 129) by calling her a 'bona stabularia', 'good stable-maid/ innkeeper' (lines 119–20). Constantius is drawn to Helena's virtuous character (rather than solely to the political advantages of a match with her or being driven by sheer lust as in earlier sources) and wins her. They marry, but this occurs after the birth of their son, Constantine (lines 125–8), as is suggested by some of the late-Roman sources. Unlike the early and medieval accounts, Jocelin portrays a politically powerful married Helena: she is declared *imperatrix* (line 134) upon her marriage to Constantius, and rules Britain in her own right after his death, as caretaker before Constantine comes of age (lines 165–71).

Jocelin cleverly weaves together a number of competing legends into a coherent narrative. He exploits Helena's legendary connection with the city of Trier without compromising her British origins, by saying that Constantius constructed a wonderful palace for her in Trier (lines 149–53), and that she is remembered in many places (lines 154–5), but she still loved her birthplace, Britain, above all others (lines 153–4). Jocelin consciously ignores the competing claims of Drepanum and Trier as her birthplace, and mentions Constantine's and her own nationality and origins in Colchester or Britain in a rhetorically emphatic manner (e.g. lines 99, 166, 173, 169, and 181). He is the first writer to integrate the hagiographical and historiographical traditions relating to Helena, employing Geoffrey's account of Helena, daughter of Old King Cole, as a prelude to the *Inventio* and Silvester legends. He exploits the high social status of this figure in order to emphasise Helena's great humility, as well as to stress the noble bearing of the mother of Constantine and finder of the Cross. Although her role as mother of the emperor is made explicit, and Constantine's achievements are mentioned, these sections of the narrative are provided in the context of their bearing on Helena's saintly development rather than as examples of the impingement of more powerful legends on this one.

Helena's British origins are emphasised in the initial portion of her biography, especially when Jocelin calls her 'Helene de Britannia' (line 89) to differentiate her from Helen of Troy, but the legend is not reiterated later (the last mention of Britain is on line 436). Rather, the saint is referred to as 'our Helena' (e.g. lines 748, 815, 821, and 913), which might denote possession by the Christian community, or, what is more probable, specifically encode a British appropriation. Her British aristocratic birth constitutes part of the fine qualities marking Helena out for sainthood, reinforced by her strong will and powerful personality. Jocelin recounts incidents which demonstrate the influence she exerts over her son, even after he has become emperor. Constantine yields to the plans of his mother (lines 155–6) and later she accompanies her son in order to advise him in his battle against Maxentius (lines 203–6). Jocelin's Helena makes her mark as a powerful and successful woman who knows her mind and dominates those around her, but this character does not continue to dominate the story.

Beyond the initial sections of the narrative, Jocelin broadens the scope of his story to include material relating to Constantine. After recounting the conversion of Constantine according to the version of Lactantius in which the emperor sees a vision of the Cross in a dream (lines 207–51), Jocelin briefly recounts Silvester's cure of Constantine's leprosy (lines 252–77); the subsequent glorious rule of the emperor, including his founding of Constantinople (lines 439–83); and the outcome of the Council of Nicaea (lines 519–83). Then Jocelin, unlike other biographers of Helena who are often more interested in Constantine, refouses on his female subject, although he had not left her out of the narrative completely prior to this. When Constantine is being converted by Silvester, Helena is in Bithinia, where she has converted to Judaism (lines 280–7), a frequently cited element in legends of Silvester. Jocelin includes in his text an account of the dispute between the Jews and Christians designed to convince Helena to convert to Christianity. Contrary to other versions of the story, where Silvester wins through a miraculous demonstration involving a bull alone, here he claims victory more by sheer rhetorical skill (lines 311–15). Only afterwards does he demonstrate his miraculous power, when he effects the removal of demons from possessed bodies (lines 315–17). He then converts and baptises Helena.

From now on, Jocelin refers to his subject as 'Beata Helena' (e.g. lines 322, 328, 346, 520, 726, 800, 842, 849, and 854), or 'Sancta Helena' (e.g. lines 356 and 484), though he had used these descriptions in his preface; occasionally, she is referred to anachronistically as 'regina' (lines 145 and 502). Once she has been converted, however, the conventional hagiographic adjectives 'blessed' or 'saint' are most commonly applied, in order to encode her activities more firmly in the Christian context. Jocelin also conforms to generic expectations in his narrative structure, concentrating on Helena's contribution to the institution of the Christian Church, as well as on her spiritual life. Her role in the promotion of her new religion is the subject of the following section of his text. Jocelin focuses on Helena's humility and holy virtues, stressing her contribution to Christianity. Recalling the cosmic imagery of his prefatory remarks, he refers to the Greek etymology of her name, likening her, in his typically flamboyant way, to a star illuminating the world of Christendom, both for her piety, but also on account of the many services she rendered to the Church as an institution (lines 322–4). Of course, the most prominent of these acts was her finding of the Cross, although Jocelin places this service in the context of her promotion of Christianity more generally. He provides a relatively brief account of the *Inventio* (lines 649–702), then moves on to the construction of churches under her guidance in Jerusalem (lines 725–5) and Rome (lines 824–40); and her ministration to the virgins (lines 782–97). His comparison of Helena and another legendary figure associated with seeking the Cross, the Queen of Sheba (lines 798–823), has much in common with Altmann's *vita*, a possible source, though he does not follow its structure or relate the same range of narrative material.[65] He then incoporates several conventional hagiographical elements, including her preparation for death (lines 853–81), her death and burial (lines 882–901); and post-mortem miracles (lines 902–16). Constantine is brought back into the narrative in the final section dealing with his fulfilment of his mother's wishes (lines 917–31). The text might be incomplete, as the final anec-dote about the fisherman ends more abruptly than other versions of this episode, though there is no indication in any of the manuscripts that anything is missing.[66] For the narrative of the translation of Helena's relics to Hautvillers (lines 932–1056), Jocelin relies on Altmann's account for his main facts,[67] though his own version is quite different from it: Jocelin's account is very abbreviated and stylistically distinct. It includes evidence of Helena's sanctity in the form of miracles attributed to her, based on Altmann's account of her posthumous miracles.[68]

Jocelin's *vita* of Helena is very much concerned with her temporal accom-plishments, including her role in the *Inventio*; her support for Christianity in the Empire; her role in Constantine's building programme in Constantinople and Rome; and her interaction with other ecclesiastical and secular female figures. He successfully integrates many of the exisiting strands of legendary narrative concerning Helena, without subsuming her biography into *vitae* of either Constantine or Silvester, or representing her merely as an agent of the *Inventio*. The British legend is part of this agenda, but it does not dominate his narrative. Rather, her alleged British nationality is presented as a factual part of both her biography and also the political history of Britain. Jocelin successfully presents a portrait of an imperial British saint, a rhetorically powerful confluence of Geoffrey's secular history and *Inventio* narratives. Most importantly, he has endowed Helena for the first time with her own sacred and political identity, creating a persona which could be exploited in many arenas of later medieval literature. Although it is difficult to gauge the impact of Jocelin's text on contemporary and later writers and audiences, the existence of two copies of the text in full and one abbreviated version attests to some degree of interest. Furthermore, Jocelin's choice of subject matter is itself indicative of interest in Helena and belief in the British story in England during the early thirteenth century. Helena's legendary British origins, once they had been incorporated into texts such as Jocelin's sacred biography, became an established part of her profile both in secular and ecclesiastical contexts.

---

65 Cf. Altmann, *Vita*, AASS, Aug. III, p. 590 (Ch. III, esp. para 34), BHL 3772.
66 Sharpe lists the text as 'incomplete' (*A Handlist*, p. 198), but the Go MS, which concludes at the same point as the C MS, includes the following rubric: 'Explicit translacio sancte Helene Regine' (fol. 213v, col. B), suggesting that the text was considered complete. Altmann's account of the posthumous miracles also concludes with the fish story (Aug III, p. 617C).
67 Altmann, *Historia translationis*, AASS, Aug. III, pp. 601–3, BHL 3773.
68 Altmann, *Miracula*, AASS, Aug. III, pp. 612–17, BHL 3774–5.

National Legendaries

Despite the rhetorical value of Jocelin's achievement, his *vita* did not put Helena immediately onto the hagiographical agenda. The balance of evidence suggests that although the British Helena story circulated freely in many textual incarnations both before and after Jocelin's contribution, it was never widely credited, at least by religious writers and administrators. Perhaps because she was not generally believed to have been British, St Helena did not feature in collections of narrative English saints' legends until the sixteenth century, when her *vita* appeared in a revised version of the *Nova legenda Anglie*, an influential Latin collection of English saints' lives.[69] This collection ultimately derives from the *Sanctilogium Angliae, Walliae, Scotiae et Hisperniae*, a Latin compilation of 156 saints' legends arranged according to their feast days by John of Tynemouth at the end of the fourteenth century, concentrating on saints from the British Isles.[70] Tynemouth collected his material from a wide variety of sources, including *vitae*, chronicles, and histories, modified with his own comments.[71] He appears to have participated in an exclusively English phenomenon of appropriating and promoting allegedly local saints for rhetorical purposes. Horstmann observes that a legendary like the *Nova legende Anglie*, based exclusively on national affiliation, rather than encompassing the saints of the Catholic Church as a whole, is a uniquely typical product of English national sentiment.[72]

Tynemouth's *Sanctilogium* was lightly revised in the fifteenth century and rearranged alphabetically by saint. Görlach notes that this practice of reproducing *vitae* unchanged was a feature of Latin texts, but not of vernacular ones.[73] The revision, still called the *Sanctilogium Anglie*, has been attributed, on no substantial evidence, to John Capgrave (1393–1464), the English writer of many biblical commentaries, chronicles, and theological treatises.[74] It was again revised anonymously in the early sixteenth century and edited by Wynkyn de Worde as the *Nova legende Anglie* in 1516, printed by Richard Pynson. This revision was more thorough. In this redaction, still in Latin, a prologue and 15

---

[69] Horstmann, ed. As suggested above (p. 16), the re-emergence of the *Panegyrici Latini* might have encouraged interest in the British Helena legend from the fifteenth century, but only when such 'evidence' was being actively sought out, as the references are sufficiently brief and ambiguous to be otherwise not susceptible to such an interpretation.

[70] John of Tynemouth was probably not the first to compile a national legendary: see Manfred Görlach, ed., *The Kalendre of the Newe Legende of Englande* (Heidelberg, 1994), pp. 7–8. Horstmann, ed., *Nova legenda Anglie*, I.ix, however, asserts that Tynemouth's idea, in his production of the *Sanctilogium*, was original as he was unaware of an earlier collection of 47 English saints' lives.

[71] Görlach, ed., *Kalendre*, p. 7.

[72] Horstmann, ed., *Nova legenda Anglie* (*NLA*), p. x. I intend to investigate this phenomenon more fully in a forthcoming study on early hagiography produced in Engand.

[73] Görlach, ed., *Kalendre*, p. 9.

[74] Peter J. Lucas, 'John Capgrave and the *Nova legenda Anglie*: A Survey', *The Library*, 5th series 25 (1970), pp. 1–10; Peter J. Lucas, *From Author to Audience: John Capgrave and Medieval Publication* (Dublin, 1997), Appendix 3 'Capgrave and the *Nova legenda Anglie*', pp. 294–306.

new saints' lives were added, including, for the first time, a lengthy 'St Helena'; and some existing *vitae* were shortened.[75] Horstmann notes that the additions were late, as they do not appear in the Tanner manuscript datable to 1499.[76] It appears, then, that it was not until the beginning of the sixteenth century that Helena was considered eligible to be included in an English national saints' legendary and when her *vita* does occur, it is in a collection with an organising principle specifically based on national pride. The British legend was a catalyst for the legitimation of her cult.

The *Nova legenda Anglie* version of *St Helena*, under her feast day, 18 August, is a compilation from a number of sources, including Geoffrey of Monmouth's *Historia regum Britannia*, the *Acta beati Silvestri*, legends relating to the finding of the Cross, and the *Historia trium regum* (a legendary account of Helena's translation of the relics of the three kings of the nativity story from India to Constantinople).[77] It comprises a prologue of 24 lines and a main text of 319 prose lines in Horstmann's edition, presenting a detailed and comprehensive compilation of legends relating to St Helena. Not surprisingly, this text concentrates on her spiritual life. The narrative recounts her British birth, stressing her regal connections: 'Empress by marriage, queen by birth; she was the only daughter of Cole, King of Britain.'[78] This information is provided in the context of the opening remarks of the Prologue which acknowledges competing legends surrounding Helena: 'Different people are accustomed to believe different things concerning this most holy woman and her origin and the course of her life.'[79] This account silently rejects Ambrose's version of the 'good stable-maid', prefering to transmit 'ancient . . . histories, which are more appropriate and much more authoritative'.[80] By endorsing the British legend with this stamp of authority, the *Nova legenda Anglie* selectively transmits details which construct a newly 'appropriate' figure of the empress Helena, finder of the Cross. In doing so, this text relates Constantine's vision and baptism (as well as her conversion from Judaism) by St Silvester after the disputation with the 12 Jewish elders;[81] Helena's finding and veneration of the Cross;[82] and her translation from India of the bodies of the three kings, Jaspar, Melchio, and

---

75 Görlach, ed., *Kalendre*, p. 10.
76 Horstmann, ed., *NLA*, p. xvii.
77 Horstmann, ed., *NLA*, II.13–21. The *Historia trium regum* was published in English by Wynkyn de Worde in 1499. According to legend, the kings' relics were translated to Cologne: see AASS, Aug. III, pp. 569–71; and Pohlsander, *Helena*, pp. 53, 136–7.
78 'Ex marito imperatrix; ex patre regina; Cloelis regis Britannie unica fuit filia' (Horstman, ed., *NLA*, II.14, lines 21–2).
79 'Solent diuersi diuersa sentire de hac sentissima muliere eiusque origine ac vite cursu' (Horstmann, ed., *NLA*, II.13).
80 'Antiquas . . . historias, ea que conuenientiora sunt magisque autentica' (Horstmann ed., *NLA*, II.14).
81 Horstmann, ed., *NLA*, p. 16, line 28; from the *Actus beati Silvestri*.
82 Horstmann, ed., *NLA*, p. 17, line 34. Helena is directed to the Invention by a dream, as in Rufinus and Socrates.

Balthazar, as well as of parts of the Cross to Constantinople;[83] her premonition of death, and the removal of her body to Constantinople (and the admission that some say it is in Venice).[84] This narrative collection now comprises a dominant version of her legend.

The *Nova legenda Anglie*, an attempt at a complete survey of British saints (by birth or residence), was translated anonymously into English and heavily abridged as the *Kalendre of the Newe Legende of Englende* in 1516.[85] The justification for the translation, which was provided for those unlearned in Latin, is given in the Prologue.[86] This most ambitious hagiographical project was also, because of its proximity to the Reformation, 'the last effort of its kind', as Görlach notes.[87] Here, Helena retains her place as a British saint, and her story is available to a much wider audience in the vernacular.

This narrative of 'St Helena' in the *Kalendre*, again under her feast day of 18 August, condenses the story of the *Nova legenda Anglie* version into just 40 lines as is typical of its abbreviated style. The *Kalendre* omits the prefatory material, opening with the remark: 'Seynt Helyn was doughter of Cleoll Kyng of Grete Brytayn',[88] and follows the narrative sequence of the *Nova legenda Anglie*, where Helena is converted by St Silvester. It is evident from the opening remark and the story-line of this version that in the late Middle Ages the secular elements of the Helena legend provided by Geoffrey of Monmouth had merged with the religious details of the *Inventio* and Silvester legends, as they had in Jocelin's *vita*. It is significant that her conversion and baptism by St Silvester are featured in this version. The narrative foci of these later *vitae* of Helena imply that it is not until her legend becomes grafted to the Silvester cycle that it attains legitimacy, if only partially, with the Church. Unlike Continental attempts to appropriate Helena, the *Kalendre* version does not claim that her relics are held locally. Typically of the *Nova legenda Anglie* and other *Kalendre* hagiographies, however, this *vita* of St Helena does provide details of her final resting place, reflecting the Continental traditions of Constantinople and Venice.

The late inclusion of Helena into this saints' calendar, however, is itself atypical: there is no 'St Helena' in the *Legenda aurea*, a much earlier and more influential collection of Latin saints' legends and biblical stories by Jacobus de Voragine (produced 1255–70), though there is an *Inventio* legend here. Jacobus was evidently aware of the British Helena legend, as well as the claims of Trier, to which he refers within the *De inventio sanctae crucis*. After recounting Helena's origins according to Ambrose, he says:

83 Horstmann, ed., *NLA*, p. 21, line 1.
84 Horstmann, ed., *NLA*, p. 20, line 38.
85 Görlach, ed., *Kalendre*, p. 7.
86 Görlach, ed., *Kalendre*, pp. 43–7.
87 Görlach, ed., *Kalendre*, p. 7.
88 Görlach, ed., *Kalendre*, p. 110 (line 1).

Thus Ambrose. Others, however, assert and we read in a reasonably authentic chronicle, that this Helena was the only daughter of Clohel, king of the Britons. When Constantine came to Britain, he took Helena to wife, and so the island devolved to him after Clohel's death. Even British sources attest this; yet elsewhere we read that Helena was a native of Trier.[89]

Jacobus's slightly reserved description of the chronicle as 'reasonably authentic' acknowledges his lack of certainty about its reliability, though this qualification seems to have been overlooked by later writers. The King Cole story achieved wide currency through the many later texts which drew upon the *Legenda aurea*, such as the early-fifteenth-century homily collection *Mirk's Festival*.[90] The inclusion of the British Helena legend in the *Legenda aurea*, and also details about Constantine's baptism by St Silvester (as well as the incongruity of the sources about the date and circumstances of this event), suggest clearly that Helena's role is perceived as that of an auxiliary to the conversion of Constantine and his proclamation of the Christian faith through the *Inventio* story. St Silvester receives his own *vita* (Ch. 12), to which this story has a cross-reference.[91] Again, Jacobus acknowledges his uncertainty and the existence of conflicting accounts of Constantine's baptism when he says, 'Many of the things stated in this account, however, are contradicted by the *Tripartite History* and the *Ecclesiastical History*, as well as by the life of Saint Silvester and the *Acts* of the Roman Pontiffs.'[92]

The absence of a 'St Helena' in this collection is a major omission, as the *Legenda aurea* was extremely popular and widely disseminated.[93] Similarly, Helena was not commemorated in the French prose translation (by Jean de

---

89 *Jacobus de Voragine, The Golden Legend: Readings on the Saints*, Engl. trans. W.G. Ryan, 2 vols (Princeton, 1993), I.281.

> Haec autem Ambrosius. Alii vero asserunt et in quadam chronica satis authentica legitur, quod ipsa Helena fuit filia Chohelis regis Britonum, quam Constantinus in Britanniam veniens, cum esset unica patria suo, duxit uxorem, unde insula post mortem Chohelis sibi devenit. Hoc et ipse Britones attestantur, licet alibi legatur, quod fuerit Trevirensis.

> (*Jacobi a Voragine: Legenda aurea*, 2 vols, ed. T. Graesse, 3rd ed. [Dresden, 1890; repr. Osnabrück, 1969], Ch. 64). Graesse's edition is still useful, though it has been superseded by P.M. Maggioni, ed., *Iacopo da Varazze: Legenda aurea* (Florence, 1998).

90 Ed. T. Erbe, *Mirk's Festival: A Collection of Homilies*, EETS, es 96 (London, 1905), pp. 142–6, at p. 144. See Pohlsander, *Helena*, p. 212.

91 This *vita* is the basis of the tale in Gower's *Confessio amantis* (ed. R.A. Peck [New York, 1966, repr. Toronto, 1986], II.3087–530). Helena is mentioned here, as Constantine's representative and church builder in Jerusalem. Gower also mentions the story in his poem, *In Praise of Peace* (*The English Works of John Gower*, ed. G.C. Macaulay, 2 vols [London, 1901], II.491, lines 339–57).

92 (Ryan, Engl. trans, I.279). 'Sed in hac hystoria multa ponuntur, quibus contradicit hystoria tripartita et ecclesiastica et vita sancti Silvestri et gesta pontificum Romanorum' (Grässe, ed., p. 305).

93 The *Legenda aurea* is extant in more than one thousand manuscripts from c. 1299, as well as many early printed editions. For a detailed study of the manuscript tradition, see Barbara Fleith, *Studien zur Überlieferungsgeschichte der Lateinischen Legenda aurea* (Brussels, 1991). Unlike the *South English Legendary* (*SEL*), which was probably written for popular consumption, the *Legenda aurea* was aimed at clerics.

Vignay, finished c. 1334),[94] nor in the fifteenth-century English translation of de Vignay's text, the *Gilte legende* (oldest manuscript is 1438)[95] nor even in Caxton's later prose translation of 1483,[96] which added some legends. Evidently, Helena was not part of the 'golden legend' group of texts, unlike St Silvester, who enjoys his own separate *vita* in each of these traditions.[97] Rather, her identity is subsumed under the feast of the *Inventio*.[98]

Just as significantly in the insular context, Helena was not an original part of the popular collection known as the *South English Legendary* (*SEL*). This national compilation of saints' lives and homiletic texts was first produced in Middle English in the south-west Midlands (Worcester/Gloucester) from about 1270, underwent a major revision around 1290, and spread north to the Midlands.[99] The *SEL* originally comprised around one hundred texts arranged in calendar order according to the subjects' feast days, in 'rhymed seven-beat couplets'.[100] The title, as well as the assumption that this diverse range of texts in various combinations and dialects formed a coherent whole, is modern.[101] It was evidently extremely popular and widely circulated: it exists in around 50 manuscripts, which comprise nine major redactions of diverse geographical origins.[102] The anonymous compiler and reviser used the *Legenda aurea* in part, though the opinion that the reliance was heavy[103] has in recent times been challenged successfully.[104] The prevailing critical view is that the *SEL* relies on the

---

94   Ed. Brenda Dunn-Lardeau, *Jacques de Voragine, La Légende dorée, Edition critique dans la révision de 1476 par Jean Batallier, d'apres la traduction de Jean de Vignay (1333–1348) de la Legenda aurea (c. 1261–1266)* (Paris, 1997).

95   Manfred Görlach, *The Textual Tradition of the South English Legendary*, Leeds Studies and Monographs, ns 6 (Leeds, 1974), p. 62. This is the most comprehensive study of the manuscript tradition of the *South English Legendary*. A new edition of the *Gilte legende* is under way, the first published volume of which is Richard Hamer and Vida Russell, eds, *Supplementary Lives in some Manuscripts of the Gilte legende*, EETS, os 315 (Oxford, 2000).

96   Ed. F.S. Ellis, The Temple Classics, 7 vols (London, 1900).

97   There are two different versions in the *SEL*: see Görlach, *Textual Tradition*, p. 217.

98   Helena is mentioned as the finder of the Cross in 'Pardon of all the Churches of Rome' from the so-called Supplemetary Lives of the *Gilte legende*, which participates in the confusion over the place of her burial by saying that Helena's body lies within the Church of the Holy Cross, Jerusalem (Hamer and Russell, ed., p. 78, lines 133–5). As in many other contexts, Helena's renown is closely tied to that of St Silvester, who is mentioned here as the one who hallowed that church.

99   Klaus P. Jankofsky, ed., *The South English Legendary: A Critical Assessment* (Tübingen, 1992), esp. 'Foreword', pp. ix–xii.

100 Manfred Görlach, 'Middle English Legends, 1220–1530', *Hagiographies*, ed. Guy Philippart, Corpus christianorum, 2 vols to date (1986–94), I.429–85, at p. 448.

101 For the view that the *SEL*, extant in many manuscripts which differ in contents, arrangement, style, and dialect, are better described as a 'corpus of versified Middle English writings for the ecclesiastical year than as a single work', see Beverly Boyd, 'A New Approach to the *South English Legendary*', *Philological Quarterly* 47 (1968), pp. 494–8, at p. 498.

102 For the complicated textual history of this compilation, see Görlach, *Textual Tradition*, which lists 25 major MSS; 19 fragments; 18 miscellanies containing *SEL* items; 5 miscellanies 'erroneously claimed to contain *SEL* items'; and 4 'now apparently lost' (pp. viii–ix).

103 Argued by M.E. Wells, 'The *South English Legendary* and its Relation to the *Legenda aurea*', *PMLA* 51 (1936), pp. 337–60. See Görlach, *Textual Tradition*, pp. 26–7.

104 Görlach, *Textual Tradition* (passim); 'Middle English Legends', p. 450; and 'The *Legenda aurea* and

Legenda aurea only for about one-fifth of the *vitae*, though the existence of the Latin text must have demonstrated the desirability of such a collection and thereby acted as an impetus to the creation of further vernacular saints' legendaries.[105] The *SEL*, then, must be considered to have a separate, and specifically vernacular, textual tradition.[106] It was possibly directed at a secular rather than an ecclesiastical audience, though liturgical use is also a possibility.[107] The *SEL* accounts for most of the hagiography produced during the thirteenth century, though a few separate individual saints' lives continued to be written in the vernacular. This collection 'dominated the verse legends in the Southwest and parts of the Midlands from at least 1280–1400', after which popular taste favoured prose over verse and the English prose translation of the French version of the *Legenda aurea*, the *Gilte legende*, gained prominence.[108]

The Middle English Verse St Elyn

Although it was not an original part of the collection, the legend of St Helena did make its way into the *South English Legendary*, but only in one small group of manuscripts, and only after the story had been modified to include the Silvester material. The Middle English *St Elyn* is a witness to the process of transformation whereby the legendary character of Helena comes to be eclipsed by the activities of St Silvester. This previously unconsidered vernacular attestation which concentrates on spiritual reorientation runs for 250 lines of rhymed couplets.[109] It was produced well after Geoffrey's *Historia* and Laȝamon's *Brut*, but before the inclusion of 'St Helena' in the *Nova legenda Anglie*, the earliest manuscript in which it appears dating from c. 1350 (London, British Library, MS Egerton 2810). How long prior to this the legend was produced is a matter of conjecture, though the northern dialectal remnants beneath the Midlands adaptation of the text signal that it is at least one step removed from the original written composition.

---

the Early History of *The South English Legendary*', *Legenda aurea: Sept siècles de diffusion*, ed. Brenda Dunn-Lardeau (Montreal and Paris, 1986), pp. 301–16.

105 Collections existed in England prior to the publication of the *Legenda aurea* and continued to be produced afterwards, though the Latin collection was '*the* decisive source for vernacular legends (not only in the form of translation, paraphrase, or allusion, but also as a pattern for arrangement)' (Görlach, 'Middle English Legends', pp. 431 and 446).

106 For detailed commentary and bibliography on these *vitae*, see Charlotte D'Evelyn and Frances A. Foster, 'Saints Legends', *A Manual of the Writings in Middle English 1050–1500*, gen. ed. J. Burke Severs, vol. II (Hamden, Conn., 1970), pp. 410–81 and 553–644. On the genre of hagiography in late medieval England, see Theodor Wolpers, *Die englischen Heiligenlegende des Mittelalters* (Tübingen, 1964); and Görlach, 'Middle English Legends'.

107 Görlach, *Textual Tradition*, p. 48.

108 Görlach, 'Middle English Legends', pp. 431 and 435.

109 The text runs for 249 lines in G, the MS on which the edition at Appendix 2 is based, though the rhyme scheme indicates that a line has been lost after line 125; line 126 has been supplied below from the later manuscript, Hx².

Manuscript evidence suggests that the Middle English *St Elyn* was not widely transmitted, but confined to a limited regional distribution: it is found in only two of the more than fifty manuscripts of the *South English Legendary* (London, Lambeth Palace, MS 223, fols 102v–105v [G] and London, British Library, MS Harley 2250, fols 81v–83r [Hx²]), and a fragment of the text has been inserted over an erasure in a third manuscript (London, British Library, MS Egerton 2810, fols 170r–170v [M]).[110] These manuscripts all belong to Görlach's 'F' redaction 'circulating in the Midlands' (Derby, second half of fourteenth century).[111] Of these manuscripts, Lambeth 223 is of particular interest, not only as the chief witness of Görlach's 'F' redaction, but also because it misnames itself *Legenda aurea* in its colophon (fol. 64v).[112] We know that this manuscript was copied for the private use of a layman, Thomas Wootton, around 1400.

All three manuscripts are collections of religious material. G and M contain exclusively *SEL* items; Hx² is a more miscellaneous collection of verse and prose religious documents. G and M are early-fifteenth-century codices; Hx² is c. 1477.[113] Manfred Görlach, in his thorough survey of the manuscript tradition of the *South English Legendary*, claims on the basis of rhymes and dialectal forms that it represents 'a southerly translation of a northern original', this provenance according with the earlier northern interest in St Helena.[114] Though this does not assist in dating the text, it is clear that *St Elyn* certainly post-dates the establishment of the elaborate legend transmitted by Geoffrey of Monmouth's and Laȝamon's histories, though there is no explicit reference to King Cole or to Colchester in the Middle English poem.

The 250–line text called in the former two codices *St Elyn* and *St Helena* respectively[115] is still little known, as the text does not appear in the manuscripts on which printed editions of the *South English Legendary* have been based.[116] A transcription of this poem is provided at Appendix 2. While only its first line makes reference to the British Helena tradition, this text, composed perhaps as late as the mid-fourteenth century, is of interest as a new witness both to the

---

[110] For a brief description of the manuscripts and references for further details, see Görlach, *Textual Tradition*, pp. 82–3, 119–20, and 90–2. Görlach treats the text of 'St. Helena' on pp. 166–7.

[111] Görlach, *Textual Tradition*, pp. 9 and 59.

[112] Thomas R. Liszka, 'Manuscript G (Lambeth Palace 223) and the Early *South English Legendary*', Jankofsky, ed., *The South English Legendary*, pp. 91–101, examines this manuscript for the light it sheds on the original compilation of the *SEL*. Görlach, too, has noted the reference to the *Legenda aurea* in the colophon (*Textual Tradition*, p. 83).

[113] Contents and dates listed in Görlach, *Textual Tradition*, pp. 46, 82–3; 90–2; and 119–20.

[114] Görlach, *Textual Tradition*, p. 276. The group of *South English Legendary* manuscripts which include 'St Elyn' (Görlach's 'F' redaction) is 'the first attempt to translate the *SEL* into a slightly different dialect' and a regrouping of the texts to bring together all those treating the Cross (p. 59).

[115] The relevant folios are headed 'Saynt Elyn' in Lambeth 223, and both 'Saynt Elene' (fol. 81v) and 'Sancta Helena' (fols 82r–83r) in Harley 2250; there is no heading at all in Egerton 2810.

[116] C. Horstmann, ed., *The Early South English Legendary*, EETS, os 87 (London, 1887); and Charlotte D'Evelyn and Anna J. Mill, eds, *The South English Legendary*, EETS, os 235, 236, 244 (London, 1956–59).

continuance of the legend in late medieval England, and to the transmission of the hagiographic narrative alongside both the secular version of the story popularised by Geoffrey of Monmouth and the legitimate historical account.

It appears that at the time of composition of *St Elyn* in *The South English Legendary* the tale of Helena's British birth is well established, for it is stated as an unembellished matter of fact in the opening line, along with a claim for aristocratic lineage: 'Saynt Elene was in Bretayn born and comen of hegh kynrade' (line 1).[117] The poet is alluding to facts which he supposes to be common knowledge, or at least would like to present as such, and expresses these credentials as the natural starting place of a laudatory biography. If he is trying to appropriate Helena as a native Briton for a specific rhetorical reason, he does not make a sustained attempt, as the matter is not mentioned again in the text, except in the vague remark that Helena's wisdom is attributable to her lineage: 'Grete heritage hir was bifallen, and þerto she was wys' (line 5). The writer clearly identifies his subject in this opening and authorises her defining attributes: British birth, aristocratic family, and wisdom.

Hagiographic and nationalistic concerns might account for this brief opening, though they cannot account for what follows. Given its locally specific beginning, it is remarkable that the remaining 248 lines of the Middle English *St Elyn* do not deal primarily with Helena or her main cause of fame, the discovery and veneration of the True Cross. Instead, the text concentrates on Constantine's illness and his miraculous cure and conversion by St Silvester (lines 26–145); and the demonstration of Silvester's miraculous powers in the bull miracle before the 12 Jewish scribes (lines 191–222). The narrative concerning Helena's conversion, baptism, and subsequent journey to Jerusalem occupies only the final 27 lines (lines 223–49), though the bull miracle is performed as proof of God's might to convince her to convert from Judaism to Christianity (lines 146–90). The introduction of this unhistorical element in the story – that Helena was initially Jewish – is a narrative feature of the hagiographic legends dealing with St Silvester. A Jewish Helena provides the greater challenge of bringing a member of a competing faith to the Christian Church through a miracle competition with representatives of the Jewish religion.[118] Here, the task of conversion appears at first particularly difficult, as Helena is vehemently opposed both to her own and Constantine's conversion and urges him to convert instead to Judaism, or threatens 'she wolde with hir power destruye him ful clene' (line 159). She argues that it is unreasonable to believe that God, as Jesus, is dead, and therefore asserts that Christian belief is worthless (lines 160–1). Helena is characterised as strong-willed, hot-tempered, and powerful, an

---

117 See transcription at Appendix 2.
118 Many scholars perceive in this a vigorous anti-Jewish sentiment in the development of the legend during the Middle Ages, paralleling the strong anti-Jewish element of the *Inventio* legend (See Jan Willem Drijvers, *Helena Augusta: The Mother of Constantine the Great and the Legend of her Finding of the True Cross* [Leiden, 1992], pp. 143–5).

extreme version of the capable and dominating character of Jocelin's text. Her violent opposition to Christianity is certainly not as explicit in other witnesses of the Silvester legends as it is here.

Perhaps reflecting the tenor of its age, the Middle English *St Elyn* may in this respect be both more anti-Jewish and more focused on the act of conversion than are other legends alluding to this event.[119] Indeed, almost the whole text is dedicated to the background of Helena's conversion from Judaism under miraculous circumstances; her prior and subsequent histories are dealt with peremptorily. This concentration is indicated near the beginning of the poem and operates as a key element in the subject's defining attributes: 'She loued truly þat lawe   þat God to Moyses made/ But ȝett she leved not God   born of Mare were' (lines 2–3). The poet is announcing early on that Helena's conversion from Judaism to Christianity will be the thematic focus, though, unlike Jocelin, there is no explanation for Helena's Judaism. She is not explicitly a convert and there is no discussion of the apparent incongruity between her British origins and her adherence to the Jewish religion. Her Jewishness does, however, serve the rhetorical purpose of providing Silvester with a greater conversion challenge, a variation on the usual pagan preconversion state of individuals in medieval Christian literature.

The narrative sequence of *St Elyn* is a based very heavily not on any hagiographic material relating to St Helena, but on part of the popular fifth-century saint's life of Pope Silvester, *Actus beati Silvestri* (or *Acta Silvestri*).[120] Legends relating to St Silvester certainly circulated in both Anglo-Saxon and post-Conquest England: Aldhelm recounts the life of Silvester in both versions of his *De virginitate*; Constantine's baptism by Silvester is recounted in the Old English *Elene* and homilies on the Invention of the Cross;[121] and later in the Cotton-Corpus legendary.[122] William of Malmesbury includes quite a lot of detail about Silvester's role in Constantine's conversion in his *Gesta regum*. William himself had produced, between 1119 and 1125, an edition of the *Liber pontificalis*, which briefly recounts this legend.[123] In this story, Silvester baptises Constantine after curing him of leprosy, and then converts Helena from Judaism after a debate with 12 Jewish scribes, won by Silvester in a miracle competition. It is dramatically different from the accepted historical version of the story, provided in sources such as Eusebius's *Vita*

---

[119] The culture of fourteenth-century England was hostile towards Jews, though perhaps somewhat less so than in other countries. The demonisation of Jews is typified by the depiction of their slaughter of a Christian child in Chaucer's *Prioress's Tale*. There would have been few, if any, Jews to observe in England at this time; they were expelled by Edward I in 1290, readmitted by Oliver Cromwell in 1655.

[120] See above, p. 24.

[121] *Elene*, lines 190–1. P.O.E. Gradon, ed., *Cynewulf's Elene* (London, 1958) construes this detail as evidence that a particular version of the *Acta Cyriaci* in the *Acta sanctorum* is the source for *Elene* (p. 18).

[122] See above, p. 33, n.54.

[123] Rodney Thomson, *William of Malmesbury* (Woodbridge and Wolfeboro, N.H., 1987), p. 137.

Constantini (IV.62.4), that the Arian bishop, Eusebius of Nicomedia, baptised Constantine at Nicomedia. In the later development of the Silvester legend, Rome was substituted for Nicomedia, Silvester for bishop Eusebius, and the sacrament was orthodox not Arian and occurred immediately after Constantine's cure rather than on his deathbed. St Silvester receives his own legend in both the *South English Legendary* (though only in a few manuscripts, including London, Lambeth Palace, MS 223, one of the three containing *St Elyn*)[124] and the *Legenda aurea*, as well as in the widely disseminated versions of the *Actus beati Silvestri*.

One important element in this legend was the debate between the 12 Jewish scribes and Silvester, widely recounted in hagiographic sources. The tale is transmitted in one distinct manuscript of the *South English Legendary*, Oxford, Bodleian Library, MS Bodley 2567 (SC 779), fol. 227r.[125] Evidently, there was concern in the minds of some writers as to how the various strands of the legends might be reconciled. In the text called *De inventio sancte crucis*[126] in the *Legenda aurea*, the author addresses the conflicting versions of historical and legendary texts treating Silvester in order to justify his acceptance of the legendary version, muddling Constantine and his father in the process. The establishment of the veracity of this account is apparently a priority of this author, perhaps indicating that the legitimate and legendary accounts of the story were still vying for supremacy in the thirteenth century. The vitality of this version of Constantine's conversion and the rapid dissemination of the Silvester legend might account for the textual focus of *St Elyn*, ostensibly a celebration of the life and achievements of St Helena, but in reality an account of the divine magic of St Silvester with an anti-Jewish rhetorical agenda.

This similarity between *St Elyn* and the legend of St Silvester was presumably apparent to a contemporary reviser of one manuscript of the *South English Legendary*, where the last 46 lines of *St Elyn* have been inserted over an erasure made at the end of the verse life of St Silvester to accommodate this inclusion (London, British Library, MS Egerton 2810, fols 170r–170v).[127] This manuscript evidence is too appropriate to be overlooked: presumably the scribal interpolator thought, quite reasonably, that he was dealing with the final miracle segment from *St Silvester* rather than the end of *St Elyn*. This proof of the subor-

---

124 Also in Oxford, Bodleian Library, MS Bodley 1486, fol. 1266r (= MS Laud 108); Cambridge, Trinity College, MS 605, fol. 269v; London, British Library, MS Cotton Julius D.IX, fol. 268v; and London, Lambeth Palace, MS 223, fol. 290v.

125 This part of the tale is based on traditional material. The *SEL* text is edited in C. Horstmann, 'Des Ms. Bodl. 779', *Archiv für das Studium der neueren Sprachen und Literaturen* 82 (1889), pp. 351–3 and 369–422, at pp. 388–94.

126 Graesse, ed., pp. 303–11.

127 British Museum, Department of Manuscripts, *Catalogue of Additions to the Manuscripts in the British Museum, 1894–99* (London, 1901), pp. 557–9. Görlach, in his description of the Helena legend, also identifies much of the narrative material as deriving from the *Actus beati Silvestri* (*Textual Tradition*, p. 166).

dination of Helena's role to that of Silvester powerfully documents the organic reliance of legendary material on other hagiographic cycles.

The Middle English poem is a rendering of the legend which is distinct from the version popularised by Geoffrey of Monmouth, yet it is also different from the bulk of medieval treatments of Helena which focus on the *Inventio* legend. Helena's finding of the Cross, unlike her British origins, is found in many vernacular sources of the Middle Ages, including other manuscripts of the *South English Legendary*, and was widely promoted liturgically and in religious art. The story of her discovery and veneration of the True Cross is recounted in the verse text called *The Finding of the Holy Cross*, which is also found in the contemporary *Legenda aurea*, and many other medieval collections including other vernacular versions. In this context, it is remarkable that the vernacular celebration of the life of St Helena, *St Elyn*, unlike the earlier poem, the Old English *Elene*, should pay so little attention to the *Inventio* legend. In fact, the finding of the Cross is not itself mentioned in the Middle English *St Elyn*, again disallowing Helena's accomplishments from overshadowing those of the real focus of interest, St Silvester (though lines 239–46 refer to the imperial use of the Cross symbol and Helena's distribution of the nails). After recounting that Helena transformed a Jewish temple in Jerusalem into the Church of St Mary's, symbolising and reiterating her own conversion from Judaism to Christianity, the emphasis of the penultimate section of the poem is on her conversion of Jews (lines 231–8), again indicating anti-Jewish rhetoric. Once converted by Silvester's dramatic miracle, Helena is as vehement a Christian as she was a Jew. She is presented as the driving force behind Constantine's faith and his promulgation of Christianity throughout the empire. Not only does she urge him to convert, but also makes him bear a cross on his banner. Hagiographic convention has produced this empowerment of an impassioned Helena, whose major role is as agent of imperial religious reform.

Despite this new narrative focus, and the hagiographic reshaping of Helena's character, the vernacular writer does not exploit the British connection. In the Middle English *St Elyn*, the subject's native status, like her role in the finding of the Cross and even her relationship to Constantine, are subordinated to her role as witness to the divine favour afforded St Silvester and a demonstration of the superiority of the Christian religion over the Jewish faith. The text is in reality part of the Silvester cycle, not a genuine witness to the cult of St Helena, though the introduction and conclusion of the poem refashion the intervening material into a celebration of Helena's legendary conversion from Judaism to Christianity. To this agenda, Helena's alleged Britishness contributes little. The opening line seems to be a nod at a local legend flimsily grafted onto an already flourishing cult of St Silvester, itself wrought from legendary material. The narrative of the poem, concentrating on the miracles of St Silvester, appears to base a claim for the legitimacy of Helena's sacred status on her conversion by St Silvester. The manuscript evidence of *St Elyn* in Egerton 2810 – the interpolation of part of the story into a text of *St Silvester* – highlights this unique reliance.

The Helena legend alluded to in the introduction of *St Elyn* offers the powerful appeal of a national connection, bringing the physical Cross on which Jesus died into direct contact with Britain through claiming Helena as a native. In such matters, the unlikelihood of Helena's native British status and the contradictory evidence of many historical sources do not play a part. Perhaps it is significant too that *St Elyn* was produced at a time when medieval verse romance flourished and itself participated in the production of the idea of nationhood in 'the discourse of the nation'.[128] The confluence of narrative elements from two separate cycles of legends built up over centuries and author-ised by mutual association lies behind the narrative structure and thematic focus of the tale of *St Elyn* in the *South English Legendary*. It is a text which illustrates the resources and methods available to the medieval vernacular poet and the intertextual dynamic of non-secular literary creation. As a witness to the legend of the British Helena, *St Elyn* represents a hagiographic strand quite distinct from the secular version popularised from Geoffrey of Monmouth, one that derived its authority from its reliance upon the legend of St Silvester. Later, these two sub-groups would coalesce into the story represented by the *Nova legenda Anglie* text, but the *South English Legendary* version, *St Elyn*, is a witness to a point at which the two parts of the tale were still separate, when not only did legend co-exist with historical fact, but rival mythical versions of the story developed throughout medieval England and farther afield.

Another contemporary textual manifestation of the legend was in some of the fifteenth-century prose versions of *The Life of St Katherine of Alexandria. Vitae* of this saint, who was possibly martyred around the time of Helena's visit to the Holy Lands in the 320s, were popular in medieval England, and perpetuated the misconception introduced into Western versions of the legend that the name of Katherine's father, 'Costus' was an abbreviation for 'Constantinus'.[129] In a further local modification, several versions of this *vita* include a genealogy for St Katherine which link her to Britain as the niece of Constantine, son of St Helena of Colchester.[130] Katherine is 'þe noble kynred of themperour Constantyne, and of the nacyon of Brytayne'.[131] This comment explains the rele-vance of the earlier references in this text to the marriage between Helena, daughter of Cole, and Constantius, the birth of Constantine, and his later reign as 'kyng of Brytayne, þat now ys callyd Englond' (lines 46–58).

Another version of the St Katherine legend, produced around 1420 and

---

128 Diane Speed, 'The Construction of the Nation in Medieval English Romance', *Readings in Medieval English Romance*, ed. Carol M. Meale (Cambridge, 1994), pp. 135–57, at p. 145.

129 Amnon Linder, 'The Myth of Constantine the Great in the West: Sources and Hagiographic Commemoration', *Studi medievali*, 3rd ser. 16/1 (1975), pp. 43–95, pp. 81–2.

130 Saara Nevanlinna and Irma Taavitsainen, eds, *St Katherine of Alexandria: The Late Middle English Prose Legend in Southwell Minster MS 7* (Cambridge and Helsinki, 1993), identify the genealogy in manuscripts which comprise their b and d versions and in the main manuscript on which the edition is based (p. 11).

131 Nevanlinna and Taavitsainen, eds, *St Katherine of Alexandria*, p. 68, lines 63–5.

known as *The Life and Martyrdom of St Katherine*, elaborates the story further. The opening chapter of this text, entitled 'Of the progenitors of Seynt Kateryn and how she was of þe Emperours blood of Rome', explains that Katherine was Roman on her father's side, being daughter of Costus, half brother of the Emperor Constantine, with the same father, Constantius, but a different mother. Although this does not make Katherine British, it does link her to the royal houses of both Rome and Britain, which themselves are united: 'Þe Brytons whiche come of the noble blood of Troye and were cosyns to þe Romayns'.[132] The inclusion of this genealogical material also provides a reason for recounting the Cole/Helena legend, which appears at considerable length in this chapter, as well as reference to Silvester's baptism of Constantine and Helena's discovery of the Cross. The focus here is Katherine's kinship to the illustrious Constantine, rather than to Helena (with whom she shares no blood relationship), but Constantine's British connection is important for establishing relevance to the English audience of the legend. Karen Winstead has interpreted the inclusion of the prefatory and genealogical material as evidence of 'the nationalism that was vigorously promoted during Henry V's reign . . . [by] . . . associating famous Romans (and by extension, Katherine herself) with England'.[133] These additions to the St Katherine story might also be interpreted as evidence of the perceived validity of the British Helena legend and the general appeal of claiming some connection to her family, even when it was not strictly relevant or altogether coherently integrated into the narrative.[134]

Witnesses to the British Helena legend suggest selective and specifically local affiliation rather than widespread appeal or acceptance. The existence of the Middle English *St Elyn* in only a small group of the *SEL* collection and in some manuscript traditions of *vitae* of St Katherine testifies to her 'boutique' status as an identifiable and occasionally appropriated saint at this time. The continued dissemination of the Colchester version of the legend throughout chronicles and histories and its elaborate representation in the Ashton-under-Lyne stained glass windows demonstrate the continued livelihood of the story, though the omissions in other contexts indicate more strongly the flagging exploitation of the legend by the end of the fifteenth century in the face of the rival forces of the flourishing *Inventio* and Silvester cycles of legends. The British myth might have outlived its usefulness for a time, but was about to be revitalised in the secular context in the sixteenth century.

---

[132] Henry Hucks Gibbs, ed., *The Life and Martyrdom of St Katherine of Alexandria, Virgin and Martyr* (London, 1884), p. 4.

[133] Karen A. Winstead, *Virgin Martyrs: Legends of Sainthood in Late Medieval England* (Ithaca and London, 1997), p. 158.

[134] Perhaps an earlier witness to the connection between the two women is implied by the juxtaposition of offices for Sts Helena and Katherine in a thirteenth-century Trier manuscript. See K.G. Van Acker, 'Ein weiterer Kodex aus dem Bistum Trier (Universitätsbibliothek Gent, Ms. 245)', *Scriptorum* 28 (1974), pp. 71–5, at pp. 73–4.

VI

The Legend Beyond the Middle Ages

GEOFFREY OF MONMOUTH'S version of the history of Britain continued to dominate throughout the late Middle Ages, though some doubts concerning his reliability were beginning to be heard.[1] These views, however, constituted a minority. Social and political circumstances of the fifteenth century, particularly the pro-British mentality fostered by the continuation of the Hundred Years War, created the ideal environment for suspension of disbelief in Geoffrey's fantasies and the active encouragement of British history. In this political milieu, Constantine was cited as a royal ideal, and Gregory of Tours' use of the expression 'New Constantine' as praise of Clovis was reiterated to refer to other monarchs in England and abroad.[2] Thomas Hoccleve (c. 1416) refers to Henry V as being very like Constantine as a mirror for princes and a champion of the faith,[3] a sentiment repeated by Richard Baxter in 1691 of William III, whom he describes as 'the new Constantine to head a national church'.[4] Even in the hostile context of the Council of Constance in 1417, originally designed to bring about the unity of the Church, the French accepted the British Helena legend (though from York not Colchester) as part of the credentials of Britain as a great nation.[5] Guillaume Fillastre's diary of the proceedings of this Council reports the English argument, based on the existence of a British Helena:

> During the second age of the world, the excellent royal house of England arose and it continues in real existence today. Among many holy palmers whom it has produced and whom we cannot here well enumerate, there are St. Helen and her son, the

---

1   Abbot John Whethamsted of St Albans, in his *Granarium* of c. 1435, is dubious about Brutus, though he does not question the British Helena legend. See T.D. Kendrick, *British Antiquity* (New York and London, 1950), p. 34; and W.J. Mulligan, 'The British Constantine: An English Historical Myth', *Journal of Medieval and Renaissance Studies* 8 (1978), pp. 257–79, at p. 268.

2   See J.H.M. Salmon, 'Clovis and Constantine: The Uses of History in Sixteenth Century Gallicanism', *Journal of Ecclesiastical History* 41 (1990), pp. 584–605.

3   *Balade* (of c. 1414–16), *Hoccleve's Works: The Minor Poems*, ed. Frederick J. Furnivall and Sir I. Gollancz, EETS, es 61 and 73 (London, 1892 and 1925), p. 41, lines 9–11, quoted in Karen A. Winstead, *Virgin Martyrs: Legends of Sainthood in Late Medieval England* (Ithaca and London, 1997), p. 157. Winstead refers to this period as one of 'national euphoria' (p. 156).

4   William Lamont, 'The Two "National Churches" of 1691 and 1829', *Religions, Culture and Society in Early Modern Britain: Essays in Honour of Patrick Collinson*, ed. Anthony Fletcher and Peter Roberts (Cambridge, 1994), pp. 335–52, at p. 339.

5   Mulligan, 'The British Constantine', pp. 265–7.

Emperor Constantine the Great, born in the royal city of York. They rescued many lands from the infidels and brought the Lord's cross in faith from the country of infidels to Christian hands.[6]

The reference to York rather than Colchester suggests a source other than Geoffrey of Monmouth, and by this time there were several in circulation. The fifteenth century was a time in which the British Helena legend seems to have been widely accepted in the secular context, particularly once the Latin panegyrics praising Constantine re-emerged after being unavailable for a millennium.[7] Once the occasion arose, these were seized upon as early proof of the legend, and reiterated for the next three centuries, though the legend was not particularly embellished or developed beyond the Middle Ages. During the early Modern period, the idea of a British Helena came to be fossilised as a tradition rather than treated as a living legend, attracting glancing or casual references rather than elaborations. It must also have continued to thrive in popular imagination, especially as St Helena was represented with the Cross in visual art and commemorated liturgically in feasts associated with the Cross and recalled in church dedications. In these contexts, her nobility and importance were stressed, even if her legendary local connections were not explicitly cited.

As a widely acknowledged tradition, however, the concept of a British Helena acquired new political resonance when Henry VIII sought a direct imperial connection with ancient Rome through his supposed descent from a British Constantine. From this time to its virtual extinguishment, at least in historical texts, by Edward Gibbon in the late-eighteenth century, the legend not only retained some currency in the popular imagination, but was deployed in some of the key social and political movements of the day: not only Tudor imperial propaganda, but the wider phenomenon of a rising national and particularly Protestant sentiment in England. As a result of these powerful associations, the legend became a target of both antiquarianism and humanist scholarship.

It was almost exclusively in written sources that Helena's British birth was promulgated. The portrayal of Constantine as an ancestor of Tudor monarchs is of interest only on account of an imputed direct connection with England, through his mother. While Constantine's half-British pedigree and birth in Britain are promoted in this context, the other elements of the story, such as the character and accomplishments of Helena, are unimportant. As was the case in earlier deployments of the British legend, Helena's position is subsumed by her son's imperial status, and here the idea of the Augusta is not so much constructed as implied by her subservient role as the provider of British lineage to Constantine. Helena's diminishing position in popular as well as literate culture was certainly also contingent upon her role as a saint and legendary

---

6 'Fillastre's Diary of the Council of Constance', *The Council of Constance: The Unification of the Church*, Engl. trans. L.R. Loomis, ed. J.H. Mundy and K.M. Woody (New York and London, 1961), pp. 341–2. Cited by Mulligan, 'The British Constantine', p. 267.
7 See above, pp. 15–16.

finder of the Cross being undermined in a Reformation environment in England. Her crucial relationship linking Constantine to King Cole of Colchester is her sole appeal in this new context.

Henry VIII and the Imperial Connection

When Henry VIII styled himself as the possessor of the 'imperial Crown' of the realm of England in 1533, he was claiming imperial authority for himself as British monarch on the basis of Constantine's legendary dual position as both emperor of Rome and King of Britain. Henry's language in the well-known 'Preamble' to the *Act in Restraint of Appeals* connotes his inherited, and documented, imperial status:

> Where by divers sundry old authentic histories and chronicles it is manifestly declared and expressed that this realm of England is an empire, and so it hath been accepted in the world.[8]

Although the wording of this proclamation is vague, Henry is exploiting the legendary possession by the British monarchy of imperial power from Constantine via King Arthur in order to seek the constitutional right to override papal objection to his divorce. This is one of many statutes claiming an imperial monarchy, but it is unique in enunciating a proof for the assertion.[9] In this argument, a British Helena is the vital link between the Roman empire and the British throne, and provides the basis for the creation of the British empire claimed by Henry, because Constantine was both King and Emperor. Henry appeals to the force of tradition: that the wide acknowledgment of his claim of empire (presumably referring to the acceptance of Geoffrey of Monmouth's *Historia regum Britannie* and other early chronicles as genuine history) renders his own claim more legitimate. In his justification for imperial autonomy, Henry uses 'tradition' in two senses as evidence of the status of the English monarch: that traditional stories support his claim, and that his entitlement to a position in the English Church similar to that held by the Christian emperor is hereditary to the monarchy (i.e. handed down as a tradition).[10]

Henry had long nurtured a belief in the imperial status of the Crown, demonstrated by the names of his ships, *Henry Imperial* and *Mary Imperial*, and his frequent use of imperial language in other contexts.[11] He was able ultimately to

---

8 'Preamble' to the *Act in Restraint of Appeals*, April 1533, cited by: Richard Koebner, 'The Imperial Crown of this Realm: Henry VIII, Constantine the Great, and Polydore Vergil', *Bulletin of the Institute of Historical Research* 25 (1953), pp. 29–52, at p. 29. See also Alan G.R. Smith, *The Emergence of a Nation-State: The Commonwealth of England, 1529–1660* (London, 1984), p. 388.
9 Koebner, 'The Imperial Crown of this Realm', p. 30.
10 On Henry's position in the Church, see F.J. Levy, *Tudor Historical Thought* (San Marino, 1967), p. 83.
11 Koebner, 'The Imperial Crown of this Realm', p. 30, cites the compendium of literary references collected by Henry, 'intended to prove that the original traditions of the *ecclesia anglicana* are

appeal directly to the Constantinian connection precisely because it was well-known, had been made credible by the force of tradition, and had been prefigured in his own rhetorical strategies. It would be convenient to find that this reliance upon the British Constantine legend was a manifestation of a more general interest in the legendary history of Britain as effective propaganda practised by Henry VIII, but Sydney Anglo has demonstrated that this was not the case: Henry invoked the Constantinian link but did not precipitate a 'cult of the *British History*' nor a dramatic rise in Arthurianism except in the minds of some antiquarians.[12] Moreover, Henry never claims personal genealogical descent from Constantine, but rather the acquisition of the monarch's status in relation to the Church through Constantine's position: ecclesiastical sovereignty of the English Church from Rome. It is clear, however, that the (originally Welsh) Tudors did claim descent from legendary Welsh and British kings back to Brutus in order to reinforce their status which had been undermined by the dubiousness of their Lancastrian descent.[13] The rhetorical value of royal genealogy was still potent and the appeal of the legendary Tudor descent was particularly appropriate to Henry's needs, as the manifestation of the Constantine legend in the Welsh genealogies also implicitly linked Brutus and Arthur with the Tudors. The connection was further exploited in 'dynastic propaganda' after the Act of Union was legislated in 1536, bringing about the incorporation of Wales with England.[14] Writers like Dr John Dee invoked the Constantine/ Helena connection in order to promote the idea of the 'ultimate restoration of British unity'.[15]

The most immediate deployment of the British Helena legend during Henry's era was by the Italian humanist historian Polydore Vergil, who arrived in England in 1502 as a collector of Peter's Pence, and was invited by Henry's father, Henry VII, to write a history of England. Presumably, Henry VII had commissioned this history with the aim of celebrating the union of the houses of Lancaster and York and the beginning of the Tudor dynasty in his accession to the throne. Vergil fulfilled this request, producing a lengthy and careful history of England from the earliest mythological founding by Brutus down to current times, combining history and legend. His *Anglica historia*, finished in 1513 (revised and first published in Basel in 1534), was translated into English and proved immensely influential.[16] Vergil broke from tradition by rejecting much of

identical with the fundamental principles which prevailed in the Catholic Church when it had been given a legitimate status by the Emperor Constantine'.

12 Sydney Anglo, 'The *British History* in Early Tudor Propaganda', *Bulletin of the John Rylands University Library of Manchester* 44 (1961), pp. 17–48. See also Sydney Anglo, *Images of Tudor Kingship* (Guildford, 1992), p. 56; and J.J. Scarisbrick, *Henry VIII* (London, 1968), pp. 270–1.

13 Anglo, '*British History*', p. 17.

14 Peter Roberts, 'Tudor Wales, National Identity and the British Inheritance', *British Consciousness and Identity: The Making of Britain, 1533–1707*, ed. Brendan Bradshaw and Peter Roberts (Cambridge, 1998), pp. 8–42, at p. 15.

15 Roberts, 'Tudor Wales', p. 36.

16 A partial Latin edition has been published: Denys Hay, ed. and Engl. trans., *The Anglica Historia of*

Geoffrey of Monmouth's *Historia*, and was outspokenly sceptical about the King Arthur story, an ideological position which earned him much scorn among his contemporaries and precipitated an energetic revival of interest in Arthurianism by antiquarians. Vergil's denial of the Arthurian myth angered many British historians, particularly John Leland and Sir John Price, who sought to revitalise the subject as eagerly as they sought to discredit Vergil.[17] In the end, the Arthurian myth was to prove more durable than the Constantinian connection, and was not permanently undermined by Vergil's dismissal.[18]

Unlike the Arthurian legend, Polydore Vergil found support for the British Helena legend outside Geoffrey of Monmouth's *Historia* and therefore included it in his own work. He enunciates an emphatic claim for Constantine's British origins: 'He was born of a British mother, born in Britain, and created Emperor in Britain.'[19] The 1846 edition of the mid-sixteenth-century English translation of the *Anglica historia* explicitly enunciates what this patriotic rhetoric implies, saying Constantine, 'being begott of Brittishe mother, borne and made emperour in Brittaine, noe doubte made his native countrie paretaker of the gretnes of his glorie'.[20] As part of this model of reflected glory, Vergil dismisses the idea that Helena was not legally married to Constantine, saying, 'I have not thought goodd to agree with them which have left in memorie, that Helena was the concubine of Constantius.'[21] As in earlier manifestations of the legend, Vergil imposes propriety on his construction of a suitable Helena through his fabrication or selection of details to transmit.

Vergil was not granted permission to publish his history immediately, possibly because he failed to support the Arthurian story and specifically rejected the fictions of Geoffrey of Monmouth, though other reasons for the delay between completion of the text and its publication might be construed.[22] There might have been a change of heart on Henry VIII's part, based on Vergil's ability to 'offer the king valuable information concerning the notion of *imperium*'.[23] Indeed, when Vergil came to rework his manuscript in 1534, he interpreted the imperial significance of this legend for the English monarch:

Polydore Vergil, A.D. 1485–1537, Camden Series, vol. 74 (London, 1950). More useful is the edition of the first part of the early English translation of Vergil's work: Henry Ellis, ed., *Polydore Vergil's English History*, vol. I: *Containing the First Eight Books* (London, 1846), which is the source of the citations below.

17 See James P. Carley, 'Polydore Vergil and John Leland on King Arthur: The Battle of the Books', *King Arthur: A Casebook*, ed. E.D. Kennedy (New York and London, 1996), pp. 185–204, at p. 193; Roberts, 'Tudor Wales', p. 15; and Kendrick, *British Antiquity*, p. 85.

18 Colin Kidd, 'Protestantism, Constitutionalism and British Identity under the Stewarts', *British Consciousness and Identity*, ed. Bradshaw and Roberts, pp. 321–42, at p. 327.

19 'Is enim Britannica matre genitus, in Britannia natus, in Britannia Imperator creatus' (cited in Koebner, 'The Imperial Crown of this Realm', p. 35).

20 Ellis, ed., p. 91.

21 Ellis, ed., p. 90.

22 Denys Hay, *Polydore Vergil: Renaissance Historian and Man of Letters* (Oxford, 1952), p. 82.

23 Koebner, 'The Imperial Crown of this Realm', p. 33.

> The imperie remained not long after in the stocke of Constantine ... neverthelesse the maiestie of the imperie could not perishe, sithe that even at this presente the kinges of Englonde, according to the usage of their aunciters, doe wear the imperiall diademe as a gifte exhibited of Constantinus to his successors.[24]

Otherwise, Vergil did not alter his opinions, including those on the legend of King Arthur, but rather published in 1525 Gildas's *De calamitate, excidio et conquestu Britanniae*, to support his position with early historical evidence.[25] Vergil's new edition of his *Anglica historia* was eventually published, along with its dedication to Henry VIII. Although Winifred Mulligan might be overstating the case when she claims that Henry VIII abandoned King Arthur in favour of Constantine and then deliberately reversed his decision to ban Vergil's work, this scenario is not impossible.[26] Certainly, the application of the Constantinian connection to imperial politics might have influenced Henry's success, and its continued exploitation in Tudor political rhetoric argues for regal acceptance.[27] Royal approval also allowed Vergil's work to become established as a key source of British history for Elizabethan writers.[28] His account of the British Helena legend was part of this transmission, and was supported by the articulation of the same narrative in other contemporary histories, such as those produced by Juan Luis Vives and John Rastell, and the later chronicles of Cooper and Grafton.[29]

Helena herself is all but lost in this deployment of the Constantinian myth. She remains important as a crucial link between Rome and Britain, but is insignificant as she is not the bearer of imperial status herself. In this secular context, her legendary discovery of the Cross is not cited, though Constantine's Christianity is important in the construction of the founding figure of the British imperial realm. Once the Donation of Constantine came to be regarded as a forgery, Henry's imperial and sacral position became stronger.[30] The tradition that Constantine had bestowed political power in the West upon Silvester in return for a cure from leprosy had been taken to mean that the king's status was a gift of the Pope's,[31] but when this idea had been debunked, the way for political and sacral sovereignty in England became clear. One outcome of this new understanding was the dissolution of the strong connection between legends of Constantine and Helena and those concerning Pope Silvester which featured in many of the earlier texts treated above. The full impact of the Reformation upon the cult of the saints in general was to consolidate this independence of the British legend.

---

24 Ellis, ed., pp. 98–9.
25 Hay, *Polydore Vergil*, p. 30.
26 Mulligan, 'The British Constantine', p. 270; and Koebner, 'The Imperial Crown of this Realm', p. 36.
27 Koebner, 'The Imperial Crown of this Realm', pp. 45–6.
28 William Haller, *Foxe's Book of Martyrs and the Elect Nation* (London, 1963), p. 143.
29 Mulligan, 'The British Constantine', pp. 271–2.
30 Koebner, 'The Imperial Crown of this Realm', pp. 32–6.
31 On the 'Donation', see above, p. 24.

The British Helena legend continued to play a role in the patriotic rhetoric of Reformation England. Specifically, the notion that Constantine had a British mother was deployed within the Protestant discourse of England as an 'elect nation' of the late sixteenth century, especially in the writings of the Reformation propagandist John Foxe, who believed Helena to have been British.[32] In his lengthy *Acts and Monuments*, Foxe briefly recounts Geoffrey of Monmouth's version of the legend and then twice reiterates the idea that Constantine was British.[33] This repetition acquires added significance from his use of Constantine as the originator of a millennium of persecution-free Christianity, at least in Foxe's estimation. This millenarianist interpretation of history draws upon the model of Constantine as religious transformer by the emperor's own biographer Eusebius of Caesarea.[34] Foxe's acceptance and transmission of the British legend, his method of mixing the fanciful with the factual, was typical of sixteenth-century historical writing which accommodated a generous acknowledgment of the mythical component.[35]

The legend was also put to other rhetorical uses at the time. The idea that Constantine had acquired political and sacral dominion over the whole of Britain was the aspect of the legend exploited within pro-unionist documents during advocacy for the union of the British and Scottish Crowns, most energetically articulated in the 1540s as it had been for the union with Wales in the 1530s. The Scotsman John Henrisoun published a tract entitled *Exhortacion to the Scottes to conforme themselfes to the honorable, Expedient, and Godly Union Between the Two Realms of England & Scotland* (London, 1547), wherein he bases his argument for union on the premiss that Constantine was 'heire of Britayne, borne in Britayne, and created Emperor in Britayne', and therefore, that Britain as a whole was an empire to which all parts owed allegiance.[36]

Helena's British birth was reiterated in the histories and chronicles of the sixteenth century, and there was a minor revival of interest in the Arthurian legend and English national identity caused by the debate, reinforced at the

---

32 See Roger A. Mason, 'Scotching the Brut: Politics, History and National Myth in Sixteenth-Century Britain', *Scotland and England, 1286–1815*, ed. Roger A. Mason (Edinburgh, 1987), pp. 60–84, at p. 61. Haller's influential study of Foxe's work has been widely criticised for attributing the rise of nationalist sentiment to Foxe. See Andrew Hadfield, *Literature, Politics, and National Identity: Reformation to Renaissance* (Cambridge, 1994), p. 57.

33 Ed. George Townsend, 9 vols (London, 1843), I.224, I.93 and I.311. On the second occasion, he wrongly attributes the story to 'Eutropius' (which the editor has sourced to the account of Constantine's elevation to emperor in York: X.2), probably in error for 'Eumenius', once considered the writer of one of the Latin panegyrics to Constantine.

34 Howard Hotson, 'The Historiographical Origins of Calvinist Millenarianism', *Protestant History and Identity in Sixteenth-Century Europe*, ed. Bruce Gordon, 2 vols (Aldershot, 1996), II.159–81, at p. 165.

35 Patrick Collinson, 'Truth, Lies, and Fiction in Sixteeth-Century Protestant Hagiography', *The Historical Imagination in Early Modern Britain: History, Rhetoric and Fiction, 1500–1800*, ed. D.R. Kelley and D.H. Sacks (Washington, D.C. and Cambridge, 1997), pp. 37–68.

36 Mason, 'Scotching the Brut', p. 69, citing Henrisoun from J.A.H. Murray, ed., *Complaynt of Scotland*, EETS, es 17 (London, 1872), pp. 207–36.

popular level, for example, by the Welsh bardic poets and celebrating 'Tudor imperial grandeur'.[37] The legend remained unchallenged until Raphael Holinshed's *Chronicles* (London, 1577 and 1587)[38] revealed the growing seeds of doubt regarding a British Helena:

> I feare . . . that it will be harder to prooue Helen a Britaine, than Constantine to be borne in Bithinia (as Nichephorous auoucheth). But forsomuch as I meane not to step from the course of our countrie writers in such points, where the receiued opinion may seeme to warrant the credit of the historie, I will with other[s] admit both the mother and sonne to be Britains in the whole discourse of the historie following, as though I had forgot what in this place I haue said.[39]

Holinshed proceeds to relate an account combining details from genuine early sources such as Orosius and Eutropius, with the legendary account of the British Helena (Ch. 27). Each time he invokes the legend, he qualifies it parenthetically with remarks like 'as some affirme' or 'as some write', confirming his incredulity, while prevented by his patriotic agenda from refuting it outright.[40] Holinshed similarly includes other legends relating to the early history of Britain, including those dealing with King Arthur, though not without enunciating his own suspicion of them and guiding his reader likewise to regard them as unreliable fantasies.[41] John Stowe took some notice of this, for he removed the section on Helena's ambiguous nationality from his *Chronicles of England* (1580), which marks a change from his position in 1565, when he had recounted the British Helena and Constantine legend in his *Summarie* of English history.[42]

Early-modern scholarship was by no means unanimous in its rejection of the legend or in its uncertainty about its legitimacy, with the result that many subsequent writers transmitted the version recounted in Geoffrey's *Historia*. In Rome, the *Annales ecclesiastici* by the Vatican librarian Cardinal Cesare Baronius, recounts the Cole legend,[43] and was the source of several later accounts,[44] including the early-seventeenth-century English text, 'The Life of St Helena Empresse' in *The Lives of Women Saints of our Contrie of England*.[45] These

37 Roberts, 'Tudor Wales', p. 16.
38 On Holinshed's methodology, see Annabel Patterson, *Reading Holinshed's Chronicles* (Chicago and London, 1994).
39 Raphael Holinshed, *Chronicles of England, Scotland and Ireland*, 6 vols (London, 1577, repr. 1807), I.528.
40 As Arthur B. Ferguson, *Utter Antiquity: Perceptions of Prehistory in Renaissance England* (Durham and London, 1993) explains, 'the British History had become a patriotic religion which it was still, in the late sixteenth century, heretical to criticize' (p. 94).
41 See Alison Taufer, *Holinshed's Chronicles* (New York, 1999), p. 24: 'He appears to have regarded the histories of the early kings as cultural knowledge and perhaps moral instruction, but not factual information.'
42 Mulligan, 'The British Constantine', p. 273.
43 Published in Rome, 1607 (III.1–7).
44 See Richard White, *Historiarum Britanniae* (Douai, 1597–1607), and Kendrick, *British Antiquity*, p. 73.
45 In a unique MS version, London, British Library, Ms Stowe 959, ed. C. Horstmann, *The Early South English Legendary*, I, EETS, os 87 (London, 1887), pp. 30–6.

texts, predicated on the misconstrued Latin panegyrics to Constantine and the reliability of Geoffrey's narrative, present portraits of Helena, daughter of King Cole, the mother of Constantine, who was baptised by Pope Silvester. They also recount her role in the *Inventio* and, most interestingly, the fact that Constantine renamed Drepanum 'Helenopolis' because Helena had left there 'a noble monument of her pietie', a church in honour of the martyr Lucian (the empress's documented favourite).[46] This explanation for the renaming of Drepanum subtly rejects the widely held view that it was Helena's birthplace. Another innovative use to which the British legend is put is the explanation for Constantius's divorce from Helena based on her unworthiness of him once he had become emperor, not because she had been a low-born stable-maid or did not provide a family bond with another member of the Tetrarchy, as in the contemporary sources, but because she was 'no Roomane, but an externe and a Barbarian, by nation and the Roman's estimation'.[47] This plausible rationale for the divorce would have been received most sympathetically by the English audience for which this text was produced, and reinforces the validity of an otherwise unlikely legend. These alterations demonstrate the selective deployment and blending of history, legend, and individual authorial input.

Around the same time, the historian and headmaster of Westminster, William Camden (1551–1623), reacted to the growing doubt in the legend by promulgating and defending it. This apologetic effort, also based on the work of Baronius, and intended to promote the concept of an English empire,[48] proved to be rather influential. He included it in the fourth edition of his *Britannia*, a description of England, Scotland, and Ireland (Latin edition published in 1586; an English translation was made under his supervision in 1610),[49] though not without acknowledging the existence of competing claims.[50] Basing his argument on the ideas of 'our excellent historian Baronius',[51] Camden, like his source, invokes the panegyrics of Constantine which assert that he was 'created emperor' in Britain. The re-emergence of these panegyrics in the fifteenth century fuelled the arguments of historians like Camden who wished to claim historical veracity for the British Helena legend through genuine antiquarian research.[52] Their misconstrual became traditional itself, as the misinterpretation of the sentiment 'created emperor' as 'born' in Britain acquired greater validity each time it was repeated. Because the panegyrics are genuine contemporary

---

46 Horstmann, ed., p. 35, line 18.
47 Horstmann, ed., p. 30, line 25.
48 Roberts, 'Tudor Wales', p. 34.
49 The prompt translation of Camden's history, like Vergil's, implies not only the declining relevance of the Latin language as a medium of communication but also the popularity of these texts and the desire for national histories in the vernacular.
50 William Camden, *Britannia* (London, 1610), pp. 50, 340, and 351; translated, rearranged and enlarged by Edmund Gibson (London, 1695), pp. lxxv and xcix.
51 Gibson, ed., p. xcix.
52 On Camden's method and intellectual milieu, see W.H. Herendeen, 'William Camden: Historian, Herald, and Antiquary', *Studies in Philology* 85 (1988), pp. 192–210.

sources, and were widely cited after their discovery in the early fifteenth century, their status as 'evidence' for the legend of a British Helena, or at least a British Constantine, was powerful, particularly within the context of a growing interest in the Roman past enjoyed in England at the time.

In the English translation of his work, Camden particularly addresses the reasons for the early writers calling her a 'stable-maid', explaining that this was done unfairly to reproach her; her connection with the humble place of Christ's birth is to her credit, 'because the manger where Christ was laid was sought out by this pious princess and a church built by her in the place where the stable stood'.[53] Camden also acknowledges the cult of Helena in Wales, conflating the local Elen with St Helena: of Sarn Helen, he says 'it is but reasonable to suppose it made by Helena, the mother of Constantine the Great' and later calls her 'Helen Luedhog', 'Helena the Great', who instigated Constantine's programme of walling London.[54]

The British Helena legend is also alluded to in Camden's later anthology, *Remains Concerning Britain*, of 1605, where he addresses, among many other topics, the arguments of the legend's critics.[55] In his alphabetical listing of Christian names, under 'Helena' he has: 'A name much used in honour of *Helena*, mother to *Constantine* the Great, and native of this Isle, although one onelie Authour maketh her a Bithinian, but *Baronius* and our Historians will have her a Britaine'.[56] The single voice of the Bithinian side against the combined authority of Baronius and 'our historians' indicates where Camden's preference lies. Under the section called 'Wise Speeches', he mentions in passing: 'Constantius's sonne *Constantine*, invested in the Empire at Yorke (and a Britan borne as all Writers consent, beside *Nicephorus* who lived not long since and now *Lipsius* deceived by the false printed coppie of *Jul. Firmicus* . . .)'.[57] Camden is alluding to the *Admiranda* of the Belgian historian Justus Lipsius (Antwerp, 1598), which, following the *Matheos libri* of Julius Firmicus (Venice, 1497), situates Constantine's birth at Tharsus. Camden took up the issue as a personal crusade and continued to defend the legend energetically, both in print and in private correspondence with Lipsius, culminating in the last word from Camden in the revised edition of his *Britannia* in 1607, which appeared after Lipsius's death.[58]

A contemporary witness to the success of his rhetoric and the durability of the legend is a source mentioned by Camden, the 1608 *English Martyrologe*, a patriotically inspired calendar which situates legendary and actual saints in the British Isles. This text recounts the story of Princess Helena from Colchester,

---

53 Gibson, ed., p. lxxv.
54 Gibson, ed., pp. 656, 661, and 312.
55 Ed. R.D. Dunn (Toronto, 1984), and see Gibson, ed., p. lxxv, note a.
56 Dunn, ed., p. 84.
57 Dunn, ed., p. 207. The reference to Nicephorus is presumably to Nicephorus Callistus, the thirteenth-century Byzantine historian, whose work was a compilation of the ecclesiastical histories.
58 Mulligan, 'The British Constantine', p. 275; Dunn, ed., p. 421.

under her feast day, 18 August, though it also transmits Altmann's legend that she is buried in 'Rhemes in France' and recounts the translation under the traditional date, 7 February.[59] This document somewhat self-consciously insists that 'ancient Records testifie' that Helena was born in Colchester, citing (wrongly) Nicephorus, Eusebius, and Socrates.

Camden's account of British history was transmitted widely throughout the following two centuries, though with an increasing degree of defensiveness and qualification. Typically, Michael Drayton, in his *Polyolbion* (of 1612), recounts the Cole legend in a lengthy note to his long poem. He enthusiastically objects to rival versions of the story, employing emotive rhetoric:

> Doe not object *Nichephorus Callistus* that erroneously affirmes him born in *Drepanum* of *Bithinia*, or *Jul. Firmicus* that sayes at *Tarsus*, upon which testimony (not uncorrupted) a great Critique hath violently offered to deprive us both of him and his mother, affirming her a *Bithinian*; nor take advantage of *Cedrenus*, that will have *Dacia* his birth soile. But our Histories, and, with them, the *Latine* Ecclesiastique relation . . . allowed also by Cardinal *Baronius*, makes her thus a *British* woman.[60]

Like his predecessors, Drayton cites the evidence of the Latin panegyrics to Constantine and treats Constantine and Helena as national icons to be defended. Other seventeenth-century writers, like John Milton, acknowledge the (misconstrued) panegyrics but allow greater reliability to other late-Roman sources: 'To this (legend) . . . the Roman authors give no Testimony, except a Passage or two in the *Panegyrics* . . . others nearest to those times clear the Doubt, and write him certainly born of Helene, a mean woman at Naissus in Dardania.'[61] Many writers such as David Hume, Robert Brady, William Tyrrell, and William Temple, either avoid or challenge the legend, as humanistic principles push aside Geoffrey of Monmouth's version of British history in favour of examining primary sources.[62] Even literary sources of the time, which are more inclined to transmit Geoffrey's stories, particularly the Arthurian section, do not include the British Helena legend in their agendas. Spenser is an exception: although he had acknowledged that the Brut material was pure fantasy, he does recount the story of Helena, daughter of King Cole of Colchester, in his *Faerie Queen* (of 1590).[63]

The Constantinian connection became a more vexed issue during the seventeenth century, when his name became synonymous in the minds of some with ecclesiastical corruption. Constantine, as the figure traditionally responsible for

---

59 John Wilson, *The English Martyrologe containing a summary of the most renowned and illustrious saints of the three kingdoms, England, Scotland and Ireland* (n.p., 1608; repr. Amsterdam and New York, 1970), pp. 225–6.

60 J. William Hebel, ed., *The Works of Michael Drayton*, 4 vols (Oxford, 1961), IV.163.

61 John Milton, *The History of Britain* (London, 1671), p. 89 (cited by Mulligan, 'The British Constantine', p. 277).

62 Mulligan, 'The British Constantine', p. 277; On the later chronicle tradition, see Levy, *Tudor Historical Thought*, pp. 167–201.

63 Ed. T.P. Roche (Harmondsworth, 1987), II, X.58–60 (pp. 342–3). Kendrick, *British Antiquity*, pp. 127–33, discusses Spenser's attitude to the material. On the transmission of the Arthurian portion of the narrative, see R.F. Brinkley, *Arthurian Legend in the Seventeenth Century* (New York, 1967).

joining Church and State, became a topos during the Reformation of 'politico-religious corruption and the rise of the episcopacy'.[64] John Milton, for example, sees the emperor as the instigator Antichrist, unlike Andrew Marvell, who saw the bishops in this light.[65] This new negative aspect to claiming Constantine, and implicitly, Helena, as British, must have checked the exploitation of the legend in other contexts and played a part in the later reappraisal of the evidence for this claim.

Morant, Gibbon, and the Eighteenth Century

By the mid-eighteenth century, when the late-Roman sources for Helena's life had been re-examined carefully and objections expressed in many histories, serious doubts had arisen concerning the veracity of the legend, and therefore, those wishing to promote it had to do so imaginatively. Thomas Carte, in his *General History of England*, addresses this problem by introducing an innovation into the narrative when he claims that Constantine was born to a British Helena while she was travelling in Naissus with her husband.[66] Philip Morant and Edward Gibbon go back to the primary sources and tackle the matter more systematically, with quite divergent results.

The historian Philip Morant, in *The History and Antiquities of the County of Essex* (London, 1768),[67] made a detailed case for the argument that Helena was the daughter of King Cole of Colchester. As the rector of St Mary's, Colchester, Morant produced a careful but probably partisan treatment of the history of Colchester (Bk I, Ch. 2). He bases his argument on the evidence of Aldhelm's *De virginitate*, a genuine source, as well as more spurious material. First, he persuasively accounts for the name, Colchester: from Latin *colonia* 'colony' + Old English *chester* 'town'; then cites the evidence of *The Chronicle of Colchester* that Helena was a native of that city and built there Helen's Chapel (p. 34). He admits that this chronicle was written as late as the early fourteenth century, but nevertheless cites it extensively (p. 28). Morant backs up this assertion with Camden's conviction that 'all Historians who have written on the subject, except [the Byzantine chroniclers] Cedrenus and Nicephorus, affirm [this] with one voice' (p. 28). He cites Geoffrey of Monmouth and the 70 other authorities listed by 'Michael Alford, alias Griffith'.[68] Here, longevity is misconstrued as proof of accuracy: the legend is traditional, he argues, so it must

---

[64] Conel Condren and C.D. Cousins, 'Introduction', *The Political Identity of Andrew Marvell*, ed. Condren and Cousins (Aldershot, 1990), pp. 1–15, at p. 11.

[65] William Lamont, 'The Religion of Andrew Marvell: Locating the "Bloody Horse"', in Condren and Cousins, *Political Identity*, pp. 135–56, at p.150.

[66] Thomas Carte, *General History of England* (London, 1747–55), I.147.

[67] *History and Antiquities of the County of Essex*, 2 vols (repr. East Ardsley, 1978).

[68] Michael Alford, *Britannia illustrata, siue Lucii, Helenæ, Constantini, patria et fides* (Antwerp, 1641).

be true. He brushes away the idea that Constantine was born in Naissus as a fanciful story peddled by a few authors and 'grounded upon the authority of one obscure writer or two' and weakened by a lack of agreement about exactly where in the East Constantine was born. Morant bases his argument squarely on the absence of reliable information in Eusebius or any of the other ecclesiastical historians (p. 29), and on the suggestions of the fourth-century panegyrics celebrating Constantine's emergence from Britain as emperor.

More dangerously, Morant relies on the evidence of 'Fl. Lucius Dexter, who lived about the end of the 4th century' (p. 29). Although Dexter was a genuine Roman personage, reputed to have written a *Universal History*, as mentioned (though unsighted) by Jerome, none of his writings is extant today.[69] Dexter's *Chronicon*, which certainly does allude to the British Helena legend,[70] has since been shown to be a forgery produced by a seventeenth-century Spanish Jesuit, Francisco Bivarius.[71] The situation of Helena in Colchester is further proof of the author's anachronism and the document's status as a forgery. Morant was misguided in believing this to be a genuine and very early source.

Aside from Morant's mistaken views on this document, its existence as a forgery is highly interesting, as it demonstrates the attractiveness of the legend in Spain in the early seventeenth century, and the desirability outside Britain of passing it off as truth.[72] Although Bivarius was evidently transmitting Baronius's (and, remotely, Geoffrey's) version of events, as he mentions in his notes, he does add a local touch by explicitly styling Constantius the imperial governor of Spain, which is a true representation of only part of his imperial

---

69 Jerome mentions both Dexter and his father in his *De viris illustribus* (Chs 132 and 106: PL 23, cols 631–760; Engl. trans: P. Schaff and H. Wace, A Select Library of Nicene and Post-Nicene Fathers of the Christian Church, 2nd ser., vol. 3 [1892; repr. Grand Rapids, 1975]), which he dedicates to Dexter. Dexter is listed in *PLRE* 1, p. 251.

70 PL 31 (Paris, 1846), cols 479–80: 'Ab anno 306, successerat in imper. gubernationeque Hispaniæ Chloro Constantino patri Constantinus filius cognomento Magnus, ex Helena femina primaria Britanniæ.' In a note, the editor, Bivarius, cites his contemporary, Baronius, as agreeing with this information, and argues for Helena's aristocratic staus and partnership with Constantius: 'Consonat his Baronius eodem anno 306, quo loco monet invidia factum, ut filia nobilissimi Britanni apud quem Chlorus hospitio susceptus est, *stabularia* vocaretur: *concubina* vero . . .' (col. 479).

71 PL 31, cols 9–10: 'Chronicon a Bivario sub Dextri nomine evulgatum, spuritatis una voce arguunt nostræ ætatis bibliographi Jesuitæ xvi sæculi illud adscribentes.' See also A. Jülicher, 'Dexter 11', *RE*, vol. 5, col. 297: '*Chronicon Dextri* ist die grosse Fälschung eines spanischen Jesuiten vor 1620.' Bivarius (or Vivarius) (1584–1635), a well-known and prolific historian based in Madrid, claimed to be the editor of Dexter's chronicle, though it is far more likely that he composed it himself. On Bivarius, see A. Baudrillart, *Dictionnaire d'histoire et de géographie ecclésiastiques*, tome 9 (Paris, 1937), p. 38, s.v. Bivar; F. Franciscus de Bivar, in N. Antonio, *Bibliotheca hispana nova* (Madrid, 1783; repr. Torino, 1963), s.v. Bivar; and P. Guerin, in *Diccionario de historia ecclesiastica de España*, ed. Q. Aldea, T. Marin, and J. Vives (Madrid, 1972), s.v. Bivar.

72 Evidently, Helena was recognised as a saint in Spain and Portugal well before this time and her Eastern feast day, which she shared with Constantine, 21 May, was the one in use in the sailor's almanac of the Portuguese navigator Admiral João da Nova Castella, who named the Atlantic island in honour of the saint when it was first sighted on this day in 1502.

responsibility, which also included Gaul and Britain.[73] There is other evidence that Helena was venerated in Spain, at least as part of the cult of the Cross. Apart from iconographic celebration of the finding of the Cross, she is the dedicatee of a fifteenth-century altar in the Iglesia San Miguel in Estella;[74] is depicted within a series of sixteenth-century painted panels, recounting the Finding of the Cross, in a Carthusian monastery near Burgos;[75] and in a much earlier context, the *Inventio* is depicted in the eleventh-century embroidery known as the Genesis of Gerona, which includes a figure certain to be Helena and one which might be Constantine, or possibly Heraclius, the Roman Emperor (610–41) who allegedly retrieved in 629 a relic of the Cross taken during the capture of Jerusalem by the Persian King Chrosroes II, the event celebrated in the feast of the *Exaltatio* (14 September).[76]

Through the use of the Dexter forgery and other doubtful material, Morant is transmitting Geoffrey's fiction in the guise of legitimate history verified by a range of supposedly reliable sources. In his attempt to marshall as many consenting voices as possible, he calls on Aldhelm, who certainly does mention the British Constantine legend,[77] and he amasses much other support in his pursuit of outweighing the evidence for Naissus with that of Colchester, and in particular refuting the rejection of the legend by Roger Gale in a letter to the Antiquarian Society.[78] Morant deduces a good deal from the silence of Roman histories (e.g. regarding the 17 years between Constantius's first and second visits to Britain, on p. 30), only slightly reducing the absurdity of this method- ology by interspersing genuine and reliable information among these more spurious ideas. Unlike earlier writers who follow Geoffrey's narrative of a married Helena based in Colchester, he recognises that Helena was Constantius's concubine, as asserted by Eusebius, Orosius, Cassiodorus, Bede, and others; and that Constantius died in York on 25 July 306 (pp. 28 and 31). Along the way, he embellishes the portrayal of Helena in semi-hagiographical style though certainly with echoes of Geoffrey of Monmouth's portrait of a romance heroine and also with a reminder of Jocelin's charitable Helena (though it is unlikely that he had read Jocelin's *vita*):

---

[73] 'Successerat in imper. gubernationeque Hispaniæ Chloro Constantio' (cols 479–80).

[74] Barbara Baert, 'Aspects of the Invention of the Cross: Iconography Around 1400 and its Relationship with the Genre of the Classes and the Adamite Peasant', *Flanders in a European Perspective: Manu- script Illumination Around 1400 in Flanders and Abroad*, ed. M. Smeyers and B. Cardon (Louvain, 1995), pp. 309–25.

[75] The Cartuja de Miraflores, in the Chapel of the Holy Cross. See Hans Pohlsander, *Helena: Empress and Saint* (Chicago, 1995), p. 224.

[76] Barbara Baert, 'New Observations on the Genesis of Girona (1050–1100): The Iconography of the Legend of the True Cross', *Gesta* 38 (1999), pp. 115–27. Baert argues that the presence of the embroidery might suggest a local cult of the Cross (p. 125). Those who claim that the figure is Constantine arrive at this conclusion by analogy with the conventional depiction of Helena with Constantine in Byzantine art.

[77] See above, pp. 37–8.

[78] 7 July 1736 (Morant, *The History and Antiquities of the County of Essex*, p. 30).

She was the beautifullest woman in the country, extremely well skilled in music, and adorned with all other, acquired as well as natural, accomplishments. Her father, having no other child, had caused her to be educated in such a manner as might best fit her to govern. Withal she was a woman of uncommon charity and piety; and had been converted to Christianity by her son. (p. 34)

As a final attempt to claim victory, Morant resorts to the argument of comparative incongruity: 'Whatever inconsistencies or anachronism are pretended to be found in those writers which affirm that Constantine was born in Britain, and at Colchester; these are as great, if not greater, in those that he was born at Naisus' (p. 31). He is right: the vagueness of contemporary sources on Constantine's date and place of birth leaves the matter wide open for imaginative interpretation such as that offered by British writers motivated by a patriotic desire to claim Helena as a countrywoman. Morant is appealing quite unashamedly to the argument for national pride as a form of wish-fulfilment, absurdly pairing patriotism as the natural partner of truth: 'I do not contend for these things *tamquam pro aris & focis*: but for the Love and Respect I have for this place, to which I owe a great part of my Happines; and the due regard I bear to Truth, have drawn these observations from me' (p. 31).

But Morant's emotional argument, like Carte's imaginative one, appealed to a minority. Many eighteenth-century historians demurred and chose to omit the legend, which had become unconvincing in the light of the contradictory evidence of late Roman sources. Within the context of the eighteenth-century trope of the unreliability of Renaissance and Reformation historiography,[79] Edward Gibbon chose to deal with the matter more openly. He pronounced against the weight of tradition and some earlier historians in his definitive refutation of the British Helena legend. Gibbon seems to have set the English-speaking world straight on this subject, as progress of the legend in print appears to have been ultimately checked by his comments in *Decline and Fall of the Roman Empire* of 1776–88:

The place of [Constantine's] birth as well as the condition of his mother Helena, have been the subject not only of literary but of national disputes. Notwithstanding the recent tradition, which assigns for her father a British king, we are obliged to confess that Helena was the daughter of an innkeeper . . . The great Constantine was probably born at Naissus, in Dacia.[80]

Gibbon uses the same primary sources exploited by Morant, though he has interpreted them in a more analytical and detached manner, driven also by his

79 Philip Hicks, *Neoclassical History and English Culture: From Clarendon to Hume* (Basingstoke and New York, 1996), p. 1.
80 Ed. J.B. Bury, 9 vols (London, 1909–14), Ch. 14: I.428. Gibbon provides a note on this section:
   This tradition . . . was invented in the darkness of monasteries, was embellished by Jeffrey of Monmouth and the writers of the xii century, has been defended by our antiquarians of the last age, and is seriously related in the ponderous history of England, compiled by Mr Carte (vol i. p. 147). He transports, however, the kingdom of Coil, the imaginary father of Helena, from Essex to the wall of Antoninus. (n. 10)

characteristically sceptical attitude towards Christianity and his particular interest in Constantine.[81] His pronouncement was timely and convincing: the legend was not seriously entertained in later historical sources. Of course, the demise of the legend in popular tradition and even in educated circles was not so easily achieved, and a subterranean current of veracity was enjoyed by the story right into the twentieth century.[82] This continued longevity was reinforced on the religious scene, where the *Inventio* legend continued to be transmitted in written and visual contexts, and Helena continued to be closely associated with this feast in Catholic culture. It is unsurprising, then, that both the major manifestations of the story in comparatively recent literature, Evelyn Waugh's novel *Helena* and Dorothy L. Sayers's play *The Emperor Constantine*, are heavily theological.

The Legend Revisited by Evelyn Waugh

The legend was revived with a new focus redirected away from Constantine and towards Helena by Evelyn Waugh in his 1950 novel, *Helena*.[83] Waugh follows Geoffrey of Monmouth's version of events, elaborated by his own research and imaginative input. He is very much in control of the legendary material. In particular, Waugh challenges Gibbon's sceptical interpretation concerning the Christian interpretation of history. His own personal circumstances as a Catholic convert and his interest in the cosmic significance of the *Inventio* converge to produce a theological biography of a specifically British finder of the True Cross.[84] He made a conscious decision to write about Helena during his visit to Jerusalem in 1935,[85] eschewing her more famous son, whom Waugh found 'unsympathetic' and 'a shit in my book'.[86] The era in which the book was written is also encoded in it: Waugh commenced it in 1945 before he had been demobilised from the British army. In a private letter to Ronald Knox, he situates

---

[81] Mulligan, 'The British Constantine', p. 277, citing David P. Jordan, *Gibbon and His Roman Empire* (Chicago, 1971), pp. 191–212.

[82] Margaret E. Tabor, *The Saints in Art: With their Attributes and Symbols Alphabetically Arranged*, 4th ed (London, 1924), opens her entry for the saint with the statement: 'There is good authority for believing that St. Helena was a British woman, though her parentage and place of birth are much disputed' (p. 55).

[83] See the recent discussion of this novel in Jan Willem Drijvers, 'Evelyn Waugh, Helena and the True Cross', *Classics Ireland* 7 (2000), pp. 25–50.

[84] In one scene in the book he creates a weak pun on Gibbon's name when he refers to a future 'false historian' while gesturing to Helena's pet 'gibbon' on a chain (p. 116). He also refers to the site of Helena's tomb as the place where 'Edward Gibbon later sat and premeditated his history' (p. 246), as if Gibbon willingly did Helena a disservice by refuting her legends. See also Kathryn W. Crabbe, *Evelyn Waugh* (New York, 1988), p. 124.

[85] Selina Hastings, *Evelyn Waugh: A Biography* (London, 1994), p. 538.

[86] Letter to Professor Jacques Barzun, 18 December 1951, *The Letters of Evelyn Waugh*, ed. Mark Amory (New Haven and New York, 1980), pp. 361–2, at p. 361; and Letter to Lady Mary Lygon, 4 February 1946 (Amory, ed., pp. 223–4, at p. 223).

the origins of his exploration of Christian hope in the ethically fraught post-war milieu, saying, 'It keeps my mind off the Responsibilities of Peace.'[87]

Waugh's sources and methodology are enunciated modestly in his preface to *Helena*. The book, he says, is the result of his personal experience of his 'desultory reading in history and archaeology' (p. vii), though this remark does not accurately represent his evidently good grasp of a wide range of historical sources, especially Eusebius's *Vita Constantini* (III.41–7).[88] Like the sixteenth-century historians, though, Waugh freely included legendary material, especially where his sources were unclear, silent, or in disagreement, though rather for artistic reasons than from a belief in their veracity. 'Where the authorities are doubtful', he says, he has 'chosen the picturesque in preference to the plausible' (p. vii), as in his choice of Colchester over York (p. ix). He claims to have 'freely invented' details only where earlier 'authorities' do not provide the information required, but sources his own story within the twin realms of tradition and history: 'There is nothing, I believe, contrary to authentic history . . . and there is little that has not some support from tradition or from earlier documents' (p. vii). The comfortable co-existence of tradition and history in this literary model illuminates the methodology of earlier transmitters of the British Helena legend, who, like Waugh, construe the two as equivalent for their purposes.

Waugh specifically addresses the subject of Helena's origins with a casual mixture of historical interpretation, reverence for tradition, and national pride, though he obscures the criteria for likelihood when he says, 'We do not know where she was born or when. Britain is as likely a place as any other and British historians used always to claim her' (p. viii). Like Morant and Foxe, Waugh plumps for tradition, but unlike them, he does not invest too heavily in the belief that legend is fact. Waugh's choices are governed by artistic rather than historical principles, and he makes a broad disclaimer at the conclusion of his preface: 'The story is just something to be read; in fact a legend' (p. xi). This brief description of his synthesis of materials and his own input encapsulates the premiss under which many earlier accounts of Helena had been produced – that legend has a unique legitimacy and value – and expresses the need for this genre unashamedly to attract its own particular method of interpretation.

Above all, Waugh weaves the traditional tales about Helena into a coherent and sympathetic whole, embroidering legend with his own inventions, such as the detail that Helena had red hair (p. 3). He situates the British Helena legend within the Brut tradition by introducing the heroine reading the story of her namesake Helen of Troy (and, by implication, the legendary founding of Britain by Brutus) (p. 5). Like some earlier writers, he also creates a pretext for the epithet *stabularia* for Helena, embellishing details of Helena's qualities and training from Geoffrey of Monmouth, but also including some character traits of

---

87 Letter to Ronald Knox, 14 May 1945 (in Amory, ed., p. 206).
88 See the discussion in Drijvers, 'Evelyn Waugh, Helena', pp. 43–9.

the modern Briton. When Constantius first meets her, Helena is in the stables, explaining that it is the result of a national predilection for scholarship: 'I'm still being educated. I'm the king's daughter you know and we Britons think a lot of education' (p. 28). Unlike earlier writers who pass over the *stabularia* reference as quickly as possible, Waugh dwells on it. He develops the equine theme throughout the book, which has an erotic aspect here, on which he sought advice from his friend, Penelope Betjeman, the dedicatee of the book.[89] Waugh himself describes the young Helena as '16, sexy, and full of horse fantasies'.[90] Waugh's contribution of the rhetoric of desire is absent from earlier accounts, especially in view of their encoded anxiety regarding Helena's ambiguous marital status. The new emphasis on Helena's love of horses allows Waugh to connect her juvenile erotic fantasies with her later spiritual vocation, and to explain the eccentric choice of the fate of one of the nails found in the Cross. The legendary detail that Constantine had a horse bit fashioned out of one nail acquires a new significance in the charged equine motif which runs throughout the book. The horse is also an element in Waugh's larger scheme of life as a hunt, made explicit in his concluding sentences: 'Hounds are checked, hunting wild. A horn calls clear through the covert. Helena casts them back on the scent.'[91] This extended metaphor is one vehicle whereby Waugh expresses Helena's single-minded contribution to the Christian Church in her desire to place the material reality of the crucifixion in the forefront. As Christopher Sykes, in his biography of Waugh remarks, Waugh was making a 'theological statement' of great importance in this novel:

> While Christian sophists argued about Homoiousion and Homoousion the down-to-earth reality of Christ's life was being forgotten. Evelyn put these words into Helena's mouth: 'Just at this moment when everyone is forgetting it and chattering about the hypnostatic union, there's a solid chunk of wood waiting for them to have their silly heads knocked against. I'm going off to find it.'[92]

This interest in 'the literal reality of the Cross'[93] is well-served by the legend of a physical connection with Britain. In a novel which uses the colloquial speech and mannerisms of Waugh's contemporary England, the thematic importance of the Cross as material object, sought from and returned to Britain, acquires a local relevance for the legend.

Waugh puts a great deal of effort into the presentation of his heroine's character, specifically in order to illuminate her decision to search for the Cross and the determination which brings this wish to fruition. Most striking are her inde-

---

[89] In his letter to John Betjeman of 27 May 1945, he asks him, 'Will you tell her to write to me fully about adolescent sex reveries connected with riding' (in Amory, ed., p. 207).

[90] Letter to John Betjeman, 27 May 1945 (in Amory, ed., p. 207).

[91] Waugh, *Helena*, p. 247; See also the review by Frederick J. Stopp, *Month*, Aug. 1953, pp. 69–84, repr. in *Evelyn Waugh: A Critical Heritage*, ed. Martin Stannard (London, 1984), pp. 324–34, at p. 333.

[92] Christopher Sykes, *Evelyn Waugh: A Biography* (Harmondsworth, 1975), p. 430; quotation: Waugh, *Helena*, p. 196.

[93] Sykes, *Evelyn Waugh*, p. 430.

fatigable curiosity, plain speech, and common sense. Her commitment to finding concrete evidence of the Christian story is presented as specifically 'English empiricism', as Waugh's reviewers were quick to point out.[94] Her British origins are crucial to his contention that Helena's characteristically English brand of practicality allowed her to find the Cross, as if this were a national trait along with a love of education. Waugh is unique in being able to marry the British and *Inventio* legends into a coherent, psychologically dependent whole, where the former is a necessary prerequisite for the latter: Helena finds the Cross precisely because her British nationality provides her with the appropriate temperament and circumstances to do so.

Evelyn Waugh was deeply committed to this project which clearly occupied a spiritual and emotional dimension in his life. He was extremely pleased with the result of his efforts, and claimed to Nancy Mitford that *Helena* was his favourite book, a 'masterpiece',[95] though he correctly anticipated that it would not be a popular book.[96] Readers disliked the anachronistic dialogue, and the 'apparent incongruity between theme and medium',[97] and were not engaged in the serious theological implications of the story. Thematically, *Helena* centres on the heroine's preparation for her unique act of finding the Cross, and its cosmic ramifications, though the actual narrative gives proportionately little attention to this act.[98] It concentrates instead on Helena's quest for Rome, transmuted into her quest for the City of God.[99] The novel failed critically and commercially because it made uncomfortably explicit some of the implicit themes of his other 'Catholic' novel, the far more successful *Brideshead Revisited*, and lacked the satire his readers expected of him and which he provided in many of his novels. He was unable to communicate his own enthusiasm for his subject to his readers, something which puzzled and saddened him as a writer. Waugh's biographer, Christopher Sykes, reports that, 'the indifferent reception given to what Evelyn believed to be by far his best book was the greatest disappointment of his whole literary life'.[100]

Waugh's Helena is a sympathetic addition to a long list of imaginative constructions of this persona: her emotional and spiritual existences are brought to life, and the legendary and historical aspects of her *vita* are drawn together in a satisfying manner which depends crucially on the British Helena legend. Waugh demonstrates that it can all fit together quite logically. Moreover, he

94 Christopher Derrick, *The Times*, 20 April 1974, p. 14 (in Stannard, ed., pp. 334–6, at p. 335); and Crabbe, *Evelyn Waugh*, p. 120.
95 Letter to Nancy Mitford, 9 November 1949 (in Amory, ed., pp. 312–13, at p. 312).
96 In a letter to Anne Fremantle, 14 September 1949, he said, 'It will be interesting only to the very few people who know exactly as much history as I do' (in Amory, ed., p. 310); later to Nancy Mitford, 'no-one will like it at all' (in Amory, ed., pp. 312–13, at p. 312); and again to her on 16 November 1949, 'My *Helena* is a great masterpiece. How it will flop' (in Amory, ed., pp. 313–14, at p. 313).
97 Stopp review in Stannard, ed., p. 325; see also Crabbe, *Evelyn Waugh*, p. 118.
98 14% cf. 84% in Cynewulf's *Elene* (Marie-Françoise Alamichel, 'La Légende de Sainte Hélène de Cynewulf à Evelyn Waugh', *Études Anglaises* 48 [1995], pp. 306–18, at p. 313).
99 Stopp review in Stannard, ed., p. 330.
100 Sykes, *Evelyn Waugh*, p. 451.

shows the universal power of patriotic feeling and the durable appeal of cultic appropriation. As one reviewer wrote of Waugh's choice of subject-matter, the idea of even a remote British Helena was appealing:

> When one is born British, no matter how long one has been dead, there is always the chance that some British writer, looking through the nation's inexhaustible gallery of unusual characters, will come across one's name and provide it once again with body, spirit, and speech. . . . [T]he British conviction that British character never changes at all furnishes a tool sharper than any generalisation for endowing the dead with life – as long as the dead are British.[101]

In this most extreme form of appropriation, Helena has become a representative of national character, an embodiment of specifically British virtue. Waugh's construction of a Helena who found the Cross because she was British occupies a minor place in the progress of the legend's increasing patriotic resonances; as an example of rhetorical manipulation, it would be difficult to better.

Waugh's was not the last use of the subject in modern times. Just one year after the publication of his *Helena*, the writer of detective fiction and sometime playwright Dorothy L. Sayers wrote a play exploiting the legend for the Colchester Cathedral Festival (part of the Festival of Britain for 1951): *The Emperor Constantine: A Chronicle* (published London, 1951).[102] When she had been asked to write the play, she chose a Christological theme, as she had done for her earlier four plays,[103] and purposefully tied it to Colchester by incorporating the legend of the town's most famous legendary identity, King Cole, and his daughter, Helena. Sayers features Cole far more prominently than Helena in the play, particularly in the opening and closing scenes (in the latter he is a spirit), though both are very much secondary to the chief character of the play, Constantine, as the title indicates.

The focus on Constantine was a deliberate one by Sayers. In one of her published letters, she explains that the Bishop of Colchester had originally wanted a play about Helena, the patron saint of that town, but Sayers had preferred to base the play on Constantine and the Council of Nicaea, through personal choice, but also 'because there didn't seem much to say about Helena, except the story of the Finding of the True Cross – a subject in which I didn't think the average British audience would take much interest'.[104] On the other hand, Sayers co-operates with the town's official plan to commemorate its

---

[101] Governeur Polding, review of *Helena*, *New York Herald Tribune Book Review*, 22 October 1950, p. 6 (in Stannard, ed., pp. 321–3, at p. 321).

[102] Performed at the Playhouse Theatre, Colchester, 3–14 July 1951. It was abbreviated and produced by Sayers herself under a new title reflecting its thematic orientation, *Christ's Emperor*, in London at St Thomas's Church in Regent Street, performed 15–26 February 1952 (Mitzi Brunsdale, *Dorothy L. Sayers: Solving the Mystery of Wickedness* [New York, 1990], p. 192).

[103] William Reynolds, 'Dorothy Sayers and the Drama of Orthodoxy', *As her Whimsey Took Her: Critical Essays on the Work of Dorothy L. Sayers*, ed. M.P. Hannay (Kent, Ohio, 1979), pp. 91–106, at p. 105.

[104] Letter to the Rev. V. James, 19 March 1952 (in Barbara Reynolds, ed., *The Letters of Dorothy L. Sayers* [Cambridge, 2000], pp. 31, 36–9, at p. 36).

patron saint when she transmits the British legend. This choice, like other manipulations of historical stories by the playwright, was not made in ignorance of other competing versions of Helena's biography. In an explicit expression of context-specific appropriation, Sayers says: 'Naturally, the play being for production at Colchester, I chose the tradition more flattering to the Saint and to our country.'[105] Sayers had undertaken some research for the project, but deployed it selectively to fit her plan for a Colchester-based Helena. In a letter, she admits to having followed closely A.H.M. Jones's classic history *Constantine and the Conversion of Europe* (London, 1948), except for Helena's early life.[106]

Sayers was aware that she was transmitting a legend, and that this was part of the play's appeal, which makes no pretence to represent the historical facts of Helena's life:

> But one does not go to Ainsworth for one's history – any more than one would go to my own *The Emperor Constantine* for the historical facts about St. Helena. (Since it was written for Colchester, she *had* to be a British Christian princess, the daughter of King Cole. The local myth is part of the game. Though the theology is sound enough.)[107]

The final, defensive remark about theology encapsulates the real focus of Sayers's long play (three and three quarter hours in performance): the conversion of the Empire and the development of Christian doctrine, particularly during the Council of Nicaea. Helena plays a minor role in this process. When she appears, it is first in a sentimentalised reunion with her former husband Constantius (Act I, Scene 1), and then as a loving mother to her grown son, Constantine (to whom she explains in a 'conscience-stricken' manner his legitimacy and the falsity of claims that she was a barmaid). In Act I, Scene 2, she urges Constantine to marry Fausta, with whom she appears briefly in a few later scenes.

Unlike Waugh, Sayers pays no attention to Helena's spiritual development, as she depicts her as a Christian from birth, a necessary aspect of the British legend adopted for the play. But despite her reference to the story as 'myth', it appears that Sayers at least entertained the possibility that the British legend had some legitimate basis. Somewhat defensively, Sayers believes that 'the modern historians are unkind to the English tradition',[108] and explains her own ideological position in her preface to the printed version of the play: Constantine's mother, she says, was later recognised as a saint, and although early sources refer to her as Constantius's concubine,

---

105   Letter to the Rev. V. James, 19 March 1952 (in Reynolds, ed., pp. 31, 36–9, at pp. 31, 36). In the same letter, Sayers explains that she had to 'take liberties with the baptism scene', admits that she 'invented my own explanation for the killing of Crispus and Fausta', and allowed Helena to use an anachronistic prayer (p. 38).

106   Letter to the Rev. V. James, 21 April 1952 (in Reynolds, ed., pp. 39–41, at p. 39).

107   Letter to Professor H.J. Rose, 11 June 1957 (in Reynolds, ed., pp. 391, 393, at p. 393).

108   Letter to the Rev. V. James, 19 March 1952 (in Reynolds, ed., pp. 31, 36–9, at p. 31).

a barmaid, indeed, from Bithinia, [nevertheless], an ancient and respectable tradition affirms, on the other hand, that she was his lawful wife, a princess of Britain, daughter of the local chieftain 'King' Coel of Colchester. . . . If this is so – and Colchester will hear no word to the contrary – she may well have been a Christian from her birth; for in the 4th century there was already a Christian church, with a Christian bishop, at Colchester.[109]

Mistaking legend for historical possibility, the otherwise well-informed Sayers assumes that a British Helena would have been Christian, a viewpoint which obviates the need for other legends concerned with her Judaism and conversion. Even the *Inventio* is introduced only very briefly in the final scene, excluding the Epilogue: Helena dreams of finding the Cross and begs Constantine for the means of going to Jerusalem, to which he agrees. As implied in earlier sources, the journey is at least in part an act of expiation for the murder of Fausta and Crispus (and others), and represents an outward manifestation of Constantine's acknowledgment of his sin and his need for baptism.

With this quite distinct narrative structure, Sayers would not appear to have been influenced by Waugh's novel.[110] At any rate, her work on the play was well under way by the time his novel was published in 1950,[111] yet it unwittingly shares some features with the novel. Like Waugh's work, hers was personal, ambitious, and critically unsuccessful because it was too theological.[112] But perhaps the theatre-going public responded more positively to her play than the critics appear to have done. Sayers claims in her letters that audiences of the play were enthusiastically appreciative of it, especially the novelty of 'dogma as drama',[113] and Barbara Reynolds, the editor of her published letters, considers the play one of Sayers's 'great achievements'.[114]

109 Dorothy L. Sayers, 'Preface' to *The Emperor Constantine*, p. 7.
110 Sayers makes no mention of Waugh or his novel in her published letters (Reynolds, ed.).
111 Ralph E. Hone, *Dorothy L. Sayers: A Literary Biography* (Kent, Ohio, 1979), p. 172.
112 For the mixed, but primarily unenthusiastic reviews, see Hone, *Dorothy L. Sayers*, pp. 173–4. Sayers's play was not the first drama to feature Constantine. The Restoration dramatist Nathaniel Lee wrote *Constantine the Great: A Tragedy Acted at the Theatre Royal* in 1684 (ed. Walter Häfele [Heidelberg, 1933]). This play focuses on the love intrigue between Fausta and Crispus and probably contains contemporary political resonances of the Popish Plot against Charles II (see Arthur L. Cooke and Thomas B. Stroup, 'The Political Implications in Lee's *Constantine the Great*', *JEGP* 49 [1950], pp. 506–15). Like Sayers's later play, Lee's drama was not a critical success, comprising an uneasy alliance of religious, political, and romantic themes. Although Helena is not a character in the play, it does make a single reference to the British legend in the penultimate couplet; curiously, it cites Britain as the place of Helena's death as well as Constantine's birth: (Constantine): 'And Roman Arts that British Isle adorn/ Where Helena Deceas'd and I was born' (V.2).
113 Letter to Miss P.M. Potter, 19 October 1951 (in Reynolds, ed, p. 22). Sayers remarks, 'I fancy that for most people, the chief fascination lay in hearing, probably for the first time, a purely theological question argued with fire and passion' (Letter to the Editor, *The Church Times*, 25 August 1951 [in Reynolds, ed., pp. 14–15, at p. 15]); and 'I find that all sorts of people to whom theology is a closed book and Nicaea a *terra incognita* were spellbound by the homoöusios debate!' (Letter to Miss P.M. Potter, 19 October 1951 [in Reynolds, ed, p. 22]). Sayers goes so far as to say, 'The only people who, as a body, did not like it were the dramatic critics, who are (if one may say so) a class apart' (Letter to the Editor, *Drama*, 11 June 1952 [in Reynolds, ed., p. 51]).
114 Reynolds, ed., p. 9.

Sayers's *Constantine* represents a return to the much earlier status of Helena as mother of the emperor and facilitator of Christendom's success rather than as a major Christian or national figure in her own right. Indeed, Sayers judged Helena to be a subject unworthy of interest herself when she declined the suggestion that the play be centred on her. Helena's legendary British origins, however, are exploited specifically to suit the intended venue of the play, the Colchester Festival, where 'an ancient and respectable tradition' would be accepted as a reliable version of events. A British Helena is also used as a means of providing the emperor with a Christian rather than a pagan upbringing, an important element in Sayer's scheme. The introduction of King Cole, along with his three fiddlers, however, in a work so profoundly concerned with Christology (the play closes with the Apostles' Creed) is slightly absurd. Sayers has employed the legend seriously, and although her play was not lastingly successful, it does contain a coherent narrative and served its immediate purpose of celebrating Colchester's legendary history. But because it deploys the story almost incidentally and focuses on Constantine and the Council of Nicaea rather than on Helena herself, Dorothy L. Sayers's version of the British Helena legend does not rival Evelyn Waugh's account as the most recent major exploration of the topic.

Conclusion

Evelyn Waugh's Helena is outstanding as the first and only representation to draw an explicit causal connection between her legendary British origins and her success in finding the Cross. In this regard, his is the most extreme deployment of the legend within patriotic discourse. Waugh was working with his own fictional and theological agendas, but the way he embraces and elaborates the portrait of a British Helena illuminates the rhetorical power of this image when it integrates hagiographical and historiographical traditions with floating narrative elements from popular tales. Waugh is also the first redactor of the legend to concentrate on Helena as an individual, independent of her relationship with Constantine, Pope Silvester, Magnus Maximus, or the Cross, though her role in the *Inventio* is a major focus of his novel. Unlike earlier accounts of this event, Waugh creates a fictional depiction of the emotional and spiritual background and impact of this event on his subject. His portrait of Helena's psychological life contrasts sharply with the purely symbolic value of her story in earlier manifestations, and here we can identify variant literary strategies in dealing with the cult of personality: medieval and early-modern writers invoke a range of traditions associated with a name whereas the twentieth-century novelist fashions a psyche for the character. These essential differences between the modern and pre-modern incarnations of the legend underscore its value as a malleable entity: not only its flexibility and applicability to many cultural and generic contexts, but also its capacity for survival despite successive re-creation. Narrative manipulation seems not to have detracted from the successful transmission of the core legendary material, any more than contradictory historical and fictional accounts restricted each other's circulation.

Because the legend underwent so many transformations and participated in several different types of rhetorical agenda throughout its long history, it is more accurate to speak of a cluster of legendary manifestations than a singular narrative entity. Similarly, because the biography, character, and achievements of Helena were created, transformed, and manipulated according to authorial and traditional impulses, we are not dealing with a singular figure, but rather with a series of representations and constructions generated from a central idea with variations in shape and texture. A British Helena was a concept, formed and reformed for rhetorical exploitation and dependent upon the changing shape of ecclesiastical association, political affiliations, and popular imagination. The value of this kind of study exists in whatever information we can ascertain about the shaping influences of the legend, both extrinsic and intrinsic. The benefit of examining the development of a core idea throughout cultures, texts, and traditions lies in the rhetorical information which the comparison of texts, documents, artistic representations, and popular culture provide. Geoffrey of Monmouth's secular agenda and promotion of Arthur are as evident from his treatment of Helena as Camden's and Morant's patriotic hopefulness is from theirs. Similarly, the inclusion of the subject's aristocratic status, first in Altmann's *vita* and later in subsequent hagiographic accounts, owes its existence to textual expectations and the interaction between the medieval genres of hagiography, romance, and historical fiction. The attraction of Magnus Maximus into the legend in the Welsh context is a further demonstration of the agglutinative power of traditional legends, particularly those concerned with national identity: as with myths of Constantine and the cult of St Silvester, Welsh legends treating Magnus Maximus both derive power from coalescence with the British Helena legend and contribute force to the host story.

The participation of non-literary sources in the transmission and adaptation of the legend demonstrates the mutual influences of the textual tradition and popular culture. Helena's popularity as a dedicatory saint in England, her relatively frequent appearances in visual art and the persistency of the British legend in local mythology indicate the force of traditional belief in popular imagination and its power to outlive textual incarnations. Specifically, the acknowledgment of viable folk belief lies behind the offhand or brief references to the legend in written sources, providing the legitimating background to claimed ideas and the shared pool of concepts to which the text is referring. Because non-literary reminders of Helena's identity and occasionally of her alleged British origins would have reached a far wider audience than written sources, especially those in Latin, and also usually survived in more durable media, they created a more constant and unvarying form of the legend.

In all the extant versions of the legend, Helena is a symbolic figure, either an ancestral heavyweight in a politically motivated genealogy, a challenging Jewish proselyte for Silvester to convert, or a link between Britain and Rome. Not surprisingly, within *vitae* dedicated to celebrating her status as a saint, she is described in conventional and symbolic language, just as she is depicted in standard iconography, with the Cross and/or Constantine in visual art. Helena's possession of readily identifiable attributes most clearly demonstrates her value as a manipulable figure to be re-created as the context demanded. Once a range of associations surrounding her name had been established, selections from the list could be made and developed at will, and further resonances could be contributed throughout this process, as the narrative witnesses to the legend demonstrate. As the two texts produced in the appendices below show, the British legend was invoked even if was not developed or stressed. The references to Helena's British birth near the beginnings of both Jocelin's *vita* and the Middle English *St Elyn* demonstrate that the legend had become part of her identifying credentials, distinguishing her from other saints of the same name and Helen of Troy, and needing no explanation or defence. Similarly, her British birth was early and consistently cited in the context of her newly acquired aristo-cratic status and virtuous nature, suggesting a close connection between these attributes: nationality is character in this rhetorical scheme, just as hagiography can be romance.

This study, which has concentrated on textual incarnations of the Helena legend, indicates clearly that the story existed (and probably pre-existed) in non-written contexts, and continued to survive and develop in oral form, as well as in various artistic media. The success of the legend and the variety of its manifestations owed as much to floating oral traditions as to the learned, scribal culture of the Middle Ages and Early Modern period. We all know of Old King Cole, but seldom read about him. Similarly, the cult of the saints and local attempts to claim Helena relied on non-written means of communication which readily and constantly changed the legend. The organic life of the legend in these contexts was crucially dependent, therefore, on its immediate relevance as an idea to the local populace, either on a narrative or spiritual level. The fluid transformations of the details demonstrate that this referentiality determined the shape of the legend as well as its viability in a given context. The local connec-tion was important for this model, because the matter of spiritual or national identification was part of the rhetorical agenda across a range of genres in which the British legend was invoked. Helena was presented as a local patron or national heroine specifically for the domestic audience of these texts who would be less likely than external readers or hearers to question the motives for adopting her as a native. The local documentation of an individual's biography made the appropriation of saints so easy to achieve because texts and legends were produced for the local community and external scrutiny was rarely exer-cised.

Despite this local power over the livelihood of the legend, Helena was constructed as a carrier of national identity for well over a millennium precisely because her fame was international. As the finder of the True Cross, Helena appealed to the Christian community as a whole, rather than to a group defined by national boundaries or a singular ethnic identity, and it was this wider fame which made the appropriation of her by British writers and artists so attractive. The hagiographic tradition itself, with its focus on the local associations of the saint, facilitated the emphasis on this aspect of her biography, which already existed in other contexts. Similarly, the cult of relics and saintly patronage ensured a strong interest in local connections and material evidence which were also being established in other quarters. Even the competing claims for her as a local patron must have enhanced her fame and provided added symbolic signifi-cance to her name in individual locations as well as confirming her more general value as a patron.

Helena was a prime candidate for multiple appropriations because she was initially well known as an auxiliary figure in an established feast day. Although her role in the Christian Church was first as the agent in the finding of the Cross, and her acknowledgment as a British saint was a long, slow process, Helena's renown in one context ensured her desirability in the other. Her initial role as *Inventrix* also meant that national connections had not been established early in her hagiographical career, so her ethnic origins could be refashioned according to need. Like Trier, York attempted to secure Helena as a local patron in the same manner as a diocese would any prominent saint with whom an association could be established. The cult of saints thrived on this sort of local connection. Indeed, the Gallic efforts to link her with Trier, even though they were ultimately unconvincing in the wider religious sphere, at least brought her birthplace to the West, and promoted her life into the hagiographic agenda. It also provided a dynamic context in which the British appropriation occurred, according to the same logic which enhanced the value of relics which were known to have been stolen.

It seems, though, that the idea of Helena as a British princess appealed, at least initially, outside the religious context, purely because her other role, as mother of Constantine I, brought an imperial connection to Britain, and thereby provided the legend with a nationalistic dimension. When Geoffrey of Monmouth and others expanded the legend, it was for the purpose of providing an imperial link with Rome (as Henry VIII did in 1533), without mentioning the Cross. This freedom from *Inventio* associations was the decisive move in establishing Helena's own identity within historiographical tradition. It also, however, raised her profile as a saint in her own right, for it is only well after her secular fame that she came to be included in saints' calendars and liturgical documents. Jocelin of Furness unconsciously records this marriage of the secular and the sacred biographies of Helena when he recounts the Cole legend within his *Vita sancte Helene*, as well as transmitting the *Inventio*, Constantine, and Silvester legends. His text illustrates the legitimation of Geoffrey of Monmouth's romance narrative, as well as Helena's liberation from subservience to the *Inventio*, even though it is still an important part of her story.

Helena's legendary biography enjoyed wider currency than is afforded most saints, in both oral and scribal cultures, secular and ecclesiastical texts, in the vernacular as well as in Latin. This coverage of both the popular and learned audiences throughout the Middle Ages and Early Modern period ensured that most people had heard of the legend, even if it was not known in detail or necessarily believed. Such wide dissemination allowed the story to assume the force of tradition and acquire and retain a legitimacy beyond fact or reason. But the legend did not develop and change as the result of any internal dynamic; it was consciously shaped and used by writers and others invoking it who wished to claim either a glorious past for Britain, an imperial connection with the Roman Empire, or a direct national association with the discovery of the most important Christian relic. The patriotic impulse is present in each of these groups, indicating that Helena was a vector of national identity for a particularly wide range of sacred and secular texts of propaganda in which her claims to fame took on vacillating priorities, but the value of her association remained a constant feature.

Helena could do as much for secular Britain as for its ecclesiastical establishment, and she provided a pseudo-link with Rome for English writers for 600 years, most notably in the two centuries prior to the discreditation of the legend by Gibbon in 1776. The legend's longevity was probably ensured by the sheer number of places in which it had been invoked visually, cited textually in chronicles, histories, literary texts, and church offices, and by the popularity and established status of some of these texts (especially Geoffrey's *Historia*; the Middle English Prose *Brut*; and Higden's *Polychronicon*). This broad rhetorical value thrived on reconfiguration to suit immediate needs. Even in comparatively recent times, the legend survived because it remained useful. The British legend was invoked during the sixteenth to eighteenth centuries because it continued to fulfil a patriotic role, but when it came to be examined in detail under the rigours of humanist scholarship its plausibility was challenged and finally defeated. Its force as a tradition, however, ensured its livelihood beyond this time, until changing political and cultural circumstances in England rendered its appeal irrelevant. When it became less compelling in early-modern times to construct national identity or situate local pride upon the appropriation of an imperial or hagiographical connection, a British Helena was no longer a useful idea. Indeed, the legend's livelihood had been less than vigorous for some time prior to this, owing to a number of factors. In the ecclesiastical context, visual representations with their frequent inclusion of the Cross, or Constantine, or both symbolically depict Helena's subordinate role to these larger forces in Christian history and almost never transmit the British legend. Even the 20 panels of stained glass depicting Helena's life and British origins at Ashton-under-Lyne were insufficient safeguard against rededication, which occurred in the fifteenth century. The lost ground of her late and lukewarm acceptance into saints' calendars was never recovered. This evidence for the declining interest in Helena in the ecclesiastical context confirms that despite the wide range of fora in which the legend was adapted and transmitted, its momentum was checked by only selective invocation, to the subordination of this story to other cycles of legends and ultimately to external forces such as the declining currency of saints' legends after the Reformation and the scrutiny of humanist scholarship. Nevertheless, that the legend flourished in a variety of contexts, and for so long, attests to its appeal and flexibility, and explains why the fictionality of a British Helena was difficult to accept and harder to relinquish completely.

Throughout the long career of the British legend, Helena was configured as a persona bestowing glory (either patriotic or religious) by association. As a fact, her British nationality was difficult to disprove in view of the scarcity of documents concerning her life and the growing temporal distance from her actual lifetime. As an idea, her nationality developed a life of its own, a cultic status in both secular and religious contexts. The conjunction of these twin roles in a single personage was rare, if not unique (St Joan of Arc might be comparable on some points), and was to ensure the longevity of Helena's fame beyond that of her once more famous son, Constantine, especially as the cult of the Cross and her role in the *Inventio* grew in significance and facilitated the development of her own comparatively minor hagiographic tradition. This secondary role to Constantine, Silvester, and the Cross is found also in historical and documentary sources, as well as visual representations, where Helena's legendary identity and circumstances are invoked briefly, but usually not elaborated upon.

The various representations of Helena as the mother of a British emperor, romance heroine, Colcestrian princess, dowager empress, pilgrim, church builder, saint, and patron, provided a multifaceted flexibility to her image which enhanced its rhetorical usefulness. As a relatively minor saint and historical figure beyond the *Inventio* context, she could be shifted in and out of view in different constructions in a way unavailable to more independently central figures. Her greatest attribute as a local representative lay in the vagueness of her actual history. As for other national saintly heroes, such as St Patrick and St George, the legendary ingredient is the major part of identity, precisely because it is the core component around which other details can be shaped and continually refashioned according to immediate need.

The Appendices

Appendix 1 and Appendix 2 contain transcriptions of two previously unpublished narratives concerning St Helena. The first is a long Latin prose *vita* of St Helena by Jocelin of Furness, the early-thirteenth-century writer of a well-known *Vita sancti Patricii* and other hagiographies. The second transcribed text is a short, anonymous poetic treatment of her biography from three manuscripts of the *South English Legendary*, a thirteenth-century collection of versified saints' lives in Middle English. These texts are made available here both as witnesses of the popularity and diversity of legendary accounts of Helena in the central Middle Ages, and also to demonstrate the degree to which her story became bound up with those of her son, Constantine, and his legendary baptizer, Pope Silvester. Because their prime value in this context is their existence and their narrative content, the following transcriptions are conservative. Editorial emendation has been kept to a minimum to reproduce as close as possible the way the texts read in the original manuscripts.

Appendix 1

The *Vita sancte Helene* of Jocelin of Furness
(Cambridge, Corpus Christi College, MS 252)

Introductory Comments

On Jocelin of Furness, hagiographer in the late twelfth and early thirteenth centuries, see above, pp. 98–9.

This two-part, long prose text of over 11,000 words, including *vita* and *translatio*, is extant in three manuscripts:

- (C) Cambridge, Corpus Christi College, MS 252, fols 166v–183v;
- (Go) Gotha, Forschungs- und Landesbibliothek, MS Memb. I 81, fols 203r–213v; and
- (B) Oxford, Bodleian Library, MS Bodley 240, pp. 801a–804b and 808a–808b.

The first two are complete, but B contains a highly abbreviated version of the first half of the text only. B follows the main text in summary form to line 502, then adds two brief sections which do not advance the narrative but reiterate some earlier material. The first addition, provided below in full in the note to line 502, is unsourced and recounts the circumstances of Constantine's birth in Britain and later elevation there as caesar. The second addition is not provided below, as it is a very close rendering of the paragraph of the *Legenda aurea* from which it is explicitly sourced; this extract recounts Constantine's vision, conversion, and baptism.[1] Between this material and the *translatio*, B includes some unrelated extracts from the sermons of Haymo of Faversham and other similar items. B rejoins the text contained in C and Go for the translation of Helena's remains, but in a very brief fashion.

All three manuscripts were produced in the fourteenth century: C probably in the first half, Go in the second, and B in 1377. All are compilations of religious material.

The main text is previously unpublished, but an edition of the much shorter final section, *de translacione ipsius*, from the Gotha MS (rather than C as below) is: P. Grosjean, 'De codice hagiographico Gothano', *Analecta Bollandiana* 58 (1940), pp. 199–203.

---

[1] The extract is from Ch. 58 of Jacobus de Voragine, *Legenda aurea*, 'De inventione sanctae crucis', ed. T. Graesse, 2 vols (Dresden, 1890; repr. Osnabrück, 1969), I.305; Engl. trans. *The Golden Legend: Readings on the Saints*, W.G. Ryan, 2 vols (Princeton, 1993), I.279.

Appendix 1

C has been chosen as the base text because it is the earliest and least corrupt version (and see further below).

Transcription

This transcription, published with the kind permission of Master and Fellows, Corpus Christi College, Cambridge, is based on the text at CCCC MS 252, fols 166v–183v. Textual emendation has been kept to a minimum, though modern conventions of punctuation and capitalisation have been adopted. Manuscript orthography has been retained, including the distribution of *u/v*. Regular abbreviations have been silently expanded, and corrections, expunctions, and interlinear insertions have been included without comment. Rubrics are shown in italics. Several readings are supplied from the other witness of the longer version of the legend, Gotha, Forschungs- und Landesbibliothek, MS Memb. I 81, fols 203r–213v, where required, and occasionally, other editorial emendations are made. The following conventions are used:

<. . .> = words or letters omitted by C and supplied by Go, or when
       Go reading preferred
      (note in apparatus if the latter is the case)
[. . .] = words or letters in C which should be omitted
(. . .) = words or letters which have been supplied editorially

The later MS, Go, shows minor reworking and some elaborations on the text as it appears in C (itself corrected by a later hand), suggesting that the two extant versions stem from different exemplars. Major additions in Go are provided in the notes. Variant readings which constitute a possible improvement or significant alternative to the base text are recorded in the apparatus, as are the base text readings when the Go reading has been substituted. Minor variations of tense and number or word transpositions and unimportant spelling variations are not noted. Because B is so heavily abbreviated, variations from it are noted only rarely to support a variant reading from Go, with which it has more in common than C.

The aim of this edition is to provide an accurate and readable version of Jocelin's text as preserved in MS C. For ease of reference to this long text, the rubrics are listed below, in translation, with corresponding line numbers. This cue has been taken from MS Go, where the headings are listed prior to the text on fol. 203.

Line Nos	Sectional Headings
1–46	Here begins the Prologue to the Life of St Helena
47–96	Here ends the Prologue and here begins the Life
97–113	How Coel won a kingdom
114–130	How Helena bore Constantine
131–155	Helena is made Empress

Vita sancte Helene

Incipit prologus in uitam sancte Helene

Licet protoparentalis preuaricacio perniciose proscripserit posteritatem suam in huius mundi uallem tenebrosam, clementissimus tamen conditor candor lucis eterne qui iussit de tenebris lumen splendescere de ipsa massa proscripte
5 propaginis produxit plures personas utriusque sexus, quasi quedam luminaria ad cecitatis humane caliginem abigendam. Non solum patriarche ante legem aut

prophete aut ceteri iusti sub lege fide meritis et presagiis signis prodigiis noctem
mortalitatis nostre illustrarunt, uerum eciam mulieres uirtutum uidelicet
patriarchales et prophetales matrone sapiencie et sanctitatis iubare mundo
10 prefulserunt. Et ne illarum nomina silencio uideamur omnino suppre<s>sisse,
quasdam earum uidelicet: Saram, Rebeccam, Rachaelem, Deboram, Ruth,
Iudith, Hester, et Euangelicas, Elizabeth et Annam prophetissas, congruum
dicimus commemorare. Ex quo enim oriens ex uespere candor lucis ex leui nube
sol iusticie processit ex sydere, totum mundum induit sui calore et claritate.
15 Radiantibus namque signis et uirtutibus eius in omnem terram omne genus
hominum omnis etas omnis sexus omnis condicio ambulabat in eius lumine nec
fuit qui se posset abscondere a calore eius. Innumera plana multitudo non solum
uirorum forcium uerum eciam mulierum et tenerarum uirginum ac
decrepitarum uetularum quelibet tormentorum et morcium genera pro eius
20 nomine tollerauerunt, innumera utriusque sexus in pace sancte ecclesie uicia
uincentes uictimas <uiuentes>[a] diutino martyrio sese ipsi domino exhibuerunt.
Ex tunc filie regum delectauerunt in honore eius et regine in uestitu deaurato
circumdate uarietate diuiciarum et deliciarum affluenciam et <imperii> terreni
fastigium fastidientes mundialem pompam et gloriam cordis calce calcauerunt
25 pre amore eius. Inter quas immo super quas quadam meritorum prerogatiua
predicabilis sancta Helena <Constantini> Augusti mater eminet et enitet ut illam
singularem Christiane fidei propagatricem et propugnatricem ecclesia
sanctorum merito predicet. Regaliter namque nata regaliter nupta su<b>limis[b] in
terreno imperio cogitacione et auiditate studuit sategitque regi regum
30 complacere Christo. Non enim thorus thronusue regis ab amore altitroni tonantis
animum eius auertit sed pocius potestatis imperialis insigne ad gloriam Dei et
innumerabilium (167r) commune commodum conuertit. Huius gesta clarissima
in diuersis historiis ecclesiasticis et cronicis catholicis sparsim strictimque
pocius tanguntur quam describuntur et nescio a quo forma nimis <informi>[c]
35 confuse collecta referuntur. In quodam eciam libello anglice dictato eius uita
seriatim dictatur cuius auctor illum de Britannico sermone in anglicum
transtulisse se testatur. De quibus omnibus quelibet fide digna racioni consona
edificacioni congrua sedit animo diligenter colligere et collecta in unum
opusculum redigere et ad laudem Dei et honorem eiusdem sancte regine
40 commune commodum legencium stilo licet pedestri ueraci tamen posteris
transmittere. Et quamuis ad hoc agendum incitauerit me propria erga sanctam
merito concepta deuocio, uenerabilium tamen et religiosarum personarum
propellor precibus <que>[d] ad titulum sancte Elene sub regulari iugo Christi
mancipantur obsequio. Siquis ob hoc dente uenenato me mordere studuerit et
45 temptauerit attramentare atris labiis laborem meum eciam me tacente habet qui
iudicet eum.

[a] uiuentes (Go)] imminentes C   [b] sublimis (GoB)] sullimis C   [c] informi (GoB)] informa C   [d] que
(GoB)] qui C

Explicit prologus, incipit vita

Temporibus Dyocleciani et Maximiani Augustorum[2] dominabatur dux
quidam illustris Coel[3] nomine quem Anglia uocant Cole sue lingue idiomate in
50 orientalibus finibus Britannie. Ex patre Britano ortus secundum maternam
prosapiam genus duxerat ex illustri stemate Triuirorim <qui>[e] quondam urbem
insignem condiderant et a suo nomine Triuerum cognominabant. Hic eciam
ciuitatem construxerat temporis egregiam quem usque in presens patriote
uocitant ex eius nomine Colecestriam. Puellam quoque genere ac specie
55 clarissimam sororem trium magnatum Britannie in matrimonium duxit, ex qua
tantum unam sobolem unicam scilicet filiam suscepit, quam Elenam uocari
fecit. Cum autem uirago uenerabilis annos habiles ad discendum attigisset,
traditur a patre magistris litteris inbuenda ac <matronis>[f] honestis bonis
moribus instituenda. Ipsa uero ita proficiebat in studiis litterarum ut aliquanto
60 tempore emerso pectus eius liberalium arcium uideretur esse gignasium. In
musicis eciam instrumentis et cantilenis componendis et canendis supra omnes
patriotas et peregrinos magistra dicebatur inconperabilis. Erat optimis adornata
moribus et ultra quam etas (167v) illa exigebat, multimodis studebat exercendis
et adipiscendis uirtutibus. Fuit humilis et pudica, prudens, simplex et pacifica,
65 liberalis atque faceta, cunctis amabilis ac preciosa. Sed licet sedes suas in illa
collocauerat istarum uirtutum conuentus aut ceterarum similium, miseracio erga
pauperes et afflictos munifica speciale sic construxit in ea domicilium ut
tantummodo nata putaretur ad illius solius uirtutis obsequium usum et
exercitium. Unde et ex sentencia dicere potuit quod beatus Iob in sua persona
70 suisque sequacibus dixit, 'Quia mecum creuit miseracio et ex utero egressa est
mecum.'[4] Nondum salutare suscepit dupplici de causa lauacrum; repensabat
tamen quendam sacri baptismatis in bonorum operum exercitiis candidatum.
Primo quia Dyocleciana persecucio per totum orbem deseuit et multas legiones
martirum celis nolens inuexit et in Britannia sicut et in mundi partibus ceteris
75 purpuratis innumeris, sacro sanguine Christianam legem ex magna parte deleuit.
Secundo quia necdum mos inoleuit in illa ut paruuli mox nati passim
baptizarentur. Sed pocius prestolarentur intelligibiles annos nisi mortis articulo
urgente illud munus gratie expetentes consequerentur. Illustris tamen Helena
cathecumina effecta secundum posse suum et patris permissum pauperibus,
80 peregrinis, uiduis et orphanis ac infirmis beneficia multa prestabat; eis
stabulum, hoc est hospicium diuertendi ac manendi quasi xenodochium in etate

---

[e] qui (GoB)] que C   [f] matronis (Go)] racionis C

2   The tetrarchy, formed in 293, consisted of Diocletian as Augustus in the West, with Galerius as his
    Caesar, and Maximianus as Augustus in the East, with Constantius Chlorus (father of Constantine)
    his Caesar.
3   The dates do not fit, as the legendary character King Cole allegedly flourished in the fifth century
    (see above, p. 65).
4   Job 31.18.

adhuc puellari preparari fecerat. Pater eius alia sobole caruit et ideo quicquid ab eo postulauit facilius impetrauit. Preterea tocius pulcritudinis in illius forma, statura, membrorum habitudine, dispensacione, colore confluxerat coagulum ut
85 merito indicaretur nature miraculum ac uirorum spectaculum. Et quamuis pulcritudo muliebris multis multociens causa fuerit ruine uel mortis, illius tamen decor utriusque (sexus)[g] uite materiam ministrabat innumeris. Species enim Helene abducte de Grecia origo fuit et incentiuum Troiane submersionis, huius Helene de Britannia nate decor innumeris extitit ad Christum causa
90 conuersionis. Decore Iudith[5] Holofernes <illectus>[h] cum exercitu suo disperiit; populus Israel ab iminente morte liberatus, cesis hostibus, cum spoliis multis collectis ad propria rediit. Pulcritudo nicholominus Hester[6] Deo disponente fuit (168r) excepcionis materia plebis Israeletice. Helene nostre decor occasionem prebuit promocioni Christiane fidei, ecclesie Dei exaltacioni, ydolatrie
95 euacuacioni, Iudaice secte depressioni, plurimarum heresium <eliminacioni>[i]. Quod qualiter euenerit sequens nostra narracio declarabit.

Quomodo Coel regnum adquisierit
    In diebis illis Ascelepiodotus[7] Allectum regem interfecit et <s>ceptrum Britannie suscepit[j] tributum <Romanis>[k] reddere contempsit. Huius autem post
100 aliquot tempus regnantis dux Coel prefatus iniuriis et grauaminibus lacessitus rebellauit, tandemque marcium campum aduersus eum ingressus uictum uita regem expolians regni solium ascendit. Per idem tempus Constancius senator a Dyocleciano et Maximiano in consorcium et aminiculum imperatorie dignitatis regende promotus, data sibi in coniugium Theodora Maximiani filia, Gallias et
105 Hispannias, totam eciam terram circa alpes regebat; Germanniam aliquam rebellem strenue debellans sibi subiugauit. In Uenstria ciuitatem construxit quam a nomine suo Constanciam denominauit. Audiens autem Asclepiodocum Romano resistentem imperio sublatum <esse>[l] de medio gauisus est gaudio magno: collectis undecumque copiis Britanniam intrauit in multitudine graui ut
110 eam sue subiugaret potestati. Audiens rex Coel famam uirtutis et prudencie eius ueritusque a facie eius pacem cum eo composuit, consuetumque tributum se persoluturum paciens Romanis sub eo regnum tenuit. Expleto adhuc uno mense Coel in fata concessit, ipsique Constancius prenominatus in regnum successit.

---

g sexus] hominis CGo   h illectus (Go)] electus C   i eliminacioni (Go)] illiminacioni C

5 The apocryphal Old Testament Book of Judith recounts the story of the beautiful heroine's decapitation of the general besieging her town. Because the book was a part of Jerome's Vulgate, the Anglo-Saxons regarded it as canonical, and the story is the basis of an Old English poem of the same name (ed. E.V.K. Dobbie, *Beowulf and Judith*, ASPR IV [New York, 1953], pp. 99–109).
6 Like Judith, Esther was renowned for her beauty: see the Old Testament book of Esther and additions in the Apocrypha.
7 Historically, he was Constantius's praetorian prefect, who in 296 recovered Britain from Allectus (finance minister and assassin of the self-proclaimed emperor Carausius in Britain).

Qualiter Helena Constantinum genuerit

115   Cernens filia regis parentibus orbata fortune rotam uersatilem inferius se deprimere timuit sibi ne ab aliquo dispendium castitatis sustineret ignobili. Abiecto sibi cultu preciosarum uestium uultus uenustatem uelaminis abieccionis obiectu <obnubilauit>[m], assumptoque ancillari famulatu in quodam senodochio uelud stabularia effecta pauperibus, peregrinis et infirmis ministrauit. Bona
120 prorsus stabularia que illi samaritano placere sategit qui uulneratum a latronibus in humero suo <inposuit>[n] et in stabulum curandum adduxit. Ipse uero uersa uice illam de stabulo ad imperium prouexit qui de stercore pauperem ut sedeat cum principibus[o] et solium glorie teneat, erigere consueuit. Et quoniam fama uolatilis nomen uirginis et (168v) urbanitatem <et> pulcritudinem circumcirca
125 diffuderat, decorem eius Constancius concupierat. Ex ipsius ergo iussu puella queritur, quesita in stabulo demum inuenitur, inuenta ad regem adducitur, adducta ab eo cognoscitur, cognita grauidatur, grauida in <partum>[p] uirilis sexus absoluitur puerque Constantinus nuncupatur. Post hec teste sancto Ambrosio[8] nomen insigne imperatoris accepit, nam antea senatoris et rectoris
130 officium gessit.

Qualiter Helena imperatrix effecta fuerit

Post aliquod temporis spacium euolutum audiens Constancius Cole fatale munus persoluisse propriam coniugem uenerabilem Helenam[9] in uxorem duxit. Ipsa uero imperatrix effecta, humilitate ac deuocione morumque suauitate et
135 uirtutum studiis nouam Hester immo sublimiorem semet exhibuit quia non uni genti scilicet Iudeorum sicut Hester, sed pluribus regnis et gentibus occidentalis imperii ad salutem utriusque hominis profuit. In orbe orientali, principantibus Dyocliciano uel Maximiano siue Maxencio,[10] inualuerunt tenebre perse-cucionis, proscripcionis, suppliciorum et mortium genera multimoda; in orbis
140 occidui imperio regnante Constancio elegantis Helene instancia tribubus populis et linguis et maxime Christiane fidei professoribus <indulsit>[q] serenitas pacis et quietis, obuiauerunt misericordia et iusticia, arrisit rerum habundancia. Iterato igitur fetu regina concepit et peperit filiam quam Constanciam nominauit et ulterius a procreanda prole cessauit. Erat autem isdem Constancius, homo
145 magne mansuetudinis et tocius humilitatis qui et ortatu Helene regine moderate et modeste se habens seruos Christi ualde uenerabatur[11] ita ut multis occulte quod Christianus esset diceretur. Et uere dignum et iustum ut de bona radice

---

[j] suscepit] optinens Go   [k] Romanis (Go)] racionis C   [l] esse (Go)] est C (*expuncted*)   [m] obnubilauit (Go)] obnubulauit C   [n] inposuit (Go)] imposito C   [o] cum principibus] cum principibus populi Go
[p] partum (Go)] partium C   [q] indulsit (Go)] infulsit C

[8] Jocelin is referring to Ambrose's *De obitu Theodosii*, a sermon delivered in 395, on which see above, p. 20. Jocelin uses Ambrose's well-known epithet of Helena, 'bona stabularia', on lines 119–20.
[9] Go adds: 'Tum ob incomperabilem decorem tum ob uis paterne hereditatis'.
[10] Maxentius, son of Maximianus, was defeated by Constantine at the Battle of the Milvian Bridge in 312 (see below, lines 184 ff.).
[11] Go omits text from this point up to and including 'iusticiam' (line 170).

surculus optimus progrederetur et de bonis parentibus optima soboles
nasceretur. Cum autem Constancius, cisalpinum imperium gubernando,
150 diuersas regiones sepius peragraret, ad ciuitatem Treuerim diuertit illamque
regine tamquam ius hereditarium a proauis deuolutum plenarie contulit.
Construxit uero ibi mirandi operis pallacium marmorium quod dedit uenerande
Helene declinandum cum uenisset ad locum. Super omnia regna terrarum
Britanniam dilexit. Unde et in ea plus quam in aliis regionibus commorari
155 consueuit.

De obitu Constancii et regimine Helene et regno Constantini
   (169r) Creuit puer bone indolis Constantinus Deo carus et hominibus traditur
tempore oportuno litteris inbuendis. Ipse uero ualde profecit in breui in
litteraturum sciencia unccione magistra. Cum autem duodenis esset ultra alpes
160 destinatur a patre obsequiis assisturus Dyocleciani cesaris causa sapiencie
secularis et urbanitatis. Perpendens Dyoclecianus in adolescentulo Christiane
religionis culturam cum etate pubescere moliebatur illum de terra delere. Quod
puer Constantinus conpariens machinamenta filii Belial protectore Deo
beneficio fuge declinauit et ad patrem reuersus suos omnes suo reditu
165 letificauit. Post hec Constancius quintodecimo anno imperii sui in ciuitate
Britannie Choracho uiuendi metas posuit, ibique in uentrem matris omnium
ingressus Constantinum filium adhuc adoloscentulum, sub custodia constitutum
sapientissime matris eius Helene, heredem regni reliquid. Miro moderamine
pacis et quietis illustris Helena, regnum Britannie gubernabat, faciensque
170 iudicium et iusticiam in terra intus et in circuitu pacem et omnium rerum
habundancium habebat. Metropolim regni scilicet Lundonias muro
quodammodo inexpugnabili et alias per plures circumcinxit, in super et
Colecestriam in qua et ipsa nata fuit et Constantinum postmodum peperit
pulcherrimis meniis adornauit. Processu temporis Constantinus sapienciam et
175 fortitudinem induit, leoninam feri<t>atem cum agnina mansuetudine exhibit.
Seuiciam predonum nequiciam latronum exterminabat, et in legum
transgressorum tyrannide<m> grauiter uindicabat. Bonos et iustos amabat et
exaltabat; prauos et pessimos seu proditores deprimebat aut a terra delebat,
sapientissime namque matris consiliis optimis obsecundans. Hec omnia faciens
180 post factum non penitebat sed in cunctis prospere agebat. Non enim natal(is)[r]
solummodo Britannia, uerum eciam Gallia, Hispannia, Germania tota illi sponte
subdiderant propter ueritatem et mansuetudinem et iusticiam quam in illo
mirabiliter uigere cognouerant.

Qualiter Constantinus de Britannia aduersus Maxencium profectus fuerit
185   In diebus illis Maxencius malignissimus imperium orientale susceperat qui
totus ydolatrie deditus et omnibus uiciis ac flagiciis plenus eciam nature iura

---

[r] natalis] natale CGo

exuens proprium patrem a Roma turpiter expulerat. Hic inmanissimus Christianorum (169v) persecutor extiterat et innumeros utriusque sexus pro fide Christi perimens ad celos inui[c]tus[s] transmiserat. Inter quos beatissima uirgo
190 Katerina, uelud margarita celica, fulgebatur, que post multiplices agones antequam decollaretur ipsum tyrannum nefandissimum a Christicola scilicet Constantino perimendum spiritu sancto edocta predicebat. Cum enim idem prophanus multos illustrium Romanorum facultatibus denudasset uel exheredasset uel ex illo dampnasset, ad Constantinum tamquam singulare
195 refugium confugiebant, ipsumque lacrimis et precibus consiliis et monitis ad ipsos uindicandum et imperium sibi iuste iudicandum[t] efficaciter inducebant. Iustus dominus concidens ceruices peccatorum, uolens uindicare sanguinem seruorum suorum qui effusus est super terram per Maxencium, excitauit Constantinum aduersarium sibi ob imperium de manu eius auferendum.
200 Electam uero miliciam de Britannia ceterisque regnis in orientali imperio sibi subiectis collegerat transcensisque alpibus, magis munitus animi deuocione quam armis bellicis cum exercitu suo Rome iam ap<p>roximabat. Prefecerat exercitui suo disponendo tres uiros sapientes et strenuos: Ioelinum uidelicet et Traherinum ac Marinum matris sue auunculos.[12] Mater uero cum Constancia
205 filia sua filium comitabatur ut si non manu saltem consiliis et orationibus auxiliaretur.

De uisione Sancte Crucis et interitu Maxencii et uictoria Constantini
   Cumque castra collocasset, Constantinus non longius ab urbe et de im<m>inente progressu tractasset in corde, uidit in uisu noctis uexillum Sancte Crucis in celo
210 flammeo colore rutilare audiuitque angelos dicentes, 'Constantine, in hoc uince!' Euigilans signum illud uite atque uictorie in arma militaria fecit depingi et imperiale uexillum quod <Labarum>[u] nominatur in speciem crucis transformari. Ipse uero crucem de auro fabrefactam in manu portabat et confidens in adiutorio altissimi tropheum sibi iam adesse <presentiebat>[v].
215 Monebatur animo attenciusque Deum exorabat ne in ipsius solius occasione plurimorum sanguis <funderetur ne>[w] gestacione signi salutaris sanctificata manus eius Romano cruore macularetur. Votis ergo deuotis iustisque postulacionibus pii principis propicia diuinit<a>s fauit miroque modo sine congressione uictoriam ministrauit. Maxencius ut audiuit Constantini aduentum
220 causa congrediendi innumerabilem undecumque congregauit exercitum. (170r) Iusserat nichilominus <isdem>[x] uersutus iuxta pontem Molini fluuii nauium copia consterni tabulisque superpositis immo dolose quasi dolatis atque dispositis diuisibilem atque fallacem pontem constructum et non solido ponti exequari. Hoc ideo gessit ut Constantinum uel eius exercitum irruentem pons

[s] inuitus (GoB)] inuictus C   [t] iudicandum] vendicandum Go   [u] Labarum (Go)] Labatum C
[v] presentiebat (Go)] presentabat C   [w] funderetur ne (Go)] ne C (*expuncted*)   [x] isdem (Go)] isolem C

[12]   Cf. Geoffrey of Monmouth, *Historia regum Britannie*, §79, and Laȝamon's *Brut*, line 5562.

225 fragilis et falsus exciperet, ac super se gradientes repentina sui dissolucione in
profundum dimergeret. Sed teste scriptura non est sapiencia, non est prudencia,
non est consilium contra dominum, nec illa humana uersucia poterit euadere
districtum eius iudicium. Maxencius namque uir Belial quasi quibusdam furiis
agitatus immo diuino iudicio condempnatus [eum] cum quibusdam satellitibus
230 ex urbis Rome portis preuius exercitus corruit^y oblitusque machinamenti sui
pertuleranti equo incidens deceptorium fictitum pontem prefatum inequitauit.
Pons illico nauibus pondere^z inequitancium subsidentibus, dissolutis tabulis,
dissipatur homoque Deo inuisus cum suis equitibus quasi plumbum in aquis
uehe<me>ntibus submergitur. Iuxta psalmiste uocem, de talibus dicentem,
235 lacum aperuit et effodit eum et incidit in foueam quam fecit. Maledixit dominus
<s>ceptris eius, capiti bellatorum eius, Maxencium uero uelud alterum
pharaonem cum curribus dominus proiecit in mari; adiutor et protector factus est
Constantini serui sui. Illius ergo hominis interitus imminentis proelii futuras
sedes diremit, saluauitque densum sanguinem utriusque exercitus. Hiis itaque
240 gestis cateruatim senatus populus<que> Romanus cum coniugibus et liberis
letabundus et laudans occurrit, et illum tamquam patrie patrem urbis
liberatorem libertatisque pristine restitutorem suscepit. Ipse uero non sibi sed
nomini domini gloriam dedit nec ullatenus sue uirtuti[s] sed diuine potencie
hanc asscripsit uictoriam. Unde et cum senatus sibi erexisse<t> ex more
245 ymagines ob honorem triumphi, ipse uexillum Sancte Crucis in dextra fecit
depingi et subtus describi: hoc signum inuincibile esse Dei uiui. Post hec
Maximianum Hercullum multo sanguine debriatum Christianorum in oriente
regnantem et rebellantem destinato Licinio sororio suo uiriliter deuicit,
deuictum longius effugauit. Uictus uero turpiter fugit, prius uiscerum morbo
250 incurabili correptus; tandem amissis luminibus spiritum fetidum baratro
tradidit.

Qualiter Constantinus de lepra mundatus fuerit
      Constantinus constanter credens in Deum baptismum aliquanto tempore
suscipere distulit (170v) quia Ierosolimam ire et in flumine Iordane baptizari
255 proposuit. Morabatur tunc temporis Helena mater eius cum Constancia filia sua
uxore scilicet Licinii[13] et nepotibus suis in orientalibus partibus. Interea
Constantinus augustus lepra profunditur, ob cuius curacionem in crurore
paruulorum recenter effuso dum caleret a senatoribus balniari persuadetur.
Illorum denique consiliis paruuli perplures ad pallacium adducuntur, quos
260 matrones cum ploratu et ululatu multo subsequntur. Quo audito tale facinus
committendum exhorret, matribus reddi natos, datis insuper uehiculis et
muneribus, iussit redire ad propria. Quo facto in uisu noctis subsequentis

^y corruit] sui prorupit Go   ^z pondere] prependere Go

13 Licinius, Western Augustus from 308, married Constantine's half-sister, Constantia (daughter of
   Constantius and Theodora), in 312, thereby forming a close alliance with the emperor.

beatorum apostolorum Petri et Pauli sibi apparencium monitis Papa Siluester
Gentiles ritus declinando delitescens in monte Sarepti queritur, inuenitur, ad
265 Augustum adducitur, adductus ab eo reuerenter salutatur, deuote suscipitur.
Visio deinde precedens immo reuelacio pontifici sancto enarratur et ex ostensis
[a perfide][a] yconiis apostolorum <depictis>[b] ueraciter apostolica reuelacio ab
imperatore creditur. Quid plura: a sancto Siluestro Augustus catezizatus,
septimane ieiunium ob penitenciam ei indicitur, septima die post claudendum
270 ieiunium infra Later<an>ense Palacium conposito baptisterio lauacro sancto
purificatur. Cum enim ter mergeretur in nomine sancte trinitatis Christum ut
fatebatur conspexit et manum se tangentem persensit. Mox uero lepre
squalorem exuit restitutaque caro eius ut caro pueri decorem induit. Deinde
iuxta morem albis indutus sacroque Chrismate signatus ut Christianssimus
275 dilataretur instanter operam dedit prout docuit papa sanctus. In primis ergo
precepit publice per totum Romanum imperium ut ydolorum fana clauderentur
et ecclesie Dei et sanctorum eius edificarentur.

De disputacione Iudeorum cum sancto Siluestro et baptismo ab Helena
suscepto
280   Mater autem Augusti Helena tunc temporis <dum>[c] in Bithinia cum
nepotibus augustis Constancie et Constancio demoraretur a Iudeis ita fuerat
subuersa ut pene fieret Iudea. <Cum>[d] enim attencius attenderet leccionem
ueteris testamenti et prophetarum, libris a Iudeis ad litteram sibi expositis, non
estimabat aliam patere sibi uiam salutis, nisi in legis obseruancia et cerimoniis.
285 Quo circa scripsit filio suo persuadens ut Hebreorum legem susciperet, asserens
illum iccirco sospitatem adeptam non quia in Christum credidit sed quia
ydolatriam (171r) abiecit. Beatus igitur Constantinus in fide Christi fundatus et
radicatus uolens omnimodis matrem ab errore Iudaice secte reuocare et cum
consilio sancti Siluestri rescripsit matri persuadens et obsecrans ut sui copiam
290 Romam dignaretur exhibere Iudeorumque legis peritos secum adducere, ut
quatinus illorum atque Christianorum doctorum disputacione mutua mundo
ueritas irrefregabilis ex testimoniis legis et prophetarum prolatis posset
elucescere. Acceptis augustialibus litteris filii regina memorabilis Romam
profecta .xii. legis doctores a principe sacerdotum Iosia nomine missos, non
295 solum Ebreo uerum eciam Greco et Latino elimatos eloquio <secum>[e] adduxit.
Nam ipse Iosias infirmitate simulata presenti profeccioni futureque controuersie
se subduxit. Conuenerant centum et octo Iudeorum doctores .xii. prefatis
adiuncti. Affuerunt eciam cum sancto Siluestro .xl. iiiior episcopi ex diuersis
prouinciis seu ciuitatibus congregati. Eliguntur eciam ex parte Iudeorum ad
300 disputandum .xii. illi prelibati; discernitur ab omnibus totidem Christianorum
ex parte debere admitti. Sanctus uero Siluester hoc renuens[f] fieri solus contra

---

[a] a perfide] CGo, *omitted* B   [b] depictis (GoB)] depectis C   [c] dum (GoB)] cum C   [d] cum (Go)] dum C
[e] secum (Go)] sancta C   [f] renuens] reminens Go

.xii. certamen disputacionis iniit credens et asserens non in multitudine
sperandam uictoriam sed in uirtute soluis altissimi. Igitur .xii. qui conuenerant
propositis uariis capitulis, inductis multiphariis prophetis, <disputabant>ᵍ cum
310 Siluestro sed non poterant resistere sapiencie et spiritui sancto qui loquebatur in
illo. Sanctus autem Siluester omnes adiecciones Iudeorum euacuans errores
illorum confutabat cum uiuis racionum assertionibus, cum auctenticarum
scripturarum testimoniis, a tauriʰ resuscitacione, ut legitur, cum miraculo
Ihesum Christum Deum uerum Dei filium esse perdocebat et ad credendum in
315 ipsum omnes efficaciter perducebat. In illa hora multi demones ex obsessis
corporibus exibant, multeque sanitates in populo per sanctum Siluestrum
fiebant. Omnes ergo Iudei et ipsa Helena genibus sancti pape prouoluti ueniam
sibi dari poposcerunt et in proximum pascha baptizati sunt. Ex illo igitur die
ydolatria cepit a[l]boleri, fides Christiana dilatari, et decus ecclesie sublimari.
320 Sicut aurora transacte noctis tenebras radiis sue claritatis disrumpit, ita huius
opera neophiti studiosa per totum mundum infidelitatis noctem dissipauit,
idolatriam deiecit. Beata uero Helena quasi stella matutina in medio nebule et
quasi luna (171v) plena in diebus suis luxit; nomen suum quod Grece lunam
sonat lucifluis operibus adimpleuit. Adiuuante namque Christo sole iusticie
325 super celos eleuato eius labore et industria sua id est sancta ecclesia iuxta
prophetiam stetit in ordine suo.

De sancte ecclesie exaltacione
    Beata uero Helena euangelice et apostolice doctrine totum suum adhibuit
studium <dinoscende>ⁱ et adimplende exercicium, et sic pectus eius quod
330 quondam mundane philosophie fuerat armariolum iam usu sacraciori effectum
est sacre scripture sacrarium immo utriusque testamenti reconditorium. Quod
uero mater sapiens et sancta in sacro eloquio didicit, filium exercere docuit,
filiusque deuote matris monitis et consiliis adimplendis obtemperauit. Sancto
Siluestro suggerente, matre monente, plures ecclesias operis mirandi construxit.
335 Inter quas erat basilica Lateranensis quam uoluit esse capud omnium
ecclesiarum in qua baptizatus fuit. Hanc preciossimis ornamentis decorauit et
prediis ditissimis et possessionibus locupletauit. Baptisterium in ea lapide
porfiretico sanctum undique ex argento et auro purissimo uestiuit. In cuius
medio columpnam porfireticam gestantem phialam erexit in qua balsamum
340 probatissimum ardere fecit. In labro f[r]ontis aquam fundentem ex auro
purissimo fecit fieri et ad dextram agni imaginem saluatoris et ad leuam beati
Iohanis baptiste scriptum in manu tenentem et digito porrecto: 'Ecce agnus Dei
ecce qui tollit peccata mundi.'¹⁴ Thimiamatherium quoque librarum decem ex
auro purissimo cum gemmis prassinis et iacinctinis in circuitu numero .xl.

ᵍ disputabant (Go)] stabant C   ʰ tauri] tamen miraculosa tauri G
ⁱ dinoscende (Go)] dinoscese C

14 John 1.29.

345 duabus et cetera donaria multa et possessiones locupletissimas delegauit.
Hortatu eciam beate Helene in exquisito decore in eadem urbe de templo
quondam appolinis basilicam beato Petro principi apostolorum edificauit in
quam sacrosanctam corpus ipsius apostoli infra locellum argenteum ere ciprino
undique grossitudine quinque pedum circumdatum conclusit ne furtiue inde
350 tolleretur. Hoc opus perpulcrum porfireticis columpnis exornauit; eiusdem
basilice cameram auro uenustauit. Super ipsam corporis thecam crucem auream
centum quinquaginta librarum pondus continentem collacauit; calices aureos
cum gemmis preciosis insertis, altaria et candelebra et thimiamateria argentea
cum coronis argenteis, et cetera templi preciosa ornamenta dedit. Possessiones
355 quoque reddituum <ditissimas>[j] eidem ecclesie contulit (quas)[k] eciam ipsa
mater eius Helena sancta amplicauit. (172r) Beato uero Paulo doctori gencium
ecclesiam non minori decore uel honore diuiciis aut possessionibus seu
ornamentis quam beati Petri construxit in qua intra locellum per omnia parilem
priori, materia, forma, precio, auree crucis equilibris supposite eleuacione,
360 corpus ipsius recondidit. Denique incredibile memoratu uidetur quanta in matris
et filii deuocione circa sumptum edif[f]icandarum ecclesiarum feruens fuit
instancia, quam in breui utriusque studio longe lateque per totum orbem sancta
creuerit ecclesia.

De prodicione et perdicione <Licinii>[l]
365   Cum enim edicta apostolica sanxissent ut ecclesie edificarentur per totum
Romanum imperium, ad hoc peragendum ex regiis thesauris pec[c]uniam
affluentissime conferebant. Insuper et singulis ciuitatatibus imperii sui ut
Augusti prepositi populisque episcopis et regali <fisco>[m] ad construccionem
earum sufficienter ministrar<e>nt litteris augustalibus precipieba<n>t. Omnibus
370 ergo bonis amabilis sed pessimis odibilis erat quia non ui uel metu sed amore uel
religione cunctis imperabat. Proinde Licinius ambicione cecatus dyabolice
<tote>[n], actu minatus inuidie, <occultis>[o] insidiis amicum Dei Constantinum
moliebatur de medio tollere. Si queratur sue prodicionis causa nulla claruit nisi
manifesta malicia et ambicio nimia. Sororem illi in matrimonium dederat,
375 consortem illum imperii creauerat honore consilii sicut seipsum sublimauerat.
Sed insidiis eius detectis cum Deo protegente non posset propositum peruersum
perficere, bellum apertum imperatori proditor indicit; ut animum serui Christi
dolore torqueret, Christianos persequitur multosque interemit. Quo conperto
Christianissimus Augustus tot malis obuians conserto prelio circa ciuitatem
380 Chrisopolim in Bithinia tyrannum uicit, conprehendit, uinxit, et apud Tessalicam
urbem publica lege adiudicatum capitali sentencia plecti fecit, totumque
Romanum imperium in solidum solus in salutem multorum optinuit. Hanc
autem uictoriam uel tocius imperii solliditatem adeptam non sue deputabat
uirtuti sed diuine ascribebat pietati. Ab illo ergo die et deinceps erat

---

[j] ditissimas (GoB)] decimas C   [k] quas] quos CGoB   [l] Licinii (Go)] Latini C   [m] fisco (Go)] filco C
[n] tote (Go)] eo te C   [o] occultis (Go)] oculis C

385 Constantinus ubique in cunctis prospere agens, quoniam dominus erat cum eo et
omnia opera eius dirigebat sicque presciso discidii capite, hostibus discrimini
parentibus, totum imperium mundi requieuit post dominum et post
Constantinum seruum eius. In diebus autem pacis non ocio torpuit aut uacuis
spectaculis siue discursibus uenatoriis tempus perdidit sed legere et audire
390 sacras scripturas dulce et iocundum habuit. Leges eciam optimas scripsit et
promulgauit, (172v) in quibus quam deuotus in Deum, quam sollicitus et
discretus circa subditos, quam equiuolus in iudiciis fuerit euidenter
demonstrauit.

De eius sublimacione et magna humilitate[15]

395 <P>iissimus[p][16] augustus <collato> sibi celitus tocius orbis imperio licet
sublimior omnium factus, omnium erat seruus in oculis propriis humilimus. Unde
et illud propheticum ex sentencia dicere potuit, 'Domine non est exaltatum cor
meum neque elati sunt oculi mei'[17] et cetera. Ita enim bonis se amabilem, impiis
terribilem, ecclesiarum ministris subditum et pauidum, sociis et amicis
400 iocundum, pauperibus se mitem exhibuit et largum, omnibus utilem et
necessarium ut omni moribus conformari natureque congruere uideretur
hominum, et quod raro nunc inuenitur in terris, illud maxime spectare credidit et
asseruit ad cumulum regie dignitatis in ecclesia Dei nichil exercere terrene
potestatis. 'Suppremus', inquid, 'et superexcellens regis honor est in regno Dei
405 quod est ecclesia eius, se nec regem sed ciuem cognoscere, non sacerdotibus
legibus suis imperare sed legibus Christi quas ipsi sanxerunt obtemperare.'
Eructauit etiam cor eius uerbum bonum utinam cunctis principibus corde ore et
opere custodiendum. 'Nullus est', inquid, 'in principibus aut magnatibus terre
licet ethnicis tam effrenis tam seuus uidens matrem suam carnalem coram se
410 contumeliis uel verberibus affici qui non moleste accipiat, qui ira non flammet,
non statim ulciscatur. Multo magis ergo quilibet rex Christianus sancte matris
ecclesie, uidelicet illum ad regnum eternum possidendum parientis, omni animi
nisu[q] debet iniurias ulcisci, honorem <tueri, et>[r] diminucionem dignitatis eius
proposse non pati, immo pro promocione et conservacione iuris eius de regno
415 deponi exiliis carceribus membrorum mutilacionibus quibuslibet morcium
generibus debet subici.' Audiant hoc reges terre immo reguli respectu
Constantini orbis domini qui sanctam ecclesiam euiscerant, eius dignitatem
deiciunt, redditus[18] in trutina ponunt, eiusque uenales ambiciosorum oculis
exponunt. Abbacias opprimunt religiosorum, sinistris usibus insumunt,
420 ecclesias aut cenobia non solum fundare nolunt sed eciam fundatis fundos
predia census diripiunt. Non sic Constantinus qui in promocione et libertate

[p] Piissimus (Go)] Hiissimus C   [q] animi nisu] annisu Go   [r] tueri et (Go)] tantum C

[15] Go has instead 'De moribus Constantini'.
[16] This is one of several wrong capitals in this manuscript. Others are at lines 950 and 1044.
[17] Psalm 131.1.
[18] 'Euiscerant . . . red-' over erasure and more cramped than other text.

sancte ecclesie congaudebat et in basillicis extruendis sedulus insistebat. Cum
enim in celebracione uicenalium suorum diademate fastigatur, ipse totam
mundialem paruipendens pompam protinus perrexit purpuratus et ad
425 fundandam quandam basillicam. Urbem eciam Romanam (173r) cum Palacio
Lateranensi sanctis apostolis Petro et Paulo domino Pape et successoribus eius
concessit eique tamquam uicario Ihesu Christi spontaneum hominium fecit;
Romanorum rectorem pocius quam regem se sub summo pontifice
ministrantem profiteri consueuit. Ab illa ergo die dominus papa terreni
430 principatus suscepit dominium mosque inoleuit ut imperatores ab ipso coronandi
prius ei iurent fidelitatem et exhibeant hominium; sanctiuit et instituit ut omnes
ecclesie per orbem diffuse Romanum antistitem papam et summum pontificem
haberent et omnia ecclesiastica iura et appellaciones ad eius disposicionem
pertinerent. Dedit eciam priuilegia per totum imperium singulis ciuitatibus ut
435 sub episcoporum ordinacione libere domino seruiret omnis populus Christianus.
Confitebatur crebro quod dominus a Britannia ad orientales partes adduxerit
illum qualemcumque famulum suum ut eius diebus propagaretur
Christianissimus per uniuersum Romanum imperium.

De construccione Constantinopolis celitus iniuncta
440   In diebus illis edificauit sibi Bisancium ciuitatem maritimam et de suo
nomine Constantinopolim nunccupauit eam. Hec autem ciuitas qualiter reparata
fuit colligimus in libro de uirginitate a sancto Aldelmo conposito, sensum
pocius quam uerba <tenentes>[s], sicut ipse in Grecis ystoriis inuenit.[19]
Constantinus in eadem urbe soporatus uidit uetulam in fronte et facie rugis
445 anilibus aratam assistere subitoque casu clamide circumamictam imperiali in
iuuenculam refloruisse. Cuius uernantis forme decor sic imperatoris in se illexit
et animum et occulum ut non abstineret quin ei osculum porr[r]igeret[t]. Mater
eciam eius Helena ut sibi uidebatur affuit, que talia sibi uerba protulit. 'Hec',
inquiens, 'tua semper erit nec umquam morietur nisi cum seculi finis aduenerit.'
450 Augustus extruso sopore matri sancte narrat uisionem sicque utrique ieiuniis et
orationibus ac elemosinis extrahere laborant e celo sompnii solucionem.
Expletis .viii. diebus iterum Siluestrum papam paulo ante defunctum, priorem
scilicet spiritualem suum, in uisu noctis conspexit, qui dulci risu luminum quasi
filium et discipulum perstringens ait, 'Conuenienter consueta egisti prudencia
455 <ut> quod intellectum effugeret humanum expectans et expectares cum optima
matre tua soluendum adeo enigmatis nodum. Hec igitur[u] anicula est ciuitas ista
cui situ decrepita cuius <iam> uenustatem quassa menia monstrant et uicinam
ruinam minancia reperatorem desiderant. Tu uero muris eam reformabis et
opibus tuoque uocabulo reparatas (173v) insignies et mea in perpetuo regnabit

---

[s] tenentes (Go)] tenentem C   [t] porrigeret] porrrigeret C, porigeret Go   [u] igitur] igitur quam uisti Go

[19] Jocelin is referring to Aldhelm, *De virginitate* (see above, p. 37); and the Greek histories of Socrates
Scholasticus, Sozomen and Theodoret, which came to be combined in the Latin text known as the
Historia tripartita (see above, p. 11).

460 imperatoria progenies. Non tamen tuo arbitratu eius fundamenta iacies sed
    ascenso sonipede cui quondam rudis Christicola insidens Rome uisitare solebas
    ecclesias apostolorum laxatisque habenis quo uolet eundi promptum illi
    concedes arbitrium. Habebis hastam regiam in manu tua cuius cuspide in terram
    tracta murorum[v] scribentur uestigia. Consules ergo in terra sulcandis cuspidis
465 lunare magisterium quo ordine disponi debeant fundamenta menium.' Visionem
    hanc imperator clarissimus et clementissimus matri sue retulit eandemque illa se
    uidisse respondens Deum glorificauit. Augustus igitur uisioni preclue paruit et
    ciuitatem emulam equalem Rome immo precellentem constituit. Profitebatur
    quasi legem sanc[t]iendo non debere terrenum imperatorem Rome principari ubi
470 apostoli principantur a Christo <coronati>[w]. Gratum ad modum fuisse fertur
    animo imperali ut illic urbem diuino iussu construeret ubi et telluris ubertas et
    celi temperies saluti mortalium congrueret et pontus circumfluus diuiciarum et
    deliciarum ac uictualium affluenciam ex tocius mundi finibus conueheret.
    Omnes pene nobiles Romanos et ordines senatorum cum liberis suis illo
475 transtulit; murorum miris municionibus eam circumdedit, confabricis diuersis
    adornauit. Plures ecclesias in illa urbe construxit quarum unam Hyrenem
    appellauit et aliam sancto Michaeli archeangelo attitulauit. Aliam apostolorum
    fecit illuc inuehens innumera sanctorum corpora que preualerent contra incursus
    hostium, impetrare possent ciuibus celeste patrocinium. Aliam quoque Agye
480 Sophye idest Sancte Sapiencie que Christus est attitulatam inchoauit, quam orbis
    ornamentum, Christicolarum uotiuum spectaculum, decus ecclesiarum, parem
    immo pulcriorem et preciosiorem fere templo Salomonis, exoptauit et fortassis
    eius desiderium in hoc opere conpleret si diucius postea uiueret.

De Iudicio Sancte Helene inter Iudeum et Christianum

485 Iudeus quidam habitans Constantinopolim Christianum quendam debitis sibi
    obligatum inmensis uinculis detinebat, quem multe inedie et carceris squalore
    afflictum grauiter torquebat. Videns hoc adolescens alumpnus eius et
    consanguineus misericordia motus super eum rogabat Iudeum ut eum susciperet
    loco nutricii sui uinculis uinciendum donec ipse libero gressu quereret ab amicis
490 de debiti solucione aminiculum. Iudeus diu resistens tandem tali pacto annuit ut
    nisi euinculatus ille die (174r) constituto solueret debitum aut se ipsum iterum
    sibi tolleret incarcerandum aut ipsius iuuenis loco alterius iam sponte subrogati
    pedem dexterum acciperet amputandum. Iuuenis libere coram testibus hoc
    acceptauit quia confidens in homine nullatenus id uenturum sperabat. Sed teste
495 scriptura multi propter inopiam deliquerunt et a uia ueritatis errauerunt. Die
    uero prefixo homo non conparuit nec aliquis pro eo debitum soluit. Iudeus
    inmitis ut odium natiuum exercere iam posset quasi de iure Christianum, nactus
    occasionem, produxit uinctum cum testibus coram iudice ut ipsius pedem
    dextrum amputaret iuxta pacti conuencionem. Iuuenis inficiari non potuit quod

---

[v] murorum] muri Go   [w] coronati (Go)] coronatur C

500 coram tot testibus pactus fuit. Cum multis igitur lacrimis ut sibi misereretur
peciit sed inmisericordem et inflexibilem Iudeum inuenit. Interim sermo iste
uenerabili Helene regine innotuit que tunc fortuitu in illa ciuitate moram fecit.[20]
Que[x] suspenso iudicio omnem contencionem, Iudeum et Christianum, testes et
iudices presentari sibi fecit. Et auditis hinc inde allegacionibus utriusque partis
505 et attestacionibus diffinitiue pronuncians Iudeo dixit, 'Iuxta condictum pactum
abscide huius pedem sed caue in periculo capitis tui ne effundas alicuius artus
sanguinem. Si autem uel guttam cruoris ex coxa uel tibia <manantis>[y] effuderis,
consequenter capite plecteris.' Uidens Iudeus hoc inpossibile sibi faciendum
Christianum liberum dimisit et illesum, omnesque Christicole laudauerunt
510 Deum amirantes et amplexantes iudicium ex ore regine tamquam diuinitus

---

[x] que] que statim Go   [y] manantis (Go)] manentis C

[20] B breaks off at this point and includes the following additional material, as well as a summary of
Constantine's vision, conversion, and baptism from the *Legenda aurea* (Ch. 58) prior to an abbreviated version of the *de translacione ipsius*. As in contemporary Byzantine legends concerning the
circumstances of Constantine's birth, in the extract below, Constantius gives Helena half his ring prior
to returning to Rome. In other versions, he gives her his purple imperial cloak in order to recompense
her for their unlawful (sometimes forced) coupling, or to provide some means of royal identification
for the son about to be born of the union. In some texts, the gift is a cloak clasp or golden necklace.
Byzantine legends, especially popular in the ninth century, were adopted and reworked in the West.
For a discussion and translation of a ninth-century Greek version of the cloak legend, see S.N.C. Lieu
and Dominic Montserrat, *From Constantine to Julian: Pagan and Byzantine Views. A Source History*
(London and New York, 1996), pp. 97–146; on the ring/gift motif, see A. Kazhdan, ' "Constantin
Imaginaire" ': Byzantine Legends of the Ninth Century about Constantine the Great', *Byzantion* 57
(1987), pp. 196–250, at p. 215; and Samuel Lieu, 'From History to Legend and Legend to History:
The Medieval and Byzantine Transformation of Constantine's *Vita*', *Constantine: History, Historiography and Legend*, ed. S.N.C. Lieu and Dominic Montserrat (London and New York, 1998), pp.
136–76, at pp. 151 and 159. The following extract is unique to B, though the final word, *etcetera*, in
the context of other brief extracts, makes it clear that an existing legend is being cited. In this text, a
British Helena ultimately holds an imperial position in Byzantium:
>   (fol. 804) Aliter desponsata est Helena Constancio, augusto et conquestori Anglie, et de semine
>   eius se grauidam affirmans, quesiuit ab illo quid faceret si masculum filium generasset. Cesar
>   vero conspiciens ut ad Romanum celeriter rediret, imperium anulum de digito suo rapuit, et in
>   duas partes equaliter divisit. 'Accipe', inquit, 'dilecta michi anuli presentis dividium signum
>   generacionis nostre tibi pro noticia quandoque futurum. Si quoquo modo contigeret quod tibi
>   partem anuli remiserim quem mecum retineo, hiis intersignis nequaquam dubites aggredi quod
>   tibi ex consultu Romanorum mea legacione noueris intimari'. Remansit Helena gravida
>   Constanciusque mare transit oceanum et ad urbem Romanam regreditur. Mulier autem insignis,
>   emenso tempore, filium edidit eumque a patre Constancio Constatinum appelavit. Constancius
>   itaque ad aites Ausonias rediens et habenas imperii principaliter regens, se verrute consumtus
>   sangorem incidit, ex quo sibi mortem imminere prescuit. Interrogatur a senatu Romanorum quid
>   se descedente de imperii dignitate statueret cum heredem ut putarent superstitem non haberet. Qui
>   senatores blande consolans se filium ut sperabat de filia regis Britannie Helene nomine
>   procroasse non negavit, qui falces Ausonias sua, ut confido, fortitudine im(m)iniet et virtute.
>   'Mittite ergo legatos ad Britanniam et inde aduocate progeniem cum matre sua. Anulum hunc ad
>   eam referte cuius medium secui et pro signo dividium ei com(m)endam.' Quem cum videret
>   adveniet suumque filium secum adducet. Nec mora post hec imperator defungitur puerque cum
>   matre ad urbem Romuleam signorum manifestacione vocatur. Ex Romanorum protinus consultu
>   Constantinus eligitur et imperator in vrbe augustusque creatur. Qui diuiciis in imperio et iuribus
>   splenderet et armis in Grecia genitrici sue Bizancium contulit in qua urbe domina et imperatrix
>   potenter imperavit *etcetera*.

dictatum. Postea san[c]ciuit legem et a filio confirmari fecit ut nullus Iudeus uel paganus presumeret in uinculis aut in carcere Christianum aliquem mittere, sed Christianus si delinqueret Christianum haberet iudicem qui eum iudicaret secundum quod promeruit iuxta publicam legem. Post hec idem Augustus super
515 matris iudicio ualde exillaratus, ciuitatem in Bithinia restaurauit quam ex uocabulo matris sue Helienopolim[z] nunccupauit.[21] Hanc ipsa mater eius perpulcris edificiis et ecclesiis multis ac magnificis ac xenodochiis adornauit, iustis legibus et litterarum studiis et corpore beati Luciani martiris uenustauit.

De Nicena sinodo
520   Cum magnifice per totum Romanum imperium beate Helene et piissimi imperatoris[a] filii eius Constantini[b] floreret ecclesia, egre tulit dyabolica inuidia. Intrauit ergo dyabolus in cor Arrii[22] cuiusdam presbiteri Alexandrini qui speciem quidem habuit sanctitatis, uirtutem eius abnegauit, filium Dei creaturam et spiritum (174v) sanctum ab eo creatum predicauit. Ad cumulum
525 eciam erroris et dampnacionis sue addendo aiebat quod erat tempus quando filius dei et spiritus non erat. Cum autem has Arrius faceret inter patrem et filium et spiritum sanctum differencias Alexander[c] eiusdem urbis patriarcha ei resistens astruebat filium patri coeternam et spiritum sanctum tempori nuncquam obnoxium sed una cum patre et filio coeternaliter uiuere et ab
530 utroque procedere. Docebat eciam totam solide trinitatis maiestatem simplicem et indissociabiliter esse connexam ita ut nuncquam pater a filio, numquam separari possit spiritus sanctus ab utrisque. Sed cum Arrium a perniciosi erroris reuocare non posset perfidia, expulit eum ab ecclesia sua. Expulsus uero non solum resipiscere refutauit sed eciam contra pontificem sanctum sedicionem
535 concitauit. Quod comperiens Constantinus coadunari fecit sinodum sanctam in urbe Nicea anno ab incarnacione domini trecentesimo sextodecimo. Hoc fuit primum consilium uniuersale in quo trecenti et .xviii. episcopi et duo cardinales presbiteri Romane ecclesie Uitus et Uincensius missi a papa Iulio, qui tercius a sancto Siluestro ob senectutis inbescillitatem adesse non ualebat, affuerunt et
540 Machareus Ierosolimitanus et Eustachius Antiochenus et Alexus Alexandrinus prenominatus cum Athanasio archidiacono eius patriarche conuenerunt. Homo eciam Dei Pan[n]ucius ex Egypto adueniens uirtutibus apostolicis et signis gloriosus ex eorum numero quos Maximianus imperator pro Christi nomine effosso occulo abscisoque poplite dextro per metalla dampnauerat huic sancto

---

[z] Heleniopolim] Elionopoliem Go   [a] imperatoris] *omitted* Go   [b] Constantini] instantias Go
[c] Alexander] *over erasure*

21 On Constantine's renaming the Bithinian city in honour of his mother, see above, p. 12.
22 Arius (c. 260–336), by denying the complete divinity and eternity of Jesus, was condemned as a heretic by Bishop Alexander of Alexandria (c. 320). The Arian heresy was debated at the Council of Nicaea (325) called by the emperor Constantine in an attempt at imperial unification. Though initially repudiated, Arianism continued to find supporters and generate vigorous debate for decades. See M.F. Wiles, *Archetypal Heresy: Arianism Through the Centuries* (Oxford, 1996).

545 concilio <vocatus> intererat. Hunc sepius introductum in thalamum imperator
assurgens brachiis amplexabatur; occulum erutum pro fide Dei crebris osculis
permulcens ut pro se atque imperio oraret sedulo deprecabatur. Beata Helena
quoniam presenti concilio pre infirmitate sui presenciam exhibere non ualuit,
filium suum ne in ecclesia sancta catholica temporibus suis aliquam heresim
550 pullulare sineret et presens monuit et absens scriptis ac nunciis autenticis
efficaciter induxit. Ipse uero ut filius sapiens secundum Salomonem matrem
suam letificauit illius monitis obtemperando; orthodoxis patribus aurem et
animum attencius accomodauit. Episcopi ergo in sancto concilio congregati
<o>mittentes inprimis ea pro quibus acciti conuenerunt querimonias adinuicem
555 motas et scriptas Augusto porrexerunt. Ipse uero porrectas et[23] positas post
iudicium de sinu extraxit, extractis igni cremari fecit et adiecit: 'Non est meum',
inquid, 'de sacerdotibus iudicare. Vos enim sicut scriptum est dii estis; soliusque
(175r) Dei examen expectandum est de uobis. Deus, inquit, in synagoga stetit
deorum; in medio autem deos diiudicat[24] et cetera que subsequntur. Si quid ergo
560 inter uos ortum fuerit questionis uel controuersie in ecclesia, domestice tractetur
ne quippiam quod uestram (de)decorat sanctitatem ad eorum <qui>[d] foris sunt
noticiam transferatur. Ego certe si quem[p]piam de ordine sancto cernerem cum
muliere peccantem eos cooperirem proprio pallio ne qua religioni uere laicis
detrahendi daretur occasio.' Sancti deinde patres dimissis alternis querelis
565 secundum euangelicam et apostolicam doctrinam filium patri et spiritum
sanctum utrique consubstancialem et coeternum esse asserunt; nouum uerbum
sed non nouam esse creaturam <adinuenentes>[e] quod Grece dicitur homousyon
debere confiteri diffinierunt. Generali tandem iudicio tocius concilii ut arbor
arida et apta igni gehenne Arrius incorrigibilis cum suis sequacibus est
570 dampnatus et anathematizatus atque ab ecclesia[f] separatus et ab imperatore
(iuxta) sententiam illorum tamquam diuinitus prolatam[g] in exilium relegatus.
Post expulsionem ergo Sathane, post abscisionem arboris pestifere, catholicam
fidem luculenter exposuerunt, expositam conscripserunt. Sancte ergo matris
ecclesie catholice statum ob longas et multiplices paganorum principum
575 persecuciones in diuersa mutatum renouauerunt, renouatum ne a uero uacillaret
sacris institutis suffulciendo coroborauerunt. In diebus illis sanctissimi presules
et eruditissimi per orbem in sancta ecclesia floruerunt et in Egypto patres sancti,
heremite scilicet et monachi, celestem uitam in terris ducentes signis et
uirtutibus innumeris coruscantes claruerunt. In quibus precipuum locum et
580 nomen tenuit Antonius cui ut pro se suisque dominum oraret scripsit Augustus.
Non enim estimabat sibi suisque sufficere propriam aut mirandam matris

---

[d] qui (Go)] que C   [e] esse creaturam] rem Go; adinuenentes (Go] aduenientes C   [f] ecclesia] ecclesia
Dei Go   [g] prolatam] prolatam amplexante Go

[23] Go omits 'et' and includes: 'sed sedulas omnes conuoluit et conuolutas in sinu posuit'.
[24] Psalm 82.1.

sanctitatem ad salutem nisi ubique terrarum sanctorum patrum gratiam sibi conciliaret, famililaritatem adquireret, orationem expectaret.

De aduentu sancte Helene in Iherusalem

585 Post hec Helena beatissima fide feruens, animi deuocione incomparabilis, diuinitus inspirata, angelicis ammonica uisitacionibus, cum beneplacito filii sui secum multam manum militarem mittentis ministrantisque thesaurorum copiam uenit Ierosolimam causa uisitandi ac reparandi loca sancta atque inuestigandi et reperiendi dominice passionis insignia. Estuanti corde desiderabat inuenire
590 sanctam crucem in qua pro redempcione generis humani saluator perpendit, nec non et clauos quibus illud domini corpus cunctis creaturis dignius (175v) et sanctius iudaica impietas affixit. Erat autem tunc temporis locus Caluarie concius mortis ad indagandum difficilis eo quod ibi a paganis prophanare locum satagentibus phanum et in eo prophanum extructum fuerat idolum Ueneris. Hac
595 de causa ne locum honorarent uel adorarent ibidem Christicole a loco arcebantur ne pro Christo Uenerem uenerari uideretur. Erat proinde eciam circumcirca locus neglectus atque desertus et iuxta Ysaie uaticinium uepribus et spinis obsitus. In primis ergo templum Ueneris execrandum fecit destrui et ydolum abhominandum in illo minutatim confringi. Macharius episcopus prefuit paucis
600 Christianis qui illic habitabant. Nam plures Gentiles et Iudei non solum in ciuitate sed eciam in finibus ceteris Iudee degebant.

Qualiter sancta Helena convenit Iudeos et concionabatur ad eos

Sancta uero Helena prudenti usa consilio cunctos Iudeos intelligibilis etatis qui fuerant in ciuitate et ceteris urbibus et castellis Iudee fecit congregari,
605 congregatos suis conspectibus assisti, et assistentibus sciscitabatur qui fuissent in eis sue legis periti. Illi uero habito consilio regine mille uiros exhibuerunt quos peroptime nosse legem astruxerunt. Iussit iterato sancta regina illis adinuicem conuenire et exquisitos in lege doctores sibi presentare qui possent et nossent inquisicionibus suis racionem reddere. Iterato consulentes adinuicem
610 elegerunt ex se tantum quingentos quos statuentes ante sanctam Helenam astruxerunt esse in lege doctissimos. Illa uero assistentes intuens concionabatur ad eos dicens, 'Noui uos quondam electos et dilectos populumque peculiarem domini fuisse quibus erat testamentum et legis lacio et obsequium et promissum secundum patres, nunc autem ob cordis cecitatem et infidelitatis pertinacitatem
615 despectos et proiectos a facie Dei tamquam a sancta stirpe penitus degeneres. Verum namque Messiam tociens in lege et prophetis multipharie multis modis uobis promissum tandem a patre missum innumerisque miraculis se Deum comprobantem non solum [non] negastis uerum eciam suspendentes in ligno interemistis, eius memoriam delere de terra sategistis. Ipse solutis doloribus
620 mortis secundum sacras scripturas tercia die resurrexit spoliato baratro; in alta celorum potenter ascendens misso spiritu sancto omnia ad se trahit. Ecce enim totus mundus post eum abiit et, ut dignum et iustum est, in factorem et redemptorem factura redempta credit ueraque progenies uiperia in incredulitate

permanet. (176r) Adhuc eciam prouidete inter uos doctores meliores ueracius[h]
625 legis et prophetarum enigmata intelligentes qui in eas sciant et queant
abstergere ambiguitates.' Iudei tercio iam conuocato concilio quare regina erga
se ac<t>itabat uehementer mirabantur et quid questionis mouere uel quid eis
obicere uellet mutuo percunctabantur. E quibus unus Iudas nomine sapiencie et
eloquencie ac etatis maturitate ueteranus dixit ceteris auide audientibus,
630 'Coniecto et formido quod regina uult a nobis cerciorari de ligno et loco ubi
crucifixerunt Ihesum patres nostri. Omnino caueatur ne per aliquem nostrum
perueniat ad huius indaginis certitudinem ne forte quod absit ipsa uel filius eius
aut ceteri Romam iam Christiani uenientes exilem iam et exiguam tollant
nostram locum et gentem. Sic profecto nostram destru<e>nt et suam legem
635 instituent. Ego tamen a iure[i] et paterno precepto perstringor ne, antequam
inmensis suppliciis subiciar aut morti tradar, lignum crucis absconditum
patefaciam et ne inquam Christi nomine blasphemiam seu cultoribus eius
incuciam. Zacheus auus meus multa mirabilia retulit Symoni patri meo et pater
meus michi de magnitudine uirtutum eius et de diuicus bonitatis eius. Spiritualis[j]
640 patricius meus celos apertos ipsumque stantem a dextris uirtutis Dei conspexit
et cum pro nomine eius lapidaretur orans pro lapidatoribus suis in gloriam
conspectam introiuit. Saulum eciam persecutorem sanctorum suorum fecit ad se
conuersum eximium predicatorem fidei sue, immo et apostolum ad se
conuertentem multa milia populorum. Uos ergo uideatis quid uobis agendum sit
645 utrum si de ligno crucis questio mota fuerit silencie supprimendum quod
nouerimus an sit propallandum.' Hic audientes ceteri pre admiracione
opstupuerunt et circa crucis reuelande misterium ei sub legalis anathematis
<interdicto>[k] silencium inposuerunt.

De inuencione Sancte Crucis et miraculis per eam factis et clauis Dominici
650 *corporis*
        Cumque Iudei demorarentur in protrah<e>ndo concilio suo, sancta regina
fecit eos ad se accessiri; dixit accersitis ut sibi demonstrarent locum
repositorium crucis Christi. Illi uero communi consensu uoce unanimi
respondentes asseruerunt sese non habere noticiam ligni uel loci. Cum obstinate
655 perdurantes in hac sentencia nollent precibus aut minis eius emolliri, zelo
succensa regina iussit omnes flammis consumendos tradi. Omnes igitur
perturbati et exeriti Iudam prefatum adduxerunt (176v) ante regine
consistorium, protestantes illum iusti esse et prophete filium, qui sicut audiuit a
patre posset et sciret eius adimplere uotiuum effectum. Semotis itaque omnibus
660 solum Iudam nunc blandimentis mulcens nunc persuasionibus permigens nunc
terroribus pulsans conuenit ut saltem sibi designet Caluarie locum ubi
crucifixum fuisse dominum sanctum indicat euangelium. Iudam uero quia nec

---

[h] ueracius] *initial* u *over erased* m, meracius Go, *with* clarius *added in margin*   [i] a iure] auito Go
[j] Spiritualis] Stephanus Go   [k] interdicto (Go)] interdiccio C

precibus nec persuasionibus siue minis flecti uoluit iussit imperatrix incarcerari
prohibens illi cibum aut potum a quolibet ministrari donec uexacio daret illi
665 intellectum uerum confitendi. Attenuatus tandem squalore carceris et augustia
diuturne famis postulauit et impetrauit educi se de carcere quia pollicebatur se
ostensurum illis locum Caluarie. Accepto deinde fossorio Iudas preuius accessit
ad locum; assistente regina cum innumerosa[1] multitudine hominum fodit in
altum. Precibus deuotis pulsabat ad portam diuine pietatis ut aliquo signo
670 mirifico demonstrare dignaretur sibi thesaurum desiderabile absconditum in
uisceribus terre. Oratione conpleta statim commotus est locus et de loco fumus
aromatizans suauitatem odoris admirandi super omnia aromata sursum ascendit;
locum et circumiacencia eius cunctosque astantes inestimabili iocunditate
repleuit. Tres deinde cruces inuenit quas cunctis qui aderant uidendas exposuit.
675 Et quamuis Sancta Crux ex titulo Hebraicis litteris Grecis et Latinis a Pilato
conscripto potuisset a ceteris discerni, plenius tamen cupiebat regina super illius
ueritate certificari ob roborandam fidem populi. Et ecce quedam mulier
primaria ciuitatis iacebat agens in extremis. Posuerunt ergo super seminecem
crucem unam primo dehinc alteram et nichil profuit. Adhibuerunt terciam titulo
680 prefato presignitam et statim sanitate et ualitudine pristina plene recepta
surrexit, exilit, omnesque leticia perfudit. Post modice morule spacium
efferebatur iuuenis mortuus ad sepeliendum in conspectu astancium. Iterabant
alteram applicacionem patibulorum super cadauer nichilque ualuit duarum
attactus sicut prius quod non erat uox nec sensus nec eciam motus; ut autem
685 lignum uiuificum mortuo inpositum fuit, non solum uiuus sed eciam suauis et
robustus coram cunctis apparuit. Sonat in ore omnium graciarum accio et uox
laudis adoratur lignum uiuifice crucis; conuertitur ad fidem multitudo Gentilis
Iudaice plebis. Audiebatur ululatus demonum (177r) in aere uolitancium ac
uociferancium: 'Ue ue[m] nobis misellis qui domino diuturno[n] priuamur et a
690 sedibus exp(u)lsamur[o] propriis. Ecce crux Christi omnia penetrat, in celo rutilat,
in aere mundum illustrat, infernum spoliat, uirtutibus corruscat. Ecce quod per
Iudam conuersum, et consentaneum nostrum adquisiuimus, per posteriorem
Iudam a nobis auersum amisimus.' Et conuersi ad illum: 'Talionem', inquiunt,
'tibi reddemus quoniam alium regem suscitabimus aduersarium crucis Christi
695 qui te tormentis grauibus subiciet et te Christum negare faciet.' Ad hec Iudas
respondens, 'Increpet', inquid, 'Deus te Sathan teque demergat in abyssum ignis
eterni qui <hamo te>[p] cepit et perforauit armillas tuas o tortuose serpens et
lubrice Leuiatan.' Demon in umbras euanuit et Iudas Iudaice secte renuncians
exuto ueteri homine per lauacrum regeneracionis et renouacionis Christum
700 induit. Processu uero temporis discedente presule Machario per beatam
Helenam a Romano pontifice in episcopum Ierosolimorum consecratus est;
tandem eciam miraculis choruscans sub Iuliano apostota martirio coronatus est.

---

[1] innumerosa] num⸗rosa Go   [m] ue ue] ueni Go   [n] domino diuturno] diuturno dominico Go
[o] expulsamur] expolsamur C, nostris effugamur Go   [p] hamo te (Go)] amore C

De inuentione clauorum Dominici corporis

Magnificauit anima beate Helene dominum et exultauit spiritus eius in Deo
705 salutari suo quia eius labore et studio crucem sanctam reuelauit in mundum.
Ecce ad restaurandum quod Eua prothoparens admisit et amisit, sanatiuum
remedium Helena beata inuenit. Tactus enim ligni fuit Eue tangenti eiusque
propagini effectus expulsiuus de Paradyso in mundum de mundo in infernum,
crux Christi arbor uite quam Helena quesiuit et inuenit efficaciter uehiculum
710 reductiuum Eue et posteritati eius de pena ad Paradysum, de ceno ad celum.
Presumens adhuc de Dei cumulaciori miseracordia cum Iuda et ceteris
credentibus instancius dominum deprecabatur ut clauos quibus palme et
plan[c]te dominice confosse fuerant sibi propalare dignaretur. Orantibus illis lux
celestis ad instar fulguris choruscantis emicuit, claritas Dei circumfulgens,
715 Caluarie locum clauos super aurum et omnem lapidem rutilantes preciosum
cunctis exhibuit. Quos regina flexis genibus obstipo capite adorans manibus
accepit, crebra illis infigens oscula saluatorem omnium glorificauit. Interea dum
hec ageret mater Ierosolimis, filius eius imperator Sarmathos et Gothos et alias
barbaras naciones matris meritis et (177v) uirtute sancte crucis ut ipse fatebatur
720 sibi rebellantes debellauit Calcerumque tyrannum in Cipro bella molientem
conspiracionemque morientem contriuit. Vbicumque enim perrexit prospere
egit, quia dominus illum protexit. Quanto enim humilius et deuocius ex maternis
monitis se Christo subdebat tanto robustius superborum sublimiumque colla
diuina uirtute calcabat.

725 ## De reparacione Ierosolime et templi et aliarum ecclesiarum construccione

Congregans igitur beata Helena undique latomos et artifices ac lignarios
ecclesias multas et magnas construxit in quibus decoris eximii et operis preciosi
templum domini et alterum in Golgatha et aliud circa sepulcrum domini mirandi
operis edificauit.[25] In monte quoque Oliueti fecit ecclesiam perpulcre structure
730 et alteram in ualle Iosaphat operis ambiciosi in honore beatissime Marie, in qua
continetur sepulcrum eiusdem sanctum de preclaro marmore. Ciuitatem
sanctam Ierusalem Nazareth et Betlehem et alias multas in Iudea [et] reparauit,
ecclesias multas et pulcherimas[26] in urbibus et castellis reparatis edificauit, quas

---

[25] Go has a lengthy and barely legible marginal comment, which is of particular interest, as it refers to a
later *vita* of Helena and London memorial text in its opening lines:
  Legitur etiam in quodam brevi tractatu de vita sancte Helene, que est scripta apud memoriales
  sancte Helene, Londoun, post istam vitam, ubi scribitur quod cum ipsa Helena repedaret et
  augustus pelagi transsitus inevitabilis ei immineret . . .
The rest of the note describes a miracle where Helena calms a tempestuous sea by casting a nail from
the Cross into it (cf. de Voragine, *Legenda aurea*, 'De inventione sanctae crucis', Graesse ed., I.310
[Engl. trans. Ryan, I.283], where the same incident is related).

[26] Go adds a paraphrase of Eusebius's *Vita Constantini* (3.43): 'Ut Eusebius Pamphilii libro tercio de
vita Constantini sic ait, "Etenim generacionem sustinere igitur nobiscum est Deus propter nos voluit
locusque cuius incarnate generacionis nominatus est apud Hebreos Bedlem. Quamobrem Helena
Augusta domino amabilis locum ubi Dei ge(n)itrix peper[e]it memoriis mirabili(b)us adornavit hanc
sacratissimam speluncam decenter irradians." '

optimis ornamentis et lampadaris lumine uenustauit, prediis et possessionibus
735 ac ministeriis clericorum et uirorum religiosorum ordinatis ditauit, uiros doctos
et sanctos regimini fidelium assignauit. Iudeos quoque et Gentiles in Christum
credere contempnentes non solum ab Ierosolima sed eciam a Iudee finibus
eliminauit. Conuersos ad fidem possessionibus donariis numerauit,
xenodochium Ierosolimis sicut alibi in multis locis terrarum constituit, quibus
740 ad sustentacionem peregrinorum et infirmorum predia et substanciam
sufficienter contulit. Filius enim eius Augustus precepit prepositis uectigalium
et reddituum suorum ut ad libitum matris sue thesauri sufficientissime
ministrarentur <et> quod eius cordi sederat circa locorum sanctorum
edificacionem siue restauracionem plenissime perficeretur. Legitur in
745 ecclesiastica ystoria quod Helena[27] regina frumentum de Egypto allatum emerit
et tempore famis existentis sub Claudio Ierosolimis uictualia ministrauerit, pro
quo facto preclarum preconium et prope portas Ierosolime monumentum
memorabile meruerit. Sed, ut michi uidetur, ampliori preconio nostra Helena
erga Ierosolimitas digniter iudicatur cuius instancia sollitudine et opere tota
750 ciuitas (178r) illa interius et exterius restaurabatur, lignum uite ad
sustentacionem fidelium, fructum uitalis alimonie, inuentum exaltabatur.

Quid sancta Helena de ligno domini et clauis fecerit
    Lignum eciam salutare sancte crucis in duas particulas diuisit, quarum unam
auro gemmisque preciosis coopertam arcello argenteo inclusit et in templo quod
755 construxerat adorandam a populis dimisit. Dignum profecto iudicabat ut illic
adoraretur ab hominibus ubi saluator in ea redemit humanum genus. Altera
quoque porcio simili modo uestita auro et gemmis Constantinopolim ad filium
eius differtur, que magne ueneracioni usque in presens ibidem habetur. Unum
clauorum prenominatorum auro inclusum freno regio fecit inseri, confidens eius
760 presencia et beneficio iter et actus ipsius in uiam pacis et salutis dirigi, motus
illicitos per hoc debere refrenari, iudicia eciam domini timendo carnes timore
salubriter configi. Completum est illud [nichilominus][q] Zacharie prophete
uaticinium dicentis, 'In die illa erit quod super frenum equi est sanctum
domino.'[28] Alterius clam imposicione galeam imperatoris armatam muniuit ut
765 muneris tam preciosa presencia atque presidio ab armis exterioribus illesus
custodiretur, uictoria seu pax a domino sibi concederetur. Dyadema
<nichilominus>[r] ex auro purissimo preciosissimisque lapidibus ornatum
fabricari fecit in cuius fronti <s>picio signum crucis porciunculam dominici
ligni continens et tercium clauum nudum errexit. Miro satis artificio sanctaque
770 calliditate mulier sancta et prudens sublimauit ad gloriam quod Iudeorum ficcio

---

q nichilominus] CGo   r nichilominus (Go)] omnis C

27 C has an undecipherable word or two at this point, 'audeb^are marum'. Go has the equally inexplicable
    but more decipherable 'a diabolorum'.
28 Zechariah 14.20.

maligna meditabatur et machinabatur rabies Gentilis ad Christi consummari contumeliam et penam. Et quia reus regie maiestatis censebatur quisquis capud flectere et adorare imperatorem diademate fastigatum aspernabatur, nunc eciam adoraret inuitus uterque Iudeus et Gentiles dominice passionis stigmata ne
775 puniretur. Perpulcrum spectaculum apparuit ut egredientes filii et filie Syon, id est ecclesie uiderunt regem Constantinum in dyademate quo coronauit eum mater sua in diebus sollempnitatis et letiticie cordis eius ut letarentur in domino, aspicerent Gentiles et Iudei incircumcisi corde et auribus confunderentur a domino, aut ad uitam conuerterentur regnaturi cum domino. Dabat etiam in hoc
780 mater salutare documentum filio ut humiliando et obsequendo penitus se subderet (178v) summo regi Ihesu Christo pro se crucifixo.

Qualiter uirginibus sancte Helena ministrauit
    Exhibuit eciam Ierosolimis magnum sue deuocionis exemplum et religionis indicium. Inueniens enim ibi aliquas Deo sacratas uirgines inuitauit secum ad
785 prandium nec passa est aliquem ministrorum suorum aliquod inuitatis impendere obsequium. Illa namque beata licet iam octogeneria mater imperatoris et orbis domina ancillarum more <succincta>^{s} deposito pallio aquam manibus illarum infudit, mensam conposuit, cibos apposuit, potum propinauit totumque famulatum astando exhibuit et postea de reliquiis cibi
790 illarum collectis se refecit; uirginitatem in aliis nimio affectu excoluit illamque sociam angelorum asseruit et maxime ob reuerenciam beate uirginis Marie que fecunda integritate creatorem cunctorum genuit. Unde et multa monasteria uirginum in mundi uariis finibus dicitur construxisse et ne foras euagarentur in prediis et redditibus eis omnia neccesaria procurasse. Unde recte colligi debet
795 quod licet aliquando uiriles amplexus experta fuerit diligendo tamen decus uirgineum et sustenando immo multiplicando uirtutis eius preclare premio seu participio non carebit.

De collacione super regina de Saba et sancta Helena
    Censeat^t in hoc loco lector quam salubriori aduentu operisque affectu
800 fructuosiori uenit in Ierusalem beata Helena quam quondam regina de Sabba.[29] Illa namque uenit de finibus suis audire sapienciam Salomonis; audiuit et pre amiracione obstupuit. Ista lignum salutare in quo pax nostra pendens pacificauit in sanguine suo omnia que in celis et in terra sunt; querere uenit et inuenire meruit. Sabea illa aurum et gemmas et ar[r]omata preciosa dedit Salomoni. Hec
805 fide feruens et caritate sanctarum orationum odoramentis fragrans in sacris scripturis [et] in sacri templi et plurimarum ecclesiarum et xenodochiorum

---

^{s} succincta (Go)] suo cuncta ^{t} censeat] senseat Go

[29] I Kings 10.1–13; II Chronicles 9.1–12. The Queen of Sheba is associated apocryphally with seeking the Cross. Cf. Altmann, *Vita*, AASS, Aug. III, p. 590F.

edificia et ornamenta aurum et gemmas errogauit. A regina[u] Meroen[30] allata
sunt regi Salomoni ligna tyn[n]a et abiegna que ut dicunt corrupcioni et
conbustioni non sunt obnoxia. Hec imperatrix uirginum Deo dedicatarum igni
810 uenereo resistencium corrupcioni non subiacencium perplura construxit
monasteria subministratus necessaria. De lignis tynnis et abiegnis fecit Salomon
fieri (179r) liras cantoribus in domo domini et uirgines, sicut scriptum est in
apochalipsi, agnum sequentes cantant canticum nouum ceteris indicibile ante
thronum Dei et agni. Holocausta in templo Dei a rege oblata et habitacula atque
815 ministeria seruorum eius Sabea mirabatur, et Helena nostra multis sacrorum
exercitiis, ieiuniis assiduis et orationibus continuis insistens, desiderioque
martyrii si se tempus optulisset semet ipsam holocastum efficiens immo
quodam modo martir effecta clericorum et religiosorum Deo ministrancium
ordines et sacerdotum patri filium immolancium constituit et in Christo
820 amplectebatur. Multiplicibus muneribus tandem acceptis a Salomone Meroen[v]
reuertitur ad terram suam et Helena nostra multiplicium carismatum donis ditata
prius in urbem Romam ad filium et post modicum ad celestem transiuit patriam.

De nouis basilicis Rome per sanctam Helenam edificatis
825 Post hec Augustus rogatu matris Romam reuerse in pallacio susuriano
basilicam operis egregii condidit quam Ierusalem nominauit eamque titulo
dominice crucis quam nuper ipsa beatissima illuc de Ierosolimis portauerat
insigniuit. Quatuorque candelabra argentea secundum numerum euangelistarum
que ante illam dominice crucis particulam iugi lumine choruscarunt constituit
830 donaque uasorum et ornamentorum preciosorum, prediorum et possessionum et
reddituum, affluenter ecclesie ministris eius contulit. Extruxit eciam ortatu
matris in eadem urbe ecclesiam insignem uia Tyburtina in agro Uerano martiri
sancto Laurencio, quam candelis argenteis uenustauit, intrinsecus porphyreticis
marmoribus adornauit. Ecclesiam [nichilominus] beate Agneti uirgini et martiri
835 rogatu Constantine filie sue, matre eciam commonente, edificauit quam
muneribus et possessionibus amplissimis dedicatam uirginibus sacris ibidem
Christo seruituris assignauit. Item basilicam in ciuitate[m][w] Ostia iuxta portum
Rome urbis et aliam in urbe Albinensi in honorem beati Iohanis baptiste et aliam
in urbe Neapoli[m] mirandi operis condidit, in quibus singulis redditibus et
840 ornamentis sufficienter locupletatis sedes episcopales constituit.

De reliquiis a sancta Helena collectis
Beata Helena sacrosanctas reliquias undecumque poterat collegit, inter quas
erat cultellus quo dominus in sacratissima cena usus est, cunctasque in theca

---

[u] A regina Meroen] *omitted* Go   [v] regina *added in margin* C] Regina de Saba Go   [w] ciuitate (Go)]
ciuitatem C

[30] By using this adjective, Jocelin quite reasonably situates the Queen of Sheba in Meroë, in Ethiopia, a
colony of Sheba.

recondidit Romamque (179v) regressa in Galliam in qua aliquanto tempore
845 quondam morabatur illas deportare si filius permisisset proposuit.[31] Sed quia
consensum ei Augustus minime prebuit archam reliquiarum repositarum
nauigio illic transferri precepit. Nauis autem occulto Dei iudicio in Danubio
flumine submersa disperiit et archa reliquiarum baiula aquis intercepta diucius
ibidem latuit. Post annorum multorum curricula diuina dispencacione beata
850 Helena reuelante theca illa cum preciosissimis <pignoribus>[x] sanctorum inuenta
ab aquis est, sublata et in ciuitate Uesoncionum sita secus flumen prenominatum
allata et magne ueneracioni habita.

Qualiter se sancta Helena ante mortem preparauerit

Beata Helena Rome constituta iam annis et meritis <matura>[y] instar
855 euangelice Anne non discedebat ab ecclesia ieiuniis et obsecracionibus seruiens
die ac nocte. Crebris oracionibus et sacris desideriis conpellebat filias Ierusalem
ut annunciarent dilecto quia 'amore languebat continuo' et cupiens dissolui et
esse cum Christo ut ipsum uidere posset regem in decore suo. Cum autem
placuit ei qui eam segregauit ex utero gentilitatis et Iudaismi et uocauit ad fidem
860 suam per gratiam suam et in mundo per eius instanciam <propagauit>[z] et
sublimauit ecclesiam suam et reuelauit crucem suam ut educeret animam eius ex
huius mundi carcere, continuo lecto doloris decubuit attacta egritudine. Cum
uero ingrauescente molestia mortem corporis adesse sensisset, in ianuis
dispersis et datis pauperibus thesauris, testamentoque sancto, unccione sacra
865 oley remissiui et sacramentis se muniuit dominici corporis et sanguinis. Astitit
Augustus adoptans <ut> benediccio matris moriture super eum ueniret
confidensque ut benediccionem a Domino et misericordiam a Deo salutari suo per
eam ampliorem acciperet. Illa[a] uero collectis uiribus aperiens os suum docuit et
monuit eum custodire fidem et deuocionem in Deum, sollicitudinem, imperium
870 a Deo sibi commissum in pauperes misericordiam circa cunctos exercere
iusticiam, et ne a prepositis uel ministris suis pauperes opprimerentur aut
indebitis exaccionibus grauarentur multam habere diligenciam. In extruendis uel
restaurandis ditandis ornandis ecclesiis curam adhibere maximam, iuxta Dei
sacerdotes et clerum summam exhibere diligenciam et reuerenciam et super
875 omnia protegere et seruare sanctam et catholicam et apostolicam ecclesiam ab
omnimode (180r) heresis contagione immaculatam. Adiecit eciam quod si
conseruaret contra rebelles dauiticos triumphos ubique reportaret et Salomonis
quietum imperium in mundo postmodum in celo perpetuum, possideret. Hec
omnia imperator se impleturum promisit et promissum optime conpleuit; mater

---

[x] pignoribus (Go)] pigneribus C   [y] matura (Go)] natura C   [z] propagauit (Go)] propurgauit C   [a] illa]
ipsa Go

[31] Go adds: 'Dicitur etiam quod fenum in quo iacuit salvator delatum est ab Helena Rome et est in
ecclesia sancte Marie maioris.'

880 postea filium in nomine sancte trinitatis benedixit et corpus et animam illius
regno[b] celesti commendans ualefecit.

De obitu et sepultura sancte Helene

Post paululum eleuatis oculis ac manibus sursum uidit celos apertos
crucemque ineffabili fulgore choruscare Ihesumque stantem in multitudine
885 anglorum. Hec conspiciens et astantibus enarrans gracias inmensas Domino pro
uniuersis beneficiis suis sibi collatis egit et inter uerba graciarium
transferendum manibus angelicis spiritum ad celestia regna emisit. Cuius
sacrum corpus fecit imperator arromatibus preciosis condiri et a Domino papa
ac cardinalibus et clero astante senatu totaque nobilitate urbis inter duas lauros
890 in Uia Lavicana, Drepani sepelliri.[32] Collocauit illud in mausoleo et marmoreo
porphiretico mire magnitudinis et stature operose infra ecclesiam sanctorum
martirorum Marcelli et Petri. Hanc basillicam ipsa construxit et ditissimis
prediis magnificauit. Augustus etiam uasa preciosissima et altare ex auro[c]
purissimo ducentas libras ponderans cum corona aurea .xxx. librarum illic
895 donauit atque multa alia dona preciosa et ornamenta templi que regiam
decebant dignitatem addidit. Oliui etiam nardi pistici libras nongentas et
balsami libras centum singulis annis presentari constituit. Plures quoque
possessiones ditissimorum censuum diuersis in locis ad sustentament<um>
clericorum in eadem ecclesia [ab] obsequio diuino ministrancium contulit inter
900 quas in monte Gabio ipsius sancte Helene <auguste>[d] predium prestans
<annuatim>[e] mille centum triginta solidos numeratum extitit.

De miraculis post eius obitum

Inclusa lapide gleba sacri corporis beate Helene, uirtus de illa exiens includi
uel obrui non potuit sed quam placita fuerit uita eius et mors preciosa in
905 conspectu eius miraculis et creberrimis et celeberimis cunctis claruit. Nec solum
signis mirandis [nisi] ossa eius pullulant de illo sepulture sue loco, sed ubique
[orbis] terrarum ubi ecclesia uel oratorium aut eciam altare nomini suo
attitulatur, tot et talia micant magnalia quod uix queant conprehendi seu discribi
alicuius literatissimi stilo nec mirum (180v). Quia enim in uita sua bonis
910 operibus insudabat et uirtutibus quibus sanctitas adquiritur pocius quam
miraculis quibus si aliquando insumatur non tamen habetur. Nunc sanctitas eius
uirtutibus sacris acquisita signis cum prodigiis innumeris declaratur. Nulla enim
in filiabus Eue tot bona contulit mundo sicut et Helena nostra excepta sola
singulari uirgine Dei genitrice Maria. Ipsius prerogatiua <cunctarum>[f] meritis

---

[b] regno] regi Go   [c] auro] augento Go   [d] auguste (Go)] augusto C   [e] annuatim (Go)] annunciatim C
[f] cunctarum (Go)] cunctorum C

[32] Jocelin confusingly situates the Via Labicana of Rome (the most likely place of Helena's burial) in the
district of Drepanum (in some traditions her native country): on the Via Labicana, see above, p. 18; on
Drepanum, p. 12.

915 mulierum prefertur que regina celi et terre iure creditur cuius se ancillam Helena
profitebatur eique deuotissimis obsequiis famulabatur.

Quod Constantinus materna monita adimplens precepit eius promissa

Constantinus pie memorie mandata morientis matris mancipauit effectui
maternumque promissum conpletum sensit sui experimento ac tocius mundi. Eo
920 namque regnante uidebatur sol solito serenior, aer salubrior, tellus fetibus
fructibus frugibusque fecundior, nauigantibus portus pacacior piscibusque
profusior et tocius mundi facies habundanciore decore <uenustior>ᵍ et continua
pace diuturnior. Ipse uero cunctis principibus predecessoribus suis fuit felicior,
sanctitate superior, gloria et diuiciis ac potencia prestancior, in omnibus bellis
925 aut cum rara sanguinis effusione aut cum nulla triumphator. Existens eciam
supra cunctos antecessores et successores suos Christiane legis sedulus propa-
gator dies demum suos in bonum consumauit et regnum mutans non amittens de
terreno ad aliud quo benedicta mater eius precesserat regnum eternum
transmigrauit. Ad quod nos meritis et precibus sanctissime Helene et omnium
930 sanctorum suorum perducere digne[re]turʰ Ihesus Christus rex eternus qui cum
patre et spiritu sancto uiuit et regnat Deus per omnia secula seculorum. Amen.

Explicit uita sancte Helene regine. Incipit de translacione ipsius[33]

Quidam sacerdos Remensis dyocesis Theogisus nomine, Romam profectus
oracionis causa, ibidem demoratus est causa uisendi loca sancta et perquirendi
935 sanctorum sacra pignora. Erat urbs illa cladibus multis multociens obnoxia et
cumⁱ hostium irrupcionibus, cumʲ crebris pestilenciis, et cum lueᵏ mortalitatis
attrita, ut in ea uix uiderentur uetuste uenustatis uestigia. Turres erant diruteˡ,
muri dirupti, domus uacue, basilice martirum deserte. Qua de causa multe
re[li]giones et precipue Francia ditate sunt copia reliquiarum ex Roma deuecta.
940 Prefatus igitur presbiter Rome constitutus, (181r) dum frequentaret sanctorum
memorias, subiit animum eius in ecclesiam ubi corpus sancte Helene requieuit
deuenire et ipsius inde tollere reliquias ad patriam transferendas. Quod cum
indicasset quibusdam consecretariis suis propositum illud illi approbant et operi
tali peragendo neccessaria preparant. Noctis subᵐ obscuro quando sopor solet
945 occupare homines, cum socio huius rei con<s>cio latitans in ecclesia prefata,
nactus oportunitatem surgit cum quibusdam machinis, operculum mausolei
reuoluit, sacram glebam extraxit, extractam locello preparato recondidit, et
reuolutum lapidem sicut prius erat reponit; recedit et cum consortibus
repatriando maturius iter arripit.

ᵍ uenustior (Go)] uetustior C   ʰ dignetur (Go)] digneretur C   ⁱ cum] tum Go   ʲ cum] tum Go   ᵏ et
cum lue] tum assidue lue Go   ˡ dirute] directe Go   ᵐ sub] cum Go

33 Cf. Altmann, 'Historia translationis ad coenobium Altivillarense', AASS, Aug. III, pp. 601–3.

950   Digressi[n] ab urbe, pernoctabant in silua que iacet[o] ciuitati Sutrie.[34] Mane
facto cum se <procinxisset>[p] ad iter, unus comitum presbiter(i)[q], iuuenis
robustus corpore, accedens sacra pignora super a[s]sellum leuare toto conamine
uoluit sed ab effectu frust<r>atus a loco ea mouere non ualuit. Quo cognito
presbiter pauore perterritus accurrit et, licet longe uiribus inpar iuueni foret,
955 omni facilitate thesaurum illum ac si omni pondere careret apprehendit[r], sursum
leuauit, asello superimposuit, et cum suis recessit. Admirans presbiter de re que
accidit percunctatur[s] a iuuene quid in illa uia <commiserit>[t]. Ille uero
confitebatur se nullius noxe criminalis in illo itinere concium esse, nisi quod illa
nocte sompno illusus carnis lubricum se sensit protulisse. Quo in facto quilibet
960 conueniuntur qui sancta tractant ut tota diligencia corporis et cordis mundiciam
custodiant. Si enim homo iste pro lapsu forsitan ineuitabili ab accessu et
contactu sanctarum reliquiarum arcetur, quid fornicacione uel adulterio seu
flagiciis siue facinoribus polluti promerentur qui non solum accedere et tangere
sancta sanctorum, uerum eciam tractare, sumere, consecrare corpus et
965 sanguinem Domini, quo nichil in hoc mundo sanctius est, non uerentur?
      Cumque iter agentes uenissent ad rapidissimum flumen Thamem[u][35] nomine,
eius [que] uidentes impetum formidabant intrare uel transuadare. Cum autem in
ripa stantes de transitu tractantes[v] asellus sacre sarcine baiulus ac si flagellis
urgeretur aut <calcaribus>[w] flumen ingressus in directum transiuit onere suo
970 deductus. Cernens hoc presbiter qui a[s]sello statura uiribusque maiori insidebat
cum magna difficultate transuadabat (181v). A[s]sellus sui portitor pene totus
undis uidebatur inmersus, cum latera minoris precedentis, geruli reliquiarum
sanctarum, intacta cernerentur a fluctibus.
      In processu uero itineris perplures utriusque sexus sese associabant illis, inter
975 quos quedum puella dum descendunt Alpium iuga labitur in preceps acta. Que
dum miserabiliter uoluitur per deuexa, <conuiatores>[x] eius nomen beate Helene
conclamantes ipsius expetunt suffragia. Ad inuocacionem uero nominis, subito
puella in prorupto[y] latere montis delapsa adhesit[z], sicque dimissis cum funibus
fasciolis eue<h>itur ad superiora incolumis et illesa. Uiso tanto miraculo plures
980 commeancium sanctam Dei glorificauerunt et ad gestanda sacra pignora sese
deuociores et prompciores exhibuerunt. Inter quos quidam equo dissiliens selle
sacras reliquias superintulit; caballum nobili honere oneratum obambulando
minat et inducit[a]. Ueniens autem ad descensum montis, casum timens,
iumentum suum exonerat [h]onusque sacrum propriis humeris inpositum

---

[n] digressi] regressi Go   [o] iacet] adiacet Go   [p] procinxisset (Go)] procingcissent C   [q] presbiteri]
presbiter CGoB   [r] apprehendit] apprehenderet Go   [s] percunctatur] percunctabatur Go   [t] commiserit
(Go)] commiserunt C   [u] Thamem] Tharam GoB   [v] tractantes] tractassent Go   [w] calcaribus (Go)]
calcariis C   [x] conuiatores (Go)] amatores C   [y] prorupto] prerupto Go   [z] delapsa adhesit] est delapsa
Go   [a] inducit] ducit Go

[34] Sutri, north of Rome. Cf. Altmann, *Miracula*, AASS, Aug. III, p. 612C.
[35] Perhaps the river name, *Thames*, in this manuscript is a local English touch; cf. GoB *Tharam*.
Altmann has *Taro* (*Miracula*, AASS, Aug. III, p. 612F). Jocelin is probably referring to the river Taro
in Gaul (now Thérain, west of Reims).

985 tamquam securius custodiendum portat. Ingressus[b] tramitem artum et lubricum
offendens pede in preceps ruit, munera tamen sacra brachiis obstricta tenere
nullatenus omisit. Turba sequens beate Helene crebro nomen exorando
<ingeminat ut>[c] homini labenti in precipicio inter[r]itus festina succurrat. Mira
res: equus qui sacram sarcinam gestauerat propriam uilipendens ruinam
990 ruentem dominum sequens anterioribus pedibus et cruribus amplexus est,
miroque modo stans, immo diuino subnixus adiutorio, tamdiu hominem lapsum
pendulus tenuit quoadusque homines subtus degentes occurrerent[d], glaciem
ferro procinderent et cum funibus et quibusdam machinis hominem et equum in
callem rectum deducerent[e]. Omnes ergo qui uiderunt et audierunt meritis sancte
995 Helene hominis erepcionem deputantes dominum laudauerunt.

Deinde deuenientes in uillam Fallesiam[36] nomine, cum sacram glebam
posuissent in euisdem matrice ecclesia,[37] quidam lunaticus basilicam ingressus
subito torqueri uexacione cepit consueta. Cunctis ergo presentibus <uexato>[f]
diuinam medelam adesse per merita beate[g] regine petentibus, surgens homo
1000 redigitur integra sospitate donatus. In eadem uilla quidam, morbo attritus
grauissimo, grabatum fouendo tria exegerat (182r) lustra, carne ita iam
putrefacta ut .xx. tria ex eius corpore cecidisse dicerentur ossa. Qui dum ad hanc
diuinam medicatricem fuisset perlatus, uirtute diuina erectus stupente populo
recessit sanus effectus.[38]

1005 Quedam puella nomine Bana[h39], clauda ex utero matris, utpote utroque
poplite contracto, <scannis>[i] repente[j] accessit, preces fudit, thecam reliquiarum
tetigit et confestim solidatis basibus et (plantis)[k] exiliit erecta, letabunda, et
laudans recessit, et in Remensi urbe postmodum in sancto proposito monialis
effecta uitam terminauit.

1010 Alia mulier in paralisa percussa lingue manusque dextre ademerat officia.
Accedens linthiolum optulit, thecam sacra continentem tetigit, moxque pristine
salutis munera perfecte suscepit.

Quidam a natiuitate surdus ueruecem offerendo adduxit, ingressus in
ecclesiam ad missarum sollempnia stetit. Cum autem recitaretur euangelium
1015 uerba uite insolita cepit audire[l], percipere, et eo perlecto confessus est se
nuncquam euangelium audisse prius. Sicque recessit exultans quod auditui suo
gaudium et leticiam optate salutis dederit Dominus per merita beata Helene.

Aduenit eciam quidam homo pater pueri lactantis quem ad exitum uite iam

---

[b] ingressus] ingressus postmodum Go [c] ingeminat ut (Go)] ingeminatum C [d] occurrerent]
accurrerent Go [e] deducerent] reducerent Go [f] uexato (Go)] uexatam C [g] beate] beate Helene
Go [h] Bana] Gana Go [i] scannis (Go)] scampis C [j] repente] rependo Go [k] plantis] planctes C
planctis Go [l] audire] aure percipere Go

[36] Falaise, north-east of Reims. Cf. Altmann, *Miracula*, AASS, Aug. III, p. 614E.
[37] MS B omits lines 861–92, summarising: 'Ubi Christus, per merita beate Helene, multa operatus est
mirabilia et tandem maiora et in mirabi[bi]lia in Altivillarensi monasterio Remensis diocesis ad
laudem et gloriam saluatoris nostri Ihesu Christi.'
[38] Cf. Altmann, *Miracula*, AASS, Aug. III, p. 614F.
[39] Cf. Altmann, *Miracula*, AASS, Aug. III, p. 615A, *Bava*.

iamque uicinum uis impellebat egritudinis. Ipse autem precibus profusis eciam
1020 pro uita nati uotum uouit et ad sua rediit; puerulum[m] qui per quinque dies
fomenta mamme pro infirmitate non tetigerat ubera suggentem et incolumen
reperit.

Paraliticus quidam Treuerorum e finibus est aduectus qui .vii. uicibus dudum
omnium membrorum soliditatem et sospitatem fuerat adeptus sed feruens
1025 carnis desideriis deprimentibus illum ad lapsum miserabiliter est contractus[n].
Qui[o] postquam confessus fuerat peccata sua quod ante a .lxx. annis euolutis non
egerat permansura deinceps sanitate <donatus> gracias <agens> Deo et beate
regine uitam suam in posterum emendabat.

Allata est hic alia mulier in dextera parte corporis paralisi percussa ibique
1030 perfectam consecuta medelam ad sua[p] reuersa est sana. Adducta est item
<quedam>[q] ibi mulier <ceca> que mane iam hora rutilante tercia, geminata
<regreditur>[r] oculorum illuminata lucerna. Item quidam leprosus pene discissus
ibidem adductus est, <mane mundus totus effectus est>. Denique postquam
perlata est ad <prefatum>[s] Altiuallarense monasterium sanctissima gleba, hec et
1035 hiis similia et eciam maiora cotidie, que quodammo<do> propter tedium
scripto (182v) non comprehenduntur, effulserunt miracula. Euenit tamen
quibusdam in dubium fratribus, ut fieri solet, an ipsa foret Helena Constantini
Augusti genitrix lignique uitalis inuentrix Ierosolimorum reparatrix. Deinde
communi tandem assensu cum letaniis et triduano ieiunio huius rei ueritatem
1040 sibi denudari suppliciter exposcebant a Domino. Pius autem Dominus trina
reuelacione tribus similibus illud esse corpus eiusdem Helene quod habebat
indicauit et eciam aliis experimentis in aqua que[t] conscribere nolumus
declarauit.

<Missi>[u] fuerant eciam tres fratres ad Romanam urbem ad indagandam huius
1045 beate regine translacionis certitudinem. Qui reuersi sic se rem habere sicut
narratum est <de>[v] certa indagine accepisse <astruxerunt>[w] et geminantes
gaudium illorum corpus beati Policarpi presbiteri et martiris college sancti
Sebastiani secum prefato cenobio attulerunt.[40]

Beate Helene die natalicio imminente, piscatores monachorum noctu
1050 instabant capture piscium in flumine Materno[41] nomine, cassoque frustrati per
totam noctem labore <conquerendo>[x] sanctam Helenam pro sua ceperunt
<inclamare>[y] fatigacione. Tunc in Dei et ipsius nomine laxantes rete, gemino

---

[m] perulum] paruulum Go   [n] contractus] recontractus Go   [o] qui] hic Go   [p] sua] suos Go   [q] quedam
(Go)] quidam C   [r] regreditur (Go)] regendorum C   [s] prefatum (Go)] prelatum C   [t] que] quia Go
[u] missi (Go)] nissi C   [v] de (GoB)] se C   [w] astruxerunt (Go)] asterunt C   [x] conquerendo (Go)]
conquirendo C   [y] inclamare (Go)] *omitted* C

40 Cf. Altmann, 'Historia translationis', AASS, Aug. III, p. 602F. MS B ends at this point, omitting the
fishing miracle.
41 The river Marne which flows south of Reims. It appears that the relics were not translated from Rome
to Hautvillers via the most direct route, perhaps to maximise their exposure prior to arriving at their
final destination.

ditati gaudent essoce sed mox unus eorum (flumen)^z elapsus repeciit^a et gaudium illorum quodam merore interpollauit. Cumque querimoniis sanctam
1055 inclamabant^b Helenam, piscis prefatus dans saltum ab imo superiorem retis funem tenaci morsu arripuit et sic inherentem funi piscator^c gratanter accepit.[42]

^{z} flumen] flumine C, *omitted* Go ^{a} repeciit] repeciit amnen Go ^{b} inclamabant] inclamant Go
^{c} piscator] piscator eum Go

[42] Cf. Altmann, *Miracula*, AASS, Aug. III, p. 617C. In Ms Go, this text is followed by a short memorial commencing 'Helena Constantinii mater' (fol. 213v), though no mention of Britain is made.

Appendix 2

The Anonymous Middle English Verse *St Elyn*
(London, Lambeth Palace, MS 223)

Introductory Comments

This 250-line text in rhyming couplets is extant in three manuscripts:

(G)   London, Lambeth Palace, MS 223, fols 102v–105v; .

(Hx²) London, British Library, MS Harley 2250, fols 81v–83r; and

(M)   London, British Library, MS Egerton 2810, fols 170r–170v.[1]

G and Hx² contain the entire text (though line 126 has been omitted in G), and M contains only the final 46 lines (205–50), inserted over an erasure at the end of a verse life of St Silvester. Görlach notes that this inclusion is not unique in this manuscript, which has had leaves added after binding to accommodate new texts.[2]

M is the earliest of the three manuscripts, dated to c. 1350–1400, though the *St Elyn* fragment is later, after 1450; G was produced c. 1400, and Hx² at some time after 1477.[3]

All three MSS are compilations of religious material. G and M contain exclusively items from the *South English Legendary*, whereas Hx² contains, as well as verse hagiography (including *St Erkenwald*), the *Stanzaic Life of Christ*, and other religious texts in both prose and poetry.

G has been chosen as the base text as it is the earlier of the two complete versions of *St Elyn*. A full list of its contents is contained in James's *Catalogue*,[4] and the manuscript is further described by Görlach, who dates it on the basis of Secretary influence on the handwriting to c. 1400; G was written by a single scribe, in a south-east Derby dialect.[5] The beginning of each new text is indicated by a large decorated capital two lines high, and each new paragraph by a capital slightly larger than one line.

In each MS, *St Elyn* is part of a larger collection of saints' lives know as *The South English Legendary (SEL)*, though because it does not occur in those MSS

---

[1] Manuscript sigla follow those in Manfred Görlach, *The Textual Tradition of the South English Legendary*, Leeds Studies and Monographs, ns 6 (Leeds, 1974).

[2] Görlach, *Textual Tradition*, p. 91.

[3] Görlach, *Textual Tradition*, pp. 91, 83, and 119.

[4] M.R. James, *A Descriptive Catalogue of the Manuscripts in the Library of Lambeth Palace. The Medieval Manuscripts* (Cambridge, 1932), pp. 362–3.

[5] Görlach, *Textual Tradition*, p. 82.

which have been the bases of printed editions, *St Elyn* has not previously been published.[6] Görlach's claim that it was 'adapted from an existing northern legend of the *SEL* MSS circulating in the Midlands'[7] is reasonable, as all existing manuscripts containing *St Elyn* are from the north-west Midlands. The Latin Life of St Helena written by Jocelin of Furness on the Cumbrian coast in the early thirteenth century (transcribed at Appendix 1 above), attests to the existence of earlier Helena legends of this sort in the north of England and in Scotland.

Transcription

This transcription, published with the kind permission of Lambeth Palace Library and the British Library, is based on the text in London, Lambeth Palace, MS 223, fols 102v–105v (G). Selected variant readings as indicated and line 126 have been provided from London, British Library MS Harley 2250, fols 81v-83r (Hx[2]); further variants are from the fragment of the text in London, British Library MS Egerton 2810, fols 170r–170v (M), as indicated in the notes. Original manuscript spelling has been retained in readings supplied from variant manuscripts. Textual emendations have been kept to a minimum, though modern conventions of punctuation and capitalisation have been adopted. Unless it is syntactically appropriate, the *punctus elevatus* which divides the long line has been omitted, though the caesura has been retained. Scribal paragraphing has been retained, since the breaks seem to mark off movements in the narrative. Manuscript orthography has also been retained, including the distribution of *u/v*. Regular abbreviations have been silently expanded. The macron has been construed as indicating the omission of a nasal consonant. The bar through final *h* and *l* is construed as a flourish rather than a macron, as final *e* is regularly included rather than indicated by marks of abbreviation. The incidence of *ff* has been construed as indicating upper-case *F*. Significant lexical and syntactic variations from H and M and a selection of dialectic and orthographic variations are contained in the notes which follow the text.

---

6   The most recent edition is Charlotte d'Evelyn and Anna J. Mill, eds, *The South English Legendary*, 3 vols, EETS, os 235, 236, 244 (Oxford, 1956–59). Individual lives have been edited separately: see the bibliography in Klaus P. Jankofsky, ed., *The South English Legendary: A Critical Assessment* (Tübingen, 1992), pp. 177–82. Subsequent to preparing my transcription, I became aware of an earlier transcription (incomplete and not annotated) and a brief discussion in Susan G. Larkin, 'Transitions in the Medieval Legends of Saint Helena' (unpub. Ph.D. diss., Indiana Univ., 1995), pp. 292–306. For a discussion of the *SEL*, see above, pp. 110–11. An examination of the narrative contents of *St Elyn* is at pp. 111–16.

7   Görlach, *Textual Tradition*, p. 9.

St Elyn

102v   Saynt Elyn was in Bretayn born   and comen of hegh kynrade.
      She loued truly þat lawe   þat God to Moyses made
      But ȝett she leved not God   born of Mare were.[8]
      But stably she loved hit siþen,   as ȝe may after here.
      Grete heritage hir was bifallen,   and þerto she was wys.   5
      In all þe world of witt and sleȝt,   þat mayden bere þe price.
      Sich a halle she lete hir wirche,   al þurȝ hir owene þoȝt
      But efte þe temple Salomon,   sich oon was neuer wroȝt.
      Þe postes alle þai were of plane   þat faire were to biholde,
      Þer was alway lyȝt ynogh   and lee from hete and colde.   10

      Of hir godenesse in all þinges   men wist nowhere sich oon,
      Ne of hir fairnesse in þis world,   þer men han soȝt and gon,
      So þat Constantyne þe kyng   leved þe self lay.
      He was a riche mon and a noble,   and of hir herde say.
      He was so riȝtwis in his lawe   and so certeyn eke   15
      Þat al he demed riȝtwisly,   boþe hole and seke.
      And þo he of hir godenesse herde,   he wilned hir to his wif.
      He myȝt nowhere fynde non sich,   acordaunt to his lyf.

      She lived so religiously   and loved wele þe riȝt
      Þat er she were his wedded wif,   he ne stynt day ne nyȝt.   20
      And when she was his wedded wif,   her lyf with riȝt þai ladden
      So þat with þe wille of God,   a sone togedre þai hadden.
      Þat was sich a conqueror   after his fader day
      Þurȝ þe witt of Elyn his moder,   as I haue herde men say,
      Þat most part of all þis world   he wan with strengþe and gate.   25
      Þerfore men chese him emperor.   Constantyne he hatt.

      Al þus þo his fader was ded,   he traueled mony a ȝere
      Þat al was at his biddinge boun,   boþe fer and nere.
      Þo come þer þurȝ Goddes sonde   a sekenesse him vppon,
      Þat he was as mesel,   as euer was any mon.   30
      In chambre he was preuely,   for shame of his sekenesse
      And myȝt non but preuy men se   in chambre why he so wes.

---

1 Elyn] Elene H (*and passim*)   2 she] ho H (*and passim; also* M)   4 may] mowen H   7 þoȝt] þoght
H (*and passim*)   11 godenesse] godehede H (*and passim*)   16 demed riȝtwisly] dempmet H
21 when] quen H (*and passim; also* M); ladden] *supplied by* H   22 with] þurh H   28 boun] *omitted
in* H

[8]   Helena's presentation as a Jew prior to her conversion to Christianity by Silvester is traditonal (see
     above, pp. 25 and 84).

Þer was mony a sory mon;   men senden fer and negh
As wyde as þe world was   to seche leches slegh.

103r   Þe gedered leches of mony a place   and saiden as hem þoȝt   35
Hade he a baþe of childer blode,   hele him wele hit moȝt.
Hit shuld make him als clene,   boþe of flessh and felle
And as clere of hewe and hyde   as water in þe welle.

Alle þus þai were assented   and saide to þe kyng
And for þai couþe non oþer skil,   þai fonde þat lesinge.   40
Mich wo þat lesinge   hade wroȝt negh hond
And so done liþer tonges ofte   þat nyl for wrache wonde.
Anon þe kyng þurȝ þat   rede of his counseileres
Into alle londes he sent   anon his messageres
To iustices and to shirreves,   by lore and by sonde   45
To do come all þe childer   þat þen were in lond.
Soone þen was þe comyn tale,   as men about wole mele
Þat all þe childer shuld be slayn   for þe emperores hele.
Þer was sorow þen ynogh,   and wymmen maden deol
Þat all her childer shulden dye   for þe kynges euel.   50

Bayllyes oueral soghten,   boþe in lond and burgh
And broȝt hem to þe emperor,   of ych a cuntrey þurgh.
Þo alle bifore þe emperor   clene comen were
He herde about his paleys   a deolful crye and bere
Of wymmen and of childer boþe,   mony a ruful voys.   55
Þe emperor asked his chamberleyn   wherof was þat noys.
'Sire', he saide, 'wymmen ar   with her childer comen
To make þee of hir blode a baþe.   Þi baylies han hem nomen.
Þai al forlyne þis lond aboute   with mych sorowe and crye.
Lord when woltow baþed be?   Þe childer ar all redy'.   60

'Calles me my stiward',   saide þe emperor,
'My iustises and my clerkes,   þat wilnen myn honor,
And bringes me into a toure,   þe heghest þat here be,
Þat I may loke into þe lond   and all þe childer se'.
Þai broȝt hym into a toure   þat was faire and hegh.   65
Þer fel a ruþe into his hert,   þo he þe childer segh
And saide to his clerkes,   'Telles me how is þe lawe
Þat ordeyned is first þurȝ God,   by wise mennes sawe,
And after þe lawe we wole do   and oþer way wole we noȝt,
For so is best bigynne   in worde and dede and þoȝt.   70

70 dede] work H

103v If þat I sle þese childer,   lokes what falles þerto
      And telles me but þe soþe,   er þen I so do'.
      'Sire', þai sayn, 'oure lawe wole þat whoso sles a mon
      Forsoþe þe same iuggement   shal passe him self vppon'.

      'Nay', quod þis emperor,   'I nyl not worche so!   75
      Goe to þe wymmen with þe childer   and bidde hem hamward go.
      Delyuer hem expenses   til þat þai come home.
      Gif I so mony giltles slowe,   I were gretely to blame.
      Grete skaþe it were to spille so   fele for oon wrecches cors.
      And siþen þe grete God hit sent   of me is lytel fors,   80
      And siþen þat Abrahames God   to me þis sekenesse sende,
      I ressayve hit mekely   to my lives ende'.

      Anon þese wymmen with her children   wenten home agayn
      And þat þai were delyuered   so all þai were ful fayn.
      But so as þis emperor Constantyn   lay in his bed at nyȝt,   85
      Of seynt Petre þe apostle   him þoȝt he hade a syȝt.
      Him þoȝt he and Saynt Paule   stode bifore his bed
      And bede him apertly   he shuld not be adred.
      Þai saide þat: 'Abrahames God   and Moyses God also
      Bede þee gif þu wolt be safe   and haue hele of þi wo   90
      To seche þe Pope Siluestre   and after him soone sende,
      For he con graiþe þee a baþe   þis euel to hele and mende.
      Do þu as he þe biddes   without more delay
      And was þu neuer holer   ne better in þi day'.

      Þis emperor at morow ros   and hade hit wel in mynde   95
      And asked where was Siluestre   and how men shuld him fynde.
      His men anon answerde   and sayde after þen
      Þat Siluestre þen was flowen   with oþer Cristen men
      In wodes and in mounteynes.   He most him vtter drawe
      For so he most nede;   he was not at her lawe.   100
      'He leves not as we done   and is not atte þes
      And þerfore he is outlawed   and all þat with him ges'.
      'Seches him radly   and safly hym me bringes.
      I mot haue with him to do   svme nedeful þinges'.
      Anon þer were ordeyned   men ynow to seche   105
      And fond Siluestre and broȝt him   to þe emperores speche.
104r And þo þe Pope Siluestre   with the emperor was mette

---

77 expenses] dispence H   78 giltles] sakles H   79 cors] corps H; fele] mony H   91 sende] wende H
92 graiþe] make H

Doun he fel on knees   and curtesly hym grette:
'Artow Siluestre', quod Constantyn,   'þe Pope of Cristen lawe?'
'Ȝe sire', saide Siluestre,   'and haue ben mony a day'.   110
'Siluestre', he saide, 'Petre is comen   þurȝ Goddes sonde
As I at mydnyȝt lay in my bed   and did me to vnderstonde
Þat þu canst make me a baþe   of more maght
To helpe of my sekenesse   þen leches han me taght'.

   'Ȝe sire', quod Siluestre,   'and þat I vndertake   115
So þat þu do as I þe bid   and neuer a poynt forsake,
And þat þu worche in all þinge   as I shal here þe telle,
Þu shalt be more safe þen euer þu was   boþe in flessh and felle.
Leves þu sire', he saide, 'þer is a God   þat all þinge wroȝt
In all þinge myȝtful   and all has made of noȝt?'   120

'Ȝe', saide Constantyn,   'and þat he made oure lawe
Vppon þe mount of Synay   to Moyses by his dawe'.
'Ȝet þu most', quod Silusestre,   'leve more riȝtly
Þat Goddes sone toke monhede   in þe mayden Marie
And ȝede here on erthe   xxx ȝere and mo   125
And tholyd dethe on rode tre   with payned felled sore.
But all was in his monhede   þat he þoled wo,
And neuer in his godhede   he þoled peyne þo,
But þe body þurȝ þe myȝt   of his deite
Was quyk aȝeyn as hit was ere,   and alway so shal be.   130
Ȝif þat þu leves þat God myȝt do   al þus as I mene
I shal graiþe þee a baþe   to make þi body ful clene'.

'Ȝe', quod þis emperor, 'þo   I leve hit wele and triste
Þat he þat is almyȝty   may do what hym liste'.
Þo made Saynt Siluestre   a coumbe with water fette   135
And halowed hit in Goddes name   and þe emperor in sette.
And þere he folowed Constantyn,   al naked without hater
And all þe filþe of meselrye   lafte þere in þe water.

Þe emperor segh þis myracle   and cries Cristes ore.
Fayrer he was in flessh and felle   þen euer he was bifore.   140
All þat euer þis myracle segh   soone was cristned þen,
And þo þat nole not turn,   þe emperor made to brenne.
For as myche as he bifore   aȝeyn Christendome was,

---

126 *Line omitted in G, possibly due to the same rhyme in two adjoining couplets; supplied from* H
138 filþe] flume H   142 nole] wolde H

For hit he was a champioun   after in ych a place.
And all þat were aȝeynes hit,   boþe he slogh and brende   145
And helde vp Holy Chirches state,   to his lyves ende.

Now is his moder Dame Elyn   in anoþer place
And herde how Constantyn hir sone,   bicomen Cristen was.
She lete write hir leres   and tolde hym all hir þoȝt
And saide him as hir þoȝt,   þat he hade wrongly wroȝt.   150
Hir þoȝt mych wonder   where his witt was bicomen
And saide she leved witterly   þurȝ þe fende hit was nomen.
So as euer his aldres   in all tymes han ysette
Þe noble lawe of Ebrewe   þat he has foule dispised
God himself hit ordeyned   in þe mount of Synay.   155
How was he so hardy   forto chaunge his lay,
And but gif he þe raþer   wole hym repent
And turne ageyn to þe olde lawe   and leve þat foule entent,
She wolde with hir power   destruye him ful clene
For þe bileve of Cristendome   was not worth a bene.   160
'Hit is aȝeynes al skil   þat God shuld be ded.
Repent þe siþen þu hast done mys   and take a better rede.
Nowe shal al þi conquest   þurȝ wrache ende in noȝt.
And sende me radly worde aȝeyn,   wheþer þu wolt turne þi þoȝt'.

Þo Constantyne his moder wille   wist in all þinge   165
He lete pristes in Holy Chirche   boþe rede and synge
And pray ȝerne to Ihesus Crist   for his mykel myȝt,
Þat he sende his moder grace   to bileve ariȝt,
So þat she myȝt be baptizéd   and broȝt in better gate
And with hir wisdome helpe   Holy Chirch astate.   170
Siþen by his leres   he sent hir worde agayn
And bisoȝt hir if she wolde   him where mete þere gayn,
And he take with hir clerkes   of þe Iues lawe,
Þat couþe best dispute   and preve with her sawe.
And he shuld of Cristen men   bring with him also   175
And lete hem dispute togedre   of þe lawes two,
And wheþer so be þe better,   þurȝ Gode preve of riȝt
He wole assent to take him to,   þurh her boþeres syȝt.
Þo Elyn sawe þe leres   she assented soone
In all maner godenesse   as skil is forto done.   180
She sent to a bisshop   Isacar þere he was,

---

146 chirches] kirkes H (*and passim; also* M)   152 Þat ever he was with any mon so saddenly
ouercomon H   162 a better] an oþer H   170 hir wisdome] hir grete wisdome H

Þe best clerk of Iewes lawe,   and tolde him of þe cas.
He sent hir sixty clerkes   him self ne come þe noȝt
And saide he was him self seke,   wherfore so he þoȝt.
Þai busked hem on boþe halues   and sechen clerkes wyde   185
And metten at her steven stid,   as aunter may bityde.

Soone so boþe half was mette,   Saynt Elyn saide hir selue:
'I rede on aiþer syde,   we chesen no but xii
And do we vs vppon þo men   þat ar so wise of lettre
Assent we to wheþer so may   by riȝt his part preue better'.   190

'Dame', quod Saynt Silvestre,   bifore hem euerychone,
'Here shal nomon for Cristendome   dispute but I allone.
I vndertake þurȝ gode riȝt   and þurȝ gode resoun
Þat al þat euer þi clerkes sayn   is noȝt but a tresoun'.
Þen saide þe emperice: 'So ȝe may ful longe   195
Dispute on aiþer syde   boþe with riȝt and wronge
And aiþer may þurȝ clergye   wel mayntene his lawe,
And we may neuer better wete,   whether is soþe sawe.
But gif we myȝten bodily se,   þurȝ þreue of Goddes myȝt
Wheþer lawe is wrongwis and wheþer lawe is riȝt'.   200
Þan stod vp a mayster þe   of þe Iues lawe:
'Dame we shul shewe þe soþe,   in deed and eke in sawe
Þat oure lawe is better   as we in bokes preuen
Þen is þat ilke fals lawe   þat Cristen men on leuen'.
A bole of bras he lad forth,   riȝt a mydde place   205
Þat ȝede quyk lowand about;   a mervayle syȝt hit was.
'Nowe sire, Pope Siluestre', he seide,   'let se what þu can do.
Here is a syȝt ful preuy of my God   a ded þing þer to go'.
He ȝede about amonge þe men,   as a quyk best shuld.
Þe emperor and his moder   þo stoden and bihelde.   210

Þen saide þe emperice   to þe Pope Siluestre:
'Þis is a veray myracle   boþe in lyȝt and þestere,
To make of bras a quycke best;   hit is a ferly myȝt'.
'Ȝe dame', saide Saynt Siluestre,   'hit is no beste with riȝt.

---

184 wherfore so he þoȝt] querfore he no myght H   187 hir selue] in highe H   188 Let so þi clerkes
bringe hom forthe for mon are all redye H   189 and do we so vppon seche men tat bene full weleche H
190 part] skylle H   192 I allone] myn one H   195 emperice] emperors moder H   203 preuen]
breuen H   205 a bole] a bulle H; a Jew a bulle M   206 lowand] bellande M; mervayle] wonder M
207 he (HM)] se G (*The context demands a masculine pronoun*)   208 syȝt ful priuy] a verray preue
M   210 þo] boþe H; full line] þen to Pope Silvester þe emperes saide wele sone M   212 boþe in lyȝt
and þestere] þat before vse we sene done M   213 ferly] wonder M

A þinge may seme in erþely siȝt   and ȝett is hit not so,   215
As I shal shewe bifore ȝow all   what makes þe beste to go'.
105v   He ȝede boldly to þat beste   and toke him by þe horn:
'I bidde þe deuel on Cristes half   all þese folke biforn
Þat þu shewe hem what þu art   þat makes þis bole to belle'.
Þer slagh forth out of þat beste   þe quyk deuel of helle.   220
Þe bras fel doun and alto barst,   and bifore hem euerychone
Þe deuel kest half þe cite doun,   as he awey con gon.

Þe emperice þo falles doun   to Saynt Siluestres fete.
So tenderly she wepte   þat all þe place was wete.
'I aske Cristendome', she saide,   'vppon Goddes name,   225
For I haue wrongly lad my lyf   euer in synne and shame'.
Þe Pope cristned hir anon   and taȝt hir all oure fay
And mony turned with hir   to þe riȝt lay.

Nowe is seynt Elyn cristned   and at þe riȝt bileve,
And all þat were ageynes þe fay,   she con hem gretely greve.   230
A temple was at Ierusalem;   was most with Iues ysett
Þere as sacrifice was done   and childer circumcised.
She lete halowe þat ilke place   so wisely she con wirche
And pristes to rede and synge   and called hit Mary's chirche.
She made hir sone by powere   þer as no prechinge myȝt,   235
To turne men to Cristen lawe   and bileue ariȝt.
Þere as men shuld teþes   bifore þat tyme brenne
She ordeyned hem to Holy Chirche,   þat neuer was done er þen.
She made hir sone to bere þe Croys   in his baner aboute
Whiderso he went to batel,   þen þurt him not doute.   240
And so han men done hiderto   ych emperor on his day,
Save Iulian þe Renegate   þat was of fals laye.
Saynt Elyn toke þe nayls   þat God was stongen mydde.
In Constantynes helme hir sone   oon of hem she did;
Anoþer in his bridell   to batel þere he ȝede;   245
Þe þridde she kest into þe see   for mony monnes nede.
Þe sendes strengþe she þer fordid   on water and on lond

216 I shal shewe] I showe H; to] superscript G   218 half] name M   220 forth] forthe some H; beste]
bulle H   223 doun to Saynt Siluestres] on kneese þe popes M   224 wepte] grette H; And ȝerned hym
mercy and mony teres lete M   226 wrongly] euell M   228 And with her twenty þousand vppon þe
selfe day H; And xxᵗⁱ þousand with hire þat ilke day M   229 Now is . . . at] þen was . . . broȝte to M
230 fay] fayth H; faithe M   231 was most] most H; Þen was a tempulle in Jerusalem þat Jewe mycull
vsede M   232 þere as sacrifice was done] þer tai made hore sacrifice M   237 teþes] togethes H;
tendes M (*placed after* 'tyme')   240 þen þurt him not] þen hade he no M   242 Renegate] Renedyede
H; Wared M

191

Hir sone euermore while þat he lived   he hade þe herre hond.
At Rome saynt Elyn dyed,   and þere she bired is.
Oure Lord for Saynt Elyn love,   graunte vs heuen blis.   250
      Amen.

250 grante vs heuen blis] bring vs to þi blisse M

Bibliography

Editions and Pre-Modern Commentaries

Actus beati Silvestri, ed. Boninus Mombritius, *Sanctuarium sive vitae sanctorum*, 2nd ed. (Paris, 1910)

Actus Cyriaci, AASS, May I (Antwerp, 1680), pp. 445–8; Engl. trans. M.J.B. Allen and D.G. Calder, *Sources and Analogues of Old English Poetry: The Major Latin Texts in Translation* (Cambridge and Totowa, 1996), pp. 60–8

Ælfric, *Catholic Homilies, The Second Series*, ed. Malcolm Godden, EETS, ss 5 (London, 1979)

————, *Lives of the Saints*, ed. and Engl. trans. Walter W. Skeat, 4 vols, EETS, os 76, 82, 94 and 114 (London, 1881–1900; repr. in 2 vols, 1966)

Æthelweard, *Chronicle*, ed. and Engl. trans. A. Campbell (London, 1962)

Alcuin, 'Versus de sancta cruce ad Carolum', ed. E. Dümmler, *Poetae latini aevi Carolini*, MGH (Berlin, 1881; repr. 1964), p. 225

Aldhelm, *De virginitate*, *Aldhelmi opera*, ed. R. Ehwald, MGH, Auctores antiquissimi, XV (Berlin, 1919); Engl. trans. Michael Lapidge and James J. Rosier, *Aldhelm: The Poetic Works* (Cambridge, 1985); and Michael Lapidge and Michael Herren, *Aldhelm: The Prose Works* (Cambridge, 1979)

Alford, Michael, *Britannia illustrata, siue Lucii, Helenæ, Constantini, patria et fides* (Antwerp, 1641)

Altmann, *Historia translationis ad cenobium Altivillarense*, AASS (Antwerp, 1680), Aug.III, pp. 580–99; *Vita (Helenae)*, pp. 601–3; *Miracula*, pp. 612–17

Ambrose, *De obitu Theodosii*, ed. O. Faller, *Sancti Ambrosii opera*, pars VII, CSEL 43 (Vienna, 1955); Engl. trans. Mary Dolorosa Mannix, *Sancti Ambrosii oratio de obitu Theodosii: Text, Translation, Introduction and Commentary* (Washington, D.C., 1925)

Anglo-Saxon Chronicle

  A Collaborative Edition, ed. David Dumville and Simon Keynes, vol. 3. *Ms A*, ed. Janet M. Bately (Cambridge, 1986)

  A Revised Edition, ed. and Engl. trans. Dorothy Whitelock, D.C. Douglas, and S.I. Tucker (London, 1961)

  Two of the Saxon Chronicles Parallel, ed. Charles Plummer, 2 vols (Oxford, 1892–99)

Anglo-Saxon Litanies of the Saints, ed. Michael Lapidge, Henry Bradshaw Society 106 (London, 1991)

Annalibus Montis S. Michaelis, ed. Léopold Delisle, *Chronique de Robert de Torigni*, 2 vols (Rouen, 1872–73), II.207–36

Arculf, *De locis sanctis* (via Adamnan), ed. P. Geyer, CSEL 39 (Vienna, 1898)

Baronius, Cesare, *Annales ecclesiastici* (Rome, 1607)

Bede, *Chronica maiora*, ed. T. Mommsen, MGH, Auctores antiquissimi (Berlin, 1898),

XIII.495–535; Engl. trans. Faith Wallis, *Bede: On the Reckoning of Time* (Liverpool, 1999), pp. 157–237

——, 'De inventione sanctae crucis', ed. J.-P. Migne, PL 94 (Paris, 1862), cols 494–5

——, *Historia ecclesiastica gentis Anglorum*, ed. and Engl. trans. B. Colgrave and R.A.B. Mynors (Oxford, 1969)

Bertrandon de la Broquiere, *Voyage d'Outremer*, ed. G.R. Kline (New York, 1988)

Brut, Middle English Prose, ed. F.W.D. Brie, 2 vols, EETS, os 131 and 136 (London, 1906–08)

Brut Dingestow, ed. Henry Lewis (Cardiff, 1942)

Calendars

Francis Wormald, ed., *English Benedictine Kalendars after A.D. 1100* (London, 1939)

——, *English Kalendars before A.D. 1100*, Henry Bradshaw Society, 72 (1934; repr. Woodbridge, 1988)

Camden, William, *Britannia* (London, 1610); translated, rearranged and enlarged by Edmund Gibson (London, 1695)

——, *Remains Concerning Britain*, ed. R.D. Dunn (Toronto, 1984)

Capgrave, John, *Abbreuiacion of Chronicles*, ed. P.J. Lucas, EETS, os 285 (Oxford, 1983)

Carte, Thomas, *General History of England* (London, 1747–55)

Cassiodorus–Epiphanius, *Historia tripartita*
  ed. J.-P. Migne, PL 69 (Paris, 1865), cols 879–1213
  ed. W. Jacob and R. Hanslik, CSEL 71 (Vienna, 1952)

Castleford's Chronicle or The Boke of Brut, ed. Caroline D. Eckhardt, 2 vols to date, EETS, os 305 and 306 (Oxford, 1996)

Caxton, William, *Golden Legend*, ed. F.S. Ellis, The Temple Classics, 7 vols (London, 1900)

Chaucer, Geoffry, *The Canterbury Tales*, gen. ed. Larry Benson, *The Riverside Chaucer*, 3rd ed. (Boston, 1987)

Chronicon Monasterii de Abingdon, ed. J. Stevenson, Rolls Series, 2 vols (London, 1858)

Cynewulf, *Elene*, ed. P.O.E. Gradon (London, 1958)

The Descent of the Men of the North., ed. and Engl. trans. W.F. Skene, *The Four Ancient Books of Wales*, 2 vols (Edinburgh, 1868), II.454–65

de Vignay, Jean, *Légende dorée*, ed. Brenda Dunn-Lardeau, *Jacques de Voragine, La Légende dorée, Edition critique dans la révision de 1476 par Jean Batallier, d'apres la traduction de Jean de Vignay (1333–1348) de la Legenda aurea (c. 1261–1266)* (Paris, 1997)

Dexter, Fl. Lucius, *Chronicon*, ed. J.-P. Migne, PL 31 (Paris, 1846), cols 550–72

Drayton, Michael, *Works*, ed. J. William Hebel, 4 vols (Oxford, 1961)

Dream of Maxim Guletic (Macsen Wledig), ed. Ifor Williams, *Breuddwyd Maxen*, 3rd ed. (Bangor, 1928); Engl. trans. Gwyn Jones and Thomas Jones, *The Mabinogion*, 2nd ed. (London, 1974), pp. 79–88

The Dream of the Rood
  ed. M. Swanton, rev. ed. (Exeter, 1987)
  ed. Bruce Dickens and Alan S.C. Ross, 4th ed. (London, 1954)

Dugdale, William, *Monasticon anglicanum: A New Edition*, ed. John Caley, H. Ellis, and B. Bardinel, 8 vols (London, 1846)

Eulogium, ed. F.S. Haydon, 2 vols (London, 1858)

Eusebius, *Historia ecclesiastica*, ed. E. Schwartz, *Die Kirchengeschichte*, 3 vols, 1.3, GCS IX (Leipzig, 1903–9); Engl. trans. H.J. Lawlor and J.E.L. Oulton (London, 1927–28)

———, *Laus Constantini*, ed. Ivar H. Heikel, *Eusebius' Werke*, I, GCS 7 (Leipzig, 1902), pp. 195–223; Engl. trans. H.A. Drake, *In Praise of Constantine* (Berkeley, 1976), pp. 83–102

———, *Vita Constantini*, ed. F. Winkelmann, *Über das Leben des Kaisers Konstantins*, GCS *Eusebius' Werke* I.1 (Berlin, 1975); Engl. trans. Averil Cameron and Stuart G. Hall, *Eusebius: Life of Constantine*, Clarendon Ancient History Series (Oxford, 1999)

Eutropius, *Breviarium ab urbe condita*, ed. F. Ruehl (Stuttgart, 1975); Engl. trans. H.W. Bird, Translated Texts for Historians 14 (Liverpool, 1993)

Fillastre, Guillame, *Gesta*, Engl. trans. L.R. Loomis, *The Council of Constance: The Unification of the Church*, ed. J.H. Mundy and K.M. Woody (New York and London, 1961)

Flodoard of Reims, *Historia Remensis ecclesiae*, ed. Martina Stratmann, *Flodoard von Reims: Die Geschichte der reimser Kirche*, MGH, Scriptores XXXVI (Hanover, 1998)

Flores historiarum, ed. Henry Ward, Rerum Britannicarum medii aevi scriptores, 95 (London, 1890)

Foxe, John, *Acts and Monuments of these Later and Perilous Dayes* (London, 1576), ed. George Townsend, 9 vols (London, 1843)

Geoffrey of Monmouth, *Historia regum Britannie*, ed. Neil Wright, *I, Bern Burgerbibliothek, MS 568* (Cambridge, 1984)

Gesta Normannorum ducum (of William of Jumièges, Orderic Vitalis, and Robert of Torigni), ed. E.M.C. Van Houts, 2 vols (Oxford, 1992)

Gestum regum Britannie, ed. Neil Wright, *The Historia regum Britannie of Geoffrey of Monmouth*, vol. V (Cambridge, 1991)

Gibbon, Edward, *Decline and Fall of the Roman Empire*, 9 vols (London, 1776–88; repr. cd. J.B. Bury, 1909)

Gildas, *De excidio Britanniae*, ed. and Engl. trans. Michael Winterbottom, *Gildas: The Ruin of Britain and Other Works* (London, 1978)

Gilte legende, ed. Richard Hamer and Vida Russell, *Supplementary Lives in some Manuscripts of the Gilte legende*, EETS, os 315 (Oxford, 2000)

Gower, John, *Confessio amantis*, ed. R.A. Peck (New York, 1966, repr. Toronto, 1986)

———, *In Praise of Peace*, ed. G.G. Macaulay, *The English Works of John Gower*, 2 vols (London, 1901)

Gregory of Tours, *Libri historiarum X*, ed. Bruno Krusch and Wilhelm Levison, 2nd ed., MGH, Scriptores rerum Merovingicarum I 1 (Hanover, 1951); Engl. trans. Lewis Thorpe, *The History of the Franks* (Harmondsworth, 1974)

Hardyng, John, *Chronicle*, ed. H. Ellis (London, 1812, repr. New York, 1974)

Hennsoun, John, *Complaynt of Scotland*, ed. J.A.H. Murray, EETS, es 17 (London, 1872), pp. 207–36

Henry of Huntingdon, *Historia Anglorum*, ed. Diana L. Greenway (Oxford, 1996)

Higden, Ranulph, *Polychronicon*, in *Polychronicon Ranulphi Higden monachi cestrensis, Together with English Translations of John Trevisa and of an Unknown Writer of the Fifteenth Century*, ed. Churchill Babington and J.R. Lumby, 9 vols, Rolls Series 41 (London, 1865)

Historia Brittonum: see Nennius

Hoccleve, Thomas, *Balade, Hoccleve's Works: The Minor Poems*, ed. Frederick J. Furnivall and Sir I. Gollancz, EETS, es 61 and 73 (London, 1892 and 1925)

Holinshed, Raphael, *Chronicles of England, Scotland and Ireland*, 6 vols (London, 1577; repr. 1807)

Hrabanus Maurus, *Martyrologium*, ed. John McCulloh, Corpus christianorum, Continuatio mediaevalis 44 (Turnhout, 1979)

Incerti auctoris de Constantino Magno eiusque matre Helena libellus, ed. E. Heydenreich (Leipzig, 1879)

Inventio sanctae crucis, ed. Stephan Borgehammar, *How the Holy Cross was Found: From Event to Medieval Legend*, Bibliotheca theologiae practicae, Kyrkovetens-kapliga studier 47 (Stockholm, 1991), Appendices A, B and C, pp. 201–302; Engl. trans., E. Gordon Whatley, 'Constantine the Great, the Empress Helena and the Relics of the Holy Cross', *Medieval Hagiography: An Anthology*, ed. Thomas Head (New York and London, 2000), pp. 77–95, at pp. 86–92

Jacobus de Voragine, *Legenda aurea*
  ed. T. Graesse, 2 vols, 3rd ed. (Dresden, 1890; repr. Osnabrück, 1969); Engl. trans. *The Golden Legend: Readings on the Saints*, W.G. Ryan, 2 vols (Princeton, 1993)
  ed. P.M. Maggioni, *Iacopo da Varazze: Legenda aurea* (Florence, 1998)

Jerome, *Chronicon*, ed. R. Helm, *Eusebius' Werke* VII, GCS 47 (Berlin, 1956)
——, *De viris illustribus*, PL 23, cols 631–760; Engl. trans. Philip Schaff and Henry Wace, A Select Library of Nicene and Post-Nicene Fathers of the Christian Church, 2nd ser., vol. 3 (1892; repr. Grand Rapids, 1975)

Jocelin of Furness, *Vita sancti Kentigerni*, ed. A.P. Forbes, *Lives of S. Ninian and S. Kentigern* (Edinburgh, 1874)
——, *Vita sancti Patricii episcopi*, ed. J. Colgan, *Trias thaumaturga vitae, Acta sanctorum Hiberniae*, II (Louvain, 1647), pp. 64–116
——, *Vita sancti Waldevi abbatis*
  ed. AASS, Aug. I, pp. 248–74;
  ed. and Engl. trans., George McFadden, 'An Edition and Translation of the Life of Waldef, Abbot of Melrose, by Jocelin of Furness' (unpub. Ph.D. diss., Columbia Univ., 1952)

John of Salisbury, *Polycraticus*, ed. and Engl. trans. C.J. Nederman (Oxford, 1990)

Judith, ed. E.V.K. Dobbie, *Beowulf and Judith*, ASPR IV (New York, 1953), pp. 99–109

Kalendre of the Newe Legende of Englande, ed. Manfred Görlach (Heidelberg, 1994)

Lactantius, *De mortibus persecutorum*, ed. and Engl. trans. J.L. Creed (Oxford, 1984)

Laȝamon, *Brut*
  ed. and Engl. trans., W.R.J. Barron and S.C. Weinberg (Harlow, 1995)
  ed. G.L. Brook and R.F. Leslie, 2 vols, EETS, os 250 and 277 (London, 1963; repr. 1978); Engl. trans. Rosamond Allen, *Lawman: Brut* (London, 1992)

Lee, Nathaniel, *Constantine the Great: A Tragedy Acted at the Theatre Royal* (London, 1684), ed. Walter Häfele (Heidelberg, 1933)

Liber pontificalis, ed. L. Duschesne, 3 vols, 2nd ed. (Paris, 1957); Engl. trans. Raymond Davis, *The Book of the Pontiffs*, Translated Texts for Historians, Latin Series, 5 (Liverpool, 1989)

Life and Martyrdom of St Katherine of Alexandria, Virgin and Martyr
  ed. Henry Hucks Gibbs (London, 1884)
  ed. Saara Nevanlinna and Irma Taavitsainen, *St Katherine of Alexandria: The Late*

Middle English Prose Legend in Southwell Minster MS 7 (Cambridge and Helsinki, 1993)

The Lives of Women Saints of our Contrie of England, ed. C. Horstmann (London, 1886)

Mabinogion
  ed. J. Gwenogvryn Evans, *The Red Book of Hergest* (Oxford, 1887)
  ed. J. Gwenogvryn Evans, *The White Book Mabinogion* (Pwllheli, 1907)
  ed. J. Loth, *Les Mabinogion*, 2 vols (Paris, 1913)
  Engl. trans. Gwyn Jones and Thomas Jones, 2nd ed. (London, 1974)

Mandeville, John, *Mandeville's Travels*, ed. M.C. Seymour (Oxford, 1967)

Milton, John, *The History of Britain* (London, 1671)

Mirk's Festival: A Collection of Homilies, ed. T. Erbe, EETS, es 96 (London, 1905)

Morant, Philip, *History and Antiquities of the County of Essex*, 2 vols (London, 1763–68; repr. East Ardsley, 1978)

Necrologium imperatorem et catalogus eorum sepulchrorum, ed. R. Cessi, *Origo civitatem Italie seu venetiarum: Chronicon Altinate et chronicon Gradense*, Fonti per la storia d'Italia, Istituto storico Italiano (Rome, 1933)

Nennius, *Historia Brittonum*
  ed. David Dumville (Cambridge, 1985)
  ed. and Engl. trans. John Morris, *Nennius: British History and the Welsh Annals* (London, Chichester, and Totowa, 1980)

Nova legenda Anglie, ed. C. Horstmann, 2 vols (Oxford, 1901)

Oath Book or Red Parchment Book of Colchester, ed. W. Gurney Benham (Colchester, 1907)

Old English Finding of the True Cross, ed. and Engl. trans. Mary-Catherine Bodden (Cambridge, 1987)

Old English Martyrology
  ed. George Herzfeld, EETS, os 116 (London, 1900)
  ed. Günter Kotzor, *Das altenglische Martyrologium*, 2 vols (Munich, 1981)

Old English Orosius, ed. Janet Bately, EETS, ss 6 (London, 1980)

Old English Version of Bede's Ecclesiastical History of the English People, ed. and Engl. trans. Thomas Miller, 4 vols (Oxford, 1890; repr. Millwood, N.Y., 1978)

Orderic Vitalis, *Historia ecclesiastica*, ed. and Engl. trans. M. Chibnall, 6 vols, Oxford Medieval Texts (Oxford, 1968–80)

Origo Constantini, ed. I. König, *Origo Constantini: Anonymous Valesianus, Teil 1: Text und Kommetar* (Trier, 1987); Engl. trans. Jane Stevenson with introduction and notes by S.N.C. Lieu., *From Constantine to Julian: Pagan and Byzantine Views. A Source History*, ed. S.N.C. Lieu and Dominic Montserrat (London and New York, 1996), pp. 39–62

Orosius, *Historia adversus paganos*, ed. Caroli Zangemeister (Leipzig, 1889); Engl. trans. R.J. Defarrari, Fathers of the Church 50 (Washington, D.C., 1964)

Panegyrici Latini, ed. and Engl. trans. C.E.V. Nixon and Barbara Saylor Rodgers, *In Praise of Later Roman Emperors: The Panegyrici Latini. Introduction, Translation, and Historical Commentary with the Latin Text of R.A.B. Mynors* (Berkeley, 1994)

Paulinus of Nola, *Epistolae*, ed. W. Hartel, CSEL 29 (Vienna, 1894); Engl. trans. P.G. Walsh, Ancient Christian Writers 36 (London, 1967)

Philostorgius, *Historia ecclesiastica*, ed. Joseph Bidez, *Kirkengeschichte*, 3rd ed., rev. F. Winkelmann, GCS (Berlin, 1981); Engl. trans. E. Walford (London, 1855)

Ralph of Diceto, *Abbreviationes chronicorum*, ed. W. Stubbs, 2 vols (London, 1876)

Robert of Brunne, *The Story of England*, ed. T. Hearne, *Peter Langtoft's Chronicle as Illust. and Improv'd by Robert of Brunne (AD 689–1307)*, 2 vols (Oxford, 1725)

Robert of Gloucester, *Metrical Chronicle*, ed. T. Hearne, 2 vols (Oxford, 1724)

Rufinus of Aquileia, *Historia ecclesiastica*, ed. E. Schwartz and T. Mommsen, *Eusebius' Werke*, II.2 (Leipzig, 1908), pp. 960–1040; Engl. trans. (partial) Philip R. Amidon, *The Church History of Rufinus of Aquileia: Books 10 and 11* (New York and Oxford, 1997)

Sayers, Dorothy L., *The Emperor Constantine: A Chronicle* (London, 1951); also performed under the title *Christ's Emperor*

———, Letters, ed. Barbara Reynolds, *The Letters of Dorothy L. Sayers*, vol. 4 (Cambridge, 2000)

Sigebert, *Chronicon*, ed. L.C. Bethmann, PL 160 (Paris, 1880), cols 57–240; repr. MGH Scriptores VI (Hanover, 1884), pp. 300–74

Socrates Scholasticus, *Historia ecclesiastica*, ed. R. Hussey, 3 vols (Oxford, 1853); Engl. trans. A.C. Zenos, A Select Library of Nicene and Post-Nicene Fathers, 2nd ser., vol. II (1890; repr. Grand Rapids, 1973)

South English Legendary
  ed. Charlotte D'Evelyn and Anna J. Mill, EETS, os 235, 236 and 244 (London, 1956–59)
  ed. C. Horstmann, 'Des Ms. Bodl. 779', *Archiv für das Studium der neueren Sprachen und Literaturen* 82 (1889), pp. 351–3 and 369–422
  ed. C. Horstmann, EETS, os 87 (London, 1887)

Sozomen, *Historia ecclesiastica*, ed. J. Bidez, GCS 50 (Berlin, 1960); Engl. trans. A.C. Zenos, A Select Library of Nicene and Post-Nicene Fathers, 2nd ser., vol. II (1890; repr. Grand Rapids, 1973)

Spenser, Edmund, *The Faerie Queen*, ed. T.P. Roche (Harmondsworth, 1987)

Stowe, John, *Survey of London*, ed. C.L. Kingsford, 2 vols (London, 1908)

Sulpicius Severus, *Dialogi*, PL 20 (Paris, 1845); Engl. trans. F.R. Hoare, *The Western Fathers* (London, 1954), pp. 68–144

Theodoret, *Historia ecclesiastica*, ed. L. Parmentier, rev. F. Scheidweiler, GCS 44 (Berlin, 1954); Engl. trans. B. Jackson, A Select Library of Nicene and Post-Nicene Fathers, 2nd ser., vol. III (1890; repr. Grand Rapids, 1973)

Usk, Adam, *Chronicle*, ed. and Engl. trans. C. Given-Wilson (Oxford, 1997)

Valla, Lorenzo, *De falso credita et emenita Constantini donatione declamatio*, 1440, ed. and Engl. trans. Christopher B. Coleman (1922; repr. Toronto, 1993)

Vergil, Polydore, *Anglica historia*, ed. and Engl. trans. Denys Hay, Camden Series, vol. 74 (London, 1950); Engl. trans. (partial) Henry Ellis, *Polydore Vergil's English History, vol. I: Containing the First Eight Books* (London, 1846)

Wace, *Roman de Brut*, ed. and Engl. trans. Judith Weiss (Exeter, 1999)

Waugh, Evelyn, *Helena* (London, 1950)

———, Letters, ed. Mark Amory, *The Letters of Evelyn Waugh* (New Haven and New York, 1980)

Welsh Genealogies, ed. P.C. Bartrum, *Early Welsh Genealogical Tracts* (Cardiff, 1966)

Welsh Triads, ed. and Engl. trans. Rachel Bromwich, *Trioedd Ynys Prydein: The Welsh Triads*, 2nd ed. (Cardiff, 1978)

White, Richard, *Historiarum Britanniae* (Douai, 1597–1607)

William of Malmesbury, *Gesta regum Anglorum*, ed. and Engl. trans. R.A.B. Mynors, completed by R.M. Thomson and M. Winterbottom, 2 vols (Oxford, 1998–99)

Willibrord, *Calendar*, ed. H.A. Wilson, *The Calendar of St. Willibrord From MS. Paris Lat. 10837: A Facsimile with Transcription, Introduction, and Notes*, Henry Bradshaw Society 55 (1918; repr. Woodbridge, 1998)

Wilson, John, *The English Martyrologe containing a summary of the most renowned and illustrious saints of the three kingdoms, England, Scotland, and Ireland* (n.p., 1608; repr. Amsterdam and New York, 1970)

Secondary Sources

Abou-El-Haj, Barbara, *The Medieval Cult of Saints: Formations and Transformations* (Cambridge, 1994)

Alamichel, Marie-Françoise, 'La Légende de Sainte Hélène de Cynewulf à Evelyn Waugh', *Études Anglaises* 48 (1995), pp. 306–18

Alföldi, Andrew, *The Conversion of Constantine and Pagan Rome*, Engl. trans. Harold Mattingly (Oxford, 1948)

Anglo, Sydney, 'The *British History* in Early Tudor Propaganda', *Bulletin of the John Rylands University Library of Manchester* 44 (1961), pp. 17–48

——, *Images of Tudor Kingship* (Guildford, 1992)

Antonio, N., *Bibliotheca Hispana Nova* (Madrid, 1783; repr. Torino, 1963)

Ashe, Geoffrey, *Mythology of the British Isles* (London, 1990)

Astley, H.J.D., 'Mediaeval Colchester – Town Castle and Abbey – From MSS in the British Museum', *Transactions of the Essex Archaeological Society*, s. 8 (1903), pp. 117–38

Ayres, L.M., 'A Tanner Manuscript in the Bodleian Library and some Notes on English Painting of the Late Twelfth Century', *Journal of the Warburg and Courtauld Institutes* 32 (1969), pp. 41–55

Bacon, Alan F., 'The History of the Windows', *The Saint Helen Windows in the Ancient Parish Church of Saint Michael and All Angels Ashton-under-Lyne* (Ashton-under-Lyne, 2000), pp. 7 8

Baert, Barbara, '*In hoc vinces*: Iconography of the Stone Cross in the Parish Church of Kelloe (Durham, ca 1200)', *Archaeological and Historical Aspects of West-European Societies*, ed. Marc Lodewijckz, Acta archaeologica lovaniensia monographiae 8 (Louvain, 1996), pp. 341–62

——, 'New Observations on the Genesis of Girona (1050–1100): The Iconography of the Legend of the True Cross', *Gesta* 38 (1999), pp. 115–27

Bailey, R., *Viking Age Sculpture* (London, 1980)

Baker, Derek, 'Legend and Reality: The Case of Waldef of Melrose', *Church, Society, and Politics: Papers Read at the Thirteenth Summer Meeting and the Fourteenth Winter Meeting of the Ecclesiastical History Society*, ed. Derek Baker (Oxford, 1975), pp. 59–82

Baring-Gould, S., *Lives of the Saints*, 16 vols (Edinburgh, 1914)

——, and John Fisher, *The Lives of the British Saints*, 4 vols (London, 1911)

Barnes, T.D., *Constantine and Eusebius* (Cambridge, Mass. and London, 1981)

——, *The New Empire of Diocletian and Constantine* (Cambridge, Mass. and London, 1982)

Bartlett, Robert, 'Jocelin of Furness', *New Dictionary of National Biography* (forthcoming)

Bartrum, P.C., *A Welsh Classical Dictionary* (Aberystwyth, 1993)

Bassett, Steven, 'Church and Diocese in the West Midlands: the Transition from British to Anglo-Saxon Control', *Pastoral Care before the Parish*, ed. John Blair and Richard Sharpe (Leicester, 1992), pp. 13–40

——, 'Churches in Worcester before and after the Conversion of the Anglo-Saxons', *The Antiquaries Journal* 69 (1989), pp. 225–56

Bately, Janet M., 'Old English before the Reign of Alfred', *ASE* 17 (1988), pp. 93–108

Baudrillart, A., *Dictionnaire d'histoire et de géographie ecclésiastiques*, tome 9 (Paris, 1937)

Bieler, Ludwig, *Ireland and the Culture of Early Medieval Europe*, ed. Richard Sharpe (London, 1987)

——, *Studies on the Life and Legend of St. Patrick*, ed. Richard Sharpe, Variorum Reprints (London, 1986)

Biggs, Frederick M., 'Inventio Sanctae Crucis', *Sources of Anglo-Saxon Literary Culture: A Trial Version*, ed. F.M. Biggs, T.D. Hill, and P.E. Szarmach (Binghamton, 1990), pp. 12–13

Binns, Alison, *Dedications of Monastic Houses in England and Wales, 1066–1216* (Woodbridge, 1989)

Bischoff, Bernard, and Michael Lapidge, eds, *Biblical Commentaries from the Canterbury School of Theodore and Hadrian*, CSASE 10 (Cambridge, 1994)

Blumenfeld-Kosinski, Renate, and Timea Szell, eds, *Images of Sainthood in Medieval Europe* (Ithaca and London, 1991)

Bollandists, *Bibliotheca hagiographica latina antiquae et mediae aetatis*, 2 vols, Subsidia hagiographica 6 (Brussels, 1898–1901); *Novum supplementum*, ed. H. Fros, Subsidia hagiographica 70 (Brussels, 1986)

——, *Catalogus codicum hagiographicorum latinorum antiquorum saeculo XVI . . . Bibliotheque Nationale*, 3 vols (Brussels, 1889)

Bond, Francis, *Dedications and Patron Saints of English Churches: Ecclesiastical Symbolism, Saints and their Emblems* (London, 1914)

Booth, James, 'Sceattas in Northumbria', *Sceattas in England and on the Continent: The Seventh Oxford Symposium on Coinage and Monetary History*, ed. David Hill and D.M. Metcalf (Oxford, 1984), pp. 71–111

Borgehammar, Stephan, *How the Holy Cross was Found: From Event to Medieval Legend*, Bibliotheca theologiae practicae, Kyrkovetenskapliga studier 47 (Stockholm, 1991)

Bosworth, J., and T.N. Toller, *An Anglo-Saxon Dictionary* (Oxford, 1898); *Supplement* by T.N. Toller (Oxford, 1921); *Enlarged Addenda and Corrigenda*, by A. Campbell (Oxford, 1972)

Boyd, Beverly, 'A New Approach to the *South English Legendary*', *Philological Quarterly* 47 (1968), pp. 494–8

Braunfels, Wolfgang, *Lexikon der christlichen Ikonographie*, 2nd band, *Ikonographie der Heiligen* (Rome, 1974)

Breeze, Andrew, *Medieval Welsh Literature* (Dublin, 1997)

Brewer, Derek, 'The Archaic and the Modern in Laȝamon's *Brut*', *From Anglo-Saxon to Early Modern English: Studies Presented to E.G. Stanley*, ed. D. Gray, M. Godden and Terry Hoad (Oxford, 1994), pp. 188–205

Brewer, George F., and Bedwyr Lewis Jones, 'Popular Tale Motifs and Historical Tradition in *Breudwyt Maxen*', *Medium Ævum* 44 (1975), pp. 23–30

Brinkley, R.F., *Arthurian Legend in the Seventeenth Century* (New York, 1967)

British Museum, Dept of Manuscripts, *Catalogue of Additions to the Manuscripts in the British Museum, 1894–99* (London, 1901)

Bromwich, Rachel, 'The Character of the Early Welsh Tradition', *Studies in Early British History*, ed. H.M. Chadwick et al. (Cambridge, 1954), pp. 83–136

Brooke, Christopher N.L., 'Geoffrey of Monmouth as a Historian', *The Church and the Welsh Border in the Central Middle Ages*, Studies in Celtic History 8, ed. D.N. Dumville and C.N.L. Brooke (Woodbridge and Wolfeboro, N.H., 1986), pp. 95–106

Brooke, George C., *English Coins from the Seventh Century to the Present Day*, 3rd ed. (London, 1950)

Brooks, C. and D. Evans, *The Great East Window of Exeter Cathedral* (Exeter, 1988)

Brown, Carleton, and R.H. Robbins, *The Index of Middle English Verse* (New York, 1943)

Brubaker, Leslie, 'Memories of Helena: Patterns of Imperial Female Matronage in the Fourth and Fifth Centuries', *Women, Men and Eunuchs: Gender in Byzantium*, ed. Liz James (London and New York, 1997), pp. 52–75

Brunsdale, Mitzi, *Dorothy L. Sayers: Solving the Mystery of Wickedness* (New York, 1990)

Bruun, P.M., *The Roman Imperial Coinage*, vol. VII: *Constantine and Licinius, AD 313–337*, gen. eds C.H.V. Sutherland and R.A.G. Carson, 10 vols (London, 1966)

Budny, Mildred, *Insular, Anglo-Saxon, and Early Anglo-Norman Manuscript Art at Corpus Christi College, Cambridge: An Illustrated Catalogue*, Medieval Institute Publications, 2 vols (Kalamazoo, 1997)

Bulloch, J.P., 'Saint Waltheof', *Records of the Scottish Church History Society* 11 (1952), pp. 105–32

Butler, Alban, *Lives of the Saints*, 4 vols, rev. ed. H. Thurston and Donald Attwater (London, 1956)

Callu, Jean Pierre, ' "Ortus Constantini": Aspects historiques de la légende', *Constantino il grande: Dall'antichità all'umanesimo*, Colloquio sul cristianesimo nel mondo antico, ed. G. Bonamente and F. Fusco (Macerata, 1990), pp. 253–82

Campbell, A., *An Old English Grammar* (Oxford, 1959)

Campbell, James, *Essays in Anglo-Saxon History* (London and Ronceverte, 1986)

Carley, James P., 'Polydore Vergil and John Leland on King Arthur: The Battle of the Books', *King Arthur: A Casebook*, ed. E.D. Kennedy (New York and London, 1996), pp. 185–204

Cassidy, Brendan, ed., *The Ruthwell Cross* (Princeton, 1992)

Caviness, Madeline Harrison, *The Windows of Christ Church, Cathedral Canterbury* (London, 1981)

Chadwick, H.M., *Early Scotland: The Picts, the Scots, and the Welsh in Southern Scotland* (Cambridge, 1949)

———, et al., eds, *Studies in Early British History* (Cambridge, 1954)

Chance, Jane, *Woman as Hero in Old English Literature* (Syracuse, 1986)

Chevalier, U., *Sacramentaire et martyrologe calendrier, ordinaire et prosaire de la metropole de Reims (VIIIe–XIIIe siècles)* (London, 1910)

Clark, Cecily, 'Towards a Reassessment of "Anglo-Norman Influence on English Place Names" ', *Words, Names and History: Selected Writings of Cecily Clark*, ed. Peter Jackson (Cambridge, 1995), pp. 144–55

Bibliography

Coatsworth, Elizabeth, 'The Robed Christ in Pre-Conquest Sculptures of the Crucifixion', *ASE* 29 (2000), pp. 153–76

Colker, M.L., 'A Gotha Codex Dealing with the Saints of Barking Abbey', *Studia Monastica* 10 (1968), pp. 321–4

Collinson, Patrick, 'Truth, Lies, and Fiction in Sixteeth-Century Protestant Hagiography', *The Historical Imagination in Early Modern Britain: History, Rhetoric and Fiction, 1500–1800*, ed. D.R. Kelley and D.H. Sacks (Washington, D.C. and Cambridge, 1997), pp. 37–68

Condren, Conal, and A.D. Cousins, 'Introduction', *The Political Identity of Andrew Marvell*, ed. Conal Condren and A.D. Cousins (Aldershot, 1990), pp. 1–15

Consolino, Franca Ela, 'L'Invenzione di una biografia: Almanno di Hautvillers e la vita di sant' Elena', *Hagiographica* 1 (1994), pp. 81–100

Constable, Giles, 'Troyes, Constantinople, and the Relics of St Helen in the Thirteenth Century', *Mélanges Rene Croze* (Poitiers, 1966), pp. 1035–42; repr. in G. Constable, *Religious Life and Thought (11th–12th Centuries)* (London, 1979), item XIV

Cooke, Arthur L., and Thomas B. Stroup, 'The Political Implications in Lee's *Constantine the Great*', JEGP 49 (1950), pp. 506–15

Coon, Linda L., *Sacred Fictions: Holy Women and Hagiography in Late Antiquity* (Philadelphia, 1997)

Cooper, Janet, ed., *History of the County of Essex*, vol. IX: *The Borough of Colchester*, Victoria History (Oxford, 1994)

Courcelle, Pierre, *Late Latin Writers and their Greek Sources*; Engl trans. Harry E. Wedeck (Cambridge, Mass., 1969)

Couzard, Abbé R., *Sainte Hélène: D'après l'histoire et la tradition* (Paris, 1911)

Crabbe, Kathryn W., *Evelyn Waugh* (New York, 1988)

Cramp, Rosemary, *Corpus of Anglo-Saxon Stone Sculpture*, vol. 1: *County Durham and Northumberland* (Oxford, 1984)

Crick, Julia C., *The Historia regum Britannie of Geoffrey of Monmouth, III: A Summary Catalogue of the Manuscripts* (Cambridge, 1989)

———, *The Historia regum Britannie of Geoffrey of Monmouth, IV: Dissemination and Reception in the Later Middle Ages* (Cambridge, 1991)

Croce, Elene, 'Elene', *Bibliotheca sanctorum*, 12 vols (Rome, 1961–68)

Curley, Michael J., *Geoffrey of Monmouth* (New York, 1994)

Curtis, Tony, *Wales: The Imagined Nation. Studies in Cultural and National Identity* (Bridgend, 1986)

D'Evelyn, Charlotte, and Francis A. Foster, 'Saints' Legends', *A Manual of the Writings in Middle English, 1050–1500*, gen. ed. J. Burke Severs, vol. II (Hamden, Conn., 1970), pp. 410–81

Drake, H.A., *Constantine and the Bishops: The Politics of Intolerance* (Baltimore and London, 1999)

Drijvers, Jan Willem, 'Evelyn Waugh, Helena and the True Cross', *Classics Ireland* 7 (2000), pp. 25–50

———, 'Helena Augusta: Exemplary Christian Empress', *Studia Patristica* 24 (1993), pp. 85–90

———, *Helena Augusta: The Mother of Constantine the Great and the Legend of her Finding of the True Cross* (Leiden, 1992)

Dumville, David N., 'Kingship, Genealogies and Regnal Lists', *Early Medieval Kingship*, ed. P.H. Sawyer and I.N. Wood (Leeds, 1977), pp. 72–104

————, ' "Nennius" and the *Historia Brittonum*', *Studia Celtica* 10/11 (1975/76), pp. 78–95

————, 'Sub-Roman Britain, History and Legend', *History* 62 (1977), pp. 177–92

Echard, Siân, *Arthurian Narrative in the Latin Tradition* (Cambridge, 1998)

Eckhardt, Caroline D., 'The Presence of Rome in the Middle English Chronicles of the Fourteenth Century', *JEGP* 90 (1991), pp. 187–207

Elliott, Alison Goddard, *Roads to Paradise: Reading the Lives of the Early Saints* (Hanover and London, 1987)

Ensslin, W., 'Maximus (Usurpator)', *RE*, vol. 14, cols 2546–55

Fairless, J., *Northumbria's Golden Age: The Kingdom of Northumbria, AD 547–735* (York, 1995)

Faral, Edmond, *La Légende Arthurienne: Études et documents*, 3 vols (Paris, 1929)

Ferguson, Arthur B., *Utter Antiquity: Perceptions of Prehistory in Renaissance England* (Durham and London, 1993)

Fleith, Barbara, *Studien zur Überlieferungsgeschichte der Lateinischen Legenda aurea* (Brussels, 1991)

Flint, Valerie, 'The *Historia regum Britannie* of Geoffrey of Monmouth: Parody and its Purpose. A Suggestion', *Speculum* 54 (1979), pp. 447–68

Foster, Frances A., *Studies in Church Dedications, or England's Patron Saints*, 3 vols (London, 1899)

Fowden, Garth, 'The Last Days of Constantine: Oppositional Versions and their Influence', *Journal of Roman Studies* 84 (1994), pp. 146–70

Gameson, Richard, *The Role of Art in the Late Anglo-Saxon Church* (Oxford, 1995)

Geary, Patrick J., *Furta sacra: Thefts of Relics in the Central Middle Ages* (Princeton, 1978; rev. ed. 1990)

————, 'The Ninth-Century Relic Trade: A Response to Popular Piety?', *Religion and the People, 800–1700*, ed. James Obelkevich (Chapel Hill, 1979), pp. 8–19

Giesen, J., 'Die Helena de Britannia: Des Meisters von St. Severin', *Jahrbuch des kölnischen Geschichtsvereins* 25 (1950), pp. 142–52

Gillingham, John, 'Henry of Huntingdon and the English Nation', *Concepts of National Identity in the Middle Ages*, ed. S. Forde, L. Johnson, and A.V. Murray, Leeds Texts and Studies, ns 14 (Leeds, 1995), pp. 75–101

Goffart, Walter, *The Narrators of Barbarian History (A.D. 550–800): Jordanes, Gregory of Tours, Bede and Paul the Deacon* (Princeton, 1988)

Görlach, Manfred, 'The *Legenda aurea* and the History of *The South English Legendary*', *Legenda aurea: Sept siècles de diffusion*, ed. B. Dunn-Lardeau (Montreal and Paris, 1986), pp. 301–16

————, 'Middle English Legends, 1220–1530', *Hagiographies*, ed. Guy Philippart, Corpus christianorum, 2 vols to date (Turnhout, 1986–94), I.429–485

————, *The Textual Tradition of the South English Legendary*, Leeds Studies and Monographs, ns 6 (Leeds, 1974)

Gransden, Antonia, 'Bede's Reputation as an Historian in Medieval England', *Journal of Ecclesiastical History* 32 (1981), pp. 397–425; repr. in A. Gransden, *Legends, Traditions and History in Medieval England* (London and Rio Grande, 1992), pp. 1–29

————, *Historical Writing in England, c. 550–c. 1307* (Ithaca, 1974)

————, *Historical Writing in England II: c.1307 to the Early Sixteenth Century* (Ithaca and New York, 1982)

Grant, Robert M., *Eusebius as Church Historian* (Oxford, 1980)

Greenfield, Stanley B., and Daniel G. Calder, *A New Critical History of Old English Literature* (New York, 1986)

Greenway, Diana E., 'Henry of Huntingdon and Bede', *L'Historiographie médiévale en Europe*, ed. J.-P. Genet (Paris, 1991), pp. 43–50

——, 'Henry of Huntingdon and the Manuscripts of his *Historia Anglorum*', *Anglo-Norman Studies, IX: Proceedings of the Battle Conference*, ed. R. Allen Brown (Woodbridge and Wolfeboro, N.H., 1987), pp. 103–27

Grierson, Philip, *Byzantine Coins* (London, 1982)

——, 'The Tombs and Obits of the Byzantine Emperors (337–1042)', *Dumbarton Oaks Papers* 16 (1962), pp. 3–60

——, and Mark Blackburn, *Medieval European Coinage, with a Catalogue of the Coins in the Fitzwilliam Museum, Cambridge*, 13 vols, vol. I, *The Early Middle Ages (Fifth to Tenth Centuries)* (Cambridge, 1986; repr. 1991)

Grosjean, P., 'De codice hagiographico Gothano', *Analecta Bollandiana* 58 (1940), pp. 90–103

Guerin, P., 'Bivar', *Diccionario de historia ecclesiastica de España*, ed. Q. Aldea, T. Marin, and J. Vives (Madrid, 1972)

Gurney Benham, W., 'Legends of Coel and Helena', *Journal of the British Archaeological Association* 25 (1919), pp. 229–44

Hadfield, Andrew, *Literature, Politics, and National Identity: Reformation to Renaissance* (Cambridge, 1994)

Haller, William, *Foxe's Book of Martyrs and the Elect Nation* (London, 1963)

Hanning, Robert W., *The Vision of History in Early Britain: From Gildas to Geoffrey of Monmouth* (New York and London, 1966)

Harbus, Antonina, 'Dream and Symbol in *The Dream of the Rood*', *Nottingham Medieval Studies* 40 (1996), pp. 1–15

Hastings, Selina, *Evelyn Waugh: A Biography* (London, 1994)

Hay, Denys, *Polydore Vergil: Renaissance Historian and Man of Letters* (Oxford, 1952)

Healey, A. diP. et al., *The Dictionary of Old English* (Toronto, 1986–)

Hebgin-Barnes, Penny, *The Medieval Stained Glass of the County of Lincolnshire* (Oxford, 1996)

Heffernan, Thomas J., *Sacred Biography: Saints and their Biographers in the Middle Ages* (New York and Oxford, 1988)

Herendeen, W.H., 'William Camden: Historian, Herald, and Antiquary', *Studies in Philology* 85 (1988), pp. 192–210

Heydenreich, Eduard, 'Constantin der Grosse in den Sagen des Mittelalters', *Deutsche Zeitschrift für Geschichtswissenschaft* 10 (1893), pp. 1–27

Hicks, Philip, *Neoclassical History and English Culture: From Clarendon to Hume* (Basingstoke and New York, 1996)

Hone, Ralph E., *Dorothy L. Sayers: A Literary Biography* (Kent, Ohio, 1979)

Hotson, Howard, 'The Historiographical Origins of Calvinist Millenarianism', *Protestant History and Identity in Sixteenth-Century Europe*, ed. Bruce Gordon, 2 vols (Aldershot, 1996), II.159–81

Houwen, L.A.J.R., and A.A. MacDonald, eds, *Beda venerabilis: Historian, Monk and Northumbrian* (Groningen, 1996)

Hughes, Kathleen, 'The Welsh Latin Chronicles: *Annales Cambriae* and Related Texts', *Publications of the British Academy* 59 (1973), pp. 233–58

Hunt, E.D., *Holy Land Pilgrimage in the Later Roman Empire: AD 312–460* (Oxford, 1982)

Hunter Blair, Peter, 'The Origins of Northumbria', *Archaeologia Aeliana*, 4th ser. 25 (1947), pp. 1–51; repr. in *Anglo-Saxon Northumbria*, ed. M. Lapidge and P. Hunter Blair (London, 1984), item III

Istituto Storico Italiano (A. Potthast), *Repertorium Fontium Historiae Medii Aevi* (Rome, 1990)

Jackson, K.H., 'The Sources for the *Life of St Kentigern*', *Studies in the Early British Church*, ed. N.K. Chadwick et al. (Cambridge, 1958), pp. 273–357

Jackson, Peter, and Michael Lapidge, 'The Contents of the Cotton-Corpus Legendary', *Holy Men and Holy Women: Old English Prose Saints' Lives and their Contexts*, ed. Paul E. Szarmach (Albany, N.Y., 1996), pp. 131–46

James, M.R., *A Descriptive Catalogue of the Manuscripts in the Library of Corpus Christi College Cambridge*, 2 vols (Cambridge, 1912)

———, *A Descriptive Catalogue of the Manuscripts in the Library of Lambeth Palace. The Medieval Manuscripts* (Cambridge, 1932)

Jankofsky, Klaus P., '*Legenda aurea* Materials in *The South English Legendary*: Translation, Transformation, Acculturation', *Legenda aurea: Sept siècles de diffusion*, ed. B. Dunn-Lardeau (Montreal and Paris, 1986), pp. 317–29

———, ed., *The South English Legendary: A Critical Assessment* (Tübingen, 1992)

Jarman, A.O.H., and G.R. Hughes, eds, *A Guide to Welsh Literature*, rev. ed. (Cardiff, 1992)

Jarrett, Michael G., 'Magnus Maximus and the End of Roman Britain', *Transactions of the Honourable Society of the Cymmrodorion* (1983), pp. 22–35

Jöckle, Clemens, *Encyclopedia of Saints* (London, 1995)

Johnson, Leslie, 'Reading the Past in Laȝamon's Brut', *The Text and Tradition of Laȝamon's Brut,* ed. Françoise Le Saux (Cambridge, 1994), pp. 141–60

Johnson, M.J., 'Late Antique Imperial Mausolea', 3 vols (unpub. Ph.D. diss., Princeton Univ., 1986)

———, 'Where were Constantius I and Helena Buried?', *Latomus* 51 (1992), pp. 145–50

Jones, A.H.M., *Constantine and the Conversion of Europe* (1948; repr. Toronto, 1982)

———, J.R. Martindale, and J. Morris, eds, *Prosopography of the Later Roman Empire*, 3 vols (Cambridge, 1971–92)

Jones, Kathleen, 'The Story of Helen as Depicted in the Windows', *The Saint Helen Windows in the Ancient Parish Church of St Michael and All Angels Ashton-under-Lyne* (Ashton-under-Lyne, 2000)

Jordan, David P., *Gibbon and His Roman Empire* (Chicago, 1971)

Jühlicher, 'Dexter 11', *RE*, vol. 5, col. 297

Kazhdan, A., ' "Constantin imaginaire": Byzantine Legends of the Ninth Century about Constantine the Great', *Byzantion* 57 (1987), pp. 196–250

Keeler, Laura, *Geoffrey of Monmouth and the Latin Chroniclers, 1300–1500* (Berkeley, 1946)

Kendon, Frank, *Mural Paintings in English Churches during the Middle Ages: An Introductory Essay on the Folk Influence in Religious Art* (London, 1923)

Kendrick, T.D., *British Antiquity* (New York and London, 1950)

Kennedy, E.D., *Chronicles and Other Historical Writings: A Manual of the Writings in Middle English, 1050–1500*, gen. ed. Albert E. Hartung, vol. VIII (New Haven, 1939)

Keyser, C.E., *List of Buildings Having Mural Decorations* (London, 1883)

Kidd, Colin, 'Protestantism, Constitutionalism and British Identity under the Stewarts', *British Consciousness and Identity: The Making of Britain, 1533–1707*, ed. Brendan Bradshaw and Peter Roberts (Cambridge, 1998), pp. 321–42

Kightly, Charles, *Folk Heroes of Britain* (London, 1982)

Kingsford, C.L., *English Historical Literature in the Fifteenth Century* (New York, 1913; repr. 1972)

Klein, R., 'Helena II (Kaiserin)', *Reallexikon für Antike und Christentum*, ed. E. Dassman et al., vol. 14 (Stuttgart, 1988), cols 355–75

Koebner, Richard, 'The Imperial Crown of this Realm: Henry VIII, Constantine the Great, and Polydore Vergil', *Bulletin of the Institute of Historical Research* 25 (1953), pp. 29–52

Kuhn, Sherman M., 'The Authorship of the Old English Bede Revisited', *NM* 73 (1972), pp. 172–80

Kurmann, Peter, *La façade de la cathedrale de Reims*, 2 vols (Paris, 1987)

Lamont, William, 'The Religion of Andrew Marvell: Locating the "Bloody Horse"', *The Political Identity of Andrew Marvell*, ed. Conal Condren and A.D. Cousins (Aldershot, 1990), pp. 135–56

———, 'The Two 'National Churches' of 1691 and 1829', *Religions, Culture and Society in Early Modern Britain: Essays in Honour of Patrick Collinson*, ed. Anthony Fletcher and Peter Roberts (Cambridge, 1994), pp. 335–52

Lang, James T., 'The St. Helena Cross, Church Kelloe, Co. Durham', *Archaeologia Aeliana*, 5th ser. 5 (1977), pp. 105–19

Lapidge, Michael, and Richard Sharpe, *A Bibliography of Celtic-Latin Literature, 400–1200* (Dublin, 1985)

Larkin, Susan Grace, 'Transitions in the Medieval Legends of Saint Helena' (unpub. Ph.D. diss., Indiana Univ., 1995)

Lavery, Simon, 'The Story of Mary the Egyptian in Medieval England', *The Legend of Mary of Egypt in Medieval English Hagiography*, ed. Erich Poppe and Bianca Ross (Dublin, 1996), pp. 113–48

Leadbetter, Bill, 'The Illegitimacy of Constantine and the Birth of the Tetrarchy', *Constantine: History, Historiography and Legend*, ed. S.N.C. Lieu and D. Montserrat (London and New York, 1998), pp. 74–85

Le Saux, Françoise H.M., *Laʒamon's Brut: The Poem and its Sources* (Cambridge, 1989)

Levison, W., 'Konstantinische Schenkung und Silvester-Legende', *Miscellanea Francesco Ehrle*, 2, Studi e testi 38 (Rome, 1924), pp. 159–247

Levy, F.J., *Tudor Historical Thought* (San Marino, 1967)

Lewis, C.T., and C. Short, *A Latin Dictionary* (Oxford, 1879)

Lieu, Samuel, 'From History to Legend and Legend to History: The Medieval and Byzantine Transformation of Constantine's *Vita*', *Constantine: History, Historiography and Legend*, ed. S.N.C. Lieu and D. Montserrat (London and New York, 1998), pp. 136–76

———, and D. Montserrat, eds, *From Constantine to Julian: Pagan and Byzantine Views. A Source History* (London and New York, 1996)

Linder, Amnon, 'The Myth of Constantine the Great in the West: Sources and Hagiographic Commemoration', *Studi Medievali*, 3rd ser. 16/1 (1975), pp. 43–95

Liszka, Thomas R., 'Manuscript G (Lambeth Palace 223) and the Early *South English*

Legendary', *The South English Legendary: A Critical Assessment*, ed. Klaus P. Jankofsky (Tübingen, 1992), pp. 91–101

Lucas, Peter J., *From Author to Audience: John Capgrave and Medieval Publication* (Dublin, 1997)

——, 'John Capgrave and the *Nova legenda Anglie*: A Survey', *The Library*, 5th ser. 25 (1970), pp. 1–10

Lyon, C.S.S., 'A Reappraisal of the Sceatta and Styca Coinage of Northumbria', *British Numismatic Journal* 28 (1956), pp. 227–42

McDonald, R. Andrew, *The Kingdom of the Isles: Scotland's Western Seaboard, c.1100–c.1336* (East Linton, 1998)

McEntire, Sandra, 'The Devotional Context of the Cross before AD 1000', *Sources of Anglo-Saxon Culture*, ed. Paul Szarmach, Studies in Medieval Culture 20 (Kalamazoo, 1986), pp. 345–56

McFadden, George, 'The *Life of Waldef* and its Author, Jocelin of Furness', *Innes Review* 6 (1955), pp. 5–13.

McKitterick, Rosamond, 'The Carolingian Kings and the See of Rheims, 882–987', *Ideal and Reality in Frankish and Anglo-Saxon Society*, ed. Patrick Wormald and Donald Bullough (Oxford, 1983), pp. 228–49

McNamara, Jo Ann, '*Imitation Helenae*: Sainthood as an Attribute of Queenship', *Saints: Studies in Hagiography*, ed. Sandro Sticca (Binghamton, 1996), pp. 51–80.

McRoberts, David, 'The Death of St Kentigern of Glasgow', *Innes Review* 24 (1973), pp. 43–50

Madan, Falconer, *A Summary Catalogue of Western Manuscripts in the Bodleian Library at Oxford*, vol. III (Oxford, 1895)

Manceaux, J.B. (l'Abbe), *Histoire de l'abbaye et du village de Hautvillers*, 1 (Epernay, 1880)

Mango, Cyril, 'The Empress Helena, Helenopolis, Pylae', *Travaux et Mémoires* 12 (1994), pp. 143–58

Marks, Richard, *The Medieval Stained Glass of Northamptonshire* (London, 1998)

——, *Stained Glass in England during the Middle Ages* (London, 1993)

——, *The Stained Glass of the Collegiate Church of the Holy Trinity, Tattershall (Lincs.)*, Outstanding Theses from the Courtauld Institute of Art (New York, 1984)

Mason, Roger A., 'Scotching the Brut: Politics, History and National Myth in Sixteenth-Century Britain', *Scotland and England, 1286–1815*, ed. Roger A. Mason (Edinburgh, 1987), pp. 60–84

Matthews, John, 'Macsen, Maximus, and Constantine', *Welsh Historical Review* 11 (1983), pp. 431–48; repr. in John Matthews, *Political Life and Culture in Late Roman Society* (London, 1985), item XII

Maurice, Jules, *Sainte Hélène: L'Art et les saints* (Paris, 1930)

Meyer, M.A., 'Patronage of the West Saxon Royal Nunneries in Late Anglo-Saxon England', *Revue Bénédictine* 91 (1981), pp. 332–58

Miller, M., 'Date Guessing and Dyfed', *Studia Celtica* 12/13 (1977/78), pp. 33–61

Morris, John, *The Age of Arthur: A History of the British Isles from 350 to 650* (London, 1973)

Mossé, Fernand, *A Handbook of Middle English*, Engl. trans. James A. Walker (Baltimore, 1952)

Mulligan, W.J., 'The British Constantine: An English Historical Myth', *The Journal of Medieval and Renaissance Studies* 8 (1978), pp. 257–79

Nelson, Janet L., 'Kingship, Law and Liturgy in the Political Thought of Hincmar of Rheims', *English Historical Review* 92 (1977), pp. 241–79

Nelson, Philip, *Ancient Painted Glass in England, 1170–1500* (London, 1913)

——, 'The Fifteenth-Century Glass in the Church of St. Michael, Ashton-under-Lyne', *The Archaeological Journal* 70 (1913), pp. 1–10

Newton, Peter A., with the assistance of Jill Kerr, *The County of Oxford: A Catalogue of Medieval Stained Glass* (London, 1979)

Niermeyer, J.F., *Mediae latinitatis lexicon minus* (Leiden, 1976)

Olsen, B.L., and O.J. Padel, 'A Tenth-Century List of Cornish Parochial Saints', *Cambridge Medieval Celtic Studies* 12 (1986), pp. 33–71

Olsen, Karin, 'Cynewulf's Elene: From Empress to Saint', *Germanic Texts and Latin Models: Medieval Reconstructions*, Germania Latina IV, ed. K. Olsen, A. Harbus, and T. Hofstra (Louvain, 2001), pp. 141–56.

Opie, Iona, and Peter Opie, eds, *The Oxford Dictionary of Nursery Rhymes* (Oxford, 1951)

Orme, Nicholas, *English Church Dedications, with a Survey of Cornwall and Devon* (Exeter, 1996)

——, *The Saints of Cornwall* (Oxford, 2000)

Parry, John J., 'Geoffrey of Monmouth and the Paternity of Arthur', *Speculum* 13 (1938), pp. 271–7

Partner, Nancy F., *Serious Entertainments: The Writing of History in Twelfth-Century England* (Chicago and London, 1977)

Patterson, Annabel, *Reading Holinshed's Chronicles* (Chicago and London, 1994)

Patterson, Frank A.P., *Middle English Penitential Lyrics* (New York, 1911)

Pearce, J.W., 'Did King Alfred Translate the *Historia ecclesiastica*?' *PMLA* 8 (1883), pp. vi–viii

Pohlkamp, W., 'Textfassungen, literarische Formen und geschichtliche Funktionen der römischen Silvester-Akten', *Francia* 19 (1992), pp. 115–96

——, 'Tradition und Topographie: Papst Sylvester I (314–35) und der Drache vom Forum Romanum', *Römanische Quartalschrift für die christliche Altertumskunde und für Kirchengeschichte* 78 (1983), pp. 1–100

Pohlsander, Hans, *Helena: Empress and Saint* (Chicago, 1995)

Raw, Barbara C., *Anglo-Saxon Crucifixion Iconography and the Art of the Monastic Revival*, CSASE 1 (Cambridge, 1990)

——, '*The Dream of the Rood* and its Connections with Early Christian Art', *Medium Ævum* 39 (1970), pp. 239–56

Réau, Louis, *Iconographie de l'art chrétien*, 3 vols (Paris, 1955–59)

Reddish, H., 'The St Helen Window Ashton-under-Lyne: A Reconstruction', *Journal of Stained Glass* 18/2 (1986–87), pp. 150–61

Reinhardt, Hans, *La Cáthedrale de Reims* (Paris, 1963)

Reynolds, L.D., ed., *Texts and Transmission: A Survey of Latin Classics* (Oxford, 1983)

Reynolds, William, 'Dorothy Sayers and the Drama of Orthodoxy', *As her Whimsey Took her: Critical Essays on the Work of Dorothy L. Sayers*, ed. Margaret P. Hannay (Kent, Ohio, 1979), pp. 91–106

Rhys, John, *Lectures on the Growth of Religion as Illustrated by Celtic Heathendom* (London, 1888)

Ridyard, Susan, *The Royal Saints of Anglo-Saxon England: A Study of West-Saxon and East Anglian Cults* (Cambridge, 1988)

Rigg, A.G., *A History of Anglo-Latin Literature, 1066–1422* (Cambridge, 1992)

Roberts, Peter, 'Tudor Wales, National Identity and the British Inheritance', *British Consciousness and Identity: The Making of Britain, 1533–1707*, ed. Brendan Bradshaw and Peter Roberts (Cambridge, 1998), pp. 8–42

Rollason, David, *Saints and Relics in Anglo-Saxon England* (Oxford, 1989)

Round, J.H., *St Helen's Chapel, Colchester* (London, 1886)

Salmon, J.H.M., 'Clovis and Constantine: The Uses of Sixteenth Century Gallicanism', *Journal of Ecclesiastical History* 41 (1990), pp. 584–605

Scarisbrick, J.J., *Henry VIII* (London, 1968)

Schaller, D., and E. Könsgen, *Initia carminum latinorum saeculo undecimo antiquorum: Bibliographisches Repertorium für die lateinische Dichtung der Antike und des früheren Mittelalters* (Göttingen, 1977)

Scott, Roger, 'The Image of Constantine in Malalas and Theophanes', *New Constantines: The Rhythm of Imperial Renewal in Byzantium, Fourth to Thirteenth Centuries*, ed. Paul Magdalino (Aldershot, 1994), pp. 57–71

Seeck, O., 'Helena 2', *RE*, vol. 7, cols 2820–3

Sharpe, Richard, *A Handlist of the Latin Writers of Great Britain and Ireland before 1540* (Turnhout, 1997)

Sigal, P.-A. 'Les Miracles de sainte Hélène à l'abbaye d'Hautvillers au Moyen Age et à l'époque moderne', *Assistance et assistés jusqu'à 1610: Actes du 97e Congrès national des sociétés savantes* (Paris, 1979), pp. 499–513

Skeat, Francis W., *The Stained Glasss Windows of St Alban's Cathedral* (Chesham and Luton, 1977)

Smith, Alan G.R., *The Emergence of a Nation-State: The Commonwealth of England, 1529–1660* (London, 1984)

Speed, Diane, 'The Construction of the Nation in Medieval Romance', *Readings in Medieval English Romance*, ed. Carol M. Meale (Cambridge, 1994), pp. 135–57

Stannard, Martin, ed., *Evelyn Waugh: The Critical Heritage* (London, 1984)

Stenton, F.M., *Anglo-Saxon England*, 3rd ed. (Oxford, 1971)

———, *The Early History of the Abbey of Abingdon* (repr. Stamford, 1989)

Stephens, Meic, *The Oxford Companion to the Literature of Wales* (Oxford, 1986)

Stevens, C.E., 'Magnus Maximus in British History', *Études Celtiques* 3 (1938), pp. 86–94

Stevens, W.O., *The Cross in the Life and Literature of the Anglo-Saxons* (New York, 1904)

Stevenson, Jane, 'Constantine, St Aldhelm and the Loathly Lady', *Constantine: History, Historiography and Legend*, ed. S.N.C. Lieu and Dominic Montserrat (London and New York, 1998), pp. 189–206

Stirnemann, Patricia, 'Two Twelfth-Century Bibliophiles and Henry of Huntingdon's *Historia Anglorum*', *Viator* 24 (1993), pp. 121–42

Swanton, Michael, *Anglo-Saxon Prose* (London, 1993)

Sykes, Christopher, *Evelyn Waugh: A Biography* (Harmondsworth, 1975)

Tabor, Margaret, E., *The Saints in Art: With their Attributes and Symbols Alphabetically Arranged*, 4th ed. (London, 1924)

Tatlock, J.S.P., *The Legendary History of Britain* (Berkeley and Los Angeles, 1950)

Taufer, Alison, *Holinshed's Chronicles* (New York, 1999)

Thacker, Alan, 'Æthelwold and Abingdon', *Bishop Æthelwold: His Career and Influence*, ed. Barbara Yorke (Woodbridge and Wolfeboro, N.H., 1988), pp. 43–64

Thomas, Charles, *Christianity in Roman Britain to AD 500* (London, 1981)

Thomas, Gwyn, 'O Maximus I Maxen', *Transactions of the Honourable Society of Cymmrodorion* (1983), pp. 7–21

Thomas, R.J., ed., *Geiriadur Prifysgol Cymru: A Dictionary of the Welsh Language* (Caerdydd, 1960)

Thomson, Rodney, *William of Malmesbury* (Woodbridge and Wolfeboro, 1987)

Van Acker, K.G., 'Ein weiterer Kodex aus dem Bistum Trier (Universitätsbibliothek Gent, Ms. 245)', *Scriptorum* 28 (1974), pp. 71–5

Vauchez, André, *Sainthood in the Later Middle Ages*, Engl. trans. Jean Birrell (Cambridge, 1997)

Vitz, Evelyn Birge, 'From the Oral to the Written in Medieval and Renaissance Saints' Lives', *Images of Sainthood in Medieval Europe*, ed. R. Blumenfeld-Kosinski and T. Szell (Ithaca and London, 1991), pp. 97–114

Vogt, J., 'Helena Augusta, das Kreuz und die Juden', *Saeculum: Jahrbuch für Universalgeschichte* 27 (1976), pp. 211–22

Walker, P.W.L., *Holy City Holy Places? Christian Attitudes to Jerusalem and the Holy Land in the Fourth Century* (Oxford, 1990)

Wallace-Hadrill, Andrew, *Suetonius: The Scholar and his Caesars* (London, 1983)

Ward, Henry, *Rerum Britannicarum medii aevi scriptores*, 95 (London, 1890)

Wells, M.E., 'The South English Legendary in its Relation to the *Legenda aurea*', *PMLA* 51 (1936), pp. 337–60

——, 'The Structural Development of the *South English Legendary*', *JEGP* 41 (1942), pp. 320–44

Werner, F., 'Helena Kaiserin', *Lexikon der christlichen Ikonographie*, 8 vols (Rome, 1974), vol. 6, *Ikonographie der Heiligen*, cols 485–90

Whatley, Gordon, 'The Figure of Constantine the Great in Cynewulf's "Elene"', *Traditio* 37 (1981), pp. 161–202

Whitelock, Dorothy, 'The List of Chapter Headings in the Old English Bede', *Old English Studies in Honour of John C. Pope*, ed. Robert B. Burlin and Edward B. Irving, Jr (Toronto, 1974), pp. 263–84

——, 'The Old English Bede', *Publications of the British Academy* 48 (1962), pp. 52–90

Wiles, M.F., *Archetypal Heresy: Arianism Through the Centuries* (Oxford, 1996)

Wilson, R.M., 'Some Lost Saints' Lives in Old and Middle English', *Modern Language Review* 36 (1941), pp. 161–72

Wilson, Stephen., *Saints and their Cults: Studies in Religious Sociology, Folklore and History* (Cambridge, 1983)

Winstead, Karen A., *Virgin Martyrs: Legends of Sainthood in Late Medieval England* (Ithaca and London, 1997)

Wolpers, Theodor, *Die englischen Heiligenlegenden des Mittelalters* (Tübingen, 1964)

Woolf, Alex, 'The Diocese of Sodor', *A New History of the Isle of Man*, vol. 3: *The Medieval Period, 1000–1406*, ed. Seán Duffy (Liverpool, forthcoming)

Wright, Neil, 'The Place of Henry of Huntingdon's *Epistola ad Warinum* in the Text-History of Geoffrey of Monmouth's *Historia regum Britannie*: A Preliminary Investigation', *France and the British Isles in the Middle Ages and Renaissance: Essays by Members of Girton College, Cambridge, in Memory of Ruth Morgan*, ed. G. Jondorf and D.N. Dumville (Woodbridge, 1991), pp. 71–113

Yarnold, E.J., 'The Baptism of Constantine', *Studia Patristica* 26 (1993), pp. 95–101

Index